STU'S SEA STORIES

FOR JOHN RESNICK
THANKS FOR THE GREAT WORK
Stu Landersman

STU'S SEA STORIES

AN AUTOBIOGRAPHY

STUART D. LANDERSMAN

To order additional copies of this book, contact:
Xlibris
1-888-795-4274
www.Xlibris.com
Orders@Xlibris.com
771190

Contents

DEDICATIONS

A number of years ago I put together a package of things that I had written and gave it to my favorite grandson Kilian Clifford Landersman so that he would have something to remember me with. After a while I thought that maybe I could do more than those twelve essays so I started my autobiography. This is for you, KC, so that you will have something to remember of your Old Grand Dad. I love you.

AND

Each of my two sons is married to a wonderful woman; David to Vicki, Mark to Jil. These two girls have made my sons very happy and they are like daughters to me. My two sons are very lucky guys as am I. This book is for both of you. I love you.

AND

How can I write anything without recognizing the great love of my life? My beautiful wife Martha, who always gave me encouragement, inspiration and love, would have given me the harshest critique of this project. I miss you, Sweetheart.

Stu Landersman

PREFACE

I hope that you've had the opportunity to read the novel I wrote, *Shellback,* before you start this book. Why? Well, *Shellback* is a novel and a novel is fiction. This book, *STU'S SEA STORIES,* is not fiction. This is as real, as true as I can recall the events of my life. Ever since *Shellback* came out people have asked me if I really did this or that, did so-and-so really happen that way and if I was really there for that. My answer has always been that *Shellback* is a novel, a novel is fiction and fiction means not true.

Long ago I read somewhere that most authors of novels, almost all, write their first novel based on their own real-life experiences; autobiographical but embellished with considerable imagination and maybe with more than a little "wanna be". I'm no exception. *Shellback* is a product of my own experiences very heavily laced with imagination. One line from the advertising says something like, "(the author) vows that he did none of these things but wishes that he had."

This book, *STU'S SEA STORIES,* is an autobiography. It is for real. This is my life. This is the way it was, the way it really happened. If you have read *Shellback* and then read this book you will see some familiar characters and situations as some of the characters in *Shellback* are composites of real people whom I have known. For instance in *Shellback,* Barney Williams, the life-long friend of

Martin Shielbrock is a composite of Otis Waterman, Jerry Fadden and Jim Williamson along with some others and some considerable imagination. I went on the Cuban Quarantine but not as does our hero. I really was a Convoy Commodore and I did an exercise at Diego Garcia but I didn't encounter Moses Farcian and his mates, they're pure fiction.

In *Shellback* Barbara Shielbrock bears close resemblance to my wife Martha and it took a great deal of fast-talking explanation by me; that Barbara was imaginary, she was not Martha, before Martha finally accepted the fictional character and conceded that the book was "pretty good," high praise from my most harsh critic.

So, having written and published my first (and only) novel, I now turn my rapidly diminishing literary focus back to where it commenced long before *Shellback*; to a project that started as a collection of events in my life. This autobiography, started more than twenty years ago, was originally intended just for my grandson, KC, so that he would know a little about the experiences of his grandfather. I didn't finish it then. Now, in the waning years of my time, I figured that it's "now or never" and I went back to work on *STU'S SEA STORIES*.

I hope that in reading *STU'S SEA STORIES* you can get just a little sense of the great joy and good fortune that I have had in living it.

Smooth Sailing,
Stu Landersman

PACKAGING

The dictionary says that an autobiography is an account of a person's life written by himself. That's what this is; the life story of Stuart David Landersman. This account takes you from his birth to the advanced age at which he put all this together; grade school through Navy retirement and long after, and after retirement there are a number of items that he wrote.

The first phase of his life is covered in Chapter One through Chapter Fourteen, from 1930 to 1953, the time from birth, through grade school, high school and college. What we might call "growing up"; the formative years.

The second phase of Stu's life is covered in Chapter Fifteen through Chapter Forty. It covers thirty years of service in the United States Navy; 1953 to 1983, what you might call the most productive years; the ships, the actions, the staffs, the Navy schools and the people. People includes marriage, family and shipmates.

The third phase of Stu's life is covered in Chapter Forty One through Chapter Forty Seven. It covers the years following Navy retirement in 1983; employment at Johns Hopkins University Applied Physics Laboratory, service as a Convoy Commodore, development of and work at shiphandling simulators, writing *Shellback* and retired life in Coronado. It could be called "The good life" but all of his life was good, better or best.

Chapter Forty Eight through Chapter Fifty Eight are some of the writings of Stu Landersman. Some were published, most were not. Some have value, some have none. Some are humorous, most are not. Perhaps you'll find some of them interesting.

Chapter Fifty Nine is the last chapter. It wraps it all up. It summarizes the autobiography; the life of Stu Landersman.

CHAPTER ONE

FIRST ADVENTURE IN LIFE

1930

I was born on May 26, 1930 at Madison Park Hospital, Brooklyn, New York. My mother was Thelma Landersman and her name is part of a story that you'll read about later, if you stay with this long enough. My father was Joseph David Landersman. You'll read more of him later, too. I couldn't realize it at the time, of course, but I was very fortunate to have these fine parents.

It's been said that life is an adventure and I suppose that's true for most lives. Most of life's adventures take place when the person is old enough to realize the experience. But for me, my first life's adventure started when I was born. It started with the issue of the birth certificate, a simple process, yes, it should have been.

An attendant at the hospital asked my mother what name she wanted to be put on the birth certificate. My mother had planned names for girl or boy and as she was told "it's a boy" she was ready with the name "Stuart" with the middle name David. But the name intended by my mother and spoken to the hospital clerk was not the name that was hand written on the birth certificate. The name written on my birth certificate was (and still is as I look at the certificate as I write this over 80 years later) Steward Landersman. Not Stuart, not even Stewart and with no middle name, simply Steward Landersman.

The name on my birth certificate really didn't matter for a number of years until my mother took me to start school; kindergarten. Even then my mother had only to show the birth certificate and spell the name she preferred; Stuart David Landersman. And so I was Stuart David Landersman from then on, through the various grade schools, high schools and colleges, on my driver's license and all the certificates, diplomas, etc.

Funny, meaningless, taken care of? Yes, but then, if you read this further you'll see that after college I went into the Navy and the Navy asked who is this Steward Landersman on the birth certificate being represented by this Stuart David Landersman. My father had to provide a notarized statement that I was who I said I was.

To the Navy a steward was, at that time, a sailor who served as a servant to officers. My mother had intended that I be linked to the Stuart royal family of England. But that was not to be. My first adventure in life was focused on my name and instead of English royalty, I was given the name of a provider of personal services.

CHAPTER TWO

GRADE SCHOOL DAYS

1935-1943

My mother took me to kindergarten near East 23rd Street and Avenue D in the Flatbush section of Brooklyn, New York, where we lived in 1935, and on the first day the teacher asked me the most simple question, "What's your name?"

I was confused, "Which name do you want?"
"How many names do you have?" the surprised teacher asked.
"Lots of them," I replied.
"What are they? Can you tell them to me?"

I rattled off, "Buddy Stuart David Landersman Boy Semila Shmuel Peter-Rabbit Butz and Kukus," the polyglot of American, Jewish, Hebrew, Christian and Yiddish slang and nick-names that I was called as a five year old.

"Well, we'll call you Stuart," and so I was Stuart at school and Buddy at home.

I went to kindergarten in Brooklyn, New York.

In 1936 my family moved from Brooklyn because my father became manager of cutting and shipping at Gottlieb Brothers, manufacturers of ladies lingerie, in Poughkeepsie, New York. The factory was on Hamilton Street next to Smith Brothers, where they made cough drops. When my parents were looking for a home to rent on the south side of Poughkeepsie my sister and I were with them. At the door of a large house that had been divided into four apartments, my Dad asked if we could look at the place with the "For Rent" sign. "No," said the owner. "I don't rent to Jews." It was my first experience with anti-Semitism.

We found a house four blocks away on Marion Avenue near Krieger School where I was in the first grade and my sister Estelle was in the fifth, and we were known as the kids with the monkey. Mike was not completely domesticated and lived in a three-foot cube wooden frame chicken-wire cage my father had built. In good weather his cage sat on the back porch.

One Spring day when my parents were away either Estelle or I left the cage lock off. Mike had hands like a human so it was easy for him to open the hasp and the cage door, and he was off into the trees. We called and tempted, threw ropes and rocks and tried to climb the trees, but Mike wouldn't come down. Neighbor kids and grown-ups tried to help. Nothing worked. A fire truck arrived and firemen tried ladders, nets and fire hoses, but Mike stayed in the trees all day, looking down at us, chattering away until we all gave up. The fire truck left, neighbors went home and Mike stayed in the trees all night. My parents came home that night and in the morning my mother put some food in Mike's cage. He climbed down, ran into the cage and my mother closed and locked the cage door. Our monkey escape was reported in the school newspaper.

The woman next door was very pregnant and very superstitious, fearing that if she saw the monkey her child would look like one, so great care was taken to keep Mike from her sight. One morning while she was away Mike got out of his cage and jumped into an open window of her house. At my mother's call, Dad came home from work, climbed into the house and chased Mike until finally, in the woman's upstairs bedroom, Mike was cornered. As Dad reached with his left, Mike jumped to Dad's right. Dad swatted him in the air with a rolled up magazine and knocked out Mike who was returned to his cage where he promptly recovered. A month later when the woman next door delivered, my Mom said the baby boy looked just like a monkey, and twenty years later she said he still did.

In grade school, high school and college I played basketball, and in the Navy, and I grew from a kid that couldn't catch, throw, dribble or shoot the ball to a college all-star. At first basketball was separate from education but gradually the two came closer and eventually it was basketball that determined where, when and how I graduated from college. The college degree led to a commission in the Navy, and the Navy became my career and led to family, so basketball was a major determinant in the path of my life, and it started in grade school when Otis Waterman let me be a Wildcat.

From 1937 to 1944 my family rented the house at 14 College View Avenue in a pretty residential area in Arlington, a suburb of Poughkeepsie. Sometimes my father would put the rent money, $40, in an envelope and I would take it to Mrs. Lyons, three houses up the street at 11 College View Avenue and wait for her to fill out a receipt form. The south side of the street was a long low stone wall backed by tall trees forming one side of the Vassar College campus. Across the street from the campus were wooden houses like ours, old but well cared for, close together with small front lawns and separate garages in the rear. The houses were numbered in sequence, so ours was the 14th house on the street from Raymond Avenue, one house from Fairmont Avenue. After Fairmont Avenue the street went on to a dead end beyond which lay more of the Vassar College campus.

Vassar was a prestigious girls' college, often socially associated with the men's Ivy League colleges. It had a large beautiful campus with fine buildings and grounds. Many of the girls came from wealthy families and the locals used to joke about the stereotypical Vassar girl wearing Levi's with a mink coat. All the Vassar girls had bicycles with license plates and many of us kids used to try to buy graduating seniors' bicycles for a couple of dollars to fix them over the summer and sell them to incoming freshmen for ten dollars. Some kids would steal the bikes as we all knew the seniors' plates and they wouldn't be back the next year. Herbie Redl from LaGrange Avenue was rumored to steal bikes. He was later a team-mate of mine and super-star in sports at Arlington High School and much later a millionaire business man. I never stole any bikes but I learned how to fix them in that process.

Vassar girls would buy flowers if I could get some from neighbors' yards. The best way to sell flowers was to sit next to the gate across the street from my house and have my dog with me. The Vassar girls would always stop to pet the dog. That was better than just saying, "Wanna buy some flowers?" as they walked by. Some were snobs and wouldn't respond. The younger you were the easier it was to get their attention. As I got older I learned that you had to have a gimmick to get the attention of a Vassar girl. Later I learned that applied to getting the attention of any girl. You could make 25 cents for a bunch of lilacs if you had a gimmick or a good enough line.

In the winter all of us kids would shovel snow, making 25 cents clearing neighbors' walks and up to a dollar and a half for driveways, and in the good weather months we would mow lawns and rake leaves.

To get to grade school each morning I would walk west on College View Avenue, take a right at the corner of Raymond Avenue, go three blocks and cross at Davis Avenue to the Arlington Grade School. After our first year the College Drug Store on the corner of Raymond Avenue moved a few doors north and the Juliet Theater was built on the corner. I would see a lot of movies at the Juliet over the next six years.

Fritz Jordan, basketball coach at Arlington High School, came to conduct a boy's gym class when I was in the fourth grade. He showed us fundamentals; how to throw a bounce pass, how to catch a basketball, how to make a lay-up and how to play defense; his zone defense that had won many county championships for his high school teams.

Fritz Jordan was to us fourth graders the ultimate in sports. This was Zeus coming down from Mount Olympus to spend 45 minutes imparting his god-like lore upon us. I clung to his every word and realized that I could actually know where I was on a basketball court, to whom I was supposed to throw the ball and which basket was mine. I learned that Arlington played a 2-1-2 zone defense and every Arlington boy had to know that defense, even in the fourth grade, because some of us, if we practiced very hard and were very fortunate, would be playing for Fritz Jordan at Arlington High School in a few years and would win the Dutchess County Scholastic League championship.

Playing for Fritz Jordan at Arlington and winning a county championship became a distant dream at that time, unattainable as the moon to an awkward nine-year-old. I was tall and skinny with big feet, clumsy, slow, weak and generally poorly coordinated. I had trouble catching a basketball and had developed a habit of deflecting the ball down to the floor before catching it, using up my dribble, so I had to pass it away immediately. Most of the time I didn't know where to pass it and I was too weak to shoot beyond a lay-up. I couldn't dribble unless I looked at the ball with full concentration which made running and passing difficult. I was the classic kid that couldn't walk and chew gum at the same time and when the kids chose up teams I was the last selected.

I practiced as much as I could, wherever I could find a ball and a basket, without much improvement. When I was in the sixth grade I put up a basket on a telephone pole down the street, towards the dead end on the college side. I nailed some boards together for a small backboard and used a fruit basket that came apart after a dozen shots. The people living across from my basket asked me to remove the ugly boards from the pole.

Three blocks away on Davis Avenue a group of kids about my age had a real basket on a telephone pole. Raymond Tuton was in my class at school, was a very good player and I would visit him there looking to be included in the games. After many pickup games spent sitting on the curb watching Tuton's friends play they would include me but

I improved very little and most of my time was spent waiting for a chance to get into a game.

Often sick as a child, I had headaches, coughing, sore throat, runny nose, colds and all the childhood diseases that came along. When I was 14 the doctor told my parents that I should live in Arizona or New Mexico where the dry air would be good for my sinus and would allow me to get stronger. I refused to leave Arlington and during the winter months I would go through a periodic painful draining of the sinus in which a doctor armed with a long steel tube would vacuum deep in my nasal passages.

Although we didn't keep a kosher house, my mother felt that most gentile food couldn't be trusted and if Estelle or I ate a hot dog we would have to swallow a tablespoon of Milk of Magnesia as soon as we got home. We soon learned not to tell her and only had to face the laxative if Mom was with us when we ate "trafe," trash in Yiddish.

At least once a week my sister and I used to go to the Juliet Theater at the corner of Raymond Avenue and College View Avenue. Sometimes Estelle would get in free because she loaned records to the movie operator to be played between showings. She always had the most popular records and she didn't miss many movies. My Dad gave me an allowance of 25 cents a week and it cost 15 cents for the movie and 10 cents for popcorn, so the allowance didn't go far unless I would sneak in the rear exit, but most of the time I paid.

One afternoon as I was leaving the Juliet Theater the usher told me that Japan had just attacked Pearl Harbor. It was December 7th, 1941. I was 10 years old, didn't know where Pearl Harbor was and couldn't believe it as the newsreel portion of the movie show I had just seen showed smiling Japanese diplomats in Washington. I ran down College View Avenue and joined my father and mother listening at the radio. World War II dominated the next five years and changed everyone's lives as there were air raid drills and we had neighborhood air raid wardens, gasoline and meat were rationed, and most of the young men either enlisted or were drafted into military service. I collected aluminum and paper, sold savings bonds and built model airplanes at school for identification training of flight crews.

Near the theater there were shops on College View Avenue, near the corner, to attract Vassar girls and when I was thirteen I got a job at one of them, an elegant dress shop. After school each day I would vacuum the shop, take out the trash and make deliveries, if any were needed, to college girls. In addition to my pay of one dollar a week, I would receive tips for the deliveries, but only when I could get past the dormitory guards. Thursday night I turned down my allowance, telling my father I now made a dollar a week.

My Dad helped me put up a better backboard with a real basket on the front of our garage, so that I could shoot baskets by myself, for hours. I improved enough so that in the seventh grade when my good friend Otis Waterman formed a team, I was included. Clearly I was not a good enough player at 12 years old to be on his team, but we were in Boy Scouts together, so Oat included me as a Wildcat. Oat had a good basket on his garage, where we practiced. There were no organized teams such as many years later in Little League. Groups of kids just got together without coaches or sponsors and formed teams, like gangs but not with that criminal connotation. Each team had a nominal head, like Oat, who sought out other teams and places to play. There were a few leagues in the area with age limits and teams could sign up to compete so we played a lot of games and won more than we lost.

The Raymond Tuton crowd from Davis Avenue, including Harold Mackey, Andy D'Angelo and John Nelson formed the best team around with shirts that said Beavers on front and a number on back. Another team was the Cardinals with some good players from out on Manchester Road, in the country. George Monroe, who later became one of my best friends, was a Cardinal.

The Wildcats did pretty well the first year, when Oat and I were in seventh grade, and even better when we were in the eighth grade. Our team included Oat and Joe Coutant at forward, Fred Schmalberger and Harry Gerth at guard. They were our best players and they carried the team. I was a substitute the first year and contributed little to nothing and did just a little better the second year, but I was growing fast, getting stronger and could, in fact, run, dribble, throw and shoot, even if I still bounced the ball before catching it.

My sister, Estelle, was four years ahead of me in school, so when I was in the eighth grade she was a senior in high school. At Arlington, the seventh and eighth grades were in the same building as the high school. My sister had troubles with her classmates, and probably the key issue was anti-Semitism as she and I were the only Jewish kids in the entire school, seventh to twelfth grades. Also, jealousy probably played a part, as Estelle was more up-to-date, more stylish than the other girls at school, and knew more about popular music, dancing and movies than the others. A boy could deal with anti-Semitism and stylishness, but a girl had no defense so Estelle took the only path she could see; she rebelled against her classmates and the school administration, getting in more trouble as a result.

Before World War II, Herbert Grimm, a boy my sister's age who lived just around the corner, would strut around in his Nazi German Youth Bund uniform; swastika, boots and all. His family attended Nazi rallies and he would call my sister names, and there were other situations, less open, that Estelle had to deal with.

For a boy, those issues were lessened by participation in school activities, especially sports. I didn't have the problems that my sister experienced at the same school because I was on the basketball, football and track teams. At Arlington the bigots would not harass a basketball player, but there was no such protection for a girl and I was accepted and she was rejected. Fifty years and more later I always looked back on my high school years with the nicest memories, while my sister always hated the thought of Arlington High School.

During the winter, on days that were cold, snow, wet and windy, the school would open the gym for dancing over the lunch hour with music provided by records brought by students, like my sister, who always had the best, most up-to-date records. She was also the best dancer and she could jitterbug the Lindy Hop or what ever was the current rage of teenagers, better than any girl in the school. One day she walked across the floor and asked the only black guy in the high school to dance. He was the older brother of a girl in my class, Cora Anderson, and he had always been at the winter noon hour dances but had never danced, as there were no black girls for him to dance with.

The high school kids watched with amazement, some with shock and even horror, as Estelle and Anderson started dancing; the kike and the nigger, and they saw dancing like they had never seen before at Arlington High School. It was something out of the movies, like Fred Astair and Ginger Rogers, Marge and Gower Champion. They whirled and twirled in time to the fast music without missing a beat or a step, as he would toss her into a spin, catch her and pull her back. It was like they had danced together a hundred times and the watching kids moved closer, crowding onto the floor and others that had been dancing stopped and watched. Soon there was only one couple dancing in the middle of the basketball court and hundreds of kids crowded into a circle watching, clapping and stomping to the rhythm. When the music ended the dancers dipped and the crowd roared, yelled and clapped, just as they did when their high school basketball team scored on that same gym floor.

My eighth grade classmates knew she was my sister and I was proud of her, just as Cora Anderson was proud of her brother, and it helped my popularity with the girls who assumed that if my sister was such a good dancer so I must be. I didn't know how to dance, but after that I asked my sister to teach me, and she tried.

Separate from my life at Arlington, I had activities with the Jewish community of Poughkeepsie. When I was nine I belonged to a Cub Scout Pack that met at the Jewish Center. I went to temple, attended Hebrew school and prepared for Bar Mitzvah, which took place at Vassar Temple, downtown near the Hudson River, on my 13th birthday. Later I played a few basketball games with the Young Hardings, a team of Jewish kids.

The school year came to a close and I graduated from the eighth grade. I had made good grades, was popular with lots of friends and had improved in basketball. Maybe I could make the junior varsity next year in high school–maybe. I was very active in Boy Scouts and would spend most of the summer at Boy Scout camp. Next September I would be a freshman at Arlington High School.

CHAPTER THREE

ARLINGTON HIGH SCHOOOL

1944-1948

At the start of the freshman year in high school each student selected a curriculum program; College Technical, College Liberal Arts, Industrial Arts, Secretarial, Homemaking, etc. Otis Waterman and I selected College Technical, which meant that we would take all the math and science offered plus those other courses needed to be admitted to an engineering college.

George McAndrews was Assistant Principal and boys' counselor but he offered little help and we used a brochure from the U.S. Naval Academy to see that we were taking the right high school courses. It wasn't that we intended to go to the Naval Academy, although that did sound good to us, but we figured that if we had the right high school courses for Annapolis we would meet the requirements of any engineering school.

During that freshman year in high School I was elected Vice President of my class and Oat was elected Treasurer, and we were both very active in Boy Scouts and later became Eagle Scouts. We played in the school band, Oat trumpet and me clarinet, the difference was Oat really could play the trumpet but I just wanted to wear the uniform and march at games and in parades as I couldn't play the clarinet at all.

Otis and I went out for junior varsity basketball our freshman year. We tried hard and survived the first cut. Basketball was very popular at Arlington High School and many kids tried out. Some were very good but I wasn't one of them, neither was Oat as we were among the last cut that year and the junior varsity coach told us it was close and encouraged us to try next year, and he told me to learn not to bounce the ball every time I caught it.

John Nelson, Marty MacIsaac, Ray Tuton and Bob Wheaton were freshman that made the JV team, but for us Oat reformed the Wildcats for a third season.

On December 15, 1944 I received an award from the Dutchess County Victory Garden Council, "in recognition of his Victory Garden vegetable production for America," the certificate read. On January 25, 1945 in the Poughkeepsie High School auditorium, I was one of about 200 awarded a Blue Star Brigade commission as Second Lieutenant by Major John Stowell, Commanding 240th Military Police Battalion, for selling War Bonds.

My sister Estelle was a "Government Girl," working for the Navy Department in Washington, DC when President Franklin D. Roosevelt was inaugurated in 1945 and my mother decided we should visit Estelle and see the ceremony. So Mom and I went to Washington by train and we stood in the cold rain and saw Roosevelt's final inauguration. My mother and father were strong supporters of Roosevelt and my mother once had tea with Eleanor Roosevelt and another time sat on a stage with her at a Red Cross ceremony for volunteers. Among other things, Mom knitted constantly for the Red Cross; scarves, mittens and winter face masks for servicemen.

Oat and I were the original two in forming a Junior Achievement company on November 26, 1943, United Manufacturing Incorporated, sponsored by Central Hudson Gas and Electric Corporation, and our company was very successful making and selling wood products. Ten kids made up the Board of Directors and were the work force of the company, each with a title; President, Vice President for this or that and we rotated the positions. We sold shares for working capital and set up shop in the basement of one of our sponsors, Henry Wengen, and the company lasted three years.

After moderate success making 25 bird houses from hollow logs and a few wooden benches, our Vice President for Marketing, Pete Purdy, got a contract from Fargo Manufacturing Company, a war industry factory in Poughkeepsie, for 25 shipping cases for shell primers. We built the boxes and got a contract for 50 more and then another 50. It would have been easy to change our Junior Achievement company from a part time program intended to teach kids business to a full time real manufacturer of shipping crates, but after over a year and five contracts-250 boxes for the same company-our sponsors encouraged us to seek other work. Pete Purdy went to another, bigger, local factory, explained our company's experience and asked if that factory needed shipping boxes. Pete was offered a contract for 20,000 boxes and had to explain that we were only ten kids in a Junior Achievement company. United Manufacturing paid shareholders ten cents on a fifty-cent share, raised salaries from five to twenty cents per hour and went back to building birdhouses.

I was Secretary of United Manufacturing 1943-44, Production Manager 1944-45, and President 1945-46. As President I attended the Annual Junior Achievement Dinner in the Jade Room of the Waldorf Astoria Hotel in New York City on June 24, 1946. S. Bayard Colgate who was Chairman of the Board, Colgate-Palmolive-Peet Company, signed the invitation. On November 20, 1946 the Board of Directors of United Manufacturing liquidated the company, returned original investments to stockholders ($2.50 each) plus a dividend, and granted bonuses to the six remaining members of the Board of Directors; Otis Waterman, Pete Purdy, George Schiavone, Stu Landersman, Ed Koch and Joe Morris. My bonus was $16.23.

The basketball season of 1944-45 saw the Wildcats win 14 of 17 games as we played in a Saturday morning league in Arlington and picked up additional games whenever we could. Otis was always our leading scorer and playmaker, and as loyal Arlington boys we always played Fritz Jordan's 2-1-2 zone defense. I could feel myself improving and by the end of the season I felt that next year, when I would be a sophomore, I could make the Junior Varsity basketball team.

A group of friends formed a close association that we called, "The Jolly Boys," from The Great Gildersleeve radio show. The group consisted of Oat and me, plus Harry Gerth, George Monroe and Jim Hauver. Sometimes Joe Morris was with us, too, and we went almost everywhere together, played on the school teams, took the same classes, and ate lunches at school together.

Oat and I made the Junior Varsity basketball team in our sophomore year as did Joe Coutant, Harry Gerth and George Monroe, so there were four former Wildcats and four Jolly Boys on the team. I was Vice President of the class and Oat was Treasurer. We were taking math and science courses, English, Social Studies, and getting good grades, Oat's a little better than mine. That school year my family moved from College View Avenue to 296 Hooker Avenue, still in Arlington but just across the street from the City of Poughkeepsie and if my parents had bought a house across the street I would have had to go to Poughkeepsie High School. The trip to school from my new residence was about a mile and a half, considerably longer than before, and I either walked or rode my bicycle but often rather than walk I would run the distance.

The Hooker Avenue house had a larger back yard than did the College View Avenue house and my father built an extension on the garage so that we could have a horse. This was not horse country, by any stretch of the imagination, as it was middle class residential and if any neighbor complained we would have had to get rid of the horse. We built a small corral and put up a backboard and basket on the side of the extended garage where I would shoot baskets often into the dark of night. JEST, we named the horse; J for Joe, E for Estelle, S for Stuart and T for Thelma, as I got the idea for the naming from Otis' family boat named KRONG, for Katherine, Ralph, Otis, Natalie and George; the Waterman family.

The horse and basketball didn't mix as the horse was frightened by the thumping of the ball on the side of her stall, and the corral often had manure piles that interfered with dribbling the basketball.

To keep the neighbors from complaining about the horse, I would deliver to them manure as fertilizer for their Victory Gardens and local small kids could get free rides and feed the horse apples picked up from around a neighbor's tree. After a year my father moved the horse to a farm south of Poughkeepsie and later I learned that the neighbors had been more annoyed by my basketball-in-the-dark than by the horse.

Oat and I sat on the junior varsity bench most of our sophomore season, but we were happy just being on the team. I got into a number of games and felt that I was stronger and could do things on the basketball court that I couldn't do before, but I still bounced the ball as I caught it.

President Franklin D. Roosevelt's home was Hyde Park, N.Y., just north of Poughkeepsie, and on Friday, April 12, 1946, his estate was dedicated as a National Park. Oat and I were among 12 Eagle Scouts that had received orders from the Dutchess County Council, Boy Scouts of America, directing us to serve as ushers to direct distinguished guests to appropriate seats. The orders told us how to be excused from school, prescribed uniform and lunch, and directed us to report to Mr. Hamilton of the National Parks Service for duty. The orders read, "Signals are to be worked out with the Director of Protocol so that you will know who you are ushering and where to direct them."

I had moved from Boy Scouts to Senior Scouts at the time, as the first Sea Scout in Dutchess County. Oat was an Explorer Scout and another Eagle of our troop, Henry Winchester, was an Air Scout and we wore our Sea, Explorer and Air Scout uniforms to the Hyde Park dedication. My Sea Scout uniform looked just like a U.S. Navy sailor's dress blue uniform which in fact it once was as there were no Sea Scout uniforms available at the time, so my dad had bought a sailor's uniform and had it modified and tailored for me. To most, maybe all, of the guests I was a tall skinny sailor among the Boy Scout ushers.

We learned the color code system of invitations and showed the guests to the appropriate seating for their status as we Eagle Scouts escorted senators, congressmen, Supreme Court justices, journalists, and members of the cabinet, to seats. Frank Sinatra created the biggest reaction of the visitors and I showed the Secretary of the Interior, Julius Krug, to his seat, but for me the most important guest I escorted was my mother, whom I sat with the senators. Fala, FDR's pet Scotty dog, was being walked before the ceremony and forever after I could say, "Shake the hand that petted Fala."

I discovered girls, and there were many nice girls at Arlington High School; Irene Van De Water, Diana Johnson, Dolores Reeder, Dorothy Owsiany, Catherine Myers, Barbara Rexhouse, Shirley Stevens, Shirley Fay, Mary Cassidy, Sue Cotter, Connie Fallon, Marie Arata and others. All were friends, good friends, and some were "girl friends" at various times. Most of us had been schoolmates since early grade school so we knew each other well, but in high school all of a sudden the girls took on a new attractiveness. Strange, for years we were schoolmates, children playing together, and all of a sudden the little girls had become young women.

George Monroe was a Jolly Boy who lived out in the country, out Manchester Road on Noxon Road, about ten miles from Arlington. Two older brothers were in service and he lived with his mother and older sister in a plain rented house among farms. George worked part time on the farm across the road. He was tall and strong, with blond hair, fair complexion, pointed features and an easy ready smile and girls and even older women thought he was very good looking and everyone liked his personality. His father had passed away a few years before and the family struggled financially. George rode a school bus but after football, basketball and track practices the bus was not available and he would hitch-hike home.

At the end of our sophomore year, George Monroe's mother died. His sister was over 18 and had graduated from high school so she was on her own, working as a clerk in Poughkeepsie. George was only 15, so the Mitchell family of Herkimer, New York, distantly related or maybe just good friends of his parents, took him into their family.

George spent his junior year at Herkimer and the Jolly Boys visited him there once. He played varsity basketball at Herkimer and did very well, had a nice girl friend and was very popular at that school. The Mitchells, with two high schoolers of their own, provided him with a nice home. But George missed Arlington and arranged to return, living at the farm across the road from his former home on Noxon Road.

During his senior year at Arlington, again on the football, basketball and track teams, he got a part time job at Howard Johnson's Restaurant near the high school and after work, which was after practice, he would hitchhike home. Sometimes I would drive him and we used to joke that he was probably the leading hitchhiker in the United States.

I grew a lot between my sophomore and junior years in high school. I was about six feet two inches tall and didn't want Coach Jordan to see me until school started, so during the summer when I saw him down the street I avoided him. At school in September I went out for football, which took some convincing of my mother who didn't want to sign the permission slip as she was afraid I'd get hurt. I talked her into it though, as I had made up my mind to be an end in football so that I would learn to hold onto the ball. Fritz Jordan also coached football. Otis also went out for football and we were both on the third team, Otis the quarterback. I played end on offense and corner linebacker in a 5-3-2-1 defense, with Otis a defensive back or safetyman. We were on the sidelines most of the season but enjoyed being on the team and the conditioning was good for basketball that followed.

I got a car in my junior year and the Jolly Boys all shared it for transportation and chipped in for gas. First I had a '33 Plymouth, then a '36 Ford that sported a large maroon and gold letter A on the front grill. The letter originated as a borrowed Juliet Theater marquis piece from which I made a pattern in metal shop, then sand cast from scrap aluminum. I couldn't get the shop class into my academic schedule but the shop teacher, Mr. Wizeman, was also the JV basketball coach and he let me participate on my own time.

New York State had Junior Drivers Licenses for 16 year olds that allowed driving only in daytime and only when assisting in a business, so I carried in my car an empty box from my father's factory, Kathel Manufacturing, Inc.. At night I was careful to avoid Arlington policemen, as they knew my car. The Junior Drivers License also did not allow driving in New York City, so the few times my friends and I went there I parked far uptown near Van Courtland Park in the Bronx at the end of the subway line, which was elevated there. We rode the subway into the city, to Ebbets Field, home of the Brooklyn Dodgers or to the Polo Grounds to see the New York Giants and to Yankee Stadium.

I was elected President of my junior class, Otis was Treasurer and Ray Tuton Vice President. Our football team won seven out of eight games, losing only to Kent School, a prep school in Connecticut by a score of 12-7. I got into some of the games, made a few tackles and caught a couple of passes, learning to hold onto the ball.

Otis and I began the 1946-47 basketball season, our junior year, on the junior varsity starting team. Also on the team were former Wildcats Fred Schmalberger, Joe Coutant and Harry Gerth.

The most exciting junior varsity game that season was with Roosevelt, one of our biggest rivals. With the score tied during the final minute, Oat described the action as he remembered it fifty years later:

"As I recall, you stole the ball three times with less than a minute to go and having been imprinted (like the birds) threw it to me each time. I dribbled the length of the court each time but; the first time I missed the lay up but was fouled and missed both shots. The second time the ref called me for walking but no one could hear the whistle and I had made the lay up. The third time I either made or missed the lay up, but the ref had blown the whistle again before my shot–this was for a foul which I finally made with about ten seconds left. I did lose my cool just a bit!!!

"The ref, I believe was Frank Fitzpatrick who Jinny and I became great friends with many years later (He and his wife). His and our kids grew up together. C'est La Vie."

Each time Oat went down the court without a score he became angrier with the referee and he did lose his cool "just a bit." I had to restrain him from getting called for a technical foul and that, as I recall, was my major contribution to our winning the game. If I had stolen the ball I surely would have thrown it to Oat as had been "imprinted" on me from Wildcat days.

Half way through the season I was moved up to the varsity basketball team so I was not on the JVs when, near the end of the season, my former teammates Oat, Carl Redl (Herbie's younger brother) and Bobby Martin played in a tournament in Poughkeepsie. They knew that players on high school teams were not eligible. They were kicked off the Arlington junior varsity by Coach Wizeman and forfeited their tournament games. If I had been on the JV team I would have been with them.

As second or third team varsity center I didn't get as much game time as I had on the JVs, but I was on the Arlington High School varsity basketball team playing for Coach Fritz Jordan. The ultimate! At basketball practice one day Coach Jordan was unhappy with the effort being put forth by the first team, so he had a five-minute practice game, first team versus second team, and announced that the winning team would start in the next regular game. The starters continued to loaf but we on the second team played hard and won.

Coach Jordan kept his word and as we huddled on the court before the next game he told us that we would stay in until the other team scored. We were leading 8-0 when they made a foul shot and the crowd roared in salute as we left the court and even more as our first team came on. There was no lack of effort as our first team ran up the score and we substitutes played most of the second half. We won the Dutchess County Scholastic League Championship with a starting team of Harold Mackey, Duncan MacIsaac, Andy D'Angelo, Herbie Redl and John Nelson.

After basketball season I didn't want to be idle, as I had been going to football and basketball practice all year every afternoon, so I went out for track. I didn't know what I could do on the track team but it looked like fun, out in the sunshine running around in spiked shoes wearing loose fitting sweat suits. Otis and I tried a number of events. Soon Otis learned that distance running was too much work, he was better at sprints, but not quite fast enough for the short sprints and he settled on pole vaulting. I tried high jump, shot put, discus and mile run before I settled on the half mile. It seemed like a lot of work, running every day at practice, but I liked the track meets.

I developed a bad concept in that junior year on the track team; do as little as possible at practice, just enjoy yourself all week and then run your heart out on Saturdays, the day of the meets. I felt that I could beat most half milers that way. As far as race strategy goes; get behind the best runner, stay there until the final hundred yards and beat him down the stretch. Walter Neidhardt, the track coach had a theory on timing each eighth of a mile and running according to a plan. Dick Moore was our best half miler and I would get behind him and try to stay there, and it worked fairly well. Dick Moore won most of the races and I came in second and third a few times, which meant points for the track team.

The school year of 1947-48 I was President of my Senior Class, Harry Gerth was Vice President, Diana Johnson was Secretary and Otis Waterman was Treasurer. Class officers were elected but really it was arranged in advance by Kathy Myers, who was like a political leader, deciding who the class officers should be and influencing others to vote for those she had chosen. That's how I was elected Vice President the first two years and President in my junior year. In our senior year, though, Kathy Myers wanted Mike Wirhowski to be President and I ran without her support. There wasn't any campaigning as the kids just voted on popularity and I won the only close election for any position in our four years.

The New York Herald Tribune held an annual Forum for High Schools and I was Arlington High School representative on Saturday, March 6, 1948 at the Waldorf Astoria Ballroom in New York. I didn't pay any attention to the speakers and just tried to meet some of the good-looking girls.

Marty MacIsaac and Bob Rogers were the starting ends on the football team and I was their substitute. In a pre-season practice game with New York Military Academy, a prep school for West Point, I took a kick-off and started up field but a cadet tore the ball loose and took it in for a touchdown. I thought he had taken my arm along with the ball. A few years later that cadet was an Army star football player.

In the early season against Roosevelt Central School, one of our big rivals, Harry Hahn threw me a short pass for our third touchdown as we won 20-0. In another game I scored an extra point on a pass. Half way through the season we lost a tackle, Coach Jordan shifted Marty MacIsaac to that position and I became starting end. Marty was like a personal coach for me, telling me my assignments and showing me how to catch passes. At times in the huddle when a seldom-used play was called Marty would look across and say, "Cross block and get the guard," or "run a square pattern." He really looked after me.

My first start was against Highland Falls, the high school just outside West Point, and their quarterback was Bobby Blaik, son of the famous Army coach Earl "Red" Blaik. We played a 5-3-2-1 defense with the ends as corner linebackers. On the first play from scrimmage Blaik came around my end with an army of blockers ahead of him. It took a bunch of them to take out Fred Lockner at tackle and I pushed through the others and pulled down Blaik for a loss. They didn't try my end again for most of the game. In the second half on offense I was lined up in a three-point stance with my head down and as soon as the ball was snapped the Highland Falls player opposite me threw a handful of dry dirt in my face. I was blind, choking and coughing and learned to keep my head up after that.

The last football game of the season was against Wappinger Falls, our biggest rival, and in the third quarter we were ahead 19-0 and they were on our three yard line. I was positioned right on the goal line in my linebacker position as they came right at me. I moved a step forward, put down my head and shoulders and caught the runner square on. He took me with him across the goal line and knocked me into the end zone, and I thought that maybe I was too light to play football. On the final play of the game, with Wappinger Falls five touchdowns behind and passing in desperation, I intercepted a pass. The newspaper report of the game included:

"Stuart Landersman, big reserve end, brought the fans to their feet late in the game when he intercepted a Wappingers pass on the Arlington 10 yard line and raced 90 yards to a score."

Final: Arlington 39, Wappinger Falls 7. On that last play Gene Pultz, one of our best, saw a Wappingers player in front of him about to tackle me. Pultz reached out, collared the guy from behind and dragged him down, figuring; we're ahead, it's the last play of the game and maybe Stu can go all the way if it's not called. It was the longest run for a touchdown by an Arlington end on an intercepted pass, and I owe that run to Gene Pultz.

As the 1947-48 basketball season started, my senior year, Coach Jordan started various combinations in the first few games. I got to start against Haldane High School of Cold Spring and scored 11 points but after that I was back on the bench. In our first league game Wappinger Falls trounced Arlington 52-26, one of the most humiliating defeats ever experienced by my school. In that game Wappingers tried to get Arlington to come out of our zone defense by holding the ball and the score at the end of the first quarter was 3-2 Arlington. At the half it was 12-11 Arlington. Coach Jordan's philosophy was that when we're ahead we'd stay in our zone defense as long as they stay out there and hold the ball. There was no shot clock in those days.

In the second half Wappingers changed their game plan and came out shooting and the roof fell in on us. The newspaper report of the game said,

"—the Wappingers outfit poured it on with Bob Foster, Bill Tulley, Cosmo Pugliesi and Bob Meyers building up the 26 point difference. Fans admit they have seldom seen a high school team shoot with such deadly accuracy. The Fallsmen ripped Arlington's zone defense apart with a flurry of sets. Foster and Meyers proving adept at the outer ranges."

The most effective weapon against a zone defense is the long shot. Most high school teams couldn't hit the long shot often enough and couldn't penetrate the zone, which is why Arlington won so many games, but against a hot shooting team we could be beaten, and were as Wappingers gave up trying to get us out of the zone and shot over it. Clearly Coach Jordan had to make some changes if we were going to have a successful season and success at Arlington meant winning the county championship.

In the practices that followed I found myself with the starting team and at the next game, in the pre-game huddle at the end of the court with our hands piled together, Coach Jordan looked across at me and said, "Stu, you're our starting center from now on. We're going to sink or swim with you. Get out there and play the way I know you can." We won the game.

More than sixty years later I still get a lump in my throat and a tear in the eye when I think back of that huddle and hear Coach's words. It was an emotional moment for me in 1948 as it was some 30 years later at a class reunion, the last time I would see Coach Jordan, when we discussed that moment. I was thrilled that he remembered it exactly as did I and especially considering that he coached thousands of young men in more than 20 years. He added that he was confident in giving me that position because I had improved so much and so fast, and that I did as I was told. I was "very coachable" in his words.

Arlington beat Catskill, Roosevelt (twice), Highland, Millbrook, and St. Mary's of Hudson, and then we met Wappingers on their court, to decide the winner of the Central Section of the Dutchess County Scholastic League.

The game got a great deal of publicity in the local media. We were interviewed on local radio and the sports page of the Poughkeepsie New Yorker of Thursday, February 26, 1948 headlined:

MAROON, FALLSMEN DUEL HEADS CAGE SLATE

WAPPINGERS FIVE GIVEN SLIGHT SCORING MARGIN

"Action in the Central Section of the Dutchess County Scholastic League will hit a crescendo tomorrow night at the Wappingers Central School gym when the Fallsmen collide with the Arlington Maroons in a game to decide the champion. A sellout crowd is assured for the duel which will have the Wappingers club favored to down the AHS squad for the second time this season. The Margin of victory, however, is not expected to attain that of the previous meeting of the two rivals which had the Fallsmen trounce the Maroon 52-26.

"Arlington will probably start Bob Martin and Herb Redl at forwards, Stewart Landersman at center, and John Nelson and Don Willis at the guards. Coach Jordan has inserted Landersman into the starting five since the Falls tilt and the big boy has been turning in good scoring jobs."

"Arlington, a team that has beaten Roosevelt twice, took heart from the FDR win over the Fallsmen. The sting of the humiliating defeat before a home town crowd was alleviated somewhat at that time. Maroon fans claim the club had an 'off night' in the first meeting."

The sports page of the Poughkeepsie New Yorker of Saturday, February 28, 1948 read:

ARLINGTON NIPS WAPPINGERS FALLS

CAPTURES CENTRAL SECTION TITLE IN SENSATIONAL OVERTIME BATTLE

"Arlington High School's Maroons reign as champions of the Central Section of the Dutchess County Scholastic League today following their pulse-pounding 44 to 42 verdict over Wappingers Falls last night at the Falls gym. A capacity crowd jammed into the gym was turned into a screaming mob as Dil De Marco, a reserve who entered the tilt with 30 seconds to play, netted a lay-up all alone underneath the Maroon basket with five seconds on the clock, tying the score at 38 to 38 and sending the uproarious conflict into a three minute overtime period.

"The Jordanmen, humiliated by a 26 point defeat in the first meeting of the two ancient rivals, instead of suffering a letdown in the extra heat, promptly jumped ahead, 42 to 38 on field goals by Herbie Redl and Stewart Landersman, and held on for the amazing triumph. Maroon fans mobbed the six players who blended in a fine show of spunk and playing ability when the buzzer sounded an end to the tense struggle. It was a game that will long be remembered by those who saw it and those who played it."

Millbrook, winner of the Hudson Valley Section beat Staatsburg, the Harlem Valley Section winner and now Arlington would play Millbrook for the Dutchess County Scholastic League championship. The game was played on a neutral court, the Poughkeepsie Armory, on Friday, March 12, 1948. We had beaten Millbrook in a regular season game.

The Saturday, March 13, 1948 sports page headline read:

ARLINGTON CAGERS BEAT MILLBROOK, 47–36

LANDERSMAN LEADS MAROON CLUB TO COUNTY LEAGUE CHAMPIONSHIP

"Arlington High School's Maroon cagers surged to the 1947-48 championship of the Dutchess County Scholastic League last night at the Armory, spilling Millbrook Memorial School, 47 to 36, before more than 1,500 fans. Lanky Stuart Landersman, who was a second-stringer at the start of the season, covered himself with glory as he gathered 18 points in pacing the Maroons to another county title. Stu, termed by Coach Fritz Jordan as the most improved player on the squad, blended with Herbie Redl, Don Willis, Johnny Nelson and Bobby Martin to pull away from the Millbrookers in the third period and further expand the margin during the opening minutes of the last period."

Defeating Millbrook for the county championship was the most important game but actually it was an anti-climax to the win over Wappingers. Revenge for that humiliating 26 point loss to Wappingers and winning the Central Section title was the real highlight of the season, especially when a comparison would have shown that Wappingers really had better players. Our best all around player was Herbie Redl and he was comparable to Bob Foster, the best of Wappingers, but after that at every position Wappingers was better than Arlington. The reason Arlington won was that Coach Jordan out-coached the Wappingers coach. Any other coach, having suffered a humiliating loss would have changed his defense but not Jordan. He had faith in his zone defense; knowing that Wappingers couldn't shoot as well as they did in the first game. He had us maintain our zone defense, Wappingers couldn't penetrate it and their long shots were not good enough and Arlington won.

The morning of that Wappingers game a friend told me that Bob Myers, the Wappingers player who would be guarding me, was out late the night before drinking with a girl in Highland. Highland was across the Hudson River from Poughkeepsie in a different county where the bars stayed open 'til 3 AM, and most kids under the legal age of 18 could find a place to drink. My friends and I knew the process well from experience. I knew Myers would not be rested and from the very start of the game I kept on the run, Myers staying with me in a man-to-man defense. He did well for the first two quarters but by the fourth quarter and in the overtime I could see that he was really dragging and I moved around even more. He couldn't stay with me. Forty years later Otis Waterman met Bob Myers at a social event and Myers told of how Stu Landersman stayed on the run and he couldn't keep up.

Joe Morris took my mother to the Millbrook championship game, the only time she ever saw me play. The next day she told me that she really enjoyed it, was glad I didn't get hurt and thought that I had been very rough on those Millbrook boys. My father never saw me play a game.

For Coach Jordan it was the ninth league championship in eleven years at Arlington and he won more in the years that followed. For me it was the realization of a dream that started back in grade school when I couldn't walk and chew gum at the same time, when I was the last kid taken as teams were made up. I was named to the 1948 Dutchess County all-star first team along with teammate Herbie Redl, Bob Foster of Wappingers, Tony Sinibaldi of Staatsburg and Nick Benza of Millbrook. Much later, in 1980, I was elected into the Dutchess County Basketball Hall of Fame.

Oat and I were on a college basketball team while we were in high school! Well, not exactly "on" a team, maybe "with" a college team would be more accurate. Vassar College was a girl's school but had accepted fifty veterans after World War II to help with the flood of servicemen that got out of the military and used their GI Bill college benefits. Oat found that there were seven or eight Vassar vets trying to form a team to compete against the vets at the other girl's colleges but they didn't have enough men to practice. So, just as he had always done in the Wildcat days, Oat recruited some friends to play basketball wherever and whenever. This time it was at the Vassar College gym on Sunday mornings and his friends were from the

Arlington High School team that had just won the Dutchess County Scholastic League championship.

On the second Sunday of Vassar College practice, as we walked out of the dressing room, who was on the court to greet us but Coach Fritz Jordan, brought in to help the Vassar Vets. Our initial thought was, "Now we're in for it, in trouble for playing basketball else-where than the Arlington team," and we remembered that Oat and others were kicked off the JVs in our junior year for playing else-where. But Coach Jordan put us at ease right away by telling us it was good of us to help and he used us to demonstrate as he coached the Vassar Vets that Sunday.

Years later as a civil engineer Oat served as the Vassar College Director of Public Works and he retired from that position. He never told anyone that he had been with the first Vassar College men's basketball team in 1948, twenty one years before the college went co-ed. And not many, if any, people know that Fritz Jordan was the first men's basketball coach at Vassar.

Track season followed basketball and Dick Moore, Arlington's best half-miler the previous year, had graduated so in my senior year I was the top half-miler. Oat was our leading pole-vaulter and he jumped well in some meets. I won a number of races in local meets with times that were not impressive, still using my tactic of following the lead runner and sprinting in the final stretch. At practice during the week I'd loaf, relying on my good condition from football and basketball to carry me in the Saturday races, but in the big regional track meets I didn't do well, coming in fifth in one, fourth in another as my sprint wasn't good enough against real runners.

When I read that the New York Giants were to play a preseason baseball game at West Point against the Army team, the Jolly Boys loaded into my car and off we went. Unfortunately that meant cutting track practice, but I had to see my favorite baseball team. We also saw Glen Davis, "Mr. Outside" of the famous football combination of Davis-Blanchard, who played baseball for Army. Next day Coach Neidhart told me that I was off the track team for missing practice. Otis suggested that I offer an apology and the following day I appealed to Coach Neidhart, who let me apologize to the team and I was forgiven.

The best half-miler in the county was from Wappingers and in the final track meet of the season I got behind him and stayed there even though he slowed, trying to get me to take the early lead. As we came into the final stretch I sprinted, as did he, and for a while it looked like he could hold onto the lead, but gradually I drew even with him, then edged ahead and won the race. It was a county record for the half-mile; 2 minutes 10 seconds, slow but worth 5 points for Arlington as we won the Dutchess County Scholastic League track championship. Among those on that track team were Otis Waterman, Herbie Redl, Don Willis, Gene Pultz, Fred Lockner, Jim Hauver and George Monroe, teammates from other sports.

Margaret McGrath went to Poughkeepsie High School. She was tall, thin and beautiful with long auburn hair and was my girl friend for part of my senior year. Her mother was very protective with plans for Margaret to marry a wealthy Catholic and I clearly didn't fit into those plans. Margaret gave me a graduation picture, "Love from Margaret to Stu, June 13, 1948." I dated Diana Johnson and Marie Arata part of the year and took Dolores Reeder to the Senior Prom.

Among the traditions of Arlington High School was a day designated as Old Clothes Day. Near the end of each school year the senior class would wear old clothes to school, very old clothes, more like costumes and each year the members of that senior class would try to outdo those of past years. The AHS class of 1948 was certainly no exception and a great deal of planning and costuming took place. I wore an outfit patterned after the comic strip character Lil Abner with torn off shirt sleeves, pants too small with one suspender, big shoes and the main prop; I carried an aged, badly rusted and useless shot gun, or what had been a gun at least 100 years before. All the Jolly Boys, all the senior class, were dressed, maybe clad would be a better description, in appropriate attire for Old Clothes Day. Clearly we were the best ever at AHS.

As I went to my last morning class the teacher told me that I couldn't come into her class in my outfit. My attempt to explain the

Old Clothes Day tradition was to no avail as the teacher only said that I had gone too far. I used up the hour in the library and then it was lunch hour, a time for planning, Jolly Boy planning.

Just before the bell rang to end lunch hour and start the afternoon session, the Jolly Boys went around to all of the groups of seniors. All of the senior class, every one, instead of going to their classrooms went out onto the football field which was located alongside, just below and parallel to the school building. As the bell rang to start the afternoon session, we were assembled around the 50 yard line, the whole senior class, and every window in the school facing us was filled with students watching this strange boycott.

I told the seniors about being refused entry into the class and that we had to be firm and united to save Old Clothes Day. They cheered me. When I told them to stay on the field and that I was going in to negotiate with the principal, Mr. Stormes, they all cheered as I trotted in to the school. (I might note here that Mr. Stormes' daughter was one of our classmates and she was in full support of our boycott.)

Mr. Stormes smiled as he received me and asked what this was all about. I explained my complaint and offered that Old Clothes Day was an accepted tradition at AHS; we shouldn't be expelled from a class for our outfits. Mr. Stormes looked serious, said he agreed with me and offered that if I would leave my ancient gun in his office until after school we would have no problems. I left the gun there, ran back to my classmates, told them that our grievance had been settled and we all ran back into school cheering all the way.

Shirley Fay was valedictorian and Mary Cassidy salutatorian of our class. Oat was number three and won prizes for, "Doing the most for the school while getting the most out of it," RPI medal for math, excellence in band, Kiwanis medal for math and science, and some others.

At the graduation ceremony, as Class President, I read off the names of each graduate as they came onto the stage to receive their diplomas. Joe Morris's mother had heard us discussing the problem of gas money for my car for the past two years, and she told me that if I included Joe's middle name she would buy me a tank of gas. I took the bribe, the only graduate whose middle name was included was Joseph Shane Morris and the Jolly Boys had gas for all the partying that week, including trips across the river 'til 3 AM.

College had been a consideration since the start of high school. A Boy Scout executive had taken Oat and me to visit Columbia University in New York and we had seen West Point a number of times. I was interested in Michigan, Purdue, Renseelear Polytechnic Institute, Worchester Tech in Massachusetts, and Clarkson College of Technology in Potsdam, New York. Oat and I read about the Naval Academy but when we found that 20/20 vision was required we couldn't qualify, as both of us wore glasses at times. Many years later when I was on duty at the Naval Academy I learned that Naval Academy requirements could be waived, but in 1948 no one at Arlington High School knew that.

I applied to Renseelear (RPI), Worchester and Clarkson, and was accepted at Worchester and Clarkson. RPI rejected me and I couldn't understand why. In my senior year at Arlington High School I was:

President, Class of 1948
Vice President of the Technical Club
Football team-county champions
Basketball team-county champions-all-star team
Representative to Herald Tribune Forum
Track team-county champions-set county record half mile
Honor Key-honors graduate academics

In addition I was an Eagle Scout and had been President of Junior Achievement, and I knew that I had all the required high school courses. So why did RPI reject me? A family friend said RPI had a quota for Jews that probably had been filled when I applied. Sorry, no more Jews allowed.

George Monroe was working full time at Howard Johnson's when school ended, spending most nights at my house, and he agreed to join in my summer plans. We went to New York to get jobs as deck hands on a merchant ship and tried a shipping company where they sent us to the union hall. There we were told we had to have a job and that took seaman's papers that came from the Coast Guard, who told us we had to be hired before we could get papers. We tried a non-union shipping company and were told we first had to have papers. We couldn't break into the loop; papers, job, and union, so we gave up that plan.

My next idea was to configure my car for living, long before the days of the RV, and go on a driving trip around the country. I found that this would cost too much and the work on the car would take too long. Hitch hiking was my next plan. We used to joke about George Monroe being one of the most accomplished hitch hikers in the country, but that was all on short ten mile trips. To prepare for long distance travel, George and I hitch hiked to Myersville, my family's summer place in New Jersey.

Selling flowers to Vassar girls had taught me that you had to have a gimmick, so I modified a two-gallon Penrod Oil can with a hinged top and hasp. In Penrod we carried food and clothes, but alongside the road with our thumbs out we looked to every driver like young college boys who had run out of gas and it worked like a charm. Every driver that stopped asked, "What'd ya do, run out of gas?" We would not reply until we were in the car and underway, then we'd say, "No, we just carry this can to make it look like we ran out of gas, so you'd give us a lift," and show them the can. Every one of them laughed and thought it was a great idea and we made it easily to Myersville and back, over 200 miles, after spending the night.

Having proven that we could do long distance hitch hiking on the Myersville trip, George and I got ready for the Big Time. Penrod was too small for what we had to carry cross country so, still looking like college boys on the road, we carried one small suitcase with a tent and two blankets and another with our clothes. The Poughkeepsie newspaper carried a tiny item:

"George Monroe and Stuart Landersman, 296 Hooker Avenue, left here Friday to tour the west and southwest. Both were honor graduates last month from Arlington High School."

Worchester or Clarkson? I couldn't decide but as I was getting ready to leave on my hitch hiking trip I solved the problem by asking Oat to make all arrangements for me with him at Clarkson, and he did. After a summer of hitch hiking around the country with George Monroe, in September 1948 it was off to Clarkson College of Technology for Oat and me.

I never felt that I was really "in," really one of the group. I never felt fully accepted. There always seemed to be something different between the others and me. There was very little overt prejudice, very little identifiable anti-Semitism, but once in a great while, just often enough to remind me, an occurrence would take place. I experienced very little prejudice from my schoolmates and none from the Jolly Boys as clearly I was fully accepted by my five close buddies.

When I would participate in an event with the Jewish community of Poughkeepsie I was the kid from Arlington as all the others were from Poughkeepsie. I went to a different school, lived in a different area, not economically different but geographic and maybe with a little cultural difference.

At Arlington there were other differences. I had been a new kid in the second grade while most had been together since kindergarten. There was the Jewish difference and there was an economic difference as my father made more money than most of the others. Still, I was elected to class office, played sports, was popular and led events and did well in academics so there was no reason to feel excluded or different, but I did. I didn't discuss or analyze my feeling of difference at the time and maybe I was not capable of doing so but probably I would have learned that every kid, maybe everybody, had differences. The feeling persisted in college and in the Navy.

Early in school I knew I was inept at sports and felt inferior. I knew that I was not as good a camper as the other Scout leaders and that's why I wasn't accepted in the Order of the Arrow. I wasn't admitted by Renseelear and knew that my grades were not all A's but I felt wronged. Still, I had confidence that I could do almost anything and was willing to try, and that I could deal with my differences. I came out of high school feeling that I could do anything, eager to try anything.

CHAPTER FOUR

BELL BOTTOM TROUSERS
COAT OF NAVY BLUE

1944

Head held high, the flat hat defied gravity perched on back of his head, and the broad bell bottom trousers flapped with the rhythm of his long strides and outboard pointed feet. Elbows bent, his hands were tucked in the slash pockets of his coat of navy blue. A classic British sailor, Limey, Tar, Gob, he was one of thousands of seamen of the Royal Navy sent to a rest camp near Peekskill, New York while their ships were being repaired at shipyards in the New York City area during World War II.

The camp was a former Civilian Conservation Corps facility, and now that President Franklin D. Roosevelt and World War II had taken America out of the Depression the CCC was not needed. All of the men had jobs in military service or working in factories making military equipment, so the camp was used by British sailors sent to the country to relax from the rigors of sea duty.

On weekends the British sailors would come to Poughkeepsie, my town, the nearest town of any size, for that other kind of rest and relaxation that sailors have sought for centuries; drinking and girls. When it was time for them to return to camp they lined the highway, thumbing for rides, some sitting on the roadside, others holding shipmates whom had partaken too heavily of Poughkeepsie beer.

This particular sailor swaggered out from La Grange Avenue and took a left on Fairmount Avenue in Arlington, the residential suburb where I lived, an area not frequented by members of the Royal Navy. It was winter of 1944, World War II was in full swing. I had just left home and dinner on my way to the high school where I was a 14 year old freshman to watch a basketball game. The junior varsity game started at 6:30 P.M. and I didn't want to miss it, having failed to make the team that year, so I was walking fast as was the Tar as our paths intersected at the corner of La Grange and Fairmount. In winter it was dark at that hour.

"Eh, mate. Ow d'y get t'the rood t'Pikskill, d'y know?"

The cockney clearly was lost but he was headed in the right direction, the same direction as I was going, so I took this as an opportunity, as the British sailors had fascinated me since they started coming to my town, and I offered to show him the way. He accepted with appreciation and we walked together on the lighted sidewalk, he with his broad bell-bottom trousers and coat of navy blue returning to his rest camp, me to high school. It was my first chance to talk at any length with a British sailor.

He was my age I learned, 14 years old, and he didn't like being called Limey. He had been serving in a Royal Navy destroyer on convoy duty for over a year and as his ship was being repaired in Brooklyn he had been sent to the rest camp along with a number of his shipmates. He told me of actions his ship had been in and certainly he could have made them up, sailors can exaggerate or even originate I would learn, but at that time I was much impressed. What impressed me most was his age, 14, the same as me, but while I was in school he was a navy war veteran.

That night at home I spoke to my mother about the inequity of that 14-year-old British guy serving his country in the war while I was going to school. If she would sign for me I was big for my age and could pass for 17 and get into the Navy. No, she wouldn't sign and she explained to me that in his country it was his duty to join the Navy, but here my duty was to go to school and after I had an education, if there was still a war, I could go into service.

She was right. Nine years later I graduated from college, the draft was still in effect, there was a war in Korea, and I joined the Navy. I served in the Navy for 30 years and had a full and rewarding career. Often I thought of that young British sailor and I hoped that he survived the war and had a good life.

CHAPTER FIVE

IN THE GOOD 'OLE SUMMER TIME

1933–1947

Joseph David Landersman at 34 had a good job as a cutter in the garment district of Manhattan and even though the country was in a depression he could provide pretty well for his family with $40 a week. The summer of 1933 he decided that he could afford to get his family out of the stifling oppressive heat of Brooklyn, into the cool mountain air of New Jersey. Thelma and the kids would enjoy Camp Amity in Myersville, in the Watchung Hills.

Mrs. Veinger ran the family camp, twelve bungalows arranged in two rows of six facing each other with a large grassy area, sometimes muddy, between the rows. Each two-bedroom bungalow had a screened porch and wide steps across the front. They were little more than shacks but they provided the Jewish families with escape from the city. The camp also included a large mess hall used for recreation and social events; singing, dancing and organized activities for the kids. Myersville was an area of scattered simple houses and small farms in low mountains, woods and dirt roads.

After that first summer Joe and Thelma decided Myersville was where they wanted to spend their summers but not at Camp Amity, so they bought a small piece of property up the hill from the camp and had a small one room bungalow built. Myersville would be their summer place for the next ten years. Estelle and Buddy spent each summer there from the time school got out in June until just after Labor Day, when school was about to start.

There were other bungalows around the camp, owned and used as summer escapes by families like the Landersmans, and over the years the families got to know each other pretty well, forming an informal community, sharing resources and cooperating on improvements. Almost all the houses were for summer use only, unfinished with 2X4 framing showing inside, kerosene lamps and stoves, and hand pumps for water, but after a couple of years most families took advantage of the running water service that was provided and later there was electricity.

Many of the houses had outside showers; square high wooden fenced enclosures with water tanks on top to be heated by the sun. Originally the tanks were filled by hand pump, and many of those outside showers remained in use long after the houses had running water. Of course kids would sneak peeks through knotholes in the shower fences, depending on who was showering.

Electricity came to the area after the first few years. Before that kerosene stoves and lanterns were used.

Thelma's brother, Morris Domes, became the unofficial chief of maintenance and repair of the Jewish community of Myersville. Moe could do electrical, plumbing, carpentry, painting, even automobile repair, and he soon became one of the best known and most important members of that small community. Anyone who wanted anything repaired or improved sought Moe's counsel and he would either do it himself or recommend an outsider for the project. Also, he didn't hesitate to give his opinion, asked for or not.

"Why do you want to install that? It won't work."
"That won't look good. You should paint it white."

"Bottled gas is better than electrical."

"Gravel will just wash away."

"Two by fours won't be strong enough. Use 2X6."

"You don't need a new one. I can fix this one."

—and the people listened to him because they thought that he was the expert.

—and Buddy would hang around Moe as his "helper." At first there was little a 4 or 5 year old could do but get in the way, but after a few years Buddy learned to fetch tools, hold wood for sawing and get a cold drink when needed, all this without asking too many questions because Moe didn't like a lot of talk when working.

Moe lived with the Landersmans in Brooklyn and went with them to Myersville in the summer. He worked at various jobs in and around New York in the winter, mostly as an electrician, and in 1936 he went to fight in the Spanish Civil War, returning wounded in 1937. So Buddy didn't have his "big brother" those two summers, and when the following summer Moe took a job as head maintenance man at a children's camp, where he met Silvia, Buddy didn't see much of him again that year.

The first few summers Joe would take the train from New York each Friday evening to spend the weekend with his family. Thelma would drive their Model A Ford convertible with the kids in the rumble seat to pick up Joe at the Gillette train station, and her herky-jerky clutch operation was a constant joke for Buddy and Estelle as they exaggerated the jolting action of the car.

After a few years Joe drove to Myersville every Friday after work in New York, arriving about 8:30 PM, and the kids would listen for the high pitch of his down-shifted car laboring up the hill, scattering stones on the dirt road, and they would run to meet him and receive hugs and candy. After handy-work on house improvements all day Saturday and Sunday, Joe would drive back to New York for a week of work, looking forward to joining the family next Friday night. When the Landersmans moved to Poughkeepsie the same summer routine was followed, but Joe had to drive much further, arriving at 10 or 11 PM Friday nights. Vacations were for the family not the breadwinner.

There were three swimming places available. Gillette was nothing more than a mud and clay quarry hole filled with dirty water with a railroad station alongside, about a mile away via shortcut through the woods. Sterling was a tiny village with a much better swimming facility, a sand and mud beach on a small lake about two miles away. Watchung was a small town about five miles away with the best swimming, a dam forming a nicely kept sandy river bank plus a chlorinated pool with admission fee. Groups of kids could walk to either Gillette or Sterling, but could go to Watchung only by car. Buddy learned to swim at Gillette, slipping on the clay bank into the water, going under and coming up dog paddling.

Saturday shopping was at either Plainfield, eight miles to the south or Morristown eight miles to the north. It was at Plainfield with Moe and Silvia that Buddy first ate "ah-beets," and later learned that everyone else called it pizza.

After Moe and Silvia married, in the summers they were at Myersville with the Landersmans, Moe reclaiming his chief-of-maintenance status, Silvia controlling everyone. Moe made his living doing odd jobs in the community and he improved and expanded the Landersman bungalow so that it had a rear space with kitchen and bathroom, a sleeping loft and a large enclosed side porch that doubled the size of the house, with electricity and water, even a hot water heater. It remained unfinished inside with framing showing and without heat, but one year Moe put an old kerosene stove in the middle of the main room so that Silvia and he could live there through the winter.

The Landersmans spent each summer in Myersville from 1933 through 1943, eleven summers. When Buddy was thirteen and involved in Boy Scouts, Estelle 17 and finished with high school, and gasoline rationing making it difficult for Joe to drive each week from Poughkeepsie and back, the Landersmans decided to stay at home the summer of 1944.

Buddy was called Stu at school and at Camp Nooteeming, the Boy Scout camp of Dutchess County, which he attended for two weeks, completing First Class requirements and earning some merit badges. He had just finished the eighth grade and would be a freshman at Arlington High School in the Fall.

The following summer, 1945, Stu and Otis Waterman, Stu's best friend, were Life Scouts with only a few merit badges needed for Eagle. Both of them were selected as junior camp counselors, spent the full summer at Camp Nooteeming and became Eagle Scouts. Bird Study merit badge was Stu's final requirement and Oat was a counselor for that badge when Stu completed it and became an Eagle Scout dated August 17, 1945.

Counselors were given off one day a week and it didn't matter to Stu which day, so when Oat needed to change his day off for a dental appointment, Stu was glad to exchange days. On the morning of August 14, 1945 Oat left camp and went to Poughkeepsie. That afternoon someone came into camp with big news, so Stu and some others went to a car with the only radio in camp and listened to reports of the celebration of VJ Day. Japan had surrendered. World War II was over and Oat was enjoying himself on Main Street in Poughkeepsie on what would have been Stu's day off. Stu lay on the car fender listening to descriptions of the festivities and said, "I'll never let him forget this!" Next day Oat made it worse by telling of the excitement, "–and you should have seen all the girls!" "Yeah, I should have," was all Stu could reply.

Following their sophomore year in high school, Oat and Stu were again counselors at scout camp, this time as Eagle Scouts with Ralph Waterman, Oat's father, who was Camp Director that summer. They were merit badge counselors and lifeguards, and conducted training sessions in the various Boy Scout activities. Near the end of the summer a ceremony was held for Order of the Arrow and Otis and Ralph Waterman were among those initiated into the honor society but not Stu. It was his first taste of failure but Stu dried his tears, tried not to show his disappointment and congratulated Oat,

Mr. Waterman and the others who had been selected. There would be other failures in life.

Every city in the United States, no matter the crime, poverty, abandoned buildings and slums has a decent section of homes. No matter the level and extent of urban decay, in or near every city there is a nice area in which to live. Every city, that is, except Beacon, New York, a small city 12 miles south of Poughkeepsie, across the Hudson River from Newberg, Beacon was all trash from city line to city line, a jungle of slum and deterioration unbroken by a decent structure. So it was not a unique situation in which Aaron found himself as a new executive of Debway Hat Company, Beacon, New York. With no reasonable place to live in or near Beacon, he had to find a home for him and his wife at some distance in the country because their apartment in Brooklyn was too far away from his office at the hat factory. He found a nice small inexpensive summer cottage on a pond that would be nice for a couple of months until he could work out more permanent housing. Trouble was, Aaron didn't have a car and neither he nor his wife could drive because they had always been big city dwellers and in The City one didn't need a car. Now, in the country, lack of transportation was a problem.

Aaron and his wife met Moe and Silvia Domes who always had solutions to everyone's problems. Moe's nephew had a car, would soon be out of school for the summer and was looking for a summer job. If Aaron could use a young man at the hat factory, chauffeur services could be provided. Stu Landersman was employed as a shipping clerk by Debway Hat Company for $40 a week and Aaron paid him an additional $20 a week for chauffeur service that involved pickup each morning, drive to work in Beacon and return home each evening. Stu's '33 Plymouth put on a lot of mileage that summer but the good money meant new tires and it went smoothly.

At Debway, Stu found that he was the shipping department. After a 20 minute training session he was all alone on the fourth floor the remainder of summer work days, boxing hats, putting the boxes in large crates and filling out and attaching address labels. Then he would take the crates down a freight elevator to a truck loading dock.

The summer of 1947 slid by too fast and soon it was time to start the senior year at Arlington High School.

CHAPTER SIX

MEYERSVILLE

1932 and After

The following was written by Estelle in 1985. Some of her memories are not consistent with mine but, hey, she was four years older than me. She passed away in 2011 and I never had a chance to question her about any of this. For instance, the property my father bought was much less than an acre, more like a half acre, and he didn't pay ten cents. I recall being told that he paid something less than a dollar but that was because the purchase price included construction of the original one room shell, as she calls it, for a couple of hundred dollars. Anyway, it's good for you, dear reader, to get someone else's views and I promise that I have not changed it in any way. These are Estelle's words.

P.S. I can't help but add this thought: Estelle describes Mom's difficulties driving the Model A and the question of her driver's license. I seem to remember being told that Mom knew she could never pass the driving test and so she got someone else, I don't know who, to take the test for

her, in her name, and it worked because, as Estelle says, she only drove
around Myersville and was never stopped.

Estelle (Landersman) Snyder writes the following:

I was 5 years old when I first went to Meyersville, probably the
summer of 1932. My father was working for a lingerie manufacturer,
Gottlieb Brothers; that was before the Gottlieb brothers split, on
Madison Avenue in Manhattan; we were living in Brooklyn at 2245
East 23rd Street.

My mother and her sister, Bertha, were friendly with a group of
people, they were all socialists, who used to like to hike and camp
out and Meyersville was the place they used to camp out at. It was all
woodsy, undeveloped, dirt roads, the real boonies. At the intersection
of where Meyersville began (4 roads intersecting from north, south,
east and west came together) was a tavern called "Clark's Oasis."
Diagonally across the street from Clark's was a general store, post
office and what-have-you-all. Across the street from the general store
was a small hotel with cottages run by a Mrs. Engel, who also had a
small grocery store.

Four dirt roads going uphill constituted the whole of Meyersville,
which was located in the Watchung Mountains. My father bought
a piece of property at the top of the third hill for (if you can believe
this!) ten cents an acre! He bought his acre and wanted to go to
Meyersville to check out his property.

I know ten cents an acre sounds pretty unbelievable. That's what
Mom told me back then, but I wonder if she was just telling me
something to shut me up and not ask questions. You're right, at that
price, why didn't Pop buy ten acres for a dollar? Of course, back then,
a dollar might buy a week's worth of groceries.

Halfway down the hill from our place was a summer camp for
families with cottages plus a large dining hall, all run by Mrs. Veinger
who was an unfriendly, sour-looking person. It was all very rustic,
the cottages all screened in, with beaverboard flaps with hooks to
fasten down in case of rain. Surprisingly, each cottage had a toilet,

sink, kerosene stove and icebox, but no electricity. Mrs. Veinger used her dining hall for Saturday night get-togethers of the guests at the camp and the people who had summer bungalows in the surrounding hills, and she would provide coffee and pie ala mode at the end of the evening. I don't think she gave it away; I'm sure there was a charge. The Saturday night get-togethers were just a social evening. Nothing extraordinary occurred; not until years later when we danced, after a juke box was brought into the dining hall. During one of my later summers at Meyersville, someone decided to put on a musical revue and I was delegated to sing and dance. Why me? I don't remember why. Our neighbor Mr. Meyers was the director. In any event, I sang and danced with a top hat and cane and sang "Without my walking stick, I'd be insane….can't look my best, I'd feel undressed, without my cane…"

During our first summer in Meyersville we rented one of Mrs. Veingar's cottages and experienced a severe thunderstorm. With our window flaps left up, we all became soaked in no time and my mother and father rushed around to let down the beaverboard flaps to keep the rain out. We only stayed a week then, but next summer we came back and stayed in a cottage for the whole summer. On weekends, when my father came up, he started building the summer bungalow that we occupied for ten summers.

Pop paid to have the original shell built; just one large room with studio couches for us to sleep on, a kerosene stove and kerosene lamps to see by. During our initial stay at the camp, our first year, Pop and Moe built the first addition, a back porch that turned out to be the kitchen and a bathroom. Over several years, other additions were made to the original shell; a loft that Moe and Sylvia used; two additional rooms on the side of the house, one of which was a porch, the other a back bedroom. Pop also spent a lot of time cutting down trees and using the logs to put in steps to the house (on both sides of the house) plus clearing a small driveway on the side of the house. With all the additions and improvements made to the house, the inside walls of the original shell were never finished. While we did eventually have electricity and refrigerators were finally invented, no more ice boxes, we never did have heat. But, of course, it was a summer bungalow and why would we need heat. We never planned on Moe and Sylvia spending their first winter in Myersville!

Mom always told the story that Stuart (he had to be about 2 years old then) awoke from his afternoon nap, decided he was hungry, climbed down from his cot and wandered to the icebox. Mom was visiting with some of the ladies outside the cottage so she didn't hear Stuart (then "Buddy") moving around in the cottage. By the time she came back inside, Buddy had bitten into everything he could bite into in the icebox. Mom learned to drive in Meyersville; I think Moe taught her. Moe was with us a lot; he helped Pop build the house. This was before he married Sylvia. Mom got a 1930 Model A Ford coupe, standard transmission only, of course, with a rumble seat. Unfortunately, Mom never learned to coordinate the clutch and the gas and we would jerk up whatever road we happened to be on at the time, until Mom could finally get into third gear. Mom wanted to get a license in New York, but she never could pass the test (probably the uncoordinated clutch and gas problem). New Jersey took pity on her and gave her a license. To my knowledge, however, she never drove in New York, not even when we lived in Poughkeepsie. On one of our return trips to Brooklyn, we made an extra stop in Whippany, New Jersey and visited with Auntie Anna and Aunt Dorothy at a large boarding/road house where Auntie Anna was the cook. Apparently, they had not ever been in touch and I don't know how Pop found them or knew where they were, because this was the first time I ever met them. Aunt Dorothy was Pop's stepsister, and was the female image of pop; same nose, also. Auntie Anna must have been Pop's stepmother; one of his father's wives. (I think Pop said he had 2 or even 3 wives).

I remember Auntie Anna telling me I had to eat my carrots so I would grow up and be beautiful like Aunt Dorothy. To this day, carrots are not one of my favorite foods. I remember looking at Aunt Dorothy after Auntie Anna passed that remark and pushed my plate away. Unfortunately, while Aunt Dorothy was a nice enough person, she was not my idea of beautiful and I certainly did not want to grow up and look like her. Of course, I never said that to Auntie Anna or Aunt Dorothy.

The Wasserbergs were Silvia's family and often came to Meyersville. I remember Auntie Anna and Sylvia's mother, who, incidentally, was also an excellent cook and baker, sitting together, preparing food, talking and laughing a mile a minute. Sidney Wasserberg, who was unmarried at that time, used to come to Meyersville also. He was a lot of fun and gave me my first cigarette. He told me I could have it if I could inhale it. Needless to say, trying to inhale resulted in a choking and coughing fit.

My 9th birthday–Mom couldn't make a birthday party for me. I was sick with German Measles. I remember dancing around in the back yard around the bonfire because the rash was finally gone. I think Sylvia was with us at that time. Moe was always in Meyersville with us and when he got back from Spain he brought Sylvia with him. When they decided to get married, we drove to Michiana Shores (between Michigan and Indiana) from Meyersville because Sylvia's family was vacationing there and she wanted her family to be at her wedding. I remember the trip, with Sylvia and I singing the Andrews Sisters version of "I'll Be With You In Apple Blossom Time….". It was definitely one of our favorites.

Pop flew back to New York from Chicago on one of the early commercial flights. We were all excited about him doing that. Commercial flying was not as commonly used then as it is today.

I had an "Estelle" experience during my last year in Meyersville. Mrs. Veinger had hired a young black man to work in the dining hall, that I became friendly with. It turned out he could play a little jazz piano and used to play and sing some songs. Also, he taught me how to jitterbug and it was one Saturday night that I insisted he dance with me. Of course, you can imagine what happened. Mr. Most got a hold of me after the dance and told me that dancing with blacks, he said "negroes," was not to be done and the next day, my black friend was gone. Mrs. Veinger had fired him.

CHAPTER SEVEN

JOSEPH DAVID LANDERSMAN

1899 and after

Joseph David Landersman was born May 2, 1899 and had an abbreviated childhood. His father and mother died when he was eleven and, following Jewish law, Joe as the oldest son had an immediate Bar Mitzvah to become the man of the surviving family. His younger brother Nat was sent to be brought up by the well-to-do Lazarus family, their mother's side, and Joe went to their father's parents who lived in poverty in the lower east side of New York, in the slums.

The Landersmans lived in a single room shack storefront between two large buildings, an eight-foot wide alley-filler from which during the day they sold two-cent soda and candy to passersby on the street. At night they dropped the lid to the street and the same room served as home for Joe and his two grandparents who spoke only Yiddish. His grandmother kept a Kosher home in that hovel, cooking on a single hot plate and washing in a bucket. From this Joe developed a life-long revulsion for greasy food and an objection to eating leftovers and undercooked meats. At night he would carefully arrange his only school pants under the rolled-out mattress so that the pants would be creased in the morning.

When Joe was faced with the early Bar Mitzvah after his father's death, the Lazarus grandfather, who owned a boys clothing factory, refused to give Joe a suit for the ceremony and Joe wore his only clothes. His Bar Mitzvah ceremony was like the funeral that had preceded it with families and friends crying and lamenting the loss of father and mother, of two young boys orphaned and split-up. Although the families had little to no contact after that, the two brothers, Joe and Nat, kept in contact over all the years that followed.

At twelve years of age Joe quit school and went to work full-time in the garment district of New York in a small factory, a sweat-shop, the first of many that would follow and immediately brought more money to the alley-filler shack of his grandparents than they made on two cent seltzer. Reading, writing and especially 'rithmatic had come easily to him at school but they had to eat, so he dropped out of school in the fifth grade and from then on supported his grandparents working twelve hours a day six days a week.

Joe could add, subtract, multiply and divide like a machine even as a boy. He could run a pencil down a foot-long column of four digit numbers and write the total when he reached the bottom. He could add up grocery prices in his head and tell the clerk how much change he was due. He could take a deck of cards and add up face values as fast as he could flash them down on a table and he could play cards. He loved to play cards. In gin rummy and poker he counted cards, memorizing what cards had been played and which ones remained and into the game he could tell what cards were held by the other players, what cards they needed and what the odds were on every hand.

Tilly Domes caught Joe's eye when he was twenty. He was a cutter and she was a sixteen-year-old stock girl in the cutting and shipping department of a ladies lingerie factory. She was short and cute, full of energy and spirit with snappy remarks and when she had to cross the cutting department, rather than walk around the long tables she would jump up and over, scampering across each table and laughing at the cutters stacking layers of fabric. They dated and as they grew to know and love each other Joe confided that he didn't like the name Tilly, he preferred Thelma and so that became her name. They were married in Newark, New Jersey on November 24, 1920. The family always celebrated their anniversary at Thanksgiving.

Joe was then supporting his grandmother (his grandfather had passed away), wife and wife's brother Moe, as he would be supporting family and extended family most of his life.

The 1930's; The Depression; Joe Landersman had been out of work for six months and his last job had been temporary; two weeks escorted through Jersey City picket lines, threatened every day until the strike was settled and he and the other scabs were fired. The country was in a deep depression, there were no jobs to be had and Joe, like thousands of others, spent most of his time calling on the countless small sweatshops in the garment district of New York looking for work. Just getting someone to talk was a rare success so it was difficult to hide Joe's surprise and excitement when this manager said he needed a cutter, but Joe was a poker player and knew how to maintain composure when holding a good hand or bluffing with a weak one.

Joe calmly outlined his considerable experience as a cutter in the garment trade; lay-up, pattern maker, marker and cutter with knife and circular and up-and-down machines. He had done it all; men's, women's, children's and undergarments. This job was ladies undergarment and yes, he had done it before, better than most, maybe better than anyone, and he could make up a marker tighter than anyone and that would save goods and make more money for the shop. Joe was good at what he did and he knew it but the problem was convincing the manager.

Twenty dollars a week! An actual offer of employment in his trade at the going rate after months of search during which his house had been foreclosed and he had scraped by with odd jobs, night work and taxi driving, barely paying the rent and putting food on the table for his family. Now a real job. Joe sat thoughtful for a moment, about to jump at the offer, smile, shake hands with the manager and accept with pleasure, but then the poker player took over.

"Twenty dollars? I couldn't take a job like this for less than forty."

Now it was the manager's turn to be surprised. "Twenty dollars is good money and jobs like this are hard to come by. This is a solid shop. You'd do well with us here."

Joe stood up and shook hands. "Thanks. I'll take my chances. I think I can do better elsewhere," and he walked toward the freight elevator used for entry and exit for the fourth floor shop.

"You'd have a steady job here. Times are tough. You're making a mistake, y'know." The manager spoke to Joe's back.

Joe pushed the call button for the freight elevator and waited. What am I doing, he thought, am I really making a mistake? He waited. The elevator took a long time coming and Joe's wish was like a prayer; come on, say something to me, tell me to come back, elevator take your time. Joe pushed the button again, could hear the elevator coming but still hoped, his heart pounding.

"Just a minute. What makes you think you're worth forty bucks?" the manager asked Joe's back.

Withholding a great sigh of relief while still maintaining his poker face, Joe turned away from the elevator. "'Cause I'm that good. I'm better than anyone you can find and I'll make you more than forty bucks, a lot more."

"Come back here and sit down," the manager asked and Joe knew he had a job for forty dollars a week.

In his next job a few years later the money was good for 1936 and it was an adventure for Joe to accept the Gottlieb brothers' offer to move away from New York to the small town of Poughkeepsie and be a co-manager of their ladies lingerie factory. Compared to the sweat shops in The City, Gottlieb's factory was very large and Joe would share the manager duties with Nat Landau, a man with whom he had worked before and who really knew the "rag business." A hundred dollars a week in 1936 put Joe in the high pay category and he knew that they could live very nicely on that money, especially in a small town. In addition to the salary, if the plant had a good year there would be a Christmas bonus. The plant did very well, better than the Gottlieb brothers had hoped and Joe received a five thousand dollar bonus. Not bad! A years pay as a Christmas present and the Landersmans went to Florida for Christmas vacation.

Jiggs was a purebred German Shepherd; a beautiful specimen and a great watch dog, but not the kind of dog to have in a small house with very little area in which to run. So the Landersmans' large pet became the watchdog of Gottleib Brothers and Jiggs stayed as the most loyal employee of that factory for almost 15 years. He made the rounds with the night watchman and on a few occasions chased away would-be break-ins. Every morning, Monday through Friday, he would stand with the watchman at the gate as workers entered, but if a stranger or a new worker approached Jiggs would block entry and growl until the watchman said, "Okay Jiggs," and the dog would step back. After that the "cleared" person could enter every morning. Jiggs never made a mistake in all those years with over 300 workers.

The Landersmans got a new dog, Fluffy; a small mutt with lots of long white hair that Joe told the kids was a Siberian Fluff because he looked like a cold climate dog. Fluffy was with the family for 15 years and was known by neighbors as the dog that could sing.

A dog that could sing? Well, not exactly. Estelle took piano lessons and every time she played Fluffy would be put out on the front porch where he would point his nose at the sky and howl with all his might, varying his tone slightly as if he were singing to the piano music. The family never knew what caused him to howl but it probably was that the frequency of some piano notes hurt his ears and he tried to drown them out. Buddy often told Estelle that she played so badly that the dog couldn't stand it.

As Joe had never had a boyhood of his own, he was fascinated with Buddy's toys, games and activities. Anything Buddy wanted to do was okay with Joe. They hiked in the woods when Buddy expressed an interest and Joe bought cookout equipment, boots, clothing and food for the event. When Buddy said he needed to shoot basketball a hoop and backboard went up on the garage. Archery? Joe bought a nice set and mounted a target.

Willie Domes, Thelma's older brother, worked for Lionel electric trains and brought various sets to Buddy on every visit, so Joe built a 4 by 12 foot table, similar to the cutting tables he was accustomed to at work, in their unfinished cellar for a fine electric train set. There was also a pin-ball machine in the basement and when Joe heard that a pool hall was going out of business he bought a professional quality subway pool table for $50. The specialist from Albany charged him $200 as he had to cut the table frame in half to get it into the cellar and reassemble it. Against a wall of that same unfinished cellar Joe set up a small rifle range where Buddy and he carved away stone and mortar firing .22 short ammunition.

When Buddy wanted a bicycle they went to the Rocket Store on Main Street where friend Jack Shafran discounted the best, a magnificent thing with two springs operating an articulated front wheel fork. Buddy learned to be careful when asking anything of his Dad because what he got could make others jealous. A year later his beautiful bike was stolen and Buddy replaced it with an $8 plain used bike like everyone else's.

Building model airplanes had been a hobby of Buddy's for some time, rubber band propeller driven models of balsam wood frame covered with paper and he got any model kit and supplies he asked for. After Buddy had finished a six-foot wingspan glider he expressed an interest in building a gas powered model plane. Joe thought that was a great idea and joined in the project.

Buddy's bed was moved into his sister's room (to some considerable chagrin by teen-aged Estelle) and Joe built a 4 by 8 foot table to make Buddy's former bedroom into a model plane shop. In three months a beautiful high wing monoplane model with six-foot wingspan was built with the best accessories and powered by a fine Super Cyclone gas engine. Having completed the model, Joe took the worktable apart, moved Buddy back into the room and never built another model.

When Buddy wanted pigeons a large coop was built in the attic for four pigeons and when he thought it would be nice to have a horse an extension was built on the garage for Jest, the Landersman's horse.

By the time Buddy was old enough to drive he was called Stuart and he got a car, paying for half of it. Some might have thought that Buddy/Stuart was spoiled, he got everything he asked for, but he had learned early to be careful because he might get too much.

Joe never denied anything Stu asked; activities at school, athletics, Boy Scouts, newspaper route, travel, jobs, camping, car, applying to college, even trying to get a job on a merchant ship and hitch hiking across the country. Joe approved and even encouraged it all.

Joe's friends and many of his business associates knew of Stu from local sports press coverage and when asked what Stu was doing for the 1948 summer after graduation from high school, Joe would proudly reply, "He's hitch hiking across the country." A common response would be, "Gee, that's something I always wanted to do," and Joe would ask, "Then why didn't you?" Joe was pleased and proud that his son was getting to do and to have everything that a boy wanted, all the things that Joe never had.

Joe was always interested in everything that his son, Stuart, did or wanted to do. At home after a basketball game Joe would ask how the game went and how Stu did. Years later Stu realized that even though Joe had expressed interest in everything that his son did, Joe never saw his son play in a single basketball game, not one. Also, Joe never saw his son play football or run in a track meet and he didn't attend any of the school events including the high school graduation ceremony at which Stu was class president.

Joe was always very interested in horse racing. Along with cards, poker and gin rummy, horse racing fit with his gambling interests and was consistent with his early boyhood skill with arithmetic. Remember, Joe never went beyond the fifth grade but he understood mathematics by his own reasoning and his patternmaker experiences. Horse racing for Joe Landersman presented challenges for the gambler that he was; odds, betting, past performances, lineage, track conditions, trainers, he would study it all and place his bets. Like all gamblers, you win some and you lose some. And like most gamblers, Joe came to realize that the track, or the bookmaker, made more money most of the time than the horse player.

Joe had developed a friendship with Irving Friedman who ran a cigar store on the corner of Hamilton and Main streets in Poughkeepsie. Joe found early that the cigar store was a reasonably successful business selling, as the name implies, tobacco products, as well as gift candies and cookies, newspapers and magazines. The store also had a small soda fountain with four stools, two pin-ball machines and a punch-board was usually available. It all looked legitimate.

Beneath the appearance of innocence Irv Friedman ran a bookmaking operation in his cigar store. A player could place a wager on any horse, at any track in the country anytime prior to post-time, and for any amount of money. At the race tracks the minimum bet was two dollars but Irv would take one dollar bets. It was common in those days to bet on "the numbers" for pennies or on a baseball game for larger amounts and Irv Friedman would take your money and hold the bet. Often the soda fountain stools were occupied with men studying horse racing sheets and the same might be going on on the pin-ball machines. If anyone was fortunate enough to win free-plays on the pin-ball machines, they could either play the games or ask Irv to pay-off at five cents a game. Of course all the gambling was illegal, so where was the law enforcement? Poughkeepsie policemen and detectives were among Irv Friedman's best customers.

Joe Landersman became one of Irv Friedman's best customers and then his best friend. They grew so close, in fact, that Irv asked Joe to join him in the bookmaking business. And so Joe became a bookie and made a lot of money. Joe still operated his ladies lingerie business, Kathel, and the bookmaking was just like a hobby, but a profitable one. Joe's bookmaking "hobby" started in 1947, which is significant because Stu started college in 1948. Many years later Joe told Stu that all of Stu's college costs were covered by bookmaking.

Irv and his wife Bessie, and Joe and Thelma took trips together; Miami, Saratoga, Boston, Las Vegas, always with some race track or other gambling as recreation and all paid for by bookmaking profits. Irv Friedman was a slick New Yorker and when he traveled he always wanted to stay in the best hotels and eat in the best restaurants. Joe Landersman loved it.

Joe loved to play poker. A group of Jewish men played each Wednesday night at the home of one of the players. The regular players included a couple of doctors, a dentist, an assistant district attorney plus another attorney, a clothing store owner, a retired security guard, a hardware store owner and some others like the electrician Moe Domes. There were two or three substitutes like Joe Landersman, who could be called upon to play if needed. One of the only rules of the loose club was that there be eight players. The home played at rotated each week and the host was responsible for providing light refreshment and for ensuring that the right number of players, eight, were available for that night's game. Usually the host's wife arranged the refreshment and then did a hasty retreat. This was a man's poker game. No women.

One afternoon Joe received a call from one of the regular poker players–I can't play tonight–can you fill in for me–the game is at Moe Domes' house. Joe accepted the offer and assured the player that he would be at Moe's game that night. A routine process. No problem.

Joe arrived at Moe's home, just around the corner from his own home, fifteen minutes before time for the game. Moe answered the door, looked surprised and said, "What the hell are you doing here? We don't need you."

It was Joe's turn to be surprised. "Sid can't make it tonight and he asked me to sit in for him."

"Well, we don't need you. Stop trying to crash the game." And Moe closed the door on Joe.

Now, we have to put this in context. This was Moe Domes, Thelma's brother, closing the door on Joe Landersman. From times past, frequent rough economic times that Moe Domes had no income, no place to sleep, nothing to eat, he lived in the home of Joe. Through The Depression Moe lived with Joe. When he came back from Spain without work, Joe gave him a place to live. When he couldn't get a job during and after WWII and when he started his electrician business, Joe gave Moe and Silvia a place to live. All of these times Joe had never asked Moe for a cent–live rent free. And Joe was married to Moe's sister who had taken care of him as a child. Moe closed the door on Joe and for no good reason.

Well, maybe to Moe there was a reason. The irony of the door closing was not lost on Joe. He realized that charity often is accepted with hidden humiliation and just as often the recipient is embarrassed later when conditions are improved. Joe and Moe never spoke again, nor did their wives and Thelma Landersman, Moe's sister, would privately cry as if she had lost her brother.

World War II caused big shortages of consumer goods as the nation's industry focused on military production. The lingerie produced by Gottlieb Brothers was sold before it was made and was only limited by the availability of fabric. Joe Landersman and Nat Landau knew how to produce the merchandise and they knew how to obtain sub-contract work from other lingerie factories. They started a business of their own, Kathel Manufacturing Corporation, named for Katherine and Thelma, in a small loft in Wappinger Falls and later they moved the plant to a larger place in Poughkeepsie. At the start there was a third partner, whose wife was Katherine, hence the business name; Kath for Katherine, thel for Thelma. The third partner ran the plant in Wappinger Falls as Joe and Landau were still at Gottlieb's all day, but when Kathel moved to Poughkeepsie they bought out the third partner.

The Gottliebs were very angry with Nat Landau and Joe for starting Kathel and issued an ultimatum: close Kathel immediately and stay with Gottlieb Brothers or you're both fired.

Years later Joe said that one of the biggest mistakes of his life was not staying with Gottlieb, for if he had he would have been manager of that business with much more money. Kathel stayed viable for about the next five years and then Joe and Landau felt there was not enough business for both of them. Landau offered to buy out Joe but the bargaining led to a reversal and Joe bought out Landau. It took all the money Joe could assemble to complete the buy-out and he never fully recovered financially from that transaction.

Kathel did fairly well over the next ten years and Joe hoped that his son, Stuart, after college and navy, would join him, learn the trade and take over the business, but Stuart had other ambitions. Eventually Kathel went out of business and Joe often said that another of the big mistakes of his life was not taking Nat Landau's money and walking away from Kathel but Joe had always been a gambler and sometimes even the best gamblers lose.

Joe Landersman had parlayed his career and his finances from an orphan selling two cent soda in the slums of the East Side to a substantial business of his own with family, comfort and happiness despite setbacks such as The Depression, leaving Gottlieb and buying out Landau. Life's gambles had paid off well for him, almost all of them.

CHAPTER EIGHT

MOE AND SILVIA

1936 and after

The American Communist Party was well established in New York during the tough economic times of the 1920s and 1930s; Depression times. The labor force was out of work, times were tough and many turned to various organizations that promised remedy for the nation's ills.

Morris Domes, the youngest brother of Tilly Domes, was known as Moe to his friends and family. As a strong labor union supporter he read the literature, attended meetings, listened to the speakers and decided that the economic and social problems of the country and the rest of the world could only be solved by communism. As a young electrician in New York the only work he could get was through his union which was controlled by individuals in the Communist Party. Moe Domes became a very strong supporter of the union and of the Communist Party.

The Spanish Civil War was advertised as a conflict of fascism versus socialism and then communism in 1936, and when the

International Brigades were being formed, Moe volunteered. He was sent by ship to France then by truck and foot across the border into Spain as a member of the Abraham Lincoln Brigade. As encouragement, his well-off communist friends Mr. Marcy and Joe Resnick in New York had promised Moe a good job upon return from Spain. All he received when he got back two years later was some brief treatment for his wounds and he was more broke than when he left and still without a job. While Moe had been fighting in Spain, Marcy and Resnick had stayed safe in the good 'ole U. S. of A. and had made a lot of money.

Moe was a handy-man and could always find work even if it was short-term. He could do anything with tools and as America prepared for and entered World War II there were plenty of jobs in war work. Problem was he had been an active member of the Communist Party and had fought for communism in Spain, so even though he was a combat veteran he was persona non grata by the U.S. military and businesses engaged in war work. The FBI had a file on him and even knew his Spanish alias, Maurice Dumas.

Before we proceed with the Moe Domes story, let's take a moment for your humble writer to insert a family rumor, maybe a myth or maybe even a fact; but it's worth telling at this point because we have just learned that Moe Domes used the name Maurice Dumas in Spain. Why did Moe use that name?

The name Dumas is very well known in literature as there were Spanish brothers, Nicholas and Alexander Dumas, who were famous authors. The name Domes is close to Dumas.

Over the years, from time to time, Thelma Landersman, nee Tilly Domes, would describe to her children that long ago her Jewish family had lived in Spain and their name then was Dumas. Their family name was changed to Domes when the family came to America. Also, Tilly Domes often stated that some of their Jewish Dumas family stayed in Spain and changed–converted–to Christianity during the Spanish Inquisition. Another part of that family left Spain rather than convert and we, the Domes now Landersmans, are a part of that family. This means that according to Thelma Landersman her children,

Estelle and Stuart, are related to the Spanish authors Nicholas and Alexander Dumas. Taking this a generation and more some steps further, the Ravitz children, their children and David, Mark and Kilian Landersman are all related to the famous Spanish authors. Remember, in Jewish lore it is matrilineal descent that counts–the female line is dominant–in our case the Domes line. What did the Dumas' write? How about *The Three Musketeers* and *The Count of Monte Christo*. Three Musketeers like David, Mark and Kilian?

The family story goes on to touch on some very sensitive areas. It's well known that most of the conversions in Spain were forced and yet were sincere but that some of the Jewish *conversos* did so only in outward appearances and practiced their Jewish faith in secret. Some of the family that stayed behind in Spain might have been truly converted or some may have continued to be Jews in secret. Some were discovered by the Inquisition and killed. Some got away with it. We'll never know.

Back to our story of Moe and Silvia.

Silvia Wasserberg married Moe in 1939 and together they traveled from New Jersey to Florida to Chicago to Poughkeepsie as Moe tried various occupations, always successful until his red background was discovered and then they would move on. When World War II ended they were in Poughkeepsie living with Joe and Thelma Landersman, as Thelma was Moe's older sister. Moe decided to go into a plumbing and electrical business with Dave Brandt, a handyman more experienced in plumbing.

Domes and Brandt lasted about a year and then Moe was in business himself as an electrician, a business he stayed in for the rest of his life. During that time Moe and Silvia lived first in the Landersman's attic on Hooker Avenue, then in a rented apartment for a few years and then they bought a house on Parkwood Boulevard, around the corner from where the Landersmans lived.

There were four Domes siblings; William, Esther, Tillie and Morris. Willie, the oldest, as a young man was in vaudeville and had performed with Al Jolsen and knew Jimmy Durante. Then he was with carnivals and circuses, and ended up as a salesman in the toy business. Willie was a comedian and a con man, knew how to manipulate money and games, and could keep people in stitches telling one story after another while taking their money. He could do card tricks and pickpocket.

One day while visiting the Landersmans, Willie had five year old Buddy get an egg from the kitchen. "Now, look at that light fixture on the ceiling," he said as he slipped the egg into Buddy's pocket and smacked his thigh. As the boy beheld his gooey wet leg Willie said, "Don't trust anyone." Buddy ran into the kitchen crying and from Thelma came, "Willie, what have you done?" in mild reprimand. She was accustomed to her brother's antics.

Another time Willie had Buddy get ten one-dollar bills from his Dad. "Now hold out your hand," and Willie quickly counted out the ten ones. "How many did I give you?" "Ten," Buddy replied. "Count them!" and an amazed Buddy found that he held only nine bills. Willie had palmed one from the bottom of their overlapping hands. "Next time you might only get eight."

Willie lived as man and wife with a gentile woman for almost fifty years, until he died. He wouldn't marry her because of the religious difference, they had no children and none of his family ever met her. He visited Thelma's family two or three times a year in Brooklyn, Poughkeepsie or Myersville and paid a lot of attention to the children but always by himself. When Ringling Brothers Barnum and Bailey Circus would come to Madison Square Garden, Willie would take Estelle and Buddy and for ten years at Thanksgiving time he took Buddy to the Macy's Parade.

Esther, Thelma's sister, had been killed in an automobile accident in the Pennsylvania mountains before Estelle was born. She had been an activist for socialism and women's rights and Estelle had been named for her, perhaps an explanation for Estelle's liberalism.

Moe was the youngest of the four Domes and Thelma, whose name had been changed from Tillie, often said that she had raised him. Well, maybe she helped because she was only a few years older, but she always had the older-sister to younger-brother ties to Moe, which is probably why he lived with the Landersmans so many years and why Thelma was in tears when the family split up.

Moe had lived with and been partially supported by Joe and Thelma Landersman at various times, single and married, in Brooklyn, Myersville, and Poughkeepsie over a span of almost 30 years and he was like a brother to Buddy. From his earliest years Buddy had followed Moe around, getting in the way most of the time, helping as he could, learning to use tools and fix things, so Buddy learned from Moe to be a handy-man but, most difficult of all, he learned to work for Moe.

As Buddy grew older, whenever he wanted to work all it took was a phone call and Moe would take him on as his assistant with good hourly pay for a day or a week. Silvia used to say that Buddy was the only person who could work for Moe. She was right because many had tried but no one could put up with Moe's demands and eccentricities, no one but Buddy. Moe hoped that after college and Navy, Buddy (Stuart) would return to Poughkeepsie, work with Moe and eventually take over Moe's electrician business.

Silvia and Estelle were as close as sisters, maybe closer, but Silvia was a very controlling person and very jealous of the dominance she continually practiced over family and friends. Silvia was a close friend to many people as long as they allowed her to lead. When Estelle was talked into marrying Jerry Ravitz by her mother and Jerry's mother, Silvia saw a threat to her control. She had had no voice in the marriage and she would be loosing control of Estelle.

Jerry was getting ready to ask Joe Landersman for his daughter's hand in marriage in the traditional way, as Jerry's mother had advised him, but Silvia said he shouldn't do that, it was foolish. No one thought it strange for Silvia to object to such a harmless act except Estelle, who promptly and properly put Silvia in her place by telling her to mind her own business. This was just not done to Silvia, whose authority had not been previously challenged even in her own family and she could not tolerate such rebellion in her followers. Estelle and Silvia had a huge argument, just short of violence, drawing in long withheld feelings, disclosures and accusations involving the rest of the family and covering far more than a simple request for a daughter's hand in marriage. Joe asked Moe and Silvia to move out of his house, they did not come to Estelle's wedding and Silvia and Estelle never again spoke.

CHAPTER NINE

A COLLEGE ESSAY

1949

As the heading below describes, the following piece was written in 1949 by Stu Landersman in his freshman English class at Clarkson College. The hitchhiking trip took place right after graduation from high school and this piece was written two months later. The trip is mentioned near the end of an earlier section of this work; Arlington High School. No changes or editing has been done from the original essay.

Stuart D. Landersman   Clarkson College of Technology
October 4, 1949   Essay, Freshman English Class

GO WEST, YOUNG MAN

Ever since Horace Greeley said, "Go West, young man," it has been the ambition of almost every young American boy to see the West. Few go, however, their reasons are lack of money and lack of time.

It is possible to fly from New York to Los Angeles or San Francisco for $99.00 plus tax, but not many fellows today have $99.00. It is possible to hitch hike the same distance for about $20 to $30 in a couple of weeks. I met a boy who made it in three and a half days (day and night). I did it myself in nine days. Others take three or even four weeks, but there is no reason for taking so long, other than poor planning or poor methods. So why don't more people hitch hike West?

Some say they can't see anything while hitch hiking. What does the auto tourist see on a trip? Miles of endless roads, rivers, mountains and forests. Most tourists never find out the name of this mountain, that stream, or what kind of trees are in that forest. Mr. Hitch Hiker has the advantage in this. The people he rides with; truck drivers, salesmen and farmers, generally know a lot more about the surrounding country than a tourist could find out from maps, and a local person is only too willing to relate stories of their locality to an interested listener.

The hitch hiker meets very interesting people on his travels and has as many interesting experiences. While hitch hiking last summer, I met some of the most interesting characters I have ever known. My companion and I spent a night in Cody, Wyoming on a park bench. Not so interesting in itself, but a real story-book hobo slept on the next bench and kept us up all night while he told some very interesting stories. We rode with lumberjacks, oilmen, cowboys and a sailor on his way home, for the first time in over a year, to marry his pregnant girl friend.

Yes, there are interesting people to be met and experiences to be had all over the country, but the regular tourist seldom comes in contact with them. Every day is to the hitch hiker a new and exciting novel. True, there are times when long hours are spent waiting for rides. This taxes one's patience and often leads to thoughts of giving up, but inevitably the law of averages catches up and helps you out of a jam.

The long hours of waiting for rides makes one look around. "There must be another way to get out of this spot," and there generally is.

Freight train riding is a subject in itself, which I shall not go into very far. It may be a little more dangerous than hitch hiking, but it can be faster and generally more dependable. I tried it and didn't fair too well, so I gave it up. The characters and experiences encountered in freight train riding far overshadow those in hitch hiking.

People who have never done any hitch hiking consider a person "bumming a ride" a lazy individual. This is a mistake. Long distance hitch hiking calls for long distance walking. Half of the rides end in the center of towns and the economical traveler is obliged to walk to the edge of town before commencing the thumb exercises. It may be only three or four blocks walk in each town, but three or four blocks in fifteen or twenty towns a day add up to a long distance. It is hard on shoe leather and hard on the hands that carry that twenty to thirty pound suitcase.

A little saying of unknown origin states, "Position is everything in life," and it is surely true of the hitch hiker. The place you stand with your thumb out constitutes at least seventy five percent of getting a ride. A straight fast road is no good, as cars won't stop when going too fast. On a curve is no good either, as drivers can't see you soon enough to decide. The bottom of a hill is even worse, as cars want to get up speed to make the hill. There are very few ideal locations for hitch hiking. The thumber has to try to pick out the best.

The method used in hitch hiking is very important. I divide hitch hiking methods into three classes: (1) The Straightforward, (2) The Trick, and (3) The On the Spot.

The Straightforward is the kind most often used. It includes all thumbing done while standing by the road and not trying to fool the drivers. Sometimes a sign is used to advantage in this method.

The Trick method is very rarely used with any degree of success. You have possibly tried it by limping along the road while hitch hiking, using a cane or a crutch, or even having a friend lay down alongside the road. These never work very well because they are obviously artificial.

A Trick Method that has been used with great success is carrying a two gallon oil can. Some of you may have read in Reader's Digest of a hitch hiker down South who used this system. I used it few years ago on two trips and found that it worked very well. The driver gets the impression that you are carrying gasoline for your car and is generally willing to help out a fellow driver. Once in the car you can tell the victim the joke you have played on him. I used this method in getting about a hundred rides and not once did anyone get angry because they had been fooled. They laughed and considered it a good joke. The can need not be used just for getting rides. The one I used had the top fitted with hinges and a hasp and made an ideal carrier for sandwiches and clothing.

The On the Spot Method can only be used when hitch hiking near gas stations or traffic lights. When the car stops for the light or gas, the hitch hiker asks for a ride. The driver with a big empty car is put "on the spot" and quite often says okay.

When your trip is over and you return home everyone will ask, "What did you see? What did you learn?" You will have little to answer. The sights you saw may not be as much as the auto-tourist. You can't point out facts and say, "Here is what I learned," but the knowledge you will have acquired by a month on the highways will give you a better understanding of people, conditions and the country in general, knowledge that could never be acquired by book or lecture.

If you want to learn a lot about not very much and spend some time wandering, combine Horace Greeley's advice and mine, "Go West, young man, hitch hike West."

CHAPTER TEN

CLARKSON COLLEGE
OF TECHNOLOGY

1948-1951

At the start of his hitchhiking summer Stu Landersman had asked his good friend Otis Waterman to include Stu in the arrangements to go to Clarkson College of Technology far upstate in Potsdam, New York. Oat took care of everything and when the hitchhiking was done and just after Labor Day in early September 1948 Stu Landersman and Otis Waterman started their college educations at the freshman branch of Clarkson which was in Malone, New York, thirty miles east of Potsdam.

FRESHMAN YEAR 1948-1949
They roomed together in a three bedroom house in a quiet residential street. All three bedrooms and the only bathroom in the house were upstairs and all three of the bedrooms were rented to Clarkson freshmen; two young men in each bedroom. A little close

perhaps, maybe a little bit more togetherness than any of them would have preferred but not too bad maybe.

Maybe it really wouldn't have been too bad were it not for the landlady and the business she ran downstairs. Oh no, not that kind of business, a legitimate business of hairdresser–a hair salon–as a further stretch; a beauty parlor. And the landlady with her ten year old son lived downstairs in the beauty parlor. And when the landlady's husband came home weekends from his traveling sales job, which fortunately was not often, he too, slept guess where? You guessed it, in the beauty parlor. And remember, the only bathroom in the house was upstairs with the rented rooms, so the landlady had a tiny potty and wash basin room installed in, guess where. You guessed it again, in the beauty parlor, for use by clients or customers, the landlady, her family and the one employee. There was a lot of togetherness with frosh living in Malone, New York.

Clarkson was basically an engineering college and the most popular academic program led to a degree in civil engineering. That's the program that Otis took. Stu took the mechanical engineering program. Other programs offered at Clarkson were electrical engineering, chemical engineering and chemistry. The only academic program offered that was not in engineering or science fields was business administration and that was taken by most of the recruited athletes.

The curriculum for all the engineering disciplines was the same for the first two years, so all engineering students took the same courses in their freshman and sophomore years. The academic program emphasized basic math and science, necessary for all engineers. In the third year, the junior year and after that in their senior year, students took courses in their specialized engineering field. This made it easy at the freshman branch of Clarkson at Malone; everyone took the same subjects. Well, everyone but the business administration students.

Remember Oat and Stu in high school playing basketball, or rather practicing, with the GI Bill veterans at Vassar College? Well, that had come about because in 1948 all, well almost all colleges were filled to capacity with the GI vets. Clarkson was no exception and couldn't accommodate all the applicants on the Potsdam campus so the Malone branch, an extension, was established to take advantage of this increase in tuition income. The GI Bill brought great financial income for all colleges in the nation. This also meant that with a large segment of the student population as veterans, the average age of the freshman class was higher than it had been and many freshmen were more mature than those in the past. The Clarkson freshman class at Malone was about fifty percent veterans.

The freshman branch of Clarkson at Malone was located in what had been a school for sight and sound handicapped. Crude townies had called them "deaf and dumb" but with the school now used by Clarkson college boys, including many veterans, the vulgar terms were no longer heard.

In college sports of that time, by NCAA rules, freshmen were not allowed to play on varsity teams, so with a separate freshman campus it was easy for Clarkson to have freshman teams. Ice hockey was the main sport of Clarkson and with proximity to Canada it was natural that most of the hockey players were recruited from Ontario and Quebec.

Older Clarkson hockey fans spoke of past freshman teams, teams with some players that spoke French better than English and most that couldn't pass freshman courses. The fans spoke of freshman teams that beat the varsity teams in practice games. And those fans would moan, "Oh, what hockey teams we would have had if we could have kept all of those freshmen!" Or did they mean Frenchmen? Each year a few of those freshmen Canadian hockey players survived to play varsity in the following seasons and even with those few each year Clarkson was able to put excellent hockey teams on the ice. In other sports Clarkson was not so good.

Dutch Prochelle was a short, stocky and very cocky ex-Marine who walked with a bow legged swagger and coached football, basketball and baseball at the freshman branch, so Stu played football and basketball for him. There was a separate freshman hockey coach; a young Canadian.

In freshman football, Stu was an end on the second team and got in on some limited game action. He enjoyed the practices, his team mates and the atmosphere of freshman college football and, as in high school, he considered football part of his preparation for basketball, which was more important to Stu. At practice one afternoon he fell on his knee. It hurt, was red and swelling but of course one did not quit practice on Dutch Prochelle's team. So Stu hobbled through the rest of the practice, showered, dressed and went to dinner. There was homework every evening.

The next morning Stu's knee was swollen, red and ached. It hurt more to walk. Stu limped to a doctor on the same street as his rooming house. The doctor shook his head and gave Stu some pain pills. "Well, you're finished with football that's for sure."

Stu asked, "You mean for the rest of the season?"

"I mean for good. There'll be no more football for you, this season or ever." The doctor was very sure of himself.

"How about basketball? I'm really more interested in playing basketball. Will I be okay by basketball season? Now Stu was really worried.

The doctor didn't ease Stu's concern. "Basketball! Maybe you didn't understand me. You won't be playing anything more active than poker or chess from now on. No, no basketball."

Stu was very concerned. Basketball was very important to him and he didn't like the prospect of not even getting a chance, never even finding out if he could play college basketball. He went to see Coach Prochelle.

"What do you mean, you went to a doctor? You get hurt with me, I take care of it. You don't go to a doctor." Dutch sneered as it seemed to Stu that Dutch was always angry. "I'm gonna take you to a guy who knows these things, a chiropractor. He can fix you, quick and easy. C'mon."

The "guy who knows these things" surely did. A twist of the knee, a bend and another twist and it felt better. The ache was gone and over the next two weeks the swelling subsided. Stu walked without limping. His college football was finished but by the start of basketball season he was healthy and ready to go.

At the start of basketball season Dutch announced, "I don't need tryouts. I can tell a ball player by how he walks out onto the court." And however he picked his team; Stu didn't care because he was selected to be on the freshman team. To Stu this was college basketball, with the hope of maybe varsity next year.

Stu sat on the bench a good deal, started a few games and played both center and forward and was generally satisfied that, as he had through high school, he would improve during the season so that he could make the varsity next season.

Dutch was primarily a baseball man and had played semi-pro third base. When he had to lay out the baseball diamond for his first practice session, he drew a polygon in the dirt for home plate and with no measurements walked to where he indicated the pitcher's mound. He did a left turn and walked to where he thought third base should be, picked up a stone and threw it across the field, across where he had indicated the pitcher's mound. "There! Where that rock hit! That's first base."

The Clarkson players were engineering students with scientific mentality that couldn't accept Dutch's crude measurements without verification and after practice (when Dutch had left) with a tape measure they found that he was more arrogant than accurate. Dutch's diamond was far off; especially his third to first base throw. The student engineers made it right.

Stu completed his freshman year with fairly good grades in all courses in both semesters and had a good time living in Malone, even living in the crowded rooming house above the beauty salon. After the freshman year it was to Potsdam, to the main campus of Clarkson, for the start of the sophomore year.

SOPHOMORE YEAR 1949-1950

In Potsdam, Oat and Stu roomed in the home of Thomas Perrin and his family on Elm Street, a quiet residential area of large old homes. The Perrin family had been long time family friends of Otis' family, the Watermans. Their wooden house was very large and very old with five bedrooms and two bathrooms upstairs, all five bedrooms rented to Clarkson men; two to a room, all five bedrooms larger than those in Malone. The Perrins lived downstairs with adequate rooms, unlike the Malone beauty parlor. Kate Perrin took good care of her tenants and even tried, for a while, to provide a simple breakfast for 35 cents, but that didn't last long.

Tom Perrin was an attorney with a local practice and he was also the local Justice of the Peace, which played an important role later in the Clarkson student activities–but more on that later. The Perrins were good to their student-tenants and their son, young Tommy Perrin, got to know most of them.

A couple of months into the first semester of the sophomore year, Otis decided that he preferred a room in the front of the house and so Jerry Fadden agreed to swap with him. That brought Stu a new room mate. Stu had known Jerry Fadden from the previous year in Malone on the freshman football team. Being roommates now brought Stu and Jerry closer and they became very good friends. Stu and Oat remained good friends but after that change of rooms it was the Stu and Jerry team.

The fraternities at Clarkson were all local, that is they were not affiliated with fraternities at other colleges, they were not national. Jerry and Stu had decided to be in the same frat and they were pretty sure that they would be accepted into any of the fraternities they chose and so the matter of choice required careful analysis. One frat was Sigma Delta to which all the Clarkson football players belonged and Jerry was a football player. Another was Lambda Iota which had all the basketball players and Stu was on the basketball team. Then there was Omicron Pi Omicron with all the hockey players.

Analysis showed Jerry and Stu that O Pi O, with the Canadian hockey players, had the wildest parties so that frat became their favorite. Further analysis suggested that if Sig had a party, Jerry probably would be invited by his football team mates and if Lambda had a party, Stu probably would be invited by his basketball team mates. Both of those frats knew that Jerry and Stu hung out together so probably both would be invited. If all that worked out it would mean that Jerry and Stu would be included in all of the parties at all three of the most active fraternities. And that's exactly how it worked out. Jerry and Stu pledged to and became brothers of O Pi O and seldom missed a party at three fraternities.

Initiations had always seemed foolish to Stu and he did what he could to avoid them. Fraternity initiation for O Pi O was no exception and he did what little he could to keep a low profile and stay out of the all-day all-night foolishness. The final initiation stunt called for the pledges individually to carry out foolish prescribed functions. At midnight, with the pledges all cowering in the large attic of the fraternity house, each was given a scrap of paper with a directive, a project that had to be completed by five AM. Stu's project was to measure a bridge located twenty miles out of town, to measure the bridge in condom lengths. He read the paper and shook his head in disgust. He had no intention of walking or hitch-hiking out to the bridge for such foolishness.

Peanut Sellers was not small. He was six feet tall. The nickname had some-how hung on to him from childhood. He was a member of the O Pi O fraternity, a GI Bill veteran in his senior year at Clarkson and he, like Stu, didn't think much of initiations. He saw Stu looking at the scrap of paper, clearly in disgust, and asked what the project was. Stu read it to him.

"Have you seen that bridge?" Peanut asked.

After Stu's affirmative reply Peanut asked, "How long would you say it is?"

Stu thought for a while, considered where Peanut was going with this and said, "It's exactly 120 feet long."

Peanut smiled. "Okay, how long is a condom?"

Stu returned the smile. "Rolled out for use, a condom is six inches long."

"You must be some-what handicapped with short equipment but six inches does divide very evenly into a foot, doesn't it?" And Peanut walked away.

Stu wrote on the paper, "240 condom lengths," put the paper in his pocket and went to sleep on the attic floor. At a quarter to five that morning Stu woke up and turned in the bridge measurement. Initiation was over. He was an O Pi O brother.

Basketball season–college basketball–not freshman, but varsity–a brief try-out and Stu was on a college varsity basketball team! A number of the best players from the freshman team had been lost–drop-outs–but some of the previous year's best from the freshmen team made the varsity team:

Ed Siedlecki–center–big strong army veteran
Bob Hodge–forward–tall thin–son of Clarkson coach
Lee Colavito–forward–fast ball handler–army veteran
—along with Stu Landersman and a couple of others.

College varsity basketball! Stu was very pleased. Mostly he sat on the bench but he got into a few games, did reasonably well and knew that he would continue to improve. Next season he would be a college junior with a year's varsity experience and, as in all college sports, the senior classmen on the team would be gone and he could move up, less bench time, maybe even start.

The Director of Athletics at Clarkson was Hank Hodge who coached basketball and baseball, with baseball his favorite. Some of his players had gone into professional baseball and Hank was particularly proud of one, Jackie Phillips, who played first base for the Brooklyn Dodgers. At the end of basketball season Hank Hodge asked Stu to be on the baseball team, laying out a two-year program to make a pitcher out of Stu. One of the mistakes of Stu's life was turning down that opportunity.

Being from Buffalo, New York, it was natural that flashy Bill Goudy would be known as Buffalo Bill, the closest thing to what many years later was "The Fonz" of TVs "Happy Days," with DA hairstyle, leather jacket and hip-jive-beebop talk. Buffalo Bill was somewhat of a loner who walked around snapping his fingers with, "Bee-bop-sha-bam-sha-booby-op." In basketball he was fast, could drive and handle the ball well but couldn't shoot and he worked out with the team but didn't make it, nor did he make the baseball team. But Bill Goudy helped Stu develop a hook shot in basketball, emphasizing dance-like steps with graceful arm movement and follow-through and that hook shot became Stu's signature shot, his most effective shot for all the basketball that followed.

Buffalo Bill was the best softball pitcher at Clarkson and Stu Landersman and Jerry Fadden, Stu's roommate, jumped at the chance to be on his intramural softball team, even passing up their fraternity team. The Buffaloes won the intramural softball league as Bill struck out almost every batter. Stu in left field handled the ball twice all season; two ground balls in different games. In a Buffaloes practice Bill was trying to improve Stu's hitting. "Hold your bat out across the plate and keep your eye on the ball," Bill told Stu, and he hit Stu's bat with the pitch. "This time swing your bat across in the same place and keep your eye on the ball," and Bill's next pitch hit Stu's bat again. "Now this time I'm not going to hit your bat. You're going to have to keep your eye on the ball and hit it," and it worked. Stu's hitting improved.

Winning the intramural league meant that the Buffaloes would play the winner of the fraternity league and that was Lambda, the frat of basketball players. So Stu got to play softball against his basketball team mates. It was all good fun with lots of razzing but Lambda won.

By the end of his sophomore year at Clarkson, partying had replaced both academics and basketball in importance to Stu. With his room mate Jerry Fadden, they never missed a party and on nights when there were no fraternity parties they hung out at McManus' Bar. Still, Stu received passable grades in his subjects and finished his sophomore year satisfied and looking forward to being a junior.

JUNIOR YEAR 1950-1951

Of all the basketball games he played from the Wildcats, through high school and two colleges, one game has stood out in Stu's memory. It was at Clarkson against their big rival St. Lawrence, junior year,

1951. In the Navy there were a few memorable games but you'll read about them later.

In those days it was very common for professional basketball (NBA) teams to promote interest by playing some regular season games in nearby towns. Also, they would play some exhibition games against nearby college or town teams. St. Lawrence had just opened a very fine field house for basketball and hockey and an exhibition game was arranged with the Syracuse Nationals. In front of a packed field house, the Syracuse professional players loafed and laughed away the first half and the St. Lawrence college team had a big lead. In the second half the Syracuse professionals tried to catch up but the college team played their best, hung on to the lead and won the game. St. Lawrence beat the Syracuse Nationals of the NBA!

A week later that same St. Lawrence team met their big rivals Clarkson in a regularly scheduled game. The game was played in the tiny old Clarkson basketball court. Stu, as backup center and forward didn't get into the game in the first half. Early in the second half it was obvious that Clarkson center Ed Siedlecki was tired and Stu went in for him. Stu was doing well so when Bob Hodge needed a break, Siedlecki came back in and Stu shifted to forward and played the rest of the game. At the end of regular time the score was tied; overtime. At the end of the overtime the score was again tied; another overtime. It took three overtimes but Clarkson finally beat the St. Lawrence team that had beaten the Syracuse Nationals; the same Syracuse Nationals that had gone on the following week to beat the NBA champion Minneapolis Lakers in a regular season game. So, being engineering students, remember, and relying on mathematical reasoning, the Clarkson basketball team and student fans could claim by comparative scores that the Clarkson basketball team was better than the best professional team. Clarkson could claim to be the best basketball team in the nation, in the world! Two weeks later on their own court in their new field house, St. Lawrence beat Clarkson by twenty points. Mathematical reasoning and comparative scores came crashing down.

In social activities Stu's junior year at Clarkson was a continuation of his sophomore year–but no–in social activities it was even more intense. More partying, more drinking and of course that meant even less time for academics. Books were much less important than booze and basketball.

Stu developed a priority list of those things that were important to him; the five B's:

1. Basketball
2. Booze
3. Broads
4. Bucks
5. Books

Clearly, basketball and booze didn't go well together and the late nights that usually accompanied drinking tended to reduce the effectiveness of athletics. Then there were broads, third on the priority list, broads a crude reference to those of the female gender. The most convenient source of feminine companionship was Potsdam State Teachers College right in the same small town as Clarkson. It was very easy for Jerry Fadden and Stu to get dates at the last minute from a sorority house and go to parties at any of the fraternity houses or to dinner. But if it were to be a dinner date that took money and Jerry and Stu didn't have much of that which was number four on the list; bucks. Stu had decided that he would minimize his requests for money from home and Jerry lived on his small GI Bill, so they both were always on the lookout for part time–one time–jobs with which to finance their social activities. All of these first four priorities took time and effort away from number five on the list; books–academics. Of course our dangerous duo gave no consideration to the very simple fact that they were in college to get an education, to get a diploma, not to play sports and to have a good time.

So, as could be expected, the five Bs led to a big bust, a disaster and Stu departed Clarkson College of Technology at the end of his junior year. He returned home to Poughkeepsie, got a full time job at Daystrom Electric Corporation and a night-time job at Van Nardsdal's Service Station and prepared to be drafted into the army.

But he wasn't drafted so he didn't go into the army. There was a phone call.

CHAPTER ELEVEN

DAKOTA WESLEYAN UNIVERSITY

1951-1953

Stu Landersman parked his ten year old Pontiac convertible, got out and stretched. It had been a long drive from Poughkeepsie, New York to Mitchell, South Dakota with a night's sleep in Chicago and he had pulled in front of the Mitchell Drug Store on Main Street to get directions and a coke.

A week ago he had been working at his night job, Van Nardsdal's Service Station, when a phone call came from a Bob McArdle who introduced himself as Athletic Director of Dakota Wesleyan University. Stu asked Joe Morris to take care of a customer that had just pulled up to the pumps as he dealt with the only long distance phone call he had received at the station.

Pete Purdy, who knew Stu well from Arlington High School and Clarkson Tech was attending Dakota Wesleyan University and had told McArdle that Stu was a good basketball player, was not going back to Clarkson and perhaps could be talked into coming to DWU. Pete had been a year ahead of Stu in high school and they had been together in Junior Achievement. After high school, Pete had turned down a baseball offer from the St. Louis Browns, opting to go to Clarkson on a baseball scholarship. He had been Stu's "Big Brother" in the Omicron Pi Omicron fraternity initiation, but after two years at Clarkson, Pete transferred to Dakota Wesleyan University and played semi-pro baseball in Mitchell, South Dakota.

McArdle had called Stu's home where his mother gave the service station phone number. McArdle explained to Stu that DWU was one of nine colleges in the South Dakota Intercollegiate Conference (SDIC), which belonged to the National Association of Intercollegiate Athletics (NAIA). Unlike the better known organization for big schools; National Collegiate Athletic Association (NCAA), the NAIA allowed member conferences to determine their own eligibility rules. SDIC rules allowed transfer students to play sports without sitting out a season, as required by NCAA rules and the SDIC allowed professional baseball players to participate in other college sports. So the SDIC colleges had many transfer students and professional baseball players on their teams. College basketball season fit nicely between the end of one baseball season and the beginning of the next, so professional baseball players could play college basketball on the SDIC teams.

If Stu were to register at DWU this quarter, which had already started, as a transfer student he could play basketball this coming season, whereas in almost any other school or conference he would have to sit out, to miss a season. Also, the SDIC did not recognize freshman sports so Stu's season on the Clarkson freshman team would not count as one of the four years of eligibility allowed by the SDIC. McArdle explained all this to Stu and offered part time jobs and student loans that would cover most if not all school and living expenses if Stu would come to Dakota Wesleyan.

After discussing the South Dakota offer the following day with his parents and his boss at the electroplating shop of Daystrom Electric Corporation, his daytime job, Stu made up his mind to go to Dakota Wesleyan University. At both of his jobs his bosses agreed that he was doing the right thing and wished him well. He notified McArdle, quit both jobs and two days later was on the road west in his ten year old Pontiac convertible.

Stu walked into the drug store in Mitchell, South Dakota and found clerks and customers in back of the store around a small radio listening intently to a baseball game. It was October 3, 1951 and the New York Giants were at bat in the ninth inning of the final playoff game with the Brooklyn Dodgers. While traveling Stu had been unable to follow the three game playoff caused by the Dodger-Giant tie at the end of a dramatic National League season. At Ebbetts Field the Giants had won the first game 3-1 and the Dodgers had taken the second game, played at the Polo Grounds, 10-0. Now, at the Polo grounds as the Giants came to bat in the ninth inning of the deciding game with the Dodgers leading 4-1, Stu quietly joined the group listening to the radio broadcast of the game.

During the past summer Stu and friends had gone to New York to see baseball games, to Ebbetts Field in Brooklyn to see the Dodgers and to the Polo Grounds in the Bronx to see the Giants. Stu was a Giant fan primarily because Wes Westrum, the Giant catcher, lived in Poughkeepsie. Westrum, originally from Minnesota, had been stationed near Poughkeepsie while serving in the Army during World War II and had married the daughter of a woman who worked in Stu's father's factory. Also, Westrum knew Arlington High School Coach Fritz Jordan and had participated in football practice with the high school team.

Alvin Dark led off the Giant ninth with a single and Don Mueller followed with a double. After Monte Irvin popped out to Dodger catcher Roy Campanella, Whitey Lockman doubled scoring Dark. With one out and the score Dodgers 4 Giants 2, Ralph Branca came in to pitch for the Dodgers. What happened next is one of the most dramatic moments in sports history, especially because the Giants had come from 13 1/2 games back in mid August with a 16 game winning streak to eke out the tie and force a playoff. Bobby Thompson hit a home run off Ralph Branca, scoring Lockman and Mueller ahead of him, and the Giants won the 1951 National League pennant.

Reaction in the Mitchell Drug Store was similar to that all over the country. Smiling laughing baseball fans supporting the New York Giants jumped, cheered, clapped and shook hands as team mates mobbed Bobby Thompson at home plate. Manager Leo Durocher jumped, yelled and waved his arms in glee. Saddened Dodger fans shook their lowered heads in disbelief as "Dem Bums" blew it.

October 3, 1951: Bobby Thompson's "Shot heard round the world" and Stu Landersman's arrival in Mitchell, South Dakota.

Bob McArdle, DWU Athletic Director and basketball coach, was only a few years older than Stu but had been in the Navy to get the GI Bill, finished college at River Falls, Wisconsin where he had played football and had tried out with the New York Giants professional football team. McArdle had been offered a contract by the Giants for $3200 a season as a guard. When he told Giants coach Greasy Neal that he could make that much or more coaching high school football, Neal told him to grab a high school job if he could. Pro football players had to have jobs in the off season and most were lucky to get work as bar tenders.

The only one Stu knew in Mitchell, South Dakota, was Pete Purdy who had told the athletic director about him, which led to the phone call which led to his coming to this small western city. Stu found Pete and he helped Stu get a room and get settled. Pete shared a room with Darwin Rodi, better known to all his friends as "Dag" and Dag had a girlfriend, Pat Moses, who was in the nursing school associated with Dakota Wesleyan University and the local hospital. Pat lived with two other nursing students in an apartment and Stu was invited to their Saturday night party.

He found the apartment, knocked on the door and was greeted by a short very cute young woman. "I'm Stu Landersman and I've been invited to your party."

Pat Moses smiled and said, "Yes you have and I'm so glad that you're here," and with that she stepped out of the apartment, joining him as she closed the door behind her. Stu was confused. He had been welcomed and yet they were both standing in the hall outside her apartment. She laughed as she could see his confusion.

"This is a poetry party and that means that before I can let you in you have to recite a poem to me, right here in this hall, any poem, your choice."

"What if I don't know any poem," Stu asked.

The cute little girl looked up at him with a sad little girl expression. "Then I'm afraid you can't join the party."

"Well, we can't have that." Stu dropped his head in thought for a couple of seconds and then stood up straight.

"Here's Gunga Din by Rudyard Kipling," and he went into the poem.

> *"You may talk o' gin and beer*
> *When you're quartered safe out 'ere,*
> *An' you're sent to penny-fights an' Aldershot it;*
> *But when it comes to slaughter*
> *You will do your work on water,*
> *An' you'll lick the bloomin' boots of 'im that's*
> *got it."*

And Stu went on through all five sections of the classic poem ending with:

> *"You Lazarushian-leather Gunga Din!*
> *Though I've belted you and flayed you,*
> *By the livin' Gawd that made you,*
> *You're a better man than I am, Gunga Din!"*

She was agape with eyes wide open as she had stared at Stu through his entire recital.

She threw open the door. "Come on in!" and as he followed she announced to all the party, "You're not going to believe this guy!"

That was the beginning of Stu's social life at Dakota Wesleyan University in Mitchell, South Dakota and it got even better.

Stu's enrollment at Dakota Wesleyan was complicated because most of the subjects he had taken during three years at Clarkson were in mechanical engineering and Wesleyan was a liberal arts school. There were not many subjects that could be transferred relevant to liberal arts. The first problem was to establish a "major" and that was solved by choosing sociology, a far cry from mechanical engineering.

Why sociology? Bob Pennington was head of the Sociology Department, a WW II veteran and PhD, he had been assigned as Stu's academic advisor. It was no coincidence that he was a good friend of athletic director Bob McArdle. Pennington worked out an academic program that enabled Stu to achieve graduation in two school years. The program required that Stu take two sociology courses every quarter to build the major. The academic program also included some courses in Government which were taught by Dr. Pennington's brother-in-law, another PhD, George McGovern. Does that name sound familiar? He later served as Senator from South Dakota and ran for President a few years later.

Pennington and McGovern were both young PhDs, South Dakota native sons, WWII veterans, alumni of DWU, department heads at DWU, basketball fans of DWU and they were married to twins. There were other courses including a few taught by Bob McArdle but in two years Stu graduated from Dakota Wesleyan University with a Bachelor of Arts Degree, major in Sociology and minor in Physical Education.

Two years meant two basketball seasons and, as Stu had played one season of freshman ball and two seasons of varsity at Clarkson, he asked McArdle about eligibility as it would total five years. McArdle told Stu that the South Dakota Intercollegiate Conference did not recognize separate freshman basketball, so Stu could play four varsity seasons, and he did.

DWU had a good basketball team for the 1951-1952 season. Besides Stu there was Whitey Mayer; a transfer from South Dakota State, Ronnie Wiblemo; transfer from Bimiji in Wisconsin and also had been a professional baseball player, and Jim Millay; good high school all-around athlete. Those were the starters with the fifth varying among three or four others.

Stu was second high scorer in the SDIC that season. The high scorer in the conference was Gene Smith from Yankton College. He was the number three scorer in the NAIA, the small colleges in the nation that season. First was Clarence "Bevo" Francis from Rio Grand College and second was Johnnie O'Brian from Seattle University. The college won the conference and DWU came in second. Stu averaged 23 points per game that season.

Academics at DWU came easily for Stu. He got good grades in all subjects, so good that upon graduation he received an award for "Scholarship and Athletics."

During the basketball season of 1952-53, Stu's second and final year at Dakota Wesleyan University, Northern State Teachers College won the South Dakota Intercollegiate Conference (SDIC) title and went to the National Association of Intercollegiate Athletics (NAIA) tournament in Kansas City. There were two professional baseball players on the Northern basketball team, both with the Boston Red Sox, Dick Gernert the starting first baseman and Fayne Throneberry a reserve outfielder. They both played during the regular college basketball season, as SDIC rules permitted professional baseball players to do so, but they were not allowed in the NAIA tournament and Northern was eliminated in the first round.

Gernert at 6' 3" and over 200 pounds was a gifted athlete and went on to a 12 year major league baseball career as a power hitter, mostly with the Red Sox, then as a coach and scout. Fayne Throneberry spent 8 years in the majors but was better known as the brother of "Marvelous Marv" of the New York Mets. When Northern came to Mitchell to play Wesleyan in the Corn Palace the Northern coach asked Bob McArdle for a private dressing room for Dick Gernert, reasoning that it wasn't fitting for the starting first baseman of the Boston Red Sox dressing and showering with college boys. McArdle responded that Gernert was not entitled to anything better than anyone else.

With the first possession against Northern, Stu took a pass in the post-position and made a beautiful hook shot with Dick Gernert guarding him closely. As they ran to the other end of the court

Stu started on Gernert. "Did you see that? I hope you were paying attention 'cause I'm gonna teach you how to play this game. I can't do anything for your baseball, but maybe you can get this right."

Gernert took a pass, moved across the key guarded by Stu and put up a hook shot that missed as Stu cleared the rebound. They went up court and Stu continued, "You weren't watching, were you? I told you to watch. Now I'm going to show you again. Pay attention." Stu made another hook shot and as they went to the other end of the court, "There, did you see that? That's how it's done. This isn't baseball. You have to learn how to play this game. The Red Sox won't help you here." Gernert missed another hook shot and Wesleyan brought the ball up court with Stu continuing the insulting chatter.

Three times Stu made hook shots moving across the key and three times Gernert missed similar shots with Stu continually prodding with verbal barbs. Gernert never replied and after his third miss called time out, sat down and told his coach he was out of the game. He didn't come back and Wesleyan won the game.

Stu Landersman had been subjected to frequent innuendo, chatter and trash talk from opposing players in previous games, "Eastern hot shit," "Big time New York nothing," and he had learned to take it and to reply with chatter of his own. Against Southern, with the referee about to toss up the ball to start the game Stu stepped back out of the circle and said, "Hold it. What's that smell?" Referee and players looked around confused as Stu stepped back into the circle saying, "Oh, I'm sorry, its just the cow shit on his shoes," pointing to the opposing center's feet. "You'd think he would have cleaned it off when he left the farm."

There were professional baseball players on most of the college basketball teams in the South Dakota Intercollegiate Conference. Northern had the Red Sox players, Southern had some minor leaguers with the Cardinals and there were others in the conference. On Stu's DWU team was Ronnie Wiblemo, a Mitchell home towner transfer from Bemidji State College in Wisconsin who had played minor league professional baseball.

1952-1953, a good season but no cigar, Northern won the conference championship and lost in the first round at Omaha. DWU again came in second in the SDIC. Stu led the SDIC in scoring with 22 points per game. The Minneapolis Lakers inquired of Bob McArdle if he thought that Stu could play for the Lakers. McArdle replied that he certainly could but he was going into the service. The Lakers told McArdle to have Stu contact them when he got out.

Stu was not at DWU for his graduation. He had completed all requirements to graduate the previous quarter and had returned home to Poughkeepsie. Prior to departing South Dakota and knowing that he had to go into the armed service, he had started the process of joining a Navy officer program.

Oh yes, the Navy officer program, let me tell you about that. About a month before the end of the quarter, Stu put a 4 by 6 card on the bulletin board at DWU. "Anyone with a car interested in joining the Navy or the Marine Corps officer programs? Willing to share expenses. Navy to Omaha. Marine Corps to Minneapolis. Contact Stu Landersman."

Two guys responded. One had a car. Both were interested in the Navy not the Marine Corps. So they agreed on the timing and the expenses and went to Omaha, stayed at the Hill Hotel and the next morning went to the Office of Navy Officer Procurement. The morning was spent filling out forms and going through a physical examination. At the end of the physical a doctor was measuring Stu's height. "Oops," he said. "You're six feet five and the height limit is six feet four. Let's measure you again." Stu could feel the measure bar pressing down on his head and he squinched lower. Just as the medic was about to call out the height an apparent friend poked his head into the room and asked the doctor about lunch. "Just a minute. I've got a height problem here," and he called out, "Six foot four and a half inches. Still too tall." His friend at the door was anxious and volunteered, "You've got to round off to the nearest whole inch. Drop the half. He's six foot four. Let's go to lunch." So Stu passed the physical as did the other two and the three started back to Mitchell, South Dakota.

But it was not directly back to Mitchell as the three decided to stop at a college, visit a friend of one of them and spend the night. The visit developed into a party with drinking and carousing with a controversial liquor purchase, dispute with police and charge of disorderly conduct. Stu found himself in jail for the night. In local court the next morning Stu was found guilty of disorderly conduct and fined $25. The DWU threesome drove to Mitchell.

Now it might have meant nothing in the normal course of things but first, Stu's coach Bob McArdle was very angry because the college was a big rival of DWU and McArdle felt that if anyone in the college athletic department found out that Stu Landersman of Dakota Wesleyan had spent a night in their jail, it would be very embarrassing for DWU. And second, as McArdle also pointed out to Stu, "You now have a police arrest record and you're trying to get a commission as an officer in the Navy."

The first fear of McArdle's didn't come to be a problem. The college either didn't find out about Landersman in their city jail or else they chose not to make an issue of it. McArdle's second issue did have a longer range effect, though. In all the processing for the Navy that Stu Landersman went through, before he was commissioned and even after, when he was serving in the Navy, on all the forms in all the years that followed, Stu had to write of the 1953 disorderly conduct arrest, night in jail and $25 fine in South Dakota.

CHAPTER TWELVE

TRANSPORTATION

1953

The first year that I spent in Mitchell, South Dakota I had my own 1941 Pontiac convertible. That chariot had carried me from New York to South Dakota and provided transportation during that school year. When time came to go home for the summer I had the oil changed in preparation for the long drive. Disaster! Two hundred miles after leaving Mitchell, as I was nipping along at 65 mph and singing aloud to myself, I heard a loud crack followed by mechanical clanking as the car lost power. I coasted onto the shoulder of the highway as the engine and the clanking stopped. I knew without looking what had happened.

The garage guy who had changed the oil in the Pontiac the day before had not put the drain plug back in properly. A few hundred miles of vibration and the drain plug worked loose and fell out. Then the engine oil ran out and with no lubrication a bearing froze, broke a rod and threw it right out through the side of the engine block. Mechanics say, "It threw a rod."

I was stranded in farm country. No cell phone in those days, not even CB radios. I walked to a farm house about a half-mile away. With great sympathy for the plight I was in, the farmer took me in, gave me a cup of coffee and called the tow-truck service he knew in the nearest town; Beresford, South Dakota.

My Pontiac convertible was towed into town. The tow-truck driver bought it from me for fifty dollars, helped me package up my belongings from the car and I rode Greyhound bus to Poughkeepsie.

Summer was coming to a close as the next school year approached and I was approached by two of my high school team-mates; Bobby Martin and Lefty Vincent. They were a few years behind me in high school and now in college as they had been attending St. Lawrence University the previous school year and didn't plan on going back. They wanted to know about Dakota Wesleyan. I told them about the school and they decided to go with me. Bobby Martin had a car and in September, just after Labor Day, the three of us were off to South Dakota.

Although Bobby Martin had a car, as I said, he didn't like to drive. I drove. I drove to Mitchell and I drove around Mitchell for most of that school year. That's why I needed transportation to recruiters and to home when I was finished with college. The car that I had been using belonged to Bobby Martin and he and Lefty Vincent were staying for the next quarter. I was finished with college and wanted to go home. So that brings us to the problem of how to get home.

The quarter ended and basketball season was over. I had completed all academic requirements for graduation with a BA degree, major in sociology. The graduation ceremony would be at the end of the next quarter in June. Acceptance in the Navy officer candidate program was pending. There was no reason to stay in Mitchell any longer as the best estimate from the Navy recruiter was that it would be a few months before I would hear of the next steps; acceptance, physical exam and orders to Officer Candidate School in Newport, Rhode Island.

How to get home, back to Poughkeepsie? I couldn't take Bobby's car. Remember that when I needed transportation to Navy or Marine

Corps recruiters I put a note on the school bulletin board and "presto" a ride to Omaha for the Navy. Now I needed transportation to Poughkeepsie and I knew that a note on the bulletin board wouldn't work for that. But remember, Bob McArdle had arranged a number of part-time jobs for me. So many jobs, in fact, that during both of my college years at Wesleyan I always had enough money for all my expenses, all my expenses including all my recreation, play and girls. I had a good time in Mitchell, South Dakota and completed my education so that I could get a commission in the Navy. It didn't cost my parents a cent. But I digress.

Among the many small and part time jobs that Bob McArdle arranged for me was one job that was not small but was part-time. I did job printing in the building that contained the preparation and printing of the local newspaper, the Mitchell Daily Republic. I had nothing to do with the newspaper but a small platen press was in a corner of the large room that contained the huge printing press that put out the daily newspaper.

What's a platen press? The dictionary says, "A printing press with a flat plate for pressing the paper against the inked type or plate to produce an impression." This one must have been a hundred years old but it worked just fine.

My job was to go into the printing room via the back door, go to the platen press and complete the projects ordered. Most of the time it was business envelopes, sometimes it would be advertising flyers, lots of things. Best of all, besides paying a nice hourly rate, I could do this work any time, any day even Sundays. I could go into the shop after basketball practice or at three in the morning. The shop was always open and even if I missed a day the projects would be there waiting.

Working for the Mitchell Daily Republic had some benefits for me. I was entitled to a newspaper every day and as I didn't need one delivered to my rooming house the paper was mailed to my home in Poughkeepsie. That way my parents kept track of me during basketball season.

Another benefit came as a surprise. I had become acquainted with most of the staff and the workers at the newspaper and I knew that the editor, Ez Brady, came to all of our home games in the Corn Palace. He liked to talk with me about the games. In one conversation he asked me what I was going to do after I graduated. When I told him that I planned to go into the service he nodded and suggested that while I was waiting for that to come through I could work as a reporter for the newspaper.

"A reporter? I've never done any journalism. Why would you want to hire me as a reporter?" I was very surprised.

Ez Brady looked at me and smiled. "I've talked with Bob Pennington and George McGovern and they both told me that you're a very good writer."

Small town. Small school. It was very flattering but I still wanted to go back to Poughkeepsie before I went into service.

Now I was faced with the cost of travel home. I could have just bought a bus ticket. I had the money. Remember, a few years back George Monroe and I had hitch-hiked across the U.S. and back, and even did a little freight-train riding. I suppose it was ingrained in me from the experiences of that summer, that there were other means of travel, more economical than public transportation.

The newspaper, ah yes, the good ole' Mitchell Daily Republic came through for me. I was glancing through the paper after finishing my printing chores one night and what to my wondrous eyes did I behold but in the classifieds there be a Navy man driving back to Philadelphia from leave and looking for someone to share expenses. A trip east! There's my transportation home. We drove straight through, alternating drivers and the sailor let me off at the Philadelphia train station. Railroad to Poughkeepsie and I was home.

Back in Poughkeepsie money was no problem, there was still, as always, electrical work with Moe as I waited to hear from the Navy.

My life-long buddy Otis Waterman, at Clarkson, had taken an extra year to graduate, same as me, too much partying. Also, Oat and Jinny Wheeler had secretly married and now that they were finished with college Jinny's parents wanted a regular wedding. I was best man. At the wedding reception Oat asked me what I was going to do next, as the second marriage couple planned a wedding trip through the central lakes of New York. Oat loved fishing and Jinny would learn. I had nothing planned so they invited me to go along with them on their wedding trip. I did go with them on that wedding trip, sort of like a butler, chauffeur or maybe just a third wheel but we all had a good time.

Back in Poughkeepsie I received my orders and went to New York by train, to the Navy headquarters at #1 Broadway, where I was sworn into the Navy on 26 May 1953, my 23rd birthday.

CHAPTER THIRTEEN

OAT AND ME

2014

In October of 2014 I received a phone call from one of Otis Waterman's grandsons informing me that Otis had passed away. He had been living with Jinny in Florida. I was living in California. It was Jinny's intention to move him to Poughkeepsie for funeral and burial. Much as I would have liked to be there, I felt that I couldn't make the trip so I wrote the following piece and sent it to Jinny.

OAT AND ME

In 1937 my family moved from Marian Avenue in Poughkeepsie to just outside of town, to an area called Arlington. That meant a new school for me; a new second grade. I was a new kid in a new school and among the new friends I made was a friendly little guy named Otis Waterman. Of course we had no way of knowing this, but from that time on "Oat and me" would go through grade school and high school together, taking the same subjects, playing all sports together, belonging to the same clubs. In Boy Scouts we made Eagle Scout together and were camp counselors. We started a Junior Achievement company, chased the same girls, made trips to New York to see Dodger, Yankee and Giant baseball games, saw Glen Davis and Doc Blanchard play football at West Point.

We went to college together; same rooming houses, same fraternity, same parties–lots of parties–so much partying that it took us an extra year to graduate. By that time I was away at a different college so I wasn't there when Oat and Ginny secretly married, but I was Best Man for their repeat marriage and chauffeured them on their wedding trip.

Basketball played an important part in my young life and Oat started me on that path. In grade school, high school and college I played basketball, and in the Navy, and I grew from a kid that couldn't catch, throw, dribble or shoot the ball to a college all-star. It was basketball that determined where, when and how I graduated from college. The college degree led to a commission in the Navy, and the Navy became my career and led to family, so basketball was a major determinant in the path of my life, and it started in grade school when Otis Waterman let me be a Wildcat.

In the seventh grade my good friend Oat Waterman formed a team he called the Wildcats and even though I wasn't much of a player, he included me. Clearly I was not a good enough player at 12 years old to be on his team, but we were in Boy Scouts together, so Oat included me as a Wildcat. Oat had a good basket on his garage, where we practiced. There were no organized teams such as many years later in Little League. Groups of kids just got together without coaches or sponsors and formed teams, like gangs but not with that criminal connotation. Each team had a nominal head, like Oat, who sought out other teams and places to play. There were a few leagues in the area with age limits, and teams could sign up to compete so we played a lot of games, and won more than we lost.

The Wildcats did pretty well that first year, when Oat and I were in seventh grade, and even better when we were in the eighth grade. Oat was our best player and he coached and carried the team.

At the start of the freshman year in high school each student selected a curriculum program and Oat and I selected College Technical, which meant that we would take all the math and science offered plus those other courses needed to be admitted to an engineering college. The boys' counselor offered little help so we used a brochure from the U.S. Naval Academy to see that we were taking the right high school courses. It wasn't that we intended to go to the Naval Academy, although that did sound good to us, but we figured that if we had the right high school courses for Annapolis we would meet the requirements of any engineering school.

During that freshman year in high School I was elected Vice President of my class, and Oat was elected Treasurer, and we were both very active in Boy Scouts and later became Eagle Scouts. We played in the school band, Oat trumpet and me clarinet, the difference was Oat really could play the trumpet but I just wanted to wear the uniform and march at games and in parades as I couldn't play the clarinet at all.

Oat and I went out for Junior Varsity basketball our freshman year. We tried hard and survived the first cut. Basketball was very popular at Arlington High School and many kids tried out. Some were very good, but Oat and I weren't as we were among the last cut that year and the Junior Varsity coach told us it was close and encouraged us to try next year. Oat reformed the Wildcats for a third season.

Oat and I were the original two in forming a Junior Achievement company, United Manufacturing Incorporated, sponsored by Central Hudson Gas and Electric Corporation, and our company was very successful making and selling wood products. Ten kids made up the Board of Directors and were the work force of the company, each with a title; and we rotated the positions. We sold shares for working capital and set up shop in the basement of one of our sponsors.

Three years later the Board of Directors of United Manufacturing liquidated the company, returned original investments to stockholders ($2.50 each) plus a dividend, and granted bonuses to the six remaining members of the board. Oat and I received bonuses of $16.23 each.

The basketball season of 1944-45 saw the Wildcats win 14 of 17 games as we played in a Saturday morning league in Arlington and picked up additional games whenever we could. Otis was always our leading scorer and playmaker, and as loyal Arlington boys we always played Fritz Jordan's 2-1-2 zone defense

A group of friends formed a close association that we called, "The Jolly Boys," from The Great Gildersleeve radio show. The group consisted of Oat and me, plus Harry Gerth, George Monroe and Jim Hauver. Sometimes Joe Morris was with us, too, and we went almost everywhere together, played on the school teams, took the same classes, and ate lunches at school together.

Oat and I made the Junior Varsity basketball team in our sophomore year as did four former Wildcats and four Jolly Boys on the team. I was Vice President of the class and Oat was Treasurer. We were taking math and science courses, English, Social Studies, and getting good grades, Oat's a little better than mine.

I should say here that Oat's father, Ralph Waterman built a small boat and named it KRONG, for Katherine, Ralph, Otis, Natalie and George; the Waterman family. I had a horse once named JEST; J for Joe, E for Estelle, S for Stuart and T for Thelma, as I got the idea for the naming from Otis' family boat.

Oat and I sat on the Junior Varsity bench most of our sophomore season, but we were happy just being on the team. We got into a number of games and felt that we were getting better.

President Franklin D. Roosevelt's home was Hyde Park, N.Y., just north of Poughkeepsie, and on Friday, April 12, 1946, his estate was dedicated as a National Park. Oat and I were among 12 Eagle Scouts that received orders from the Dutchess County Council, Boy Scouts of America, directing us to serve as ushers to direct distinguished guests to appropriate seats. The orders told us how to be excused from school, prescribed uniform and lunch, and directed us to report to Mr. Hamilton of the National Parks Service for duty. The orders read, "Signals are to be worked out with the Director of Protocol so that you will know who you are ushering and where to direct them."

Oat and I had moved from Boy Scouts to Senior Scouts at the time. Oat was an Explorer Scout and I was a Sea Scout and we wore our Sea and Explorer Scout uniforms to the Hyde Park dedication. We learned the color code system of invitations and showed the guests to the appropriate seating for their status as we Eagle Scouts escorted senators, congressmen, Supreme Court justices, journalists, and members of the cabinet, to seats. Frank Sinatra created the biggest reaction of the visitors. Fala, FDR's pet Scotty dog, was being walked before the ceremony and forever after Oat and I could say, "Shake the hand that petted Fala."

At school in September Oat and I went out for football and we were both on the third team; Oat the quarterback, me an end. Fritz Jordan also coached football. Our football team won seven out of eight games, losing only to Kent School, a prep school in Connecticut by a score of 12-7. Oat and I were on the sidelines most of the season but enjoyed being on the team and the conditioning was good for basketball that followed.

I was elected President of my junior class and as the two years before, Otis was Treasurer. Otis and I began the 1946-47 basketball season, our junior year, on the junior varsity starting team. The most exciting junior varsity game that season was with Roosevelt, one of our biggest rivals. With the score tied during the final minute, Oat described the action as he remembered it fifty years later:

"As I recall, you stole the ball three times with less than a minute to go and having been imprinted (like the birds) threw it to me each time. I dribbled the length of the court each time but; the first time I missed the lay up but was fouled and missed both shots. The second time the ref called me for walking but no one could hear the whistle and I had made the lay up. The third time I either made or missed the lay up, but the ref had blown the whistle again before my shot–this was for a foul which I finally made with about ten seconds left. I did lose my cool just a bit!!!

"The ref, I believe was Frank Fitzpatrick who Jinny and I became great friends with many years later (He and his wife). His and our kids grew up together. C'est La Vie."

Each time Oat went down the court without a score he became angrier with the referee and he did lose his cool "just a bit." I had to restrain him from getting called for a technical foul and that, as I recall, was my major contribution to our winning the game. If I had stolen the ball I surely would have thrown it to Oat as had been "imprinted" on me from Wildcat days.

Half way through the season Oat and some other JV teammates played in a tournament in Poughkeepsie. I wasn't with them. We all knew that high school players were not eligible. They were kicked off the Arlington Junior Varsity and forfeited their tournament games.

After basketball season Oat and I didn't want to be idle, as we had been going to football and basketball practice all year every afternoon, so we went out for track Otis and I tried a number of events. Soon Otis learned that distance running was too much work, he was better at sprints, but not quite fast enough for the short sprints and he settled on pole vaulting.

The school year of 1947-48 I was President of my Senior Class and Otis Waterman once again was Treasurer.

As the 1947-48 basketball season started, our senior year, Oat and I were on the varsity team. We won the Dutchess County championship in a dramatic finish of the season.

Oat and I were on a college basketball team while we were in high school! Well, not exactly "on" a team, maybe "with" a college team would be more accurate. Vassar College was a girl's school but had accepted fifty veterans after World War II to help with the flood of servicemen that got out of the military and used their GI Bill college benefits. Oat found that there were seven or eight Vassar vets trying to form a team to compete against the vets at the other girls' colleges but they didn't have enough men to practice. So, just as he had always done in the Wildcat days, Oat recruited some friends to play basketball wherever and whenever. This time it was at the Vassar College gym on Sunday mornings and his friends were from the Arlington High School team that won the Dutchess County Scholastic League Championship.

On the second Sunday of Vassar College practice, as we walked out of the dressing room, who was on the court to greet us but Coach Fritz Jordan, brought in to help the Vassar Vets. Our initial thought was, "Now we're in for it, in trouble for playing basketball else-where than the Arlington team," and we remembered that Oat and others were kicked off the JVs in our junior year for playing else-where. But Coach Jordan put us at ease right away by telling us it was good of us to help and he used us to demonstrate as he coached the Vassar Vets that Sunday.

Years later as a civil engineer Oat served as the Vassar College Director of Public Works and later he retired from that position. He never told anyone that he had been with the first Vassar College men's basketball team in 1948, twenty one years before the college went co-ed. And not many, if any, people know that Fritz Jordan was the first men's basketball coach at Vassar.

Track season followed basketball and I was the top half-miler. Oat was our leading pole-vaulter and we did well in most meets.

When we read that the New York Giants were to play a preseason baseball game at West Point against the Army team, the Jolly Boys loaded into my car and off we went. Unfortunately that meant cutting track practice, but we had to see the Giants. We also saw Glen Davis, "Mr. Outside" of the famous football combination of Davis-Blanchard, who played baseball for Army. Next day Coach Neidhart told me that I was off the track team for missing practice. Otis suggested that I offer an apology and the following day I appealed to Coach Neidhart, who let me apologize to the team and I was forgiven. Arlington won the Dutchess County Scholastic League track championship.

At graduation Shirley Fay was valedictorian and Mary Cassidy salutatorian of our class. Oat was number three and won prizes for, "Doing the most for the school while getting the most out of it," RPI medal for math, excellence in band, Kiwanis medal for math and science, and some others.

College had been a consideration for us since the start of high school. A Boy Scout executive had taken Oat and me to visit Columbia University in New York and we had seen West Point a number of times. Oat and I read about the Naval Academy, but when we found that 20/20 vision was required we couldn't qualify, as both of us wore glasses. Years later I learned that Naval Academy requirements could be waived, but in 1948 no one at Arlington High School knew that.

Two techs; Worchester or Clarkson? I couldn't decide but as I was getting ready to leave on summer travel I solved the problem by asking Oat to make all arrangements for me with him at Clarkson, and he did. After the summer, in September 1948 it was off to Clarkson College of Technology for Oat and me.

Thanks for a great young life together, Otis.

Sleep well Eagle, Wildcat, teammate, brother, and in the Navy we say "shipmate."

CHAPTER FOURTEEN

THE JOLLY BOYS

The Full Story

You have read about The Jolly Boys in an earlier chapter and as I read through these past pieces it occurs to me that there was more about these young men than I had told. I can't tell you about all my classmates but if you'll give me just a few more moments I feel that I must tell the tales of the six, of which I was one, and of the guys with-whom I was closest of the Arlington High School Class of 1948.

The Jolly Boys took the name from a popular TV and radio show, The Great Gildersleeve, starring Willard Waterman as the Water Commissioner in a small town. It was light humor, situation comedy in which a small group of men got into various meaningless situations. The name was unique so we used it.

The Jolly Boys of AHS Class of 1948 were (in no particular order):

Harry Gerth
Jim Hauver
Joe Morris

Otis Waterman
Stu Landersman
George Monroe

Harry Gerth

Harry was fairly tall, very thin, very quiet and shy. He was good looking, always had a smile and never said a bad thing about anybody. He was well liked by everyone, played basketball and baseball.

His father and mother were both very good looking and his father worked in a local gas station/service station. Harry had a younger sister and the family lived in a small, very neat house. It always seemed strange to me that Harry's father; good looking, smart and hard working, worked in a gas station. I often thought that there was some drama there.

I think I told, in an earlier chapter, that a very nice girl in our class, Shirley Stevens, came to me one day and asked me to have Harry ask her to the Junior Prom. She knew that Harry was too shy. I asked Harry. He balked and said he was afraid that she would say no and that he couldn't dance. I coerced him, saying that I was sure she would accept and would be happy to teach him to dance. He asked, she accepted, she taught him to dance and they went to the Junior Prom. It didn't end there by any means as they went together forever after.

After high school Harry went to work at IBM and a few years later they married. Many years later I learned that he had retired after a full career at IBM and a few years later they moved to a retirement home.

It was about 60 years after our high school time that I received an email from Shirley Stevens Gerth telling me that Harry had passed away. The email went on to say that she never forgot that I had put them together, she knew Harry would never have asked her out and the wonderful life that they had together was all because I coerced Harry into asking her to the Junior Prom. It was heavy stuff. I was moved to tears. It's hard to imagine that those two nice kids wouldn't have gotten together by some other means, but who am I to say? I was flattered by the consideration and most happy for them.

A great guy, Harry Gerth.

Jim Hauver

Jim was of medium height, heavy-set and friendly. He played interior lineman in football and threw weights on the track team.

I never understood his family's living arrangement as it appeared that his mother, father, two brothers and a sister (and he) lived in an old railroad worker apartment building a few miles from town near an unused railroad line. He was always eager to participate in the various activities. There were only a few times that I drove him home or picked him up but I never saw the others of his family.

After high school he enlisted in the Air Force and served as what we Navy people would call a "storekeeper." He married while in the Air Force and then went to live near Denver, Colorado where he worked for a supermarket chain (storekeeper–supermarket) until he retired. We exchanged emails and phone calls off and on over a few years and one day I realized that I hadn't heard from him in a while. I couldn't connect by email or phone. In one of our last phone conversations he told me that he never forgot the great times we had as Jolly Boys. A great guy, Jim Hauver.

Joe Morris

Joe was of medium build and I guess you could say was a medium sort of guy. He was on the track team in high school. He lived in a small neat house on Ziegler Avenue which was positioned so that his back yard was a short walk to my back yard as I lived on Hooker Avenue.

His father was a plumber who worked for a large company and it was clear that in appearance Joe was the image of his father. Joe's mother was very overweight and the only times she left her house were to go to church or when her husband would take her grocery shopping. His mother had often heard the Jolly Boys questioning where our gas money would come from and just before high school graduation she offered me gas money if I would use Joe's middle name as I announced each graduate. I did so, "Joseph Shane Morris." Shane was her maiden name. We had fuel for festivities.

Both parents were very strict Catholic and had hoped that their only child, Joe, would one day be a priest. That didn't happen. After high school Joe went into the army, saw some action in Korea, used the GI Bill for college, returned to Poughkeepsie, went to work for IBM, married and lived just down the street from his parents on Ziegler Avenue.

At the 30th high school class reunion I could hardly recognize Joe Morris from the boy I knew in high school. He was self-confident, out-going and humorous. He told me that once his parents were having a discussion in which some negative things were said about Jews. He stopped them and said, "No, no, Stu Landersman isn't like that."

A great guy, Joe Morris.

Otis Waterman

I first met Otis in the second grade and we soon became best friends. I suppose you could say that we were the first of the Jolly Boys. You may have read about this in an earlier chapter. Oat and I were best friends through grade school, high school and college. We went through Boy Scouts together, were camp counselors and made Eagle Scout together and were in Junior Achievement together. Oat was elected class treasurer all four years of high school.

Oat's origin is interesting. The Waterman family has some significance in American history. One of them was a well known clipper-ship captain, Bully Waterman, who lost a highly publicized clipper-ship race from San Francisco to China and back, killed one of his crew and later founded a small city in California. Oat's grandfather was a career army officer who saw action in the Philippines in the Spanish-American War. A brother of Oat's father was a Marine Corps colonel in the Pacific island hopping campaign of World War Two. Otis's mother's maiden name was Catherine Otis, of the Otis Elevator family.

During World War One, Otis' father, Ralph Waterman, dropped out of high school, lied about his age and enlisted in the army. His father, a career army officer, was notified about this with intention to discharge him. The father said no, keep him in the army and assign him to the protection of water reservoirs in the Catskill Mountains of New York. Ralph Waterman stood that duty, very disappointed as it was far from what he envisioned as glamorous combat in France. After the war he returned to school and later was unsuccessful in an attempt to be a part of the U.S. Olympic team in the high jump.

Otis rarely paid any attention to the Waterman family history because it really wasn't his history. Why? Well it's because Otis was adopted! That's right. Otis was the adopted son of Ralph and Catherine Waterman. In later years Oat's wife Jinny spent some considerable time researching the family history but Oat never found out his origin.

Ralph Waterman, Oat's father, joined us in Boy Scouts and took us through all the requirements to make Eagle Scout. He was one of the most influential men in my young life.

Otis was short while I was tall and we often heard references to us such as, "—Mutt and Jeff over there." He was well built and very athletic and as I described in the earlier chapter before high school he formed teams and functioned as coach, scheduler, manager and star player. In high school he was in the band and played football, basketball and track. He was Class Treasurer all four years in high school. In schoolwork he was very good, graduated as number three in academics and received a number of awards.

Oat graduated from Clarkson with a degree in Civil Engineering and a commission as a second lieutenant in the Army Corps of Engineers, earned via ROTC. After a few years in the army he and Jinny returned to Poughkeepsie where Otis worked as a licensed Civil Engineer for a few years then became Public Works Director of Vassar College where he remained until he retired and moved to Florida.

There's a good story about Oat that I have to tell you. After our freshman year in Malone the remaining Clarkson years were in

Potsdam, NY, which was also the location of Potsdam State Teachers College; mostly-almost all-women, which was very convenient for Clarkson-all men. The major sport at Clarkson was hockey and with proximity to Canada, most-almost all-of the hockey team were Canadians. Most-almost all-of the hockey team were fraternity brothers of Oat and me so we did much partying with them and with dates from PSTC.

Ken Brown was a BMOC (Big Man on Campus) as he was a Clarkson senior, a Canadian hockey player, an O Pi O brother and officer, and-most important of all-he was captain of the hockey team. At a fraternity party he met a PSTC girl, Jinny Wheeler and soon they dated and dated again. Jinny and Ken Brown were going steady and were at a party when Otis Waterman exchanged some pleasantries with Jinny. At the next party they talked more and soon much more. Jinny broke up with Ken Brown and started to go out with Otis Waterman. They went steady. Otis had stolen the girlfriend of Clarkson's most popular man, the BMOC.

They married in secret and a year or so later married again, this time in public, at Jinny's home town. I was best man at the second wedding.

Oat and I stayed in contact, off and on, over all of the years until he passed away in Florida, leaving me as the only surviving Jolly Boy.

A great guy, Otis Waterman.

Stu Landersman

This whole book is about Stu Landersman so I don't have to go through it here other than to say that altogether it has been a great life. You may have seen that the Jolly Boys all had fine times in high school and in the years, in all the lives that followed. They were all great guys. All? But wait a minute! You haven't read about one more Jolly Boy.

George Monroe

Long ago there was an expression used to describe the very best of men, "A prince among men." You don't hear that description used very much any more. Maybe it's because we don't have anyone that it fits, maybe. But I think, rather, it still applies to very few people and always has. George Francis Monroe was one guy to whom the expression, "A prince among men," applied.

In high school George was very popular, did well in college-prep academics, played basketball and track and had a part-time job in the local Howard Johnson's restaurant.

When we finished high school in 1948 George was 17 years old, was 6 ft. 2 in. tall and weighed 175 pounds, long and lean, not an ounce of fat. He had straight blond hair that was always properly cut and combed. He had classic facial structure, like Roman, and by any measure or description was just plain handsome. It may seem strange for me, one of the guys, to call him handsome but it's not just me. Clearly, all the girls thought so, too. With his good looks and very fine personality, modesty and charm he was very attractive to girls. Where-as most of the other Jolly Boys had to hustle to attract girls, George seemed to have a magnetic attraction. And it was not just high school girls. My mother, as an example, would always single out George from my group and ask how he was doing. Maybe it was his looks, personality and charm that caused this attraction by females or maybe there was something else added to those features and characteristics. Maybe it was a feminine instinct, a motherly instinct.

George Monroe was an orphan. When I first met him in eighth grade he lived with his mother and older sister in a small house across the road from a dairy farm. His father had passed away a few years before and George's two older brothers were grown and gone. The summer before George's junior year of high school his mother passed away. His sister had just finished high school and was working and living in Poughkeepsie, so George was alone.

Some one decided that a 15 year-old should not be living by himself and a family that had been long-time friends of the Monroe family took George to live with them in Herkimer, New York. George was accepted into the Mitchell family, the school and the community of Herkimer. He was popular in school, played on the basketball team, did well in academics and had a very nice girl-friend. The Jolly Boys drove to Herkimer and visited George in his new residence. All was well.

At the end of his junior year at Herkimer George was 16 years old and he decided that now it was up to him to decide where he would live and he decided that he would live in Arlington. He thanked the Mitchell's profusely, it was emotional, they cried, as he had become one of their family but he wanted to be back in Arlington.

The family that owned and ran the dairy farm across the road from where the Monroe's had lived had always been very friendly and often offered part-time work opportunities to George. Now that he wanted to be back in Arlington but had no family to live with they provided George with a room. George had a place to sleep and was back with the Jolly Boys for his senior year of high school.

A place to sleep was one basic requirement and one other basic requirement was meals, but for George that problem had been solved before. The manager at the same Howard Johnson's at which he had previously worked was very happy to get him back and with a pay increase. Just as valuable to George were his hours of employment. He could work anytime he was available. That meant that he could go to school and go to basketball and track practice. Then, when the rest of us went home to dinner, George had dinner at HoJos, worked until nine and then hitch-hiked 14 miles to his room at the dairy farm.

The Jolly Boys all graduated from high school in 1948 and went their separate ways except, of course, George Monroe and I went hitch-hiking around the country for the summer. Even during our hitch-hiking summer girls were attracted to George. One evening as we were sitting on a park bench in Cody, Wyoming preparing to spend the night in that park, a pretty girl came walking through the park. She spotted George, sat down next to us and asked what we were doing there. A great adventure, she thought, and she wanted to join us, or rather she wanted to join George, but he talked her out of it.

When we were working at Jolly Joan's restaurant in Portland, Oregon, George as a busboy and me as a glass-washer, the waitresses couldn't keep their eyes (and hands they wished) off George and so we were invited to a couple of late night parties.

Summer ended, George went to work full time and I went off to college. I only saw him Christmas and summers. A year after high school George went to Syracuse University for one semester. I visited him there one weekend. After that one semester he decided that he couldn't put it all together, the costs, the academics and the part time work, so he went back to Poughkeepsie and full-time restaurant work. He had lots of friends there. Along the way he met Joan Thiessen, a very nice girl. They made a nice couple, fell in love and made plans to have a life together.

I hadn't seen George in almost a year, was home from college and I called Joan to find out where George was. She was hesitant, I thought, but told me where George was living. He had no phone and I went to see him.

I have never been so shocked. You'll remember that when George left high school he was tall, strong, handsome and charming. As I sat in a chair alongside his bed I thought that this person I saw in bed in a small room in a rooming house was hardly the George Monroe I had known so well. This person was, in a word, shriveled. He was pale, almost white. He was bald, no more blond hair and the skin was drawn tight across his once handsome face. He weighed perhaps a hundred pounds. He was in constant pain in spite of a number of medications. He forced a smile as a greeting to me and our conversation was forced.

George told me of his first indication of medical problems, going to a doctor, into the hospital and surgeries (a number of them) which failed to remove all of the cancers that had spread through his body. He had an ugly surgical scar from his neck to his crotch.

As we talked he told me that he had planned to marry Joan Thiessen and continue in the restaurant business but of course now he knew those would never be. He told me that our hitch-hiking the summer after high school was the most exciting thing of his life and he thanked me for giving him that.

I told him, "Bullshit, it was both of us. We were a great team."

George was in pain throughout my visit with him. We were both near tears. Finally he twisted toward me and said, "Stu, I want you to leave now. I don't want you to look at me or to say good-by. I don't want you to come back here to see me. I don't want you to remember me this way. I want you to remember me as I was in high school and as we hitch-hiked, and when we had those great times together as Jolly Boys."

I looked away from him, toward the foot of his bed, thought for a moment and said, "I'll always remember you that way." I got up and left.

Two weeks later Joan Thiessen called to tell me that George had passed away. He was twenty-one years old.

A great guy, George Monroe.

Summary

Although this section is titled Summary, perhaps it should be Confession. Why? Well, because in the first paragraph of this chapter I wrote that I wanted to tell you about the six Jolly Boys and I did so. But what I really intended was for you to learn about George Monroe and there was a good reason that I singled him out.

The Talmud has a line that says something like, "If a person's name is forgotten than the person is forgotten."

The other Jolly Boys all had family; sons, daughters and grand children to remember them so their names will not be forgotten. They will not be forgotten. The people who knew George Monroe, family and friends, have all either passed away or soon will. His name will soon be forgotten. He will be forgotten.

This "Prince among men" was too good a person to be forgotten. Perhaps, I offer to you, Dear Reader, that if this humble writing survives to be read by even one after we have all passed away than George Francis Monroe will not be forgotten.

CHAPTER FIFTEEN

OFFICER CANDIDATE SCHOOL

1953

I was at home in Poughkeepsie, New York, living with my parents on Woodland Avenue, working part time for my uncle Moe Domes as an electrician's assistant and earning enough money to enjoy night life with friends from high school days. I had completed all the requirements for graduation from Dakota Wesleyan University in Mitchell, South Dakota the previous academic quarter so I wasn't at the college for the graduation ceremony.

In May of 1953 a letter came from the Department of the Navy. I had been accepted into the officer candidate program. I was to report to the Navy Headquarters at Number One Broadway in New York City on May 26 for final processing and acceptance into the officer candidate program. Also, the letter included standard Navy orders to report again, this time for duty, to Number One Broadway at 0800 on a date in June.

I went to New York on May 26, completed the processing and returned to Poughkeepsie. Now, as it happens, May 26 is the date of my birth and that is the date that I raised my right hand and recited the oath, "to support and defend the constitution of the United States," that made me a part of the Naval Reserve. That date, my birthday, May 26 became my "pay entry base date" for the next 30 years and that determined year group for promotion and pay increases, all on my birthday. A nice birthday present.

On the evening in June before I was to report, my father drove me to the train station in Poughkeepsie and I went to Grand Central Station in New York, a familiar train ride for me. I slept the night on a bench in the famous station, was awakened by a policeman in the early morning and took a subway ride to the Navy Headquarters at the foot of Broadway.

A few hundred young men were waiting for the office to open and precisely at 0800 a Navy chief petty officer came out and took charge. We were herded into the building, herded through a brief processing, herded out into busses and the herd of busses headed through the city traffic and then north toward Newport, Rhode Island.

During World War Two newly commissioned officers that came through the brief officer candidate programs were called "Ninety Day Wonders." That moniker could no longer be used because the Navy had extended their officer candidate school to four months. A hundred twenty days didn't seem attractive in a derogatory nickname. So we very recently just college boys were now "OCs" and we wore classic sailor's uniforms; bell bottom trousers with 13 buttons, Navy jumpers, neckerchiefs and white hats. Some years later the uniform for OCs was changed to officer style but for my class, Class Thirteen, we wore sailor's uniforms and when we went on liberty we rolled up our sleeves one turn and positioned our hats on the very back of our heads, like real sailors.

The first day, first formation on the big drill field, the entire Class 13 was lined up and the CO of the school welcomed us. There were 1300 of us in the class, the largest ever at Navy OCS, and that number and title, the largest class, was never exceeded. At that first formation the CO asked that any of us that had signed on to Navy OCS just to avoid being drafted into the army step out of ranks at this time for processing out of OCS. I was amazed that about a dozen of our young men immediately walked over to the side and were marched away. This was during the Korean conflict and I would learn that it had to do with serving the minimal amount of time in the Navy rather than as a foot soldier in Korea.

An hour later my company was lined up beside our barracks and the Chief Petty Officer who was our overseer asked if anyone had any marching or drill experience. Although I had had some experience marching in high school band, boy scouts and Army ROTC at Clarkson, I was not about to volunteer for anything, as I had been advised by numerous service veterans. No one responded at first but after some further pursuit by the Chief, one timid sole stepped forward. Yes, he had led the marching band at college. He had been the drum major of the West Virginia University marching band. Great, we had our leader and after some further directives the Chief asked our new Company Commander to march us away.

A puzzled frown, a smile and our new leader raised his fist then punched it in front of him as he called out in a loud clear voice, "Foeward, ho-woe." The entire company of OCs broke up in laughter.

All was not laughter at OCS, however. I had some problems. Once while serving as the day's company commander (We all took a turn or two at that function) we were marching back to our barracks when it started to rain, to rain hard. Our barracks was in sight, a few hundred yards away. In my loudest and clearest voice I ordered, "Company Run!" and run they did. As we got to the barracks our Chief Overseer was waiting.

"Who is today's company commander?'

"Sir, I am, sir. Officer Candidate Landersman."

"Candidate Landersman, that stunt just cost you fifteen demerits."

"Yes sir. Thank you, sir."

No one seemed to make much of a big deal out of the demerit thing and I hadn't paid any attention to it until I received fifteen of them. What did that mean? I learned that if an OC got more than 50 demerits he was caput, gone, out of OCS. Bilging out of OCS was like dropping out that first day to avoid the draft. A former OC would then spend two years in the Navy as an enlisted man. Well, fifteen was a long way from fifty, I thought.

And I was right; fifteen was a long way from fifty. But I got ten more demerits when the Chief found dust on the shelf behind my books. That made twenty five demerits; half way to fifty but with only a month to go at OCS I felt that I could be careful and make it to graduation. And I did make it but it was not as comfortable as I had hoped.

There were 1300 men just out of college formed into 13 companies in OCS Class 13. The leaders of OCS decided that we should have a basketball tournament. The winning company would be given extra liberty on a weekend. Big prize. Important.

Every company had some that had played basketball in college. My company had five. We had guys from Penn State, Holy Cross, Lewis and Clark and Dartmouth, and of course, me from Clarkson and Dakota Wesleyan. I was really looking forward to the tournament and tried to find some extra time to practice before the tournament started. I hadn't touched a ball in a number of months. One late afternoon I squeezed in an hour between dinner and required study time and was shooting and running in the big gym next to OCS at the Naval Training Center at Newport. I lost track of the time, was late getting back to the barracks and faced the same Chief who had awarded me the earlier demerits.

"What is it with you? Are you trying to bilge out of here, because if you are I can arrange it for you?"

"Sir, no sir. I want to graduate and get a commission."

"Then why are you in trouble all the time."

"Sir, I'm trying to stay out of trouble, honest. This time I was trying to get ready for the basketball tournament and I lost track of the time."

With the mention of the basketball tournament the Chief took a renewed interest and asked me about my basketball experience. I suppose I impressed him because he finally told me that he would hold back the fifteen demerits that I should get for late study time. It was like I was on probation for that last month of OCS.

Years later, as I looked back at the basketball tournament at OCS, it occurred to me that that was some of the best basketball that I had been involved with, well, maybe nearly so because later, in the Navy, I was involved with some really good basketball with PHIBLANT, but that's another story. Enough to say, that at OCS we did pretty well but didn't win it all, so my OCS company didn't get the extra-long weekend.

I stayed clean the rest of the time at OCS and even if the Chief had slapped on the fifteen demerits for late study, I would have graduated with 40 demerits; ten short of fifty. But I did graduate from OCS on 11 November 1953 and was commissioned as an ensign in the Naval Reserve.

Just prior to graduation from OCS I had received my orders. I was to report to USS LST 542 at Little Creek, Virginia and my duty would be as First Lieutenant and Gunnery Officer. With help from some others who knew more than I did, I was able to determine that with authorized leave and travel time I would report to USS LST 542 just before Christmas 1953.

CHAPTER SIXTEEN

THAT FIRST UNDERWAY WATCH

1953

She was my first ship. Not only the first Navy ship in which I served but the first ship upon which I ever set foot. Her name was USS LST 542, and that was before LSTs had names like other ships. Later, after I had moved on, she was named USS Chelan County, as all the LSTs that were still in commission were named after counties or parishes.

USS LST 542 was a prototype, which means she was the first of her class. During World War Two over a thousand Landing Ship, Tank (LST) were built. The first class included hull numbers 1 through 541, then some changes were made and a new class was built with hull numbers starting at 542 going on until after the war when another new class was introduced, the LST 1153 Class. I served in USS LST 1153 also, but that's another story.

On 14 December 1953 I reported on board USS LST 542 moored to a pier at the Naval Amphibious Base, Little Creek, Virginia with her bow doors open and bow ramp on the slanted concrete shelf that had recently been built for LSTs. The ship had been at sea when I arrived as ordered at Little Creek and schools filled the time until her return to home port. Having graduated from Officer Candidate School 11 November 1953, I had taken some leave then traveled to Virginia.

In an evaluation of looks ranging from beautiful to ugly LST 542 would tend strongly toward the latter. Being a veteran of World War II she had been used and abused, a boxy cargo carrier that resembled an underfed workhorse with ribs showing through skin dished and dented from a thousand brushes with unyielding piers.

I walked down the ramp, put down my baggage, saluted and reported as I had been told to do at OCS, which felt odd because all I could see as I looked aft was the vast tank deck, not the stern where the U.S. flag was supposed to be, and on the forward end of that tank deck was an area serving as the quarterdeck with a petty officer in charge not a commissioned officer. This was not the setting we had rehearsed at OCS. I saluted anyway and it seemed to be the right thing to do because the Gunner's Mate Second Class returned my salute, smiled and welcomed me on board. He told me that he knew I was expected aboard and that I would be his division officer, and he had the Quarterdeck Messenger take my baggage and show me to the Executive Officer's Office, which was also his stateroom.

There was a great deal of noise and many sailors in dirty dungarees were busy scraping, banging, chipping at rust on the deck as the messenger and I walked aft through the tank deck. Some of the men looked up and smiled at me in my brand new ensign's service dress blue uniform with its single bright gold ring on the sleeve and some didn't look up or smile. They knew I would be their division officer, which was more than I knew.

The Executive officer was Lieutenant (Junior Grade) Eddie Epps, a former enlisted man who had risen through the ranks and received a commission. I was to learn that such officers were called "mustangs," and that the single silver bar on a khaki uniform meant that this mustang was a "jaygee." He welcomed me to the ship and asked if I had ever been in a Navy ship before.

There was a story told at OCS of a brand new ensign reporting to his first ship, being asked by the Exec, "Have you ever been in a Navy ship before?" And the ensign replied, "Oh, yes sir, two others." "Really," said the Exec. "Which ships?" "The two that I crossed getting to this one." The story went through my mind as I searched for a similar wise response but I had not crossed any other ships getting to this one and answered the Exec with simple truth. No, I had never been in a Navy ship before. This was my first.

The Exec told me about the ship, that I was to be the First Lieutenant and Gunnery Officer, that I would meet the Captain tomorrow and that the Senior Watch Officer would explain my watch standing duties. I started into the process of relieving the First Lieutenant and trying to learn the vast lore of seamanship and gunnery with Chief Boatswains Mate Lane and First Class Boatswains Mate Long my patient mentors trying to teach me in a few weeks some of what they knew from years of serving at sea. The Senior Watch Officer put me on watch in training to be an in-port Officer of the Deck.

I really liked living on board the ship. Having spent most of the last five years in college, living in rooming houses, eating in low cost "greasy spoons" or slightly better college dining halls, I found it very comfortable and convenient in the ship. I had a small stateroom, good meals with all I could eat, wardroom, laundry, haircuts, movie every night, companionship of officers and men and no distance to travel to work. Above all there was the excitement of learning about the ship, how to be a Navy officer, to be responsible for something other than myself and with all of this I actually received pay; $220 a month.

The Senior Watch officer, Lieutenant (junior grade) Willie Hayes, explained to me that I had to have duty a number of days under instruction so that I could be qualified as an in-port OOD, which meant I could take duty by myself. I wanted that. I wanted to be in charge, responsible for the ship for that 24 hour period as OOD in-port. So, I asked how long it took to be qualified and was told that it depended on how rapidly I learned. The Senior Watch Officer told me that normally to be qualified as OOD in-port an officer had to be qualified underway, in case he had to move the ship for an emergency, but in my case if I really wanted to become qualified there were two weeks to Christmas and if I stayed on board those two weeks under instruction I could be qualified and have duty over Christmas. What a good deal! I stayed on board for the two weeks as the other four officers, qualified in-port OODS, changed each day.

When it was Christmas Eve I had duty as OOD in-port, and on Christmas Day and that night I had duty. Only a month and a half after OCS and I was OOD in-port in a U.S. Navy ship. What a great Navy! I was so proud! I was now OOD in-port in a five-officer rotation and I was looking forward to getting underway in the ship so that I could become an underway OOD.

Some years later I would learn that the normal process of being qualified as an Officer of the Deck Underway was long and complex requiring an officer to demonstrate knowledge of rules of the road, ship handling, seamanship, communications, engineering and to stand watches as Junior Officer of the Deck and Combat Information Center Watch Officer.

USS LST 542 had six officers before I came aboard; the Captain, the Exec and four department heads who were also division officers and also watch-standers as OOD. I brought the total to seven but by mid-January when it was time to get underway for a big fleet exercise, the officer I relieved as First Lieutenant and Gunnery Officer was gone, leaving four watch standers.

With the ship underway I went to the bulletin board outside the wardroom to look at the watch bill. Jack Donahue had the 1200-1600, Willie Hayes the 1600-2000, Jeff Sanborn the 2000-2400 and Stu Landersman the 0000-0400. Great! I was elated. My first time underway and I'm an OOD with the midwatch. Never having been underway before, I didn't know how the ship operated at sea so I went to the bridge and pilot house area for an hour and watched.

The ship was operated, or "conned", at sea from a conning station, a six-foot square room with all-around view atop a tower well aft in the ship. Below the conning station was the Captain's sea cabin and below that was the pilot house, from where the ship was steered. A ladder on the rear of the tower gave access to the sea cabin and the conning station. This put the officer in control of the ship, or with "the conn" in Navy parlance, by himself using a voice tube for communications with his helmsman and other bridge watch. There was no Combat Information Center.

Much later a crewman claimed to me that one night with no other ships around the pilot house watch, suspecting that the OOD up in the conning tower was not paying attention, put the rudder over and watched the steering compass go through 360 degrees and back to the original course as the ship's wake carved a luminescent circle on the smooth sea and no one else ever knew. That was before I had come aboard so, "It didn't happen on my watch."

Fifteen minutes before midnight, as I had been taught at OCS, I reported to Jeff Sanborn in the conning station. "I'm ready to relieve you sir." He showed me the radar repeater with the explanation that it never worked and was only good to sit on and keep warm. "See that light over there? That's the guide. His bearing should be 150 if you're on station, range 5000 yards, like it shows in this formation diagram." He had a plastic covered maneuvering board with the formation drawn in crayon, called grease pencil, and he gave me a long litany on course, speed and other details.

"How do I tell the range to the guide without radar?"

"See that ship over there," he pointed to a light, "and that one. Those are here on the maneuvering board. You know they're on station so you just keep the angle between them 52 degrees."

"Is that right?" I asked. "Doesn't seem right to me, but I'll figure it out. Anything else?"

"Yeah," Jeff said. He explained about the tactical voice radio circuit that I would have to guard and how to respond and added, "You have to be alert for flashing light signals."

"Flashing light?" I asked.

"Yeah. If it's for us you give him a 'wait' and yell for the quartermaster, who's also the signalman."

"Where's he?"

"We've only got one on board so when we're underway with other Navy ships he sleeps on the chart table down below in the pilot house."

"How do you know if the flashing light signal is for us?"

"Gheesus! Don't you know anything? Our call-up is tare two, for LST 542; tare for the last letter of the type, two the last digit of the hull number. Dah pause dit dit dah dah dah, repeated over and over. Got it?"

"Yeah." If I had answered his question about whether or not I knew anything, the answer would have been "no," but I disregarded it as I didn't know enough to realize how totally unprepared I was. I asked, "How do I tell him to wait?"

"You just give him able sugar; dit dah dit dit dit repeated until he stops sending to you, then you yell down the voice tube for 'signals!'". After some further explanations I felt I had all that I could get from Jeff and gave the statement learned at OCS, "I relieve you sir." I would have saluted as I relieved him, but Jeff was not "covered," that is he wasn't wearing a hat.

Here I was, Officer of the Deck of a U.S. Navy ship at sea in a big formation of Navy ships! What a great Navy! After a few moments of self-satisfaction I realized that I didn't know what I was doing and I had better figure out some things and fast. Fortunately, fast was relatively slow with formation speed eight knots and I had time to reason through where my ship's station was and how to keep the ship on station. There was a mimeographed operation order that couldn't be read in the dark and I didn't have a flashlight, but through a combination of things learned at OCS, high school geometry and boy scouts, and what I had seen the previous afternoon, I figured out a little more.

After a while I saw that the ship was a few degrees off station. What should I do? With the maneuvering board and positioning my hands so that left was my ship and right the guide ship, I reasoned through relative motion that if I were to speed up, ever so slightly, the bearing to the guide would increase and I would be back on station. I remembered from OCS, in Lieutenant McClintok's navigation class, that an OOD didn't change course or speed without getting the Captain's permission, so I cranked the howler and put my ear to the voice tube. Immediately a voice responded, "Captain."

"Cap'n. Officer of the Deck. I'm two degrees off station and recommend increasing to 135 rpm to get us back on station." I had remembered that Lieutenant McClintok always used "Cap'n" in class when simulating a call to the Captain. It sounded like real Navy so I used it.

"Very well. Make it so," was the Captain's response.

I called the pilot house, "Add four rpm." "Add four rpm," came the response from the voice tube. Then a few seconds later, "Engine room acknowledges add four rpm, making 135 rpm, sir." "Very well," I replied.

Hey, this is all right! Now I knew how to keep station, get the Captain's approval and give orders to the helm. A few minutes later I found that I would have to change course two degrees to keep station. Same process. "Very well. Make it so," said the Captain, and so it went through the four hour watch; every few minutes I had to make an adjustment, figured out what to do, called the Captain, got permission and ordered the change. I called the Captain to tell him everything that happened. "Very well," he would reply.

From out of the dark a small flashing light seemed to be pointed right at me. I couldn't figure out the signal but it persisted and it was surely in my direction so I turned on the signal light and flashed back "wait;" dit dah, dit dit dit. The signal persisted. I sent "wait" again and the signal continued. After sending many waits I called for the signalman who climbed two decks up the ladder, looked at the light flashing in the dark then at me with disgust and said, "He's calling the 901 over there on the other side of us."

At breakfast the Captain, Lieutenant Wallace M. Riggs, said, "Mr. Landersman, stood your first underway watch this morning, didn't you? And did real well."

"Yes sir. Thank you. It was really interesting but I don't see how a Captain gets any sleep at sea."

"Well, you get used to it."

After breakfast the Exec told me to help Willie Hayes at the conning station as there would be some formation maneuvering. I didn't realize until much later that I was sent to the conning station more as a training process for me than as a help for Willie, so that when I came on watch the next time I was far better prepared, even with a red filtered flashlight.

For the rest of my time in the USS LST 542 I stood many OOD watches and wrote many log entries, many more complex than, "Steaming as before," even though the ship was diesel not steam powered.

In all my Navy time that followed I never met nor heard of an officer in any ship being qualified as an underway formation steaming Officer of the Deck with as little or no preparation as had I.

In my next ship, USS LST 1153, the Senior Watch Officer said, "If you were qualified in the 542 you're qualified here," and he put me on the watch bill as OOD in-port and underway. For three years in two ships I was an OOD with no qualification process. It wasn't that way in my first destroyer where I had to experience the entire procedure and it took me six months to qualify as OOD underway.

Years later, long after I had learned that an officer is supposed to go through an elaborate process of preparation and experience before being qualified as OOD, I met Wallace M. Riggs when he was a Captain and as we reminisced about LST 542 days I asked him about that first watch I had stood as OOD underway. He remembered it clearly.

"If you don't mind me asking," I said, "How could you let me stay on watch when you must have known that I didn't know what I was doing up there?"

He laughed. "As soon as I heard your voice I knew something was wrong. An OOD doesn't have to get permission for such minor stationing course and speed adjustments. I knew you shouldn't have been up there and I had two choices; I could go up to the conning station and sit there on the radar repeater keeping my eye on you or I could stay in the sea cabin a few steps below and see if you kept me informed. Either way I wasn't going to get much sleep. So I decided to stay in the sea cabin until I felt uncomfortable. As it developed, you kept calling me every few minutes and you told me everything that was going on and I had the whole picture so I let you keep going. Later that morning, though, I had the Exec see that you got some training and you were fine after that." Actually he had a third choice; calling the Exec or Senior Watch Officer to get a qualified officer on watch but he felt that might embarrass me and damage my confidence.

I don't know if I would have had the patience and consideration of Wallace M. Riggs, but later in my Navy career, when I had command of Navy ships I often thought of my first underway watch and tried to give young officers opportunities to conn the ship and opportunities to become qualified.

CHAPTER SEVENTEEN

USS LST 1153

1954-1956

Secretary of the Navy Josephus Daniels banned use of alcoholic beverages on board Navy ships and for over a hundred years it had been illegal to drink in a ship of the U.S. Navy. The strongest drink for a sailor at sea then was coffee, still called "a cup of Joe" after the Secretary that took away their whiskey. Navy Regulations prohibited it and so there was no drinking, at least not on surface ships and submarines. On board aircraft carriers, though, some aviators considered that the prohibition did not apply to them and they enjoyed an evening cocktail hour in the security of their staterooms.

An LST (Landing Ship, Tank) carried six officers; Captain, Exec and four department heads; Operations, Engineering, Supply and First Lieutenant. The four department heads also covered a number of important shipboard roles such as communications, damage control, finance and gunnery, and the Executive Officer served as Navigator. Every officer had collateral duties; jobs in addition to his primary job and often the collateral duties took more time than the primary.

Classified Material Custodian, Safety, Lookout Training, Recreation Fund Custodian, Landing Party, Fundraising Drive, Laundry to name a few and there were boards and committees such as the Crypto Board, Accounting Board, Courts Martial Board, Training Board, Recreation Committee, Recreation Fund Audit Board, the list went on and on. Navy shipboard requirements of these collateral duties, boards and committees were the same for all ships; battleship, aircraft carrier, destroyer or LST. In a big ship hundreds of officers were available for the tasks. In an LST there were six. Every ship was checked in a periodic Admin Inspection to ensure that every function was covered by the required appointment letters and backed by detailed log books, forms and records.

Sometimes just prior to an Admin Inspection a ship would learn of a new requirement. Ensign Jones would be given a letter appointing him as Pier Sentry Training Officer the day before the inspection and if he knew the process he would be up all night "gun-decking" records. Next morning the past three months of training for pier sentries would be displayed, the ship would receive a grade of Outstanding in the inspection and the Captain and squadron commander would be pleased that pier sentries had been trained so well.

One of the requirements was for a monthly inventory of medications held in custody of the ship's "Doc." In an LST the Sick Bay was run by a Hospital Corpsman qualified for independent duty, a First Class Petty Officer with considerable experience able to care for normal shipboard health and medical matters. If a doctor was needed the patient was referred to a big ship or ashore. At sea a prescription signed by the Captain authorized issue of controlled substances. Each month the Alcohol and Narcotics Inventory Board counted pills, measured medicines and audited prescriptions to see that Doc had not mishandled those medications entrusted to him by the United States Navy. There was no gun-decking of these records. Well, not in the usual sense.

Lieutenant Junior Grade Jim Williamson, Operations Officer, Lieutenant Junior Grade Stu Landersman, First Lieutenant, and Ensign Jim Carino, Supply Officer, were the Alcohol and Narcotics

Inventory Board. Half the officers in the ship, they assembled each month in Sick Bay as Doc opened his safe and showed what he had and what he had issued. They counted every pill, noted there were fewer than last month and Doc produced chits showing issue, all signed by the Captain. They measured ounces of liquid medicines and Doc showed chits signed by the Captain. Included with liquid medications, the ship was authorized to carry whiskey as relief for stress and exposure to adverse weather and only issued by Doc with the Captain's approval. There had been 12 issues of whiskey the past month, four ounces each and Doc had prescriptions for 48 ounces of whiskey, exactly the amount missing since last inventory.

Doc was putting his medications back in the safe and Jim Williamson was filling in the blanks on the form letter for the three officers to sign when Stu Landersman asked to see the liquor prescriptions again. Strange, he thought and pointed out to the others, "These are my men from the Deck Force, look at their names and they weren't in any cold weather or water this past month."

Doc shrugged his shoulders with an amphibious salute. "I don't know. Cap'n must have wanted them to have it. He signed the chits," and sure enough there was the Captain's signature on every one of the prescription forms.

The three officers then asked more about the whiskey inventory. They checked past month's issues and sure enough, most of the chits showed Deck Force sailors receiving whiskey for exposure to weather that was news to the First Lieutenant. Then the Operations Officer made a discovery. Every period of issue was in the first few days of the ship being underway.

Doc finally told the full story. Lieutenant Commander Leo J. Curtis, Commanding Officer of USS LST 1153 was a practicing alcoholic. When the ship got underway he was cut off from his supply ashore so he had Doc issue whiskey to him with the lame excuse that he was giving it to sailors in need and he would sign the authorizations to keep Doc's records legal. Doc explained that the Captain used about four the first day, three the second day, then two as he tapered off his use. Leo Curtis even had Doc stock his preference of bourbon.

Lieutenant Edwin J. Cantaloupe, the Executive Officer, was a mustang just as Captain Curtis. Both had served as quartermasters in destroyers on the old China Station before World War II. Cantaloupe wore long sleeve collared shirts all of the time to hide tattoos from neck to wrists and ankles. Both had been commissioned during World War II in a Navy far short of officers. When told of Curtis' use of the ship's alcohol, the Exec said he'd look into it and after that the Captain stopped using Navy whiskey, bringing his own supply on board prior to each underway period.

The four department heads were OODs underway and stood duty days in port. One of the first things a watch officer had to learn was not to call Captain Curtis for anything the first three days of any underway period, although they hadn't known why, and the Exec paid more attention to bridge matters than usual during that time. Also, when the ship was in her home port of Little Creek, Virginia, tied up at the Amphibious Base, the duty officer had to know the Captain's routine so that he could be reached when necessary.

Arriving on the ship at 1000, Curtis did paperwork at his desk until lunch at 1130. A nap followed until 1330 followed by a tour of the ship, chat with the Exec and departure at 1430. He would instruct the duty officer not to "bong" him and not break his absentee pennant until the squadron commander's absentee pennant was displayed in the flagship at another pier.

It took Leo Curtis a half-hour to reach his favorite bar on the way home and the duty officer had that phone number and knew the Captain's timing. He would be at that bar until 1730, leaving just in time to get home as his wife arrived from work. He told the Wardroom that he and his wife drank a fifth of bourbon every night, unless he had been fortunate enough to procure a case of quart bottles.

That was a little corner of the amphibious force. Legend had it that during World War II the Navy was desperate for men to man the amphibious ships, especially the many LSTs that were being built for the invasion of Europe and for the island hopping campaigns of the Pacific. So desperate was the Navy, the legend goes, that they turned to the brigs, Navy prisons, and took volunteers. This means that at least some of those WWII LSTs, ships that put troops ashore at places like Normandy, Tinian, Saipan, Iwo Jima and Okinawa, were manned by "brig rats." But of course that's just legend, sea stories, and you can't really believe everything in a sea story, can you?

While Stu had been seriously dating the lovely Martha Morehead, the Captain of USS LST 1153 invited all officers and their ladies to a Saturday night dinner at his home. Martha was very style conscious and wore her best Saturday night attire, having visited the hairdresser that day and Stu wore his only suit. Together they were "dressed to kill." After all, this was a Saturday night affair at the home of the commanding officer and Martha wanted to make a good impression. She knew that social events and an officer's wife's appearance and behavior were important in the Navy.

As promptness in an officer is a virtue, they arrived at the door of the Captain's apartment exactly on time. In response to Stu's ring the door flew open. There stood Leo Curtis, commanding officer of a U.S. Navy warship, hosting his wardroom officers and their ladies at a Saturday night dinner, clad only in faded Bermuda shorts, no shirt, no shoes or socks, a drink in his hand obviously not his first or second.

Martha's mouth dropped open, Stu stood there wondering if he had the right day and Leo Curtis yelled, "C'mon in! Why'd y'get so dressed up?"

When Stu had reported on board USS LST 1153 the Senior Watch Officer said, "If you were qualified in the 542 you're qualified here," and Stu became one of the four watch standing OODs underway and duty officers in port. That first watch qualification in the 542 made it quick.

Commander Amphibious Force, U.S. Atlantic Fleet (COMPHIBLANT) had a requirement to provide one LST to Commander Service Force, U.S. Atlantic Fleet (COMSERVLANT) and LST 1153 was the ship assigned to fill that requirement for six months in 1956. The ship carried cargo for COMSERVLANT, steaming independently on various assignments, considerably different operations than participation in Amphib exercises with lots of other ships. Service Force duty took them to places like Antigua, British West Indies and Argentia, Newfoundland. They carried Navy Construction Battalion (CB) teams home to Davisville, Rhode Island and a carrier aircraft from Roosevelt Roads, Puerto Rico to Norfolk. They were loading, unloading and underway most of the six months and visited many places not often frequented by Navy ships in normal employment. After the SERVLANT duty the ship was assigned to her home port for maintenance and to make up for the heavy operating time.

On 5 January 1956 the ship received orders to send Stu Landersman on Temporary Additional Duty (TAD) to COMPHIBTRALANT, "—in connection with Force athletics." This put Stu ashore at the Amphibious Base to play basketball for COMPHIBLANT, a "varsity" Navy team coached by a Chief Warrant Officer, Bos'n Ozzie Ahlwardt and consisting mostly of former college players taken from Amphib ships, as had Stu.

Until 1954 the Navy had a basketball rule that there could be no more than two officers of the five playing on the court at any time. This was intended to ensure that officers would not dominate playing opportunities and deny enlisted men chances to play. It meant that a coach had to consider this limitation in his team make-up and substitutions and it curtailed the effectiveness of Navy teams competing outside the service. That rule was abolished in 1955 and for the first time Navy teams could compete with others on an equal basis, using any and all players as a coach desired.

The COMPHIBLANT Gators basketball team of 1955-56 consisted of 12 players; ten of whom had played in college. Six were officers and six were enlisted men. They played a full schedule including Army, Air Force and Marine Corps teams and other Navy teams as well as a few local athletic clubs and colleges.

At the end of the season there was a tournament in which eight Type Commanders' teams of the Atlantic Fleet competed, the winner to go to the All-Navy tournament. The All-Navy winner would go to the All-Service tournament. At each level the winning team could augment their roster by taking players from other teams of that tournament, so that the team coming out of a tournament was composed of most of the best players.

Service teams at the time were comprised mostly of college basketball players. With the draft, physically fit young men coming out of college were faced with military service. It was either be drafted into the army or sign up in one of the other services. Many chose the other services, each of which had programs of similar length service as the Selective Service System obligation. When it came to varsity level competition many service teams included name players; all-this or that and some had been selected for professional teams after their college and service stints.

Mel Roach was the top player for PHIBLANT. He was from the University of Virginia where he had been a big star in three sports and he had signed a bonus contract to play baseball with the Boston Braves, soon relocated to Milwaukee and later, in 1965 to Atlanta. Mel had used his $40,000 bonus for an engagement ring and his teammates never found out if he got the ring back after the girl ditched him. After his Navy service Mel did very well playing second base for a pennant winning Braves team until he was injured, left baseball and became a stockbroker in Richmond, Virginia.

Doug Pfaff and Don Oenken had been teammates coached by Pfaff's father at a small Wisconsin college. They could have been officers but chose to serve the minimum time as enlisted men. Both intended to be high school coaches after leaving the Navy.

Bob Place and Nels Hoffman had played together at the University of Rochester where they had been commissioned from NROTC. Stu, while at Clarkson, had played against them. All three; Stu, Place and Hoffman, and their wives became good friends enjoying social activities together. There wasn't much money for recreation on LTJG pay and more than once the three couples would cash-in their soda deposit bottles, pile into one car and go to a drive-in movie.

Twenty years later, in 1976, as a brand new destroyer squadron commander, Captain Stu Landersman sat in one of his ships, USS Albert David (FF1050) and glanced at a paper on the Wardroom table.

"This officer," pointing to a note in the Plan of the Day, "Is he available now in the ship?" he asked Commander Kelsey Stewart, the skipper.

"Yes, I'll get him for you," and a few minutes later a bright young jaygee introduced himself to the Commodore.

"Is your father Ozzie Ahlwardt?" Stu asked the young officer who was smiling as he knew what was coming.

"Yes sir, and I used to throw foul shots back to you twenty years ago," was the smiling reply.

The PHIBLANT Gator coach, Ozzie Ahlwardt, had a five-year-old son Elmer who had been mascot and ball boy at practices and games. Now that freckled faced kid was a department head in a ship in Stu's destroyer squadron. Months later, when Ozzie came from Jacksonville, Florida to San Diego to visit his son, Stu met his former coach again.

At the end of the season, the Gators won their first three games in the double elimination Atlantic Fleet tournament including a win over SERVLANT in the first game, but SERVLANT came out of the losers' bracket and beat the Gators in the rematch. The two had to play again for the championship. Four of PHIBLANT's original players had been transferred during the season, leaving eight on the tournament team and Stu Landersman was on crutches with an ankle sprained against AIRLANT. Ozzie Ahlwardt had a team of only seven healthy players for the final game so Stu dressed for the game, hobbled through warm-up and sat on the bench so the team wouldn't look so depleted.

It was a close game and as they tired two Gators fouled out. Ozzie looked down the bench at Stu without saying a word, then at Stu's ankle, heavily wrapped with Ace bandage, then back at Stu.

"I'll give it a try," Stu responded to the coach's slightly raised eyebrow.

With less than a minute to play a third Gator fouled out and Stu hobbled onto the court. He could do no more than limp along with the play as SERVLANT won the Atlantic Fleet championship by two points.

Three healthy Gators (Roach, Pfaff and Oenken) augmented the SERVLANT team representing the Atlantic Fleet that won the All-Navy but lost to the Air Force in the All-Service tournament. An augmented Air Force team representing all services then competed with winners of NCAA, NAIA and AAU to form the Olympic basketball team. There had been a long path that could have lead to the Olympics but Stu never really got on that path.

Long before those follow-on basketball tournaments Stu was back in his ship and just in time for the ship to receive a new name. USS LST 1153 became USS TALBOT COUNTY (LST 1153) as all LSTs were named for counties or parishes. Her sister ship LST 1154 became TALLAHATCHIE COUNTY and Stu's former ship, LST 542, became CHELAN COUNTY.

Lieutenant Commander Robert E. Kemp, a mustang and a real gentleman, relieved Leo Curtis as Commanding Officer of USS TALBOT COUNTY and Lieutenant Charlie Sassone, a Naval Academy graduate, came aboard and replaced E. J. Cantaloupe as Executive Officer. With new Captain and Exec the ship had a completely changed personality.

Leo Curtis went to command a Naval Reserve Training Center in Tennessee and a couple of years later, after he had been passed over for promotion to commander, he was accused of intoxication and making improper advances to a woman. This sounded familiar to the former LST 1153 officers and Curtis retired rather than face charges.

On 1 November 1956 Stu Landersman was detached from USS TALBOT COUNTY (LST1153) so that he could be processed by the Norfolk Naval Base for release from active duty in the Naval Reserve. He was paid $31.32 for transportation from Norfolk, Virginia to Poughkeepsie, New York and an additional $31.32 for dependents' travel. His Honorable Discharge was recorded in the Dutchess County Clerk's Office, Poughkeepsie, New York in volume 32, page 265, Military Discharges, signed by Frederick L. Smith, Dutchess County Clerk. He was issued Selective Service System number 30-20-30-83 and assigned in classification 4-A on 5 December 1956.

CHAPTER EIGHTEEN

MEETING MARTHA MOREHEAD

1955

While serving in LST 1153 Stu Landersman met Martha Morehead.

In the early 1950's Norfolk, Virginia and the area immediately around made up the largest naval base complex in the world. Hundreds of Navy ships were home-ported at the Naval Base there. It was the location of the Commander in Chief of the U.S. Atlantic Fleet and numerous other high commands. There were two major naval air stations in the area, the largest naval shipyard, many Navy schools, communications stations, and amphibious warfare activities. Sailors out-numbered single girls fifty to one and single officers out numbered good-looking college girls more than that ratio.

Norfolk girls fell into two basic categories; enlisted men's' girls and officers' girls. There was no agency to keep this rule and there were many that passed over and back in both directions but basically Norfolk girls stayed in one camp or the other.

In Norfolk there were countless naval officers and most of the girls that dated officers had a continuous flow of them through their lives. Tall, short, talkative, quiet, funny and serious, they came from all parts of the country and all ethnic backgrounds. There were naval aviators who flew from the decks of aircraft carriers and tried to act dashing and bold, submarine officers quiet, serious and studious, and destroyer officers who could be any of the above. The girls learned their differences and the terminology of their lifestyle. If a ship was in port for upkeep it meant that he would be around for a week or two. Overhaul meant a few months. If his ship were about to deploy he would be away for many months. Forget him. Find someone else, someone who would be around to take you to dinner and dancing when you wanted.

Martha Britt Morehead had come to Norfolk with her family during World War II as her father obtained work in a shipyard. She had graduated from Granby High School and gone to two years of college at Longwood before going to work as a secretary at Southern Materials, a large supplier of concrete and then with V. H. Monnette and Company, agent for sales to military exchanges and commissaries. Martha lived with her mother and sister in a small house on Little Creek Road. Her father had passed away in 1953.

Martha was an exception to the dating pattern of Norfolk girls as she dated a few civilians and a few officers, but she knew most ships' names and schedules through her work at V.H. Monnette. She could have gone out seven nights a week if she chose, each night to a place of her choosing and each night with a different officer, but she was selective and limited her social life.

The Morehead family name reached back into American history. Morehead City was named for the first governor of North Carolina and there were buildings and endowments at the University of North Carolina that carried the name. Part of the Morehead family had migrated to Texas in early days and the Texas part of the family included Martha's father.

In the 1950s Norfolk was a dry town; no liquor was sold in bars or restaurants, so there were very few, if any, good restaurants. The officers' clubs sold liquor, beer and wine, served excellent food and provided the best dancing, often to name bands. Martha had been to all the officers' clubs in and around Norfolk as that's where a naval officer took a girl and often she met friends or shipmates of her dates. There were a few private clubs in Norfolk and a few country clubs but these were available only to members and membership was limited.

Martha had wanted a car for some time. There were city busses to and from work but it was inconvenient and when needed she had the use of her parent's car. Often there were young men with cars to help with errands but over the past few months she had developed a desire to have her own transportation. The women where she worked were known as "Monnette girls" as they were all good looking, shapely, well dressed, well made-up and very well paid, so she could well afford a car. She decided on a Chevrolet two tone convertible.

To Martha, choosing a car was like selecting a dress or a coat. It had to match her hair and coloring and it had to go well with her other clothing. The car was a part of her apparel. Turquoise and cream, the convertible driven by the striking blonde wearing a turquoise and cream ensemble caused heads to turn wherever she went as surely as they did when she walked into a restaurant.

On May 26, 1955 Martha and Richard, whose ship was soon to deploy, joined some friends for an evening at the Amphibious Base Officer's Club. Downstairs, the club did not require coats and tie and was known as a haven for junior officers. Often the large room was filled with noise and smoke, and a piano player led songs. Rowdy at times, Thursday nights had developed into the most popular night to "sing-along", as it was called. Martha, Richard and their friends had chosen this particular night at the Amphib Club, and it was as expected, crowded, noisy and smoky. All joined in as a club habitué, Joe Sullivan, belted out his favorite, "Steve O'Donnell's Wake."

> "There were fighters and blighters
> and Irish dynamiters.
> There was beer, gin, whiskey, wine and cake.
> There were men in high positions,
> There were Irish politicians,

And they all got drunk at Steve O'Donnell's wake."

Joe sang out the chorus in a loud clear tenor accompanied by the two hundred or more club patrons, then by himself in the same voice but with an Irish accent, "Oh, Stevie bie, why did you die, the weepin' widow cried, and they all got drunk at Steve O'Donnell's wake—," the singing continued.

Through the noise, singing and smoke Martha's friend Jackie leaned across the table and asked or yelled, "Have you seen those three standing at the bar?"

She had to repeat it before Martha replied. "Yes. The one in the middle, in the white tennis sweater is really something but forget the tallest one. Look at that haircut!" They laughed and turned their attention back to the singing.

The three at the bar had just come in and were feeling fortunate to find space at the bar on a Thursday night. They ordered a pitcher of beer. A second pitcher followed. In the middle was Jim "Gabe" Gabler, six foot three and 180 pounds wearing a white tennis sweater. This was his last night as an active duty Navy officer. Tomorrow he would be released to the inactive Naval Reserve, free to return home and find a civilian job having completed three years of active duty in amphibious ships.

Gabe's former shipmate Jim Williamson stood to the right wearing a tan summer sport jacket, beige shirt and maroon tie. The night out for the three of them was Jim's treat because of Gabe's last night in the Navy and also it was the birthday of the third officer, Stu Landersman. Stu was six foot five, weighed 185 pounds and wore a white shirt, light blue tie and dark blue blazer. His hair looked awful, being in a confused state somewhere between a crew cut that had been and a longer hair style that was not yet there.

Stu and Jim were ship mates in the LST 1153 and Gabe had served with Jim in a previous ship. All three played basketball at the base gym whenever they could find time and this night they had been to a seafood restaurant out in the country near Little Creek.

"Okay," Jim Williamson declared, "the dinner was on me because Gabe is leaving the Navy." He raised his glass. "To my former shipmate and team mate Gabe: Smooth sailing and a following sea." The other two followed suit and they all drank. "Now for my current shipmate and team mate Stu on his birthday, I offer a special gift. For tonight and only tonight, you get to pick out from this room any woman and I will get you her name and phone number."

"Get out a' here! If I see one I'll take care of her myself."

"No, no, really! This is a special deal for you," Jim insisted, "and I've already spotted the leading candidate. That blonde over there is just for you. She doesn't even have to stand up. I can tell she's tall and she fits your specifications."

Stu had seen her, also. "If you're going to make a move for yourself, go ahead and good luck but if it's for me, stay away from that one. I'll take care of her myself." Stu's drinks were starting to show.

"With all respect, shipmate," Jim's drinks also were having their effect, "I have seen you in this kind of action before, with minimal success and many a failure, but that woman I think is out of your league."

"We'll see."

"Now if you don't want me to arrange her for you, pick another. You have to use your birthday present."

"I'll look around, okay?" Stu scanned the smoky room as they consumed a little more beer, while keeping an eye on the blond.

"I think I'll catch her coming out of the ladies room," Stu thought aloud.

The noise, smoke and singing continued. Over in one corner a glass dropped and broke with a "clop" sound indicating that it had been full. People in the area exclaimed, laughed and jumped around. Loud voices and laughter almost drowned out the piano until a popular song was offered and the voices joined in.

Halfway through the next pitcher of beer, Martha left her table and headed to the stairs toward the ladies room.

"My move," said Stu a couple of minutes later as he left the bar and headed toward the stairs.

Off the lobby at the top of the wide carpeted stairs was the ladies room. Halfway up was a landing where the stairs reversed direction. From this landing Stu could see the top of the door to the ladies room. After a few minutes the door opened. He started up the stairs. It was someone else. He returned to the landing. Again it opened. He started up. False alarm once more. Back to the landing. The door swung out, he started up the stairs and there she was walking toward him; an elegant woman in heels and hose, she walked with an air of feminine confidence announcing clearly, "I am a woman." She looked, acted and was dressed like his favorite actress-singer Doris Day. Taller than he had expected, she was almost six feet in heels. Very nice.

"Excuse me." He stopped as did she. "I know this sounds corny and you've heard it a hundred times but I really think we've met before. Maybe it was in Washington?"

She looked at him and would have preferred a pass from his friend in the tennis sweater. Look at this guy, she thought. His hair's a mess. His face is sunburned and peeling. His clothes are very plain. His line is as corny as they come.

"You're right. It is corny. I have heard it before and I have never been to Washington. If we had met it wouldn't be very flattering if you didn't remember my name or where we met, now would it?"

"Yes," and she started to walk away. "But I mean it, really. I think we've met." Stu was desperate. He was losing her.

She stopped; thinking maybe this guy is a client of Monnette and he could have been in our office as Mr. Monnette brings in lots of supply officers. I'd better not be too flippant because maybe he did meet me there. She asked, "Are you a supply officer?"

Maybe there was hope. Stu had only recently changed jobs from first lieutenant to supply. "Yes, I am. How—? Why—?"

"What ship?" she interrupted his confusion now glad she had not given him a rude brush-off.

"LST eleven fifty three."

"Well then, I just processed your order for four cases of Hershey's chocolates this afternoon. What's your name?"

"Stu Landersman. What's yours?"

"I'm Miss Morehead of V. H. Monnette and Company. Landersman? Yes. That was the name on the order. Your Hershey's will be shipped Monday." She was just as businesslike as a Doris Day movie and she turned to leave.

"Hey, wait. That's great, so now we meet and like I said, we have met before, at least by order form and now that we're old friends and all why don't you give me your phone number so that we can go out next week? I have to retrieve my car from New York this weekend."

She hesitated. He wasn't much and she really didn't want to go out with him, but he was tall and had nice looking friends and Richard was leaving. He mentioned a car, New York, kind of humorous, bit of a hustler and might be interesting. This guy could provide transportation, meaning an opportunity to meet other officers. Even her previous transportations were better looking or had more to offer than this one. Should she? She still hesitated.

"Well," she played it safe. "Why don't you call me at work next week and we'll see. Your storekeeper has the number, V. H. Monnette and Company."

"Fine, and does Miss Morehead have a first name?"

"It's Martha, Martha Morehead." She was sure he wouldn't call. It was just a line and she really didn't care.

"There were fighters and blighters and Irish dynamiters, there was beer, gin, whiskey, wine, and cake—" Joe Sullivan was leading his Irish song again, louder than before, with more singers, each having consumed more drink. The noise level of the singing did not allow normal conversation. One had to yell to be understood. Stu, Jim and Gabe turned away from the bar, leaned their backs against it and placed the heel of one shoe on the foot-rail, cowboy style. They sang along, beer glass in hand and looked over the crowded, smoke filled room.

Martha, Richard and their friends passed in front of the bar patrons with "good nights" on the way out. As Martha was delayed by a crowd Jim asked, "Did my good friend Stu Landersman really get your phone number tonight?

"Yes, he surely did," and she smiled just like Doris Day.

Three months later, September 2nd, 1955, with Jim Williamson serving as best man, Martha Britt Morehead became Mrs. Stuart D. Landersman.

CHAPTER NINETEEN

BRIEFLY A CIVILIAN

1956-1957

Martha and I with our one year old son David continued to live in our Landsdale Gardens apartment in Norfolk, Virginia, after I had been discharged from the Navy in November 1956. I had been serving in USS Talbot County (LST 1153) when my contracted time of active service, three years, neared expiration time. To be released from active duty I had been transferred to the Norfolk Naval Station for processing. Before I had been transferred I had asked the Executive Officer of the Talbot County about remaining on active duty, maybe going regular, which meant perhaps I might transfer from reserve to regular Navy. That would mean perhaps making the Navy my career.

Charlie Sansonne had been an excellent executive officer; regular Navy, Naval Academy graduate, which were rare attributes in the amphibious force in those years, but in an LST there was little experience or knowledge of Navy career choices. Charlie talked it over with the Captain and the personnel chief and they all agreed that it would be best to transfer me to the naval station for processing and surely there would be people there who would be happy and capable of giving me all the information and do all the processing, if that were necessary, to further a Navy career.

Not so. As soon as I reported to the Naval Station I asked about staying in the Navy and the immediate response was, "No way, Mister. You've reported in here for processing for release from active duty and in three days you will be released. That's what we do here." Three days later I was a civilian.

In the months before my release from active duty I had been going through considerations of what I wanted to do when I got out of the Navy; what kind of work, what job, where to live, etc.. I knew that I could return to Poughkeepsie and go into my father's ladies lingerie business. My dad had hoped for that for a long time. I could have gone into Moe Domes' electrical contracting business. My uncle Moe would have liked that. But neither the lingerie nor the electrician business appealed to me as a career; that is for the rest of my working life. And just as important, maybe most important, there was consideration of living in Poughkeepsie for the rest of my life. In that regard there was another person to consider.

Marriage is a partnership and although Martha would have and did support me in whatever I wanted to do as for employment, she had very strong feelings of where we would live. Those feelings included an objection to living in Poughkeepsie. Why? Well, Martha had learned of the peculiar relationships between the personalities of Joe and Thelma Landersman, Sylvia and Moe Domes, Estelle and Jerry Ravitz and a dozen or so other Poughkeepsie characters. Martha knew that living in Poughkeepsie would put her right in the middle of a whirlpool of difficulties with families and friends and to avoid those problems she wanted to live elsewhere. Occasional visits would be nice but not living in Poughkeepsie. And, as later years proved, Martha was right.

So I searched for employment as we continued to live in Norfolk. Well, maybe not searched, maybe looked would be more accurate. I interviewed with Libby Owens Glass for a job in Toledo, Ohio, but that didn't turn out. I answered a few ads for employment from Navy Times. Nothing there.

I needed a job. Christmas was approaching and I saw that the largest department store in Norfolk, Sears Roebuck, was advertising for help. I applied and the Sears personnel director latched on to me not for just a Christmas time floor clerk but for their executive development program. Okay with me. Either way I started out in the Sporting Goods Department as the assistant manager. I liked it; selling sporting goods.

Years before, when I was 14 years old, my father's best friend, Irv Friedman, gave me a job for Christmas in his cigar store. Irv did bookmaking and needed someone to take care of the other customers. Bookmaking as used here is not associated with literary work. Bookmaking here refers to the illegal endeavor of off-track acceptance of wagering on horses. It meant taking bets on horses. Irv did very well with bookmaking.

Irv was very demanding and insisted that I deal with customers "his way." I was not to ask, "Can I help you?" The proper way was to see what the customer was looking at, pick it up and hand it to the customer and say, "This is a very tasty box of candy. It's filled with milk chocolate from Switzerland and the fillings are–this and that. Are you looking for something for wife or friend, etc., etc." and maybe "sell up" by showing the customer a larger, more expensive box of candy.

My first day in the Sporting Goods Department of Sears, with the department head watching me closely, I pulled a full press of Irv Friedman on a little lady customer looking for a bicycle for her grand-daughter. I sold her up to the best bike we had and convinced her to open a charge account. The customer was tickled to death and my department head was awed with his new employee. I did very well at Sears during the busy Christmas season and continued on after into the new-year. I knew that Sears was not to be my future but I couldn't decide what my future would be.

I learned of a naval reserve unit in Portsmouth, Virginia, and went to a meeting. They welcomed me and were impressed that I had served in two LSTs as a qualified OOD. I was just as impressed that with something like 20 officers that had been on active duty, none had been a qualified OOD on any ship. They put me into their training program and I felt good about being associated with the Navy again.

Each naval reserve unit had a certain number of pay billets allotted that could be assigned to those officers who met and maintained the membership requirements. Other officers could be active members of a unit without pay, usually waiting for a pay billet to open. As I was the newest, there was no pay billet available, so I became one of those serving while waiting for a pay billet to open. The CO of the unit was impressed with me and we often talked; told sea stories.

During one of my chats with the CO of the reserve unit, I told him that I had been interested in remaining on active duty a few months ago but couldn't find out how that could be done so I had been released. He asked me if I was still interested in going on active duty and I had to think fast.

"Well," I said, "I'd like to find out what kind of duty might be available."

With that much to go on, the CO of the reserve unit arranged for me to have an interview with a Captain at the Norfolk Naval Station, and the meeting was in the same building from which I had been released from active duty a few months before, where the clerk had told me, "No way, Mister. You've reported in here for processing for release from active duty and in three days you will be released. That's what we do here."

The Captain at the naval station was much more accommodating. I told him that all of my duty had been in LSTs so if I could go back on active duty I wanted to go as Executive Officer on an LST. He shook his head and explained that if I were to be a career officer I had to get duty in destroyers, so my next duty should be in a destroyer.

"So, could that be arranged? Could I go back on active duty in a destroyer?"

"If that's what you want, you'll have your orders in two weeks."

Two weeks later I received orders to report to USS Robert A. Owens (DDE 827) and I went back into active duty in the Navy.

CHAPTER TWENTY

USS ROBERT A. OWENS (DDE 827)

1957–1959

Dressed in his best service dress blue uniform and carrying a large brown manila envelope under his arm, Stu Landersman walked across the Norfolk Naval Shipyard toward where he had been told that his ship would be moored. The envelope contained his service record and orders. The service record was a copy of all the official papers of his Navy time, the originals of which resided in Washington, D.C. at the Bureau of Naval Personnel, BUPERS, as it was known, the same BUPERS that had issued him orders to report for active duty in USS Robert A. Owens (DDE 827). Orders are what send Navy people to where the Navy wants them to be.

Three years and a few months ago Stu was at home in Poughkeepsie and had received orders to report for active duty in USS LST 542 in Little Creek, Virginia, then, later, he had received orders to USS LST 1153. When his time on active duty was running out he received orders to go home and he had been released from active duty. But Stu didn't return home to Poughkeepsie. He was married by then, with a son, David, and so he stayed in Norfolk, worked at Sears for a couple of months and arranged to go back on active duty.

Now, with orders to report to Owens he was on his way to what would be, for him, a new ship, a new and different ship type, a destroyer. No more LST for Stu. Robert A. Owens was a destroyer, a special class of destroyer, and he would soon learn that destroyers were not only a different type of ship than were LSTs, but the entire destroyer force might as well be a different Navy than was the amphibious force.

USS Robert A. Owens (DDE 827) was a Gearing class destroyer that had been modified for escort-of-convoy work. Gearing class destroyers were built late in World War Two with many completed after that war. Classes of Navy ships are named after the first ship of each class, this class being named for USS Gearing (DD 710) and the hull numbers of the class ran from 710 to the last of that class, USS Meredith (DD 890). Eighteen of the hull numbers from 710 to 890 had been used for late-built Sumner class destroyers which means that there were 162 Gearing class destroyers in the U.S. Navy.

The Gearings were known as "twenty-two hundred tonners" by destroyermen, were considered to be fast and reliable, and carried three gun mounts, each mount with two five inch thirty eight caliber guns. Robert A. Owens, though, as part of her modification for convoy escort duty, had all three 5"/38 twin gun mounts removed. Mounts 51 and 53 had been replaced with twin 3"/70 gun mounts and mount 52 had been replaced with an ASW weapon launcher called Weapon Alfa.

Navy gun caliber is designated by the diameter of the bore, or inside dimension of the gun barrel and a number which, when multiplied by the diameter of the bore, gives the overall length of the barrel. A three inch seventy caliber gun accepts a projectile three inches in diameter and the length of the gun barrel is three inches multiplied by seventy or 210 inches, which is seventeen feet six inches. The 3"/70 gun barrels were water cooled because of the high rate of fire. Each mount of 3"/70 was a round armored turtle-like shell with two barrels protruding, the thin barrels peculiar with exterior coolant tubing and muzzle manifold.

The 3"/70 gun system had some other noteworthy features because the Navy had designed the gun to deal with kamikaze-like aircraft attacks; suicide attacks by high speed aircraft. Navy planners reasoned that future kamikaze attacks were not likely but this was the dawning of guided missiles and the gun that could deal with a kamikaze had a better chance of success against a guided missile than would the Navy's 5"/38. The 3"/70 gun configuration included a separate radar and fire control system for each gun mount; systems capable of dealing with high speed targets.

The 3'/70 gun had a very high rate of fire; 90 rounds per minute from each barrel and each gun mount carried two barrels, that means each 3"/70 gun mount could put out 180 rounds per minute; two mounts; 360 rounds per minute and at a much higher muzzle velocity. Destroyers with six 5"/38 guns could fire at a rate of about 12 rounds per minute from each gun with a total of about 72 rounds from all three twin mounts.

The Weapon Alfa in place of mount 52 on the 01 level just forward of and below the bridge/pilot house was part of the most up-to-date ASW configuration in the Navy. That ASW suite included the newest sonar, underwater battery fire control system, two types of ASW torpedoes, and depth charges that could be rolled over the stern or projected with the Weapon Alfa.

As Stu walked across the shipyard he passed a drydock in which a destroyer sat. Hull number 510 told him that this was a Sumner class destroyer and the Weapon Alfa launcher in place of one of her forward five inch gun mounts told him that this ship had been modified for special anti-submarine operations. ASW the Navy called it. She was no longer a DD, a general purpose destroyer. She was an escort destroyer, a DDE, like Owens but of an earlier class.

But the most unique feature of DDE 510 resting on blocks in a Norfolk Naval Shipyard drydock was that this ship was almost cut in half. Clearly, the sharp bow of another ship, probably much larger, had rammed into the side and gone, what looked like, more than half way across this poor ship. He looked over the damaged drydocked ship and then continued his walk to Owens.

Some days later, after Stu was settled in Owens, he heard more of the story of DDE 510.

Owens had been scheduled to accompany the battleship Wisconsin on some night maneuvering exercises in the Virginia Capes operating area off Norfolk, a routine training exercise for the battleship. A few days before the exercise it was discovered that Owens had a boiler problem that needed shipyard attention. The destroyer squadron commander designated another ship of his squadron, USS Eaton (DDE 510), to take the place of Owens in the battleship exercise.

The routine training exercise became anything but routine. In the dark of night the battleship Wisconsin collided with the destroyer Eaton, almost cutting through the smaller ship. Both ships required major repair and were returned to service. Wisconsin to this day has the bow that was cut off and taken from the uncompleted battleship Kentucky. Wisconsin today is a museum ship at the Hampton Roads Naval Museum in Norfolk and it is said that if you go far enough forward in Wisconsin you'll be in Kentucky.

Eaton? That could have been, maybe, Robert A. Owens.

Back to that first morning in the shipyard as Stu found his ship; from pier-side he walked across the complex brow that had been provided by the shipyard and stood on the quarterdeck of USS Robert A. Owens (DDE 827).

Stu saluted toward the stern, toward where he knew the U.S. flag would be. In port a Navy ship flies the flag from the stern. Underway it flies from the mast, up high. The flag is called an ensign in the Navy, not to be confused with the lowest of commissioned officer rank, and sometimes the U.S. flag is referred to as just the colors, and even though the flag, ensign, colors could not be seen from this quarterdeck, protocol required a salute towards the stern. Next, also according to protocol, Stu saluted the Officer of the Deck, called the OOD.

"I have orders to report aboard. Request permission to come aboard, sir."

The OOD returned his salute and offered, "Permission granted."

Stu informed him again that he had orders to report on board the Owens and gave the OOD a copy of his orders. The OOD welcomed him aboard with a smile and had the quarterdeck messenger take him to the Executive Officer.

Harry Risch was a lieutenant commander, the appropriate rank for an Executive Officer of a destroyer. He was a big guy, a grounded helicopter pilot; he had that naval aviator big smile, open friendly personality. He welcomed Stu, told him about the ship; where they would be operating and where Stu would be assigned in the ship. The XO called in a lieutenant, Bernie Duffy, and told Stu that he would be working with Bernie.

Harry Risch then took Stu to meet the Captain. Clearly Stu Landersman was not what Commander Edward G. Miller had in mind for his ship when he had asked the BUPERS detailer for an experienced OOD. After a brief discussion of Stu's Navy experience Captain Miller turned to his Executive Officer, with Stu sitting right there in the Captain's cabin, and said, "I ask the detailer for an experienced OOD and what do I get? I get a guy whose only experience is in running ships aground."

Miller didn't think much of LSTs which were, after all, built to run on to a beach and lower their bow ramp to offload marines. To Miller this was deliberately running a ship aground, something he spent a major part of his time avoiding. Destroyers and all other Navy ships did not deliberately run aground and it meant that Stu's path to be an OOD in Robert A. Owens would be more complex than in those two LSTs of his past, much more complex.

Stu had no way of knowing it at the time, but in reporting aboard Robert A. Owens he was really just then starting his Navy career. Oh sure, he had served three years in the Amphibs, been OOD underway in two ships, formation and independent steaming, qualified OOD in port, department head, at least a dozen collateral duties—and did pretty well through all that. But this was a destroyer, not an LST, and Stu soon learned that Captain Miller did not consider that qualifications or experiences in other ships, especially Amphib ships, had any relevance to qualifications in a destroyer, especially his destroyer. To Captain Miller Stu was a boot ensign, right out of OCS, who had never been on the bridge of a Navy ship. And in Captain Miller's destroyer, as in almost all destroyers of that time, there was an extensive demanding program for brand new ensigns that, if successfully completed, that is completed to the satisfaction of the Commanding Officer, would lead to that exalted status; qualified as Officer of the Deck.

Remember when Stu reported aboard the LST 542? He stayed aboard for two weeks and was OOD in port. Then the first time underway he was OOD on the mid-watch formation steaming. Just like that! And then in LST 1153, "If you were qualified in the 542 you're qualified here." Well, it wasn't like that in Robert A. Owens. Stu had to go through the complete extensive destroyer program for qualification as Officer of the Deck.

It took eighteen months for an ensign to be promoted to lieutenant junior grade and a few brand new ensigns right out of the Naval Academy serving in their first destroyer were eager and sharp enough to become qualified as OOD before that first promotion. That means that some other young officers, less motivated or maybe just less capable, might make jay gee before they were qualified as OOD. How long would it take Stu to qualify?

Owens was scheduled for a couple of months of local operations and upkeep in preparation for a deployment to the Mediterranean Sea. In the Navy, in keeping with nicknames, shortened names and acronyms for all names, the Mediterranean Sea is spoken simply as "The Med."

Stu was assigned as assistant to the Anti-Submarine Warfare Officer. (From now on let's just use ASW, that's real Navy.) Now consider this; the ASW officer in a DDE is a big deal. After all, the primary mission of the ship is ASW. The ship exercises and trains in the other warfare areas, like anti-air and anti-surface, but ASW is primary and Stu was now into ASW.

Even with three years of sea duty Stu knew little more about ASW than what those three letters stood for, but the ASW Officer of Owens was very patient and took considerable time in trying to convey to him all that he could, and that ASW Officer knew a great deal about ASW. As you might imagine, the ASW Officer in a destroyer, a destroyer that had the primary mission of ASW, was a big deal. Much more than the officers of the other warfare areas. So Stu set about learning ASW and also learning to be an OOD.

There were, and still are, schools in Norfolk for all the warfare areas, like the Fleet ASW School, and Stu attended many sessions there. The Navy's primary training school for ASW was in Key West, Florida, a six month course and every destroyer was supposed to have an ASW Officer who had attended that school. Captain Miller had decided that his ship didn't have six months before deployment to send Stu to the Key West school so he had Jim Paxton, the ASW Officer put together a program for Stu using the Norfolk schools and on-board training. So Stu learned ASW in Norfolk from the schools there and from the ASW Officer of Owens.

It's easy to say, "He learned ASW," but what he really learned was shipboard ASW. If you, the reader stays with this tome long enough you'll see that over the years Stu went much further with ASW. He learned that ASW performed by a destroyer, or a couple of destroyers working together, usually wasn't good enough. It took many more resources, time and space. It took "Combined Arms" to deal with the submarine threat.

But we're getting ahead of ourselves; back to 1958 and the new ASW Officer of USS Robert A. Owens (DDE 827). Jim Paxton, the former ASW Officer had departed the ship, having completed his active duty time and returned home. What did you know about him? Nothing? Well, he was music major from the University of Cincinnati. One day Stu told him that he had not met any officers in the Navy who were music majors. Jim laughed and said that he had been asked about that a number of times, but to him, to be an ASW Officer was closely related to music. First, when the ship was at ASW General Quarters he was the orchestra leader as he called upon the various sections to perform according to his commands; now sonar, now battery control, now CIC, now weapons, bridge, signals, he controlled the orchestra. Secondly, the submarine was detected by the ship's sonar, which is a tone of energy at a specific frequency, just like music. So to him, ASW was all based on and conducted just like music.

Jim Paxton taught Stu all that he could about ASW and then departed the ship; went home to Cincinnati, and Stu Landersman was the ASW Officer of R.A. Owens, still trying to learn that job. Also, he was trying to become qualified as OOD and the path to that qualification included qualifications as Engineering Officer of the Watch, CIC Watch Officer and Junior OOD.

After a few months of local operations in the Virginia Capes Operating Area, Destroyer Squadron 28, of which R.A. Owens was a part, deployed to the Med. Was Owens just a part of DESRON 28? Well, she was more than just a part; she was the squadron flagship. That means she carried the squadron commander, a captain in rank, and his staff.

In those days most destroyer squadrons consisted of eight ships of the same class organized into two divisions of four ships. The first division was commanded by the squadron commander and the second division was commanded by another captain with a smaller staff. Those were formal organizations; destroyer divisions such as DESDIV 281 and DESDIV 282 forming DESRON 28. In some tactical situations two destroyers would be assigned to operate as a sub-division commanded by the senior commanding officer of the two ships. A few years later divisions were done away with and destroyer squadrons were formed as five or six ship units.

With the squadron commander on board, the bridge watch and the CIC had additional functions. Besides taking care of the ship's interests the flagship had to support the squadron commander, so a qualified OOD and CICWO had to know how to provide the Commodore with needed information. Qualifications were getting tougher.

Naval forces in the Med are part of the Sixth Fleet and the exercises were more intense, more challenging because ships work-up and prepare before they join the Sixth Fleet. It makes for increased operational tempo that provides excellent qualification opportunities. Also, there are frequent visits to very nice liberty ports in France, Italy, Spain and Greece.

The squadron had just completed a fleet exercise and the eight ships were proceeding to various liberty ports when a message came to Owens; fuel and proceed to Gibraltar, intercept a Soviet task group consisting of a minesweeper and two diesel-electric submarines on the surface believed to be heading to Egypt. Owens found an oiler, fueled and headed east.

They came through the Strait of Gibraltar; three Soviet ships; a mine-sweeper leading two diesel-electric submarines in a slow sloppy formation. USS Robert A. Owens (DDE 827) was there to meet them. Owens took station a thousand yards on the starboard quarter of the Soviet group. Why starboard quarter? Why not astern?

Captain Miller explained to the Commodore, both standing on the bridge so that all the bridge watch personnel could hear, "If we were dead astern of them and one of them were to turn toward us we would be in a meeting situation according to the rules of the road and both ships would be required to turn to the right to avoid a collision. When we are in this starboard quarter position, if one of them were to turn toward us we would be in a crossing situation and the rules of the road would require us as privileged vessel to maintain course and speed and he as burdened must maneuver to avoid us.

"Now, we don't expect them or any one of them to turn toward us but just in case they do or maybe they might want to harass us, this starboard quarter station puts us in a more favorable position."

The Commodore acknowledged and the bridge watch understood including the JOOD. Stu Landersman had no way of knowing this but many years later in another part of the world and with a similar scenario, Stu would use that reasoning.

They trailed the Soviet group across the Med at a crawl; four or five knots, from Gibraltar to the eastern end. Attempts at flashing light communications with the mine-sweeper drew no response. Every few hours Owens sent a SITREP (situation report) to the Sixth

Fleet commander giving location, course and speed with little else to report.

Near the eastern end of the Med, the Soviet group went into port in Egypt and Owens was directed to refuel and go to a French port for upkeep. Upkeep really meant to prepare for the transit back to Norfolk with the rest of the squadron, to be "Homeward Bound."

DESRON 28 was in the Atlantic headed west toward Norfolk. Ships of the squadron were in a circular screen and taking turns refueling from the oiler that was accompanying them "across the pond." On the bridge of Owens, Captain Miller sat in his designated chair on the starboard side of the pilot house and the Commodore sat on the port side.

Bernie Duffy was the OOD and Stu Landersman was his JOOD. Stu had the conn, meaning that he was directing the movements of the ship by giving orders to the helm. A message came directing Owens to leave screening station and proceed to waiting station in preparation for refueling. Stu informed Bernie, the Captain and the Commodore and each acknowledged with a nod of his head. Stu increased speed, changed course and spoke with the CIC to confirm his actions. At any moment Stu expected Bernie to take the conn but as that didn't happen, he continued maneuvering, responding on the radio, and giving orders to the signal bridge. The ship arrived at waiting station astern of the oiler. Stu ordered the refueling detail to be set. When the side of the oiler was clear, Owens was ordered alongside and seeing that Bernie, the Captain and the Commodore acknowledged, each with a nod, Stu took the ship up alongside for the refueling.

It took about a half hour alongside and still neither Bernie, the Captain nor the Commodore had said a word to Stu as he ran the entire refueling process. Fueling completed, hoses returned, rigs clear; Stu took the ship back to her screening station, reporting "Alfa Station," meaning that Owens was back where she started.

A few minutes passed and then Captain Miller said, "Bernie, don't you have some paper work to catch up on?" Without waiting for a reply he added, "Why don't you turn over the deck to Stu and go below?" It was more of an order than a question.

Bernie looked at Stu with his big Irish grin. Stu stood at attention in front of him, saluted and said, "I relieve you, sir." Still grinning, Bernie returned the salute. "I stand relieved."

Stu Landersman was a qualified Officer of the Deck in a destroyer.

Meanwhile, back at the ranch, that is back in Norfolk, Martha and infant son David had been living in a two bedroom apartment in Landsdale Gardens. This was the young family's second home, the first had been a one bedroom apartment on Willoughby Spit and with the expectation of their first-born they had moved to a larger apartment.

While Stu had been away Martha had done some considerable research and planning; she had located a very nice house and had worked out all the details including, of course, the finances. With a loan of $600 from Stu's parents for the down payment (She had already cleared this with his parents) they would easily qualify for the mortgage and the monthly payments would be just a wee bit more than they were paying for the apartment.

Done deal, the Landersmans bought their first house. They had no way of knowing it at the time but that process of Stu being away, Martha arranging a new home and the deal being completed when Stu returned, would be followed many times over their Navy career years.

Back in Norfolk following the Med deployment the ship received a new CO and XO, and the departure of Bernie Duffy put Stu Landersman in the position of Senior Watch Officer. He was now also a department head; Gunnery Officer. The new Captain, Burns W. Spore, was very experienced and very capable and let Stu know that he would depend on Stu to do most of the ship handling. The new Exec, Stanley Washburn Jones, was not very experienced or capable and he let Stu know that he needed a lot of advice. This put Stu in a very nice position. He did a great deal of ship handling, ran the officers' bridge watch standing, advised the executive officer and was a department head.

One day a couple of months after Commander Spore had taken command he asked Stu if he had heard of the new program that provided officers to be designated "Qualified to command destroyers." Stu had not heard of this program. With the Captain's recommendation, Stu went through the process and was so designated. He later learned that he was one of, and maybe the first in his lieutenant's year group to achieve that qualification.

During the 1950's the Navy was going through some significant changes in mission emphasis. ASW had always been a mission and certainly the "Battle of the Atlantic" had been a primary Navy achievement in World War Two. After that war, however, the Navy went through a few years of adjustment where-in ASW took a back seat. It didn't take long in terms of Navy strategic planning, though, to realize that the Cold War opponent, the Soviet Union, had a potential submarine threat as significant as was the German U-boat of WWII.

Toward the end of WWII, one of the developments by the U.S. that contributed to the neutralization of German U-boats in the Atlantic was the creation of hunter-killer groups. These were carrier task groups in which the aircraft carrier was outfitted to support an air wing specially configured for ASW. Part of the HUK group was a destroyer squadron.

The success of HUK groups in WWII led Navy planners searching for means to deal with the Soviet submarine threat to form new HUK groups. Some WWII aircraft carriers were configured for new rolls as ASW carriers, air wings were formed for the ASW mission and destroyer squadrons comprised of DDEs were assigned to the new groups.

The first hunter-killer group of the Cold War was named Task Group Alfa. Destroyer Squadron 28 became a part of this first group and USS Robert A. Owens (DDE 827) was the flagship of the squadron commander. Stu Landersman was the Gunnery Officer of that ship and later was Operations Officer and it was with Task Group Alfa that Stu learned of coordinated ASW.

Oh, yeah, hold on a minute, please. I forgot to describe the situation that caused Stu to become Operations Officer. Remember, he was Gunnery Officer when the ship returned from the Med and became part of Task Group Alfa. Owens got a new Commanding Officer and a new Executive Officer. Bernie Duffy also left the ship and so there was a new Operations Officer and Stu, as the senior watch standing officer, assumed additional duty as the Senior Watch Officer.

Stanley Washburn Jones was the new Executive Officer and he was no Harry Risch. Stan Jones needed a lot of help and he looked to the Senior Watch Officer for that help. Stu was only too glad to give the new Exec all the help he could and to Stu it was like he was running the ship; Gunnery Officer, Senior Watch Officer and (almost) acting Executive Officer. Stu was a happy and a busy man but it didn't end there.

Stan Jones had married late in life for a Navy officer and his wife was a very nice gal but very inexperienced as to the role of an Executive Officer's wife. Just as Stan looked to Stu for help in the ship, Stan's wife looked to Stu's wife Martha for help in her role as leader of the officers' wives matters. And just as Stu enjoyed his "acting XO" role, so did Martha enjoy her role as "acting XO's wife" role, and it didn't end there.

Remember, Owens was the flagship of the destroyer squadron commander in this newly formed HUK group. As such the ship had to provide all the regular information and coordination of other destroyers but in addition the flagship had to provide significant support to the embarked squadron commander. The squadron commander had a small staff and some meager facilities in the ship but these proved to be insufficient for his role in the HUK group. He had to rely on the ship's bridge, CIC and communications for his command support. There was a steep learning curve as the ship tried to provide command support for the squadron commander as well as its own ship support.

In the first few exercises with the full HUK group it became clear that the Owens CIC was not cutting it. The Owens CO had to listen to continuous complaints from the embarked squadron commander. Something had to be done.

A normal day in port, Norfolk, between ASW exercises with the HUK group. Stu arrived as usual earlier than most and went into his normal routine; reading message traffic, checking gunnery spaces, conferring with his people. A call to come see the XO, not unusual but when he got there the brief question from the XO certainly was.

"How soon can you relieve as Operations Officer?"
A gulp and Stu replied, "I can relieve him this afternoon."
Without looking at Stu, Jones said, "Do it."

So Stu added Operations Officer to his list of duties in USS Robert A. Owens (DDE827), flagship of Commander Destroyer Squadron 28 operating with Task Group Alfa, the first HUK group since World War II. It was here that this cast-off from the amphibious force, in his first destroyer in which he learned what the letters A, S, and W stood for, would take his first steps toward becoming an ASW sub-specialist.

You will read more about coordinated ASW and Stu's role in it if you stay with this long enough. For now, though, let's move on to the next duty station as Stu received orders to the Naval Postgraduate School in Monterey, California.

CHAPTER TWENTY ONE

U.S. NAVAL POSTGRADUATE SCHOOL

1959-1960

A little background, call it history.

The idea for a graduate education program for naval officers first emerged in the late 19th century. Initially the concept found few advocates but by 1909 belief that advanced education for U.S naval officers could be valuable to the Navy gained support.

On June 9, 1909 Secretary of the Navy George von L. Meyer established a school of marine engineering at Annapolis. The original program consisting of 10 officer students and two Navy instructors would later become the Naval Postgraduate School. The Navy Secretary's order placed the fledgling school under the direction of the Naval Academy superintendent who provided two attic rooms set aside for classroom and laboratory space for the new school.

On October 31, 1912, SECNAV Meyer renamed the school the Postgraduate Department of the Naval Academy and established courses of study in ordnance and gunnery, electrical engineering, radio telegraphy, naval construction and civil engineering as well as continuing the original program in marine engineering. With the additional curricula, enrollment increased to 25.

Before World War II one of the finest luxury hotels in North America, the Hotel Del Monte, occupied the present site of the Naval Postgraduate School in Monterey, California. Samuel F.B. Morse, the president of the Del Monte Properties Company, began developing the Del Monte as a "sports empire" where guests could enjoy playing golf, polo, tennis, swimming, yachting and deep-sea fishing. Considered by some to be the most elegant seaside resort in the world, the hotel played host to world leaders, dignitaries, American presidents, film stars and famous artists until 1942, when it was taken over by the U.S. Navy and used as a pre-flight school for aviators.

During World War II, Fleet Admiral Ernest King established a commission to review the role of graduate education in the Navy and by the end of the war it had become apparent that the facilities of the Naval Postgraduate School at the Naval Academy at Annapolis would be insufficient for the Navy's future needs. In 1945, Congress passed legislation to make the school a fully-accredited, degree-granting graduate institution. Two years later, Congress authorized the purchase of the Hotel Del Monte and 627 acres of surrounding land for use as an independent campus for the school.

Step back a moment, please. That gentleman who was president of the early Del Monte Properties, did you get that name? Samuel S. B. Morse. Yes, the same Morse who is connected with the telegraph and the well-known Morse code. Dot dash, dit dah, that's him; Morse code–Monterey–PG school.

Back to our story.

In December 1951 the Naval Postgraduate School established its current campus in Monterey. Rear Admiral Ernest Edward Herrmann supervised the move from Annapolis. The main building of the former Hotel Del Monte, now named Herrmann Hall, houses the principal administrative offices of the Naval Postgraduate School.

During World War II and after, the Navy had been desperate for officers and so officer candidates were accepted with college degrees that were earned with courses lacking those considered valuable for

Navy careers. Some of those officers, lacking the desirable courses, had elected for Navy careers. Someone in Navy decision-making decided that these promising officers should be given those valuable courses. Hence, General Line School was established to provide those career intended officers whom did not get the right career enhancing subjects in their various colleges with the same educational preparedness as Naval Academy or NROTC, or nearly so.

After World War II, General Line School was established at Newport, Rhode Island and later moved to the Naval Academy at Annapolis. In 1951, along with the postgraduate school, the General Line School was transferred to the site of the former Hotel Del Monte in Monterey, California.

The Navy didn't send Stu Landersman to Monterey for postgraduate education. He went there for General Line School. What was General Line School? Well, there was a long standing policy in the Navy that career officers should have educations appropriate for naval careers. These educations should include engineering, math, science, government and others. Navy officers with career intentions and lacking in those subjects were sent to the General Line School.

The academics were not difficult, most of the subjects I had had before at Clarkson. Those subjects that were new for me were interesting. Most of those were taught by profs from the PG school and they were all very high quality instructors. But always there are exceptions, aren't there, and Line School was no exception. Some of the subjects, the Navy subjects in particular, were taught by Navy officers who had no business in front of a class room. The best example of this was a class in Leadership; very important for naval officers, but presented by a totally unqualified alcoholic naval aviator, a commander who knew absolutely nothing about leadership. The course required each student to write an essay on leadership. I wrote Damn Exec and got a C. I appealed to the instructor who grudgingly raised the grade to a B after commenting that he didn't see anything of value in it.

Damn Exec follows this chapter and at the end of that piece are some of the credentials that it earned over the years. The C to a B paper was published in the Naval Institute Proceedings and was included in a leadership text book at the Naval Academy. No other paper written at Line School ever received the acceptance of Damn Exec.

Bridge, I didn't tell you about bridge, did I? Not the passage over a river but the card game; contract bridge. Martha had always wanted me to learn to play bridge but I carefully avoided it. She got me a small book on it but I disregarded it.

We have to reach back to my time in R. A. Owens, just prior to Line School, when we got a new CO, when CDR Burns W. Spore relieved CDR Edward G. Miller. You'll remember that Captain Spore had us call on a Saturday night and we all got to know each other–a Navy tradition. The captain and his wife talked about getting together for bridge and Martha told of failed efforts to get me to play bridge. I didn't know of this discussion but at lunch aboard ship the next Friday, Captain Spore said to me, "I'm looking forward to our bridge tomorrow."

What could I say other than, "Yes sir."

I studied the little book the next morning and afternoon, and that evening I played bridge at the captain's house. Everyone helped me. I got through the evening. I played bridge many evenings after that.

So, at Monterey Martha and I found that there were people that wanted to play bridge.

We became part of a four couple group that met at one of our homes each Saturday night for bridge. The host couple had to provide a gallon of Gallo red wine and some finger food.

The men of the bridge group were classmates; Paul Daley and Gene Schultz were aviators, Archie Swartztrauber and I were black shoes. That's what the aviators called surface ship officers.

Let me tell you a story about Archie.

The first quarter of our academic year included a mathematics course that ran through algebra, geometry and the very beginning of calculus. Archie had never had any math beyond high school. He was a liberal arts major, remember, that's why Line School.

Archie studied very hard, harder than anyone that I ever knew in any of the schools I attended, and when the grades came out for the first quarter Archie had As in everything but B in math. Archie was devastated. He told me that through high school and through college he got As in everything, never anything but As. This B in math at Line School was the first and he couldn't understand how that could happen.

He went to see the prof and explained his dilemma. Could he retake the final? He explained to the prof that he had planned, before he arrived at Monterey, that he would get all As, every subject, and that he would set the record for academic achievement at Line School. This B in the first quarter shattered his dream.

The prof found it difficult to believe this enthusiasm and searched his options for a resolution to Archie's problem. Finally, "This is what I'm going to do," he said. "I'm not going to turn in the grades from your class until the end of the final quarter, and if you have As in every class by then, I'll raise your math grade to an A."

"Thank you. I really appreciate that," Archie replied.

Archie Swartztrauber got an A in every subject the rest of the academic year. He set the record of all As at Line School that was never, could never, be broken. Years later he earned a doctorate degree, retired as a rear admiral and became president of a maritime academy.

Basketball! I found that there was a basketball team at the PG school that played in the city league of nearby Pacific Grove and in a league of military bases. Having played in high school, college and in my earlier Navy time, it was natural for me to join the PG school team. Among a student body of officers you could always find ten or so who had played college basketball. And so it was at Monterey. We had a good team, did well in the city league and with the military bases. The most memorable games, though, were two games that we played at the California state penitentiary near Salinas known as Soledad.

Soledad was a maximum security prison, meaning that the prisoners were there for serious crimes of violence, they were bad dudes, hence maximum security. It was an experience just getting in, dressing for the game and walking onto the court.

The basketball court was just like most high school gyms, with folding bleachers on the sides and the bleachers were maybe three quarters filled with prisoners. But the surprise was that the prisoners in the stands cheered for us, the visitors. I asked the big fellow I lined up with why the prisoners were cheering for us and he said, "What do you think, we have school spirit here?"

Another surprise was more subtle. The prisoners we played against were very, how shall I say it, very gentle. We Navy college players were accustomed to a certain amount of rough-house, its called "contact" in some areas. We knew that these convicts had their basketball experiences on playgrounds, where the games could get pretty rough at times. But here we were playing against a bunch of tough guys and they were nearly perfect gentlemen on the court. It took me some time to learn that very few teams would come to this maximum security prison to play against violent felons, so they were careful in their play. They wanted us to come back for another game, and we did.

The second time we went to Soledad, as we lined up to start the game I said to the guy I would be playing against and whom I had played against in our previous game, "That forward, you didn't have him last time."

He smiled, "Yeah, that's right, but we got him now for a while. He's here for ten to fifteen."

They were all black; prisoners and guards. We had a young black sailor on our team, a yeoman who worked in the office of the PG school, big strong guy. The prisoners in the stands immediately made him their favorite and although they cheered for all of us, the house came down whenever he slammed a basket home. We played to him the entire games and the fans loved it.

Of all the years, in all of the games I played basketball, among the most memorable games I played were those two games at Soledad.

Well, it wasn't all play at PG school. Yes, there was basketball and bridge, even softball and many enjoyable evenings spent with classmate couples. Martha and I made many friends that we remained in contact with for many years, some for the rest of our Navy time and some for the rest of our lives. But we were at PG School for academics and that was the primary focus. We went to classes every week day, studied most evenings, read many books, wrote papers and took tests. It was just like a heavy college load, well, that's what it was at the Naval Postgraduate School in Monterey.

Toward the end of the school year I received orders to the staff of Commander Destroyer Force, U.S. Atlantic Fleet. We called it COMDESLANT in that Navy habit of abbreviating everything and often it was spoken as just DESLANT.

COMDESLANT was embarked in a ship, a destroyer tender, in Newport, Rhode Island and so the next Navy move for the three Landersmans would be from Monterey to Newport. I say the three Landersmans as Stu, Martha and David but during that last month in Monterey Martha informed me that there was another Landersman on the way. Mark would be born in Newport.

From Monterey I put an ad in the Newport newspaper concerning desire to purchase a home. Later, when we arrived in Newport, I had a notebook with about 15 listings from people who had responded to my ad. We still owned our first house in Norfolk, it was rented to a Navy family and now we were prepared to buy a second home, this one in Newport.

We drove across the country from California to Rhode Island in our 1959 Chevy station wagon, that's the one with the gull wings. We bought a house, our second one, and I reported in to the staff of Commander Destroyer Force, U.S. Atlantic Fleet.

CHAPTER TWENTY TWO

DAMN EXEC

1960

See author's notes following this chapter

The Norfolk wind was streaking the water of Hampton Roads as Commander Martin K. Speaks, U.S. Navy, Commanding Officer of the USS Bowens (DD891), stepped from his car, slammed the door, and straightened his cap. As he approached the pier head, a sailor stepped from the sentry hut and saluted.

"Good morning, Captain."

"Good morning, Kowalski," answered Commander Speaks. He took pleasure in the fact that he knew the sailor's name. Kowalski was a good sailor. He had served his entire first cruise in the Bowens and did his work well.

The Captain noticed that, over his blues, Kowalski wore a deck force foul weather jacket, faded, frayed, dirty, and spotted with red lead. "Little chilly this morning," said the Captain as he walked by. "Yes sir, sure is," replied the sailor with his usual grin.

As the Captain approached his quarterdeck, there was the usual scurrying of people, and four gongs sounded. "Bowens arriving," spoke the loudspeaker system, and Lieutenant (j.g.) Henry Graven, U.S. Naval Reserve, gunnery officer and the day's command duty officer, came running to the quarterdeck. Salutes and cheerful "Good mornings" were exchanged, and the Captain continued to his cabin.

Lieutenant Graven looked over the quarterdeck and frowned. "Let's get this brightwork polished, Chief."

"It's already been done once this morning, sir," replied the OD.

"Well, better do it again. The Exec will have a fit if he sees it this way." said Graven.

"Yes sir," answered the OD.

As soon as Graven had left, the OD turned to his messenger, "Go tell the duty boatswain's mate that Mr. Graven wants the brightwork done over again on the quarterdeck."

Later that morning, Captain Speaks was going over some charts with the ship's executive officer, Lieutenant Commander Steven A. Lassiter, U.S. Navy. The Captain had just finished his coffee and lighted a cigarette. "Steve, I noticed our pier sentry in an odd outfit this morning, He had a foul weather jacket on over his blues; it looked pretty bad."

"Yes sir. Well, it gets cold out there, and these deck force boys have mighty badlooking jackets," the Exec said.

The Captain felt the Exec had missed his point and said, "Oh, I realize they have to wear a jacket, but for a military watch like that, I'd like to see them wear pea coats when it's cold."

Lieutenant Graven was talking with a third class boatswain's mate on the fantail when the quarterdeck messenger found him. When told that the executive officer wanted to see him, Graven ended his discussion with, "There, hear that? He probably wants to see me about the brightwork. I don't care how many men it takes to do it, the Exec told me to be sure to get that brightwork polished every morning."

The executive officer indicated a chair to Graven and asked: "How's it going these days?"

Lassiter had always liked Graven, but in the past few months, since he had taken over as senior watch officer, Graven seemed to have more problems than usual.

"Okay, I guess," Graven replied with a forced grin. He knew that things were not as they used to be. It seemed strange, too, because everyone on the ship had been so glad to be rid of the previous senior watch officer, that "damn" Lieutenant Dumphy. The junior officers even had a special little beer bust at the club to celebrate Dumphy's leaving and Graven's "fleeting up" to senior watch officer. Now the Exec was always after him. The junior officers didn't help much either, always complaining about the Exec. Maybe the Exec was taking over as "the heel" now that Dumphy was gone.

"That's good", said the Exec. "Here's a little thing that you might look into. These men who stand pier watches have to wear a jacket, but the foul weather jacket doesn't look good for a military watch. I'd like to see them wear their pea coats when it's cold." Graven had expected something like this, more of the Exec's picking on him. He responded properly, got up, and left.

Graven told his first lieutenant: "The Exec says the pier head sentries can't wear foul weather jackets anymore. If it's cold they can wear pea coats," he added.

"But the pea coats will get dirty, and then what about personnel inspections?" asked the first lieutenant.

I don't know," Graven shook his head, "but if the Exec wants pea coats, we give him pea coats!"

"Pea coats!" said the chief boatswain's mate, "Who says so?"

"That's what the Exec wants," said the first lieutenant, "so let's give him pea coats."

"The Exec says pea coats for the pier sentries when it's cold," announced the chief to his boatswain's mates.

A third-class boatswain's mate walked away from the group with a buddy, turned and said, "That Damn Exec. First I got to have all my men polish brightwork on the quarterdeck, now they got to wear pea coats on sentry duty 'stead of foul weather jackets!"

Seaman Kowalski's relief showed up at the sentry booth at 1150. "Roast beef today," constituted the relieving ceremony.

"Good, I like roast beef," was the reply. "Hey, how come the pea coat?"

"Damn Exec's idea," said the relief. "We can't wear foul weather gear no more out here, only pea coats."

"Damn Exec," agreed Kowalski. "Captain, didn't say nothin' when he came by."

"The Captain's okay, it's just that Damn Exec, He's the guy who fouls up everything," complained the new sentry.

Seaman Kowalski had just gone aboard the ship when Captain Speaks stepped out on deck to look over his ship. The quarterdeck awning shielded the Captain from the view of those or the quarterdeck, but he could clearly hear the conversation.

"Roast beef today, ski."

"Yeah, I know, and we wear pea coats from now on.

"Whaddaya mean, pea coats?"

"Yeah, pea coat on the pier, Damn Exec says no more foul weather jackets."

"Well that ain't all; we got to polish this here brightwork 'til it shines every morning before quarters. Damn Exec says that too."

"Damn Exec."

Captain Speaks was shocked. "Why 'Damn Exec' from these seamen?" he thought. It was easy to see that the executive officer had passed the order along in proper military manner. It was easy to see that the junior officers, leading petty officers, and lower petty officers were passing it along saying "The Exec wants. . . "That's the way orders are passed along. Why? Because "it's easy."

"All ship's officers assemble in the wardroom," the boatswain's mate announced on the loudspeaker system. Lieutenant Commander Lassiter escorted in the Captain. The junior officers took their seats when the Captain was seated. The executive officer remained standing.

"Gentlemen, the Captain has a few words to say to us today."

The Captain rose and looked around slowly. "Gentlemen, we are continually exposed to words like administration, leadership, management, capabilities, organization, responsibilities, authority, discipline, and cooperation. You use these words every day. You give lectures to your men and use them, but if I were to ask each of you for a definition of any of these words I would get such a wide variety of answers that an expert couldn't tell what word we were defining. Some we probably couldn't define at all. We still use them, and will continue to use them as they are used in the continually mounting number of articles, instructions, and books we must read.

"If I were to ask any of you how can we improve leadership I would get answers filled with these words-undefined and meaningless.

"If we listed all of the nicely worded theories of leadership, studied them, memorized them, and took a test in them, we would all pass. But this would not improve our ability as leaders one bit. I can tell a story, containing none of these meaningless words that *will* improve your leadership.

"In 1943, 1 was secondary battery officer in a cruiser in the South Pacific. In my second battle, gun control was hit and I lost communications with everyone except my 5inch mounts. I could see that the after main battery turret was badly damaged and two enemy destroyers were closing us from astern. At the time my 5inch mounts were shooting at airplanes. I ordered my two after 5inch mounts to use high capacity ammunition and shift targets to the two destroyers closing from astern. 'But Mr. Speaks, we're supposed to handle the air targets; who said to shift targets?' my mount captain asked.

"There were noise and smoke and explosions that day, but the explosion that I heard and felt was not from a shell, but from those words of the mount captain.

"Those attacking destroyers got a few shots in at us before we beat them off. Maybe those shots found a target and some of my shipmates died. I never found out. There was too much other damage.

"I thought over the battle afterward and realized that this entire situation was my fault, not the mount captain's. I may have been responsible for the death of some of my shipmates because up to that day I always gave orders to my subordinates by attaching the originator's name to it.

"What does that mean? It means that it was the easy thing to do, to say, 'the gunnery officer wants us to shift targets.'

"In this peacetime world you may say that we no longer have this struggle on a life or death basis. Quick response does not mean life or death now, but it might tomorrow or sometime after we've all been transferred elsewhere and this ship is being fought by people we don't know.

"Whether you're cleaning boilers, standing bridge watch, or administering your training program, it's easy to say 'The Exec wants' or 'Mr. Jones says.' It's the easy, lazy way; not the right way. You can sometimes discuss or even argue with an order, but when you give it to a subordinate, make him think it is coming from you.

"Giving orders the lazy way is like a drug. Once you start saying 'The ops officer wants' you will find yourself doing it more and more until you can't get a thing done any other way. Your men will pass along orders that way, too, and it will become a part of your organization right down to the lowest level. When some problem arises and you want action, you'll get 'Who wants this?' or 'Why should we?'

"Each of you ask yourself if you have given an order today or yesterday in the lazy manner. I think almost all of us have. Now ask yourself if that order really originated with the person who gave it to you, or did he receive it from a higher level? We never really know, do we, but why should we even care?

"In almost every unit the 'lazy' ordering starts on a particular level. From personal experience I can tell you that this can be an exact measure of the unit's effectiveness. If it starts at the department head level or higher it's a relatively bad outfit, and if it starts at the chief's level it's a relatively good outfit. You can find the level below which it starts by hearing a new title preceding a primary billet. 'Damn Exec' means that the executive officer is the lowest level giving orders properly. 'Damn division officer' means that the division officers are taking responsibility for the order.

"Here I am using some of those words, responsibility and authority, those undefined terms we want to avoid, but perhaps we have helped define them.

"To be more specific, every officer does some 'lazy' ordering, but we need to do it less and less. We must try to push the 'damn' title down as far as it will go.

"Let's push the 'damn officer' down all the way to the chiefs and below, then we will have a Damn Good Ship."

AUTHOR'S NOTES:

"Damn Exec" is included in the U.S. Naval Academy leadership textbook <u>Naval Leadership, Voices of Experience</u>, edited by Karel Montor, et al., Naval Institute Press, Annapolis, MD, 1987, page 129, with the introduction:

> "DAMN EXEC," BY LT. COMDR. STUART D. LANDERSMAN
>
> The manner in which orders are relayed down the chain of command is another leadership issue, The following sea story, "Damn Exec," by Lt. Comdr. Stuart D. Landersman, was originally published in the January 1965 Proceedings and addresses the issue in a most effective manner.

Professor Karel Montor called me in1987 and we discussed his book and my article. On the letter to contributors that I received he penned:

> Hi–It was great to hear your voice. After seeing this book I hope you will still be glad that we used your article (see p. 129). In all these years–it's still the best which all refer to. Take care-Karel.

CHAPTER TWENTY THREE

ABOUT DAMN EXEC

1960

In the school year of 1959-1960 I was a lieutenant student at the U.S. Naval Postgraduate School in Monterey, California. The program I was in was called General Line School and it was for career lieutenants and lieutenant commanders who had not gone to full officer programs like the Naval Academy and NROTC. All of the students were either OCS or NAVCAD people, mostly aviators, and among the courses we took was one on leadership, taught by an overage, passed over, alcoholic grounded aviator commander. I met the requirement for an essay on leadership by writing *Damn Exec* for which the commander gave me a C.

The grade really didn't matter but I thought it was worth something higher especially when I saw some of my classmate's work and I went to the instructor and told him so. It was clear that he had no interest or understanding and grudgingly raised my grade to a B.

Soon after I noted that the U.S. Naval Institute was conducting an essay contest and I sent in *Damn Exec*. Months later I received word from an assistant editor of the *Proceedings*, Norman Polmar, that although my essay did not win the contest, he wanted to publish it in the Professional Notes section of the *Proceedings*. I agreed and received a check for $50 and considered that my leadership essay had done better than any of the essays from Line School.

Years later Norman Polmar told me that *Damn Exec* was the first fiction ever published by the U.S. Naval Institute. When the Naval Institute Press published Tom Clancy's hit novel, <u>The Hunt for Red October</u>, advertisements for the book included statements that this was the first fiction of the U.S. Naval Institute. Polmar and I knew better. The first fiction of any kind was *Damn Exec*. Clancy's was the first novel.

By the time *Damn Exec* was published in the January 1965 *Proceedings* I was a lieutenant commander and in the years after it appeared in *Proceedings* I received a number of inquiries and requests to use the essay and always gave permission. About 20 years after it was published I was asked for permission to have *Damn Exec* included in a leadership text book being edited by Professor of Leadership Karel Montor of the U.S. Naval Academy. Professor Montor called me personally, complimented me and then penned a personal note on the thank you form letter saying, "In all these years–it's still the best which all refer to." I think *Damn Exec* has overcome the grudging C to B from Line School with a "best" from the Naval Academy.

Damn Exec appears on page 129 of Montor's <u>Naval Leadership, Voices of Experience</u>, Naval Institute Press, Annapolis, 1987, followed by comment of MCPON Sanders that is intended to be explanatory and supportive but shows the Master Chief did not understand the message–perhaps like the Line School instructor some 27 years earlier. The message of *Damn Exec* is that we must take responsibility for the orders we issue. We cannot say, "Damn Exec says—," when we give an order by blaming a superior for an unpopular directive.

Taking responsibility is a matter of good leadership.

CHAPTER TWENTY FOUR

COMMANDER DESTROYER FORCE
U.S. ATLANTIC FLEET

1960-1962

Commander Destroyer Force, U.S. Atlantic Fleet was Vice Admiral Charles S. Weakley. He and his staff were embarked in a ship, a destroyer tender that spent most of her life at the Navy pier in Newport, Rhode Island. Like so many military organizations and like most government organizations, over the years the DESLANT staff had grown in numbers of personnel from that which could be accommodated in the flagship to so many more that most had their offices in a pier building alongside where the flagship was moored. The destroyer tender that served as flagship very seldom got underway so it was almost like a building at the naval station. But still, the flagship was indeed a ship and as a ship it had the ability to go to sea, so to Navy personnel management it was considered "sea duty."

Stu didn't realize it at the time but duty on the DESLANT staff was like joining a fraternity and, like a fraternity, joining it was preceded by an initiation and once a brother you were a brother for life. In Stu's case the initiation had been his tour of duty in the destroyer Robert A. Owens where he had been a qualified Officer of the Deck, Senior Watch Officer, head of two departments and, most important of all; he had been formerly declared as "Qualified to Command Destroyers." That qualification to command was very new at the time he reported to the DESLANT staff so very few officers had achieved that qualification. In Stu's year group only two officers had the destroyer qualification, two lieutenants, Virgil Snyder and Stu, and both of them were assigned to the operations section of the DESLANT staff.

Virg Snyder had come from a destroyer in a squadron dedicated to anti-air warfare and Stu came from an anti-submarine warfare squadron. Virg had been OOD, SWO and had two departments along with his qual for command, as had Stu. Together they felt that they knew it all. It took them a short time to realize that this staff, the DESLANT staff of Vice Admiral Weakley, was loaded with officers who had very impressive destroyer experiences.

A number of years later a couple of officers from that Weakley staff got together and did a rough analysis that showed that half of those staff officers, from lieutenant to captain while on that staff, reached flag officer rank. That meant that about 25 of the 50 officers who had served on Weakley's staff were selected as rear admirals. Unfortunately, Virg Snyder and Stu Landersman were not among those who later made flag rank. But what matter at the time? Both of those lieutenants had a good time, worked hard and met a lot of great people, many of whom they kept in touch with for many years. Remember; fraternity brothers for life.

The Weakley staff, besides looking after all of the more than a hundred destroyer-type ships of the Atlantic Fleet, were also part of a pet-project of their admiral; that of creating a separate community in the Navy, a community of "Destroyermen." Just as there were naval aviators who proudly wore wings of gold on their breasts and submarine officers who similarly wore dolphins, Weakley was embarked on a program to have a community of destroyermen, with their own distinctive identification badge which would be earned by an extensive program. Virg Snyder and Stu Landersman had both completed the requirements before the community had been established with their qualification for command of destroyers but the badge had not been established yet.

The operations section of the DESLANT staff, to which Stu was assigned, was located in the flagship, USS Yosemite. (Remember, most of the staff were in the pier building.) Stu's title was Assistant Operations and Plans Officer. Sounds simple doesn't it? The Assistant Operations part was easy to understand as there was an Operations Officer to assist but the Plans part raised a question as there was no Plans Officer to be the assistant to on the staff. So did Stu's billet include that of Plans Officer? Well, Stu learned early that he would carry out the functions of the Plans Officer until told otherwise.

The operations section of the staff came under the Assistant Chief of Staff for Operations and Plans; Captain Royal K. Joslin. The head of the operations section was Commander Roger E. Spreen who was filling in for CDR Robert E. Smith who had been delayed in reporting. Spreen and Smith were close friends and had been classmates at the Naval Academy. Spreen had orders to command a new guided missile destroyer being built. The senior of the assistant ops officers was LCDR John Drake, later relieved by LCDR Warren Hamm. In addition to Virg Snyder and Stu Landersman the operations section of the DESLANT staff included LTJG Jim Kvederis who looked after berthing assignments for the ships in Newport.

Joslin, Spreen and Smith had graduated from the Naval Academy in time to see action in World War Two and in Korea that followed. Joslin was a bit of a drinker and it became apparent that he had been cared for, or covered for, by subordinates through his Navy career. Still, he did his job well on the DESLANT staff and then became the first commanding officer of Destroyer School, which later became Surface Warfare Officers School.

Upon leaving the Naval Academy during World War Two, Ensign Roger Spreen had been assigned to a destroyer in the Pacific. That destroyer had been part of Arleigh Burke's famous "Little Beaver" squadron. Some years later Captain Roger Spreen had command of that same squadron while Stu Landersman had command of one of the ships in it. Later, Stu Landersman was commodore of that same Little Beaver Squadron. It's a small Navy.

The destroyer force in 1960 consisted of more than a hundred destroyer-type ships, all with designations that started with the letter D. The basic destroyer was a DD and then there were DDR and DDE, with a family of DE including DER. Most were regular Navy but some DD and DE were in various statuses as Naval Reserve Training ships.

The U.S. military at that time, especially the Navy, was heavily influenced by the 1941 December 7th Japanese surprise attack on Pearl Harbor and military planning, again especially the Navy, dealt with reaction to such a surprise attack. Strategic planners had to deal with the question of how to deal with and respond to a surprise attack on the U.S., an attack that might occur on a Sunday and which might eliminate regular communications. The Navy answer to this was called the "Notional System." It was a highly classified system of prepositioned/preplanned instructions for each Navy ship in the event of a surprise attack. The system provided each ship with instructions on what to do, where to go, who to report to, what the initial duty assignment would be and what a follow-on duty assignment might be. For the destroyer force the system consisted of notional numbers, each number referring to a detailed duty assignment. Notional numbers were assigned each month to each ship with numbers related to the ship's actual assignment and schedule as related to the emergency assignment. A destroyer operating in her regularly scheduled carrier task group would find that the notional number assigned that month would have her remain with that carrier group. A DE visiting a port in Central America might be assigned a notional number that directed that DE to proceed immediately to Norfolk for escort work.

This assignment of notional numbers each month, the maintenance of the system, the briefing of each prospective commanding officer and unit commander, and the conduct of periodic tests to ensure that ships understood the system, was the function of the Plans Officer. So, Stu Landersman conducted the Notional System for the Destroyer Force and assisted in the scheduling of Atlantic Fleet destroyers.

Every year there's a hurricane season in the Atlantic Ocean. Hurricanes are born in the Caribbean and follow a curved path towards Florida and up along the East Coast of the U.S. These hurricane paths are roughly predictable, very roughly that is, so that their curved paths can, and do, vary from right through Florida, Georgia and the Carolinas to barely touching the southern tip of Florida and then curving away from the East Coast, spinning their way north and dieing out well to sea. Once in a great while a hurricane will work its way north right along the coast, all the way north to New England as it terrorizes the populace and tears up property.

On what would have been a quiet Sunday morning in Newport, Rhode Island during hurricane season, Stu, Virg and Jim Kevederis were on the job, on board the flagship Yosemite because a hurricane was working its way north along and close to the coast. Predictions indicated Newport was in for a very rough time with some 45 destroyers moored in nests to piers. At sea Navy ships can maneuver to avoid a bad storm but moored to a pier they could sustain damage as the wind either crashed them into the pier, damaging both ship and pier, or tear them loose in the maelstrom.

The senior officers of the staff were not yet on board (remember, this is Sunday morning) so the three young officers decided that with the location and speed of advance of the hurricane there would not be time for the ships to get underway and cross the projected path of the hurricane and reach the "safe semicircle." The other option, and the option chosen by the three young officers was to get the ships underway and send them far up into Narraganset Bay, to an anchorage where they would be safe.

On board the flagship the operations section of the DESLANT staff was a madhouse as one by one the senior officers arrived. The ongoing program of sending the ships to anchorage was approved as it continued with many ships being delayed in getting steam up and dozens of other reasons. Captain Joslin, Assistant Chief of Staff for Operations and Plans, was the senior officer to make it aboard that day. Remember, he had a drinking problem that had always been covered by his subordinates and this was Sunday morning which usually follows Saturday night. Saturday night is usually a night for festivities or just plain drinking and it was clear that Captain Joslin had been involved in either or both. He was very heavily hung-over, stayed in his stateroom and consumed copious quantities of coffee as his subordinates kept him informed of the progress and problems. With each such report he would nod with a "Very well."

The hurricane passed with no ship damage and Captain Royal K. Joslin received glowing credit for his initiative in taking timely appropriate action to "save the fleet." His subordinates had saved his ass once again. The story doesn't end here with a negative for Captain Joslin because he saw to it that all of his people received superlative fitness reports, couldn't have been better. Captain Joslin really knew how to prepare a fitness report to be signed by Vice Admiral Weakley, leader of the fraternity.

Fitness Reports were very important to a career officer; actually his whole career depended on them. Early in Stu's DESLANT Staff time the Chief of Staff was called to Washington to serve on a selection board, an annual formal board to select lieutenant commanders for promotion to the rank of commander. This screening and selection is accomplished by the board members reviewing fitness reports of the eligible officers. When the Chief of Staff returned from this duty he was clearly disturbed with the process he had just been party to and the Admiral asked him to present his views on the selection process to the staff. As much of the staff as could be accommodated crowded into the briefing room as the CofS described his experience with the selection board.

Seems that the other line "fraternities" of the Navy, aviators and submariners, were writing much stronger fitness reports on their officers than was the destroyer community. That meant that in a competitive selection process those officers serving in destroyers would be less likely to be selected for advancement even if they were doing superlative jobs. The CofS explained that the fitness report served two purposes: (1) an instrument to assist the detailer in determining the officer's next duty assignment, and (2) a communication with the selection board as to the fitness of the officer for promotion to the next rank. It was the second of these purposes that concerned the CofS.

"If you want this officer to be promoted you have to make that very clear to the selection board. You have to make this officer look like a combined Chester Nimitz and John Paul Jones. I hate to use this term but you must 'inflate' the report so that your officer stands out among the others who have inflated reports. If we don't do this we are not looking after our best officers."

Admiral Weakley gave some words of agreement and the senior officers of the staff discussed the issue. Stu Landersman, a lowly lieutenant on the staff, had stood quietly in the back of the room. He had listened carefully to every word and absorbed the concept. If you want your subordinates promoted; communicate that to the selection board, inflate the report so that your guys stand head and shoulders above all the others. It was a long time before Stu had opportunity to write fitness reports but when he did they were the best!

Just as fraternities are known to have parties, so did the DESLANT staff. Every month there was a "Hail and Farewell" party to welcome newcomers and bid adieu to those departing. Stu had served in three ships and spent a year at the Navy PG school and Martha and he had been active participants, even organizers, in most of the social activities. They both loved the Navy social life and here they were at their first social event with the leaders of the entire destroyer force. They went through the receiving line, got drinks and stood– and stood–and stood. The admiral and his wife made the rounds, graciously chatting with each couple and then Martha and Stu stood some more.

Stu turned to Martha, "Let's get out of here."

Martha shook her head, "No! If these people are not coming to us, we'll go to them. C'mon."

With that Martha and Stu circulated around the room, introducing themselves to as many couples as they could, generating conversation, exchanging information and getting to know the people of the DESLANT staff. In all of the monthly Hail and Farewell parties that followed, Martha and Stu continued the introductions and circulation and from what started as neglected wall-flowers they became a very popular couple of the staff. They always focused on the newcomers so that over the months on the staff, as newbies became regulars, they all remembered the couple that had welcomed them.

When World War Two had come to a victorious close, the Navy was faced with reductions-in-force. That meant fewer ships and fewer personnel. The reductions slowed during the Korean conflict but after that the reductions continued.

The Atlantic Fleet and the Pacific Fleet were organized into what were called "Type Commands," meaning type of ships. Long before World War Two there had been a Battle Force consisting of the battleships and this force was supported by all the other type ships. When aircraft carriers became important, type commands were established for aviation. Cruisers had their type commanders as did destroyers and the Service Force consisted of ships that provided the all-important logistic support. Faced with reductions, the various Navy communities were forced to combine some commands.

When Stu Landersman reported to the COMDESLANT Staff in 1960 the Atlantic Fleet consisted of many type commands, two of which were BATCRULANT and DESLANT. The battleships had all been retired except for USS MISSISSIPPI which was used only as a platform for development of combat systems. Soon after, that last battleship, MISSISSIPPI, was retired leaving that force as CRULANT with six cruisers organized in three flotillas, two cruisers in each flotilla, not a very large force. It made sense to combine the two combatant ship force commands into one.

A committee was formed of officers from the DESLANT and CRULANT staffs to work out the administrative details of the combination of the forces. Stu Landersman was one of the officers on that committee. There were very few problems, almost none.

Attitude was probably the closest thing to a problem. The attitude of the DESLANT officers was that six ships that happened to be cruisers were becoming a part of the more than a hundred ship destroyer force, while the cruiser force officers saw the situation as the joining together of two type commands. It was six ships joining over a hundred and the commander of this new type command would be the current commander of the destroyer force in Newport. The admiral that had commanded the cruiser force in Norfolk had been reassigned.

One of the issues to be dealt with was the title of this new command. Should it be CRUDESLANT or DESCRULANT? Stu's view was that the hundred plus ship types should occupy the premier or first position; destroyers should be first. A brief discussion of the committee changed his mind because sailors would have a good time with DESCRULANT as "D' Screw Lant." Let's go with CRUDESLANT.

A generally accepted situation was naming of subordinate units. All Navy units had been numbered with odd numbers in the Atlantic, even numbers in the Pacific, so that the subordinate units in DESLANT were Destroyer Flotillas Two, Four and Six and those flotillas of CRULANT were numbered the same. Did it have to be numbers?

Stu came up with a brainstorm. Why not, instead of numbers, name the new flotillas for vicious animals or even colors, something sailors could relate to; Tiger Flotilla, Lion Flotilla or maybe Red, White or Blue.

How could this idea be supported? Another brainstorm started with a phone call to Boston.

Samuel Eliot Morison was the closest thing the Navy had to a Navy Historian. A distinguished professor at Harvard, he had been commissioned by President Roosevelt to write the history of the U.S. Navy in World War Two, which turned out to be a 15 volume project for which he received a commission as Rear Admiral, USNR, the Legion of Merit and the Presidential Medal of Freedom. Over his career Morison wrote over 40 books most on naval history. He received over ten honorary doctoral degrees and numerous literary prizes including two Pulitzer Prizes.

On the phone Dr. Morison was easy to talk with and he was interested in the project; the joining together of DESLANT and CRULANT. He laughed and understood the reasoning and failure of Stu's attempt to put destroyers first in the title. He listened carefully then gave considerable thought to the idea of names rather than numbers to the new CRUDES flotillas. He offered a few similarities such as the Royal Navy's former use of "Admiral of the Blue, etc." but could not come up with combatant ship units being identified by anything but numbers.

Nice try, good original thinking, thanks for thinking of me, a gracious nautical wish for smooth sailing and that was it from the great man. Another of Stu's brainstorms given the deep-six.

Joining together of destroyers and cruisers into one force carried an unforeseen effect on Vice Admiral Weakley's favorite project which was the creation of a community of Destroyermen. How could we call ourselves Destroyermen when we had cruisers in our force? Clumsy, awkward, yes, it slowed the project. A few years later though, when other force reductions and reorganizations led to the Service Force and the Amphibious Force joining with the cruiser and destroyer force, the path led to the formation of the Surface Force. With it came the Surface Warfare community with qualification for its identifying badge. Weakley's dream of Destroyermen had not been realized but took shape as the entire Surface Warfare community.

Remember, while at PG school in Monterey with orders to the DESLANT staff; Stu had put an ad in the Newport paper stating that he was looking for a home. That had worked very well and the Landersmans had purchased a home in Middletown (adjacent to Newport) as a result of that newspaper ad. Also, you might remember that when they left Monterey Martha was expecting. Christmas Eve 1960, late at night, Martha woke Stu and informed him it was time. From across the street came a woman who had volunteered a few days prior to look after David. The Newport area was in deep snow and Stu had tire chains on their 1959 Chevy station wagon so the ride to the Naval Hospital was easy. Mark Stuart Landersman was born Christmas Day 1960.

Stu Landersman's duty on the DESLANT staff, which had now been changed to CRUDESLANT, was a two year tour. As he approached that two year time, Stu was quite naturally concerned with what his next duty would be. Newport was the home port for two squadrons designated as escort squadrons and consisting of Dealey class DEs. These ships were commanded by officers in the rank of lieutenant commander and Stu knew that those lieutenant commanders were carefully selected members of the destroyerman community or fraternity. Executive officers in these ships were lieutenants, like Stu, and also like Stu most of them had sea going experience in ASW.

Considering the quality of the COs, the ASW mission of the ships and the role of executive officer, Stu thought that being exec of a Dealey would be a very fine next duty. Also, Martha liked living in Newport with lots of friends and a busy social life.

Even though officer detailing, that is duty assignments, were conducted at the Bureau of Naval Personnel in Washington, COMCRUDESLANT in Newport had considerable influence on who went where in his ships, in his force. Stu knew that if the admiral whom he served, via the senior staff officers, told the detailer that Lieutenant Smith should go to the USS Jones, that officer could plan on that duty assignment. The fraternity looked after its brothers.

Sometimes the best laid plans, etc. and timing just wasn't right for Stu to fit into an XO billet in a Dealey. So what was next best? The pundits at the COMCRUDESLANT staff pointed Stu toward an executive officer of a destroyer scheduled for FRAM conversion, and that's where he went.

What's FRAM? The letters stand for Fleet Rehabilitation and Modernization, meaning an extensive conversion of a World War Two destroyer into a more up-to-date ship with newer radar, sonar, weapons, and improvement of the engineering plant. It would mean at least ten months in a naval shipyard during which time the executive officer would serve as commanding officer. Commanding officer of a destroyer! Stu was still a lieutenant.

Stu received orders to: Proceed and report to USS Stickell (DDR 888) for duty as Executive Officer. Stickell's home port was Norfolk, Virginia and the Landersmans still owned that first house they bought there. The Navy family that had been renting their home had just vacated so it was a very convenient move, door to door, to Peppermill Lane in Norfolk.

Martha, David and Mark left Newport for Norfolk in the VW bug while Stu and the German Shepard named Tanker stayed for ten days in the BOQ as Stu had to turn over his staff job to his relief. After that it was off to Norfolk and reporting to USS Stickell.

Stickell's schedule was nothing to be excited about-FRAM conversion-but "The best laid plans—," have a way of being changed, like being surprised.

CHAPTER TWENTY FIVE

TURN RIGHT AT THE LIGHTSHIP

1962

The Cold War lasted for almost 50 years and the worst crisis of that tense era was the 1962 Cuban Crisis. On Sunday, October 14, 1962 the National Security Council reported to President Kennedy that U-2 reconnaissance photos showed Soviet nuclear armed missiles and launchers positioned near Cristobel, Cuba; a clear threat to the United States of America. To deal with this threat, the U.S. had four options; (1) invade Cuba, (2) destroy the missiles by air strike, (3) blockade Cuba, or (4) negotiate with the Soviets for the removal of the missiles. In the days that followed, the U.S. blockaded Cuba, negotiated with the Soviets and prepared air strikes and invasion forces, but by the end of October the Soviet Union agreed to withdraw the missiles and on November 2nd the blockade, then called "quarantine," was lifted.

The Cuban Missile Crisis involved the highest levels of government and the entire U.S. military. For the Navy it was a demonstration of rapid and powerful response. To the individual Navy ship it put into practice that which they had planned, talked about, but seldom if ever thought they would do. Navy ships had to get underway on short notice for extended operations, recall men from leave and liberty, rush to re-assemble equipment and fill supplies, and operate short handed. Destroyers supported by patrol aircraft established a blockade of Cuba, patrolling passages through which merchant ships would pass in transit from the Atlantic Ocean into the Caribbean Sea to Cuba.

Destroyer Division 262, consisting of four Gearing Class converted to radar picket destroyers; O'Hare (DDR 889), Corry (DDR817), Charles P. Cecil (DDR 835) and Stickell (DDR 888) lay in a nest moored alongside at the Des-Sub Piers, Norfolk, Virginia. O'Hare was the flagship of the division commander, Captain Roger Spreen. The eight ships of Destroyer Squadron Twenty-Six, including DESDIV 262, had returned to their home port a month ago from a six month deployment to the Mediterranean and the ships were in an upkeep status, doing repair and maintenance work with assistance of a destroyer tender at the next pier. DESRON 26 was the premier anti-air warfare squadron of the Atlantic Fleet with its seven radar picket destroyers and one of the first guided missile destroyers, USS Dewey, carrying the broad command pennant of the squadron commander. The crews had been on leave following the deployment and the ships had settled down to routines of ship's work and liberty.

Lieutenant Stu Landersman, with his wife and two sons, had traveled from Newport, Rhode Island to Norfolk, Virginia and moved into a their home some 10 miles from the Naval Base. Stu had orders to report to USS Stickell (DDR 888) for duty as Executive Officer. He was excited about the prospect of being Exec of a destroyer because he was only a lieutenant and the Exec billet called for a lieutenant commander. Also, Stickell, with her well-known logo of three 8 balls, was part of an elite squadron of anti-air warfare specialists. Newly built missile ships like Dewey were just coming into the fleet to replace the radar picket destroyers.

Stickell was a World War II destroyer, a Gearing Class, 2250 tons, 390 feet long with 40 foot beam, four Babcock and Wilcox boilers providing 600 pound steam to two turbine engines, the ship was capable of 34 knots. Seventy-seven of these ships had been built right at the end of World War II and most of them were commissioned in 1945 and 1946. Gearing Class destroyers carried three gun mounts with two barrels of 5 inch 38 in each mount, a total of 6 five-inch guns, and Stickell was one of 26 ships of this class that had been converted a few years before to radar picket destroyer and designated DDR. The DDRs were primarily anti-air warfare ships because the main feature of their conversion had been the addition of special air search radar, including a large clumsy antenna which provided the altitude of air contacts while other radar gave only range and bearing.

The National Security Council recommendations to the President regarding Cuba were not made public but the television news carried some items about concern with Cuba receiving arms from the Soviet Union. Also on TV news and of more immediate concern to some in Norfolk that weekend was a story of a serious automobile accident. One sailor had been killed and five badly injured and all six were quartermasters from USS Stickell; the entire QM gang of the ship out celebrating a shipmate's transfer.

On Wednesday October 17th 1962 Stu Landersman reported on board and relieved as Executive Officer Friday October 19th. His first act as Exec required a decision regarding weekend liberty. A hurricane had been working over Florida moving north and Navy people in Virginia were waiting to see its movement and the predictions so as to determine if normal "long weekend" liberty could be granted. Long weekend liberty meant that one section of the crew, that is one third, would be granted time off the ship from Friday afternoon to Monday morning. If the hurricane threatened Norfolk the crew had to be on the ship or nearby on short liberty in the event the ship had to get underway for storm evasion. But as the 4 P.M. predictions showed that the hurricane was no longer a threat, the new Executive Officer granted the long weekend. He didn't know it at the time but on that same Friday afternoon President Kennedy ordered the Navy to prepare for a blockade of Cuba and ordered an increase in readiness of all U.S. military.

Saturday morning the new Exec put on his khaki uniform at home and told his wife that he thought he should go to the ship because it was his first full day as Exec and he wanted to see how the ship functioned on a weekend. He would be home for lunch he told her but his next meal at home would be over two months later.

As lunch time approached the new Exec was busy and he decided to eat on the ship with three other officers in the wardroom. A phone call came telling them to make all preparations to get underway as soon as possible. Official message traffic would follow. They didn't know when the ship would sortie or where they were going but they started to get ready.

Commander Tracy Wilder, Commanding Officer of USS Stickell, was painting second floor window frames on his Virginia Beach home that Saturday when his wife called him down from his ladder to take a call from a squadron staff officer. Wilder was told to return to his ship and get ready to get underway as soon as possible for extended operations. In response to the question of where he was to go the staff officer said it was classified but message traffic would soon reach the ship giving the answer. When asked which way he should turn when he reached the mouth of Chesapeake Bay, the staff officer replied, "Turn right at the lightship." When his new Executive Officer called, Wilder had already been notified of the sortie orders.

Months later author Fletcher Knebel ("Seven Days in May") visited Stickell as part of his preparation for a series about the Cuban Crisis entitled, "The War We Never Fought." Knebel's first article started with a description of the phone call to Commander Tracy Wilder, skipper of the destroyer Stickell, at his Virginia Beach home. It told of his wife calling him down from the ladder to take a call from the staff officer and the exchange that included, "Turn right at the lightship," and Knebel used that as the title of his first piece.

Turning right at the lightship translated to heading south in the Atlantic Ocean, which meant towards Cuba as there had been bits and pieces in the news and in Navy message traffic. In his previous duty on the staff of Commander Cruiser Destroyer Force, U.S. Atlantic Fleet, Stu Landersman had frequent contact with the staff of the Commander-in-Chief, U.S. Atlantic Fleet in Norfolk. With recall and readiness procedures started in his ship and the captain on his way,

Stu went to see his former contacts on the Fleet staff where he learned the overall situation and the plans for blockade of Cuba. When the Captain came aboard Stickell knew more about what they were facing than most of the other ships making ready to depart.

Wilder was immediately very busy, involved in continuous discussions with his department heads, on the phone with various activities, seeking information and help in solving a mountain of problems that had to be overcome in putting Stickell together so they could deploy on short notice. A key element was getting the destroyer tender to return equipment and complete repairs on a Saturday afternoon. Destroyer tenders also granted weekend liberty to the crew and had the same recall problems as the ships they tended. The engineering plant had to be reassembled, boilers had to be lighted off and pumps and valves had to be tested. The ship had to transition from a scheduled upkeep status with equipment being worked on to full readiness, possibly for combat operations. The Captain focused his attention on getting the ship ready and delegated to the Executive Officer the problem of getting the crew back on board.

Stu Landersman was very anxious to be a part of this blockade operation and wanted his ship to be first to go. Every half-hour the division Operations Officer would cross the four nested destroyers asking each ship's Executive Officer how many men were missing. When it came time to get a destroyer underway the ship missing the fewest people would be first to go. As the four ships of DESDIV 262 were nested, Stickell was the last outboard, the furthest from the pier so Stickell would be the easiest to get underway from the nest.

It was impossible to get an accurate count of men on board as all departments were sending men ashore to get supplies, equipment and parts, and to go out and bring back sailors whom they couldn't contact. They held musters but no one knew precisely where their people were. Every effort was being made to get ready. Every one was busy. The Navy Supply Center was on emergency mode trying to get every ship in Norfolk everything they needed. There was a continuous flow of people trafficking across all quarterdecks, up and down the piers and car traffic jammed the base and gates where security had been increased. That Saturday afternoon was worse than the busiest rush hour. Stu's wife made it through the congestion to bring him a toilet kit, which gave him a chance for a brief good-by. She didn't know that he hadn't moved his uniforms on board.

As the staff officer came across the nest Stickell's Exec greeted him on the quarterdeck, "How are the other ships doing?"

"O'Hare's missing 150, Corry 120, and Cecil 128. How are you doing?" giving the status of others before he was told the number of men absent from Stickell. Landersman always picked a number lower than any of the other three ships. "We're missing 115," and so it went all afternoon. The Exec kept asking department heads for estimates and that's what he got, very rough estimates of the number of men accounted for. Stickell gave the staff officer a lower number than the other ships every half-hour.

There was not a single quartermaster rating on board as all had been lost to the ship in that automobile accident the previous Saturday and the Navy personnel distribution system hadn't had time to replace the losses. Captain Wilder borrowed a Second Class Quartermaster from the squadron flagship, USS Dewey, and that was the only quartermaster in Stickell for the Cuban Quarantine.

At 1800 (6 PM) on Saturday 20 October 1962 orders came to get underway. Stickell stopped men from errands ashore and set the Special Sea and Anchor Detail, and it really was "special" that evening as people were moved around and assigned to provide essential functions. Cooks, storekeepers and stewards handled mooring lines. Chief Petty Officers were on watches they hadn't stood in years. Every officer and man had an active function at Sea Detail as Stickell glided through the darkness of Hampton Roads and Chesapeake Bay and turned right at the lightship.

The Fletcher Knebel article told that Stickell sailed with 75 strange faces aboard, that the Captain, Tracy Wilder had borrowed 25 men from three different ships. Knebel was wrong. USS Dewey's quartermaster was the only strange face on board and as soon as Special Sea and Anchor Detail was secured the first accurate muster showed 90 absentees. Of 320 men assigned to operate and possibly fight the ship, Stickell had 230. All but two officers were aboard. Every Chief Petty Officer was aboard and only two First Class Petty Officers were missing. The bad news was that Stickell was missing about one-third of her crew. The good news was that most of the senior and experienced men were on board.

Of the missing, most were junior enlisted men. It was understandable that the older men should be on board as they had family and lived nearby in the Norfolk area. Younger sailors had traveled away for the long weekend and couldn't get back in time. Constructing a model months later of where these sailors were showed a polygon with corners at Atlanta, St. Louis, Chicago and Boston. There was something called an Out of Area Chit but no one paid attention to it. Sailors don't hesitate to travel on a long weekend.

Stickell was escorting an oiler south on Monday October 22 when President Kennedy addressed the nation on radio and television, telling of the threat posed by missiles in Cuba and U.S. response. DEFCON Five was normal peacetime readiness and DEFCON One meant war. The military increased readiness to DEFCON Two, the highest of the Cold War, one step less than war, and forces mobilized in preparation to invade Cuba. News reports told of Cuban mobilization of a hundred thousand men. Soviet forces were on alert.

The Ship's Organization and Training Manual included a section called, "Boarding and Salvage, Blockade and Prize Crew." These procedures had not been practiced or even looked at in a long time. The manual stated that stopping a merchant ship on the high seas as part of a blockade was a belligerent act, an act of war, so Stickell rehearsed as if to meet opposition. The ship would be prepared to stop a merchant ship with threat or actual gunfire and a boarding party armed to deal with uncooperative or even hostile merchant seamen would be ready to go aboard by boat. The Executive Officer was to be the boarding officer, armed with a .45 caliber pistol. Two big gunners' mates with Thompson sub-machine guns would accompany him, one on each side. If hostile action was needed the gunners' mates would open fire from outside in and the Exec would shoot those immediately in front of them. After Stickell had rehearsed a number of times in this scenario a message came from higher authority directing that all boarding parties be prepared to board with candy and magazines, not as belligerents. So practice started over with new teammates, no guns and with giveaways. A week later at sea, a Coast Guard officer arrived in Stickell by helicopter as part of a program to teach destroyermen how to inspect a merchant ship.

Years later it was disclosed that the issue of boarding a merchant ship armed as belligerents or giving goodies was a controversy in the President's Executive Committee between Chief of Naval Operations Admiral George Anderson and Secretary of Defense Robert McNamara.

USS Charles P. Cecil generally operated with Stickell in what was called a Sub-Division. But Stickell had departed Norfolk alone for the Cuban Crisis and the two destroyers hadn't teamed up. Still, it was natural to keep track of their sister-ship and so Stickell radiomen informally watched the fleet broadcast for Cecil messages. They found a lot. Cecil had been proceeding to her next assignment in the Caribbean when she gained a sonar contact. Over many hours into days Cecil held the contact despite orders from various higher authorities to break off and proceed. Cecil persisted. Higher authorities didn't believe a WWII destroyer with out-dated anti submarine equipment, such as old sonar, could hold contact with a submarine for so many hours. All the experts said it couldn't be a submarine but Cecil insisted it was.

Repeatedly ordered to break-off, Cecil stayed with her sonar contact. Finally, a Soviet diesel electric submarine was forced to surface proving the higher authorities wrong. The picture of a surfaced submarine, made available to the press was an embarrassment for the Soviets.

On Wednesday October 24th the Lebanese merchant ship Marcula, enroute to Cuba was stopped by two U.S. Navy destroyers, USS John R. Pierce (DD 753) and USS Joseph P. Kennedy, Jr. (DD 850) and President Kennedy directed boarding and search by radio-telephone from the White House. Marcula had first been intercepted by destroyer Kennedy and authorized to proceed. Later, inspection of the ship was ordered and Pierce was first on the scene but the boarding order was delayed until the destroyer named for the President's brother could be a participant. In the open ocean, Executive Officers of the two destroyers led a boarding party, checked manifest against cargo and after finding no prohibited materials in their selective spot verification the ship was authorized to proceed via Providence Channel to Cuba. LCDR K.C. Reynolds of Kennedy was in charge of the boarding party and LCDR D.G. Osborne of Pierce, a maritime academy graduate with merchant ship background provided his experience with ship configuration and associated papers. This U.S. Navy boarding of a merchant ship on the high seas as part of a blockade was the first such act in nearly 100 years, since the Civil War.

Three days later, Saturday October 27, 1962 has been called "Black Saturday" as the Soviets shot down a U-2 reconnaissance plane. Attorney General Robert Kennedy went to the Soviet Ambassador in Washington with an ultimatum; if missiles were not withdrawn from Cuba or if one more U.S. plane was shot down the U.S. would invade Cuba. 125,000 troops moved to Florida and Georgia. Anti air missiles were set up along the Florida coast. Marine Corps troops were at sea enroute Cuba holding plans to assault Santiago and Havana.

That Saturday was a very significant day for USS Stickell, patrolling Silver Bank Passage in the Caribbean. The Naval Reserve destroyer USS Bearss (DD 654) came over the horizon bearing 90 Stickell men, most still in their very well worn liberty uniforms and all very anxious to get back to their ship. After six and a half hours of steaming alongside conducting personnel transfers by dual high lines, Stickell had her full crew.

The next day Khrushchev sent a message to Kennedy; he would withdraw missiles from Cuba if the U.S. would remove missiles from Turkey and promise not to invade Cuba. On Friday November 2nd 1962 the Cuban Quarantine was lifted and U.S. military forces stood down from their high alert DEFCON.

Stickell men did not know of the diplomatic steps and readiness procedures beyond the ships in and near company. The general population knew more of what was going on than did those in a

Navy ship at sea, where only by getting radiomen to "copy press" (a slightly illegal process of intercepting commercial wire service news broadcasts) could a ship learn what was going on at home or in the outside world. A sailor's wedding was cancelled. Another held two tickets to an important North Carolina football game that went unused. Every one had a personal situation, an emotional drama. Stickell men didn't know that school children were practicing hiding under desks for safety, like fire drills.

The Exec had only the uniform he wore when he went to the ship in Norfolk that Saturday morning. His predecessor hadn't removed his things until the day he departed, so the new Exec's uniforms were not aboard. Every evening at Eight O'clock Reports each department reported their overall condition to the Exec and salutes were exchanged, requiring a hat. Unlike the other services Navy men only salute when covered. On the second evening underway the Exec stepped out of his stateroom to receive reports in the passageway and as he pulled on his "steamer" garrison hat the brim came off in his hand. Only friction held it as he pushed the brim back in place, returned a salute with each report and then very carefully placed the hat atop his locker. Glue and scotch tape didn't help but for three weeks that broken hat served the Exec until the ship went into San Juan, Puerto Rico and he replaced the steamer and bought underwear and khakis so he didn't have to do wash basin laundry each night.

The following has little to do with the Cuban Quarantine but is related more to a Landersman family anecdote. It's the story of Stu's uncle and aunt, Moe and Sylvia on a banana boat cruise. Instead of taking vacations like other people, like people that took cruises on luxury liners to exotic places in the South Pacific or Caribbean, Moe and Sylvia liked to book trips with United Fruit Company ships trading in bananas in Central America. These ships could carry only a dozen or so passengers and provided no entertainment. Passengers played cards, chatted and looked forward to the brief port visits in the commercial shipping trade. On one port visit to San Juan, Puerto Rico, Moe noticed that there many sailors in town and a group of Navy ships were tied up together in the harbor. He stopped a group of sailors and asked if they knew if one of those ships could be the Stickell. Moe didn't know much about the Navy but he did happen to know the name of the ship that his nephew was serving in. Surprise, surprise, yes, the sailor told Moe, one of those destroyers alongside the tender was Stickell and if he wanted to get in touch with anyone in that ship the fleet landing was right there and they had radio communications with those ships.

Stu was sitting at his desk in his tiny stateroom when the messenger from the quarterdeck knocked and entered. The messenger described that this information had come from the fleet landing to the quarterdeck of the destroyer tender and had been relayed from ship to ship across three quarterdecks: A man claiming to be Stu's uncle was at the fleet landing waiting for him. The destroyer tender had a boat ready to take Stu ashore.

Stu went ashore, met Moe and Sylvia and spent the rest of the day together with them; a family reunion as part of the Cuban Quarantine.

On that Cuban Quarantine, officers and men of Stickell performed their duties with the highest degree of dedication and professionalism. They filled in where needed, worked longer hours then ever, stood watches often without relief and did everything necessary so that the ship carried out every assignment and was always ready for more. Through it all there was a spirit of cheerfulness, élan and camaraderie that so often accompanies adversity.

They were Destroyermen.

CHAPTER TWENTY SIX

USS STICKELL (DDR 888)

1962-1964

USS Stickell (DDR 888) returned from the Cuban Quarantine to her home port, Norfolk, Virginia and had to pick up where she had left off in the process of preparation for FRAM conversion. The Cuban Quarantine had delayed her about two months and to the material/maintenance section of the type commander's staff, COMCRUDESLANT; operational functions were just a nuisance and an interference with maintenance requirements. One might give the maintenance people of the type commander's staff a motto; "We don't keep the shipyard waiting."

Stickell had kept the shipyard waiting and now had to catch up with preparations for what would be a ten month conversion in the Philadelphia Naval Shipyard. One of those preparations was a cruise to the shipyard so that the planners could look over the ship in detail and plan in detail the details of what had to done in ten months of detailed work. And so the ship got underway from Norfolk, transited north, embarked a pilot and made the long trip up the Delaware River to Philadelphia.

Stickell people thought that the trip up the Delaware River was the first of what would be four river transits for Stickell in connection with her FRAM conversion. There was this up-river trip to the Philadelphia Naval Shipyard and the return two weeks later with the ship enroute back to her home port; Norfolk. Then, two months later, Stickell would sail first to the ammunition depot to off-load all of her 5 inch 38 gun ammunition and then up-river again to the Philly shipyard. Then, if things went well with the shipyard work and the DDR would be converted to a DD, Stickell would transit one more time down-river enroute to her home port of Norfolk. That's what was expected by the Stickell men.

Remember, though, that old saying about "the best laid plans of mice and men"? Well, the Stickell people would soon learn that there would be some other down-river and up-river in their schedule. When the ship was all done, all converted and ready for sea, before she went back to the fleet the shipyard and, of course the CO of the ship and all of the people that would be serving in her and, of course the type commander, all wanted to be sure that the ship was in fact, "Ready for Sea." That meant another trip down-river, a demonstration of all the ship's systems followed by an up-river return to the shipyard.

And then it was learned that upon completion of the FRAM conversion Stickell would be inspected by a team from the Secretary of the Navy; the Board of Inspection and Survey. That inspection included a very thorough look-over at all the ship's systems and then an at-sea demonstration in which the ship would operate all of her systems and steam at full power both ahead and astern. Then it would be back to the shipyard to correct any deficiencies detected by the Board of Inspection and Survey. Navy people called that inspection team Insurv.

Four up-rivers and down-rivers? No, more likely eight river trips.

And then would it be back to the home port of Norfolk ten months later at the end of FRAM conversion? Well that was the original plan, oh yes, but remember once again, please, that in the Navy plans are made for changing and that's what happened to Stickell. Upon completion of FRAM conversion Stickell would proceed not to her previous home port of Norfolk but to her new home port; Newport, Rhode Island.

But we are getting ahead of ourselves in this story. Let's go back to our first long up-river trip taking us to the Philadelphia Naval Shipyard so that the yard planners could get an accurate appraisal of the work they would have to do to convert Stickell to a more modern destroyer.

From the Atlantic Ocean to Philadelphia the Delaware River consists of at least twenty ranges. A range is a navigation aid consisting of two large colorful markers, shapes like triangles. These markers are positioned in such a way so that when viewed from a ship in the proper river channel the two shapes are exactly aligned with each other, one on top of the other. If the ship views the shapes as being apart, that means the ship is not in the navigational channel. The markers are positioned some distance apart, one behind the other with the rear marker higher than the forward one. These range markers are a very nice aid in navigating the Delaware River as every turn brings the ship onto a new range. The pilots of the Delaware River have these ranges memorized and these pilots are confident and competent in taking large ships up and down the river. River pilots they are, pilots of the river. Why am I belaboring this river pilot thing? Well, there's a story here about river pilots of the Delaware River or maybe one such pilot.

Let's jump to the end of the FRAM conversion again. Well, not to the very end but near the end when the new commanding officer had just come aboard. Oh yes, did I not tell you this earlier? The plan for all destroyers undergoing FRAM conversion was for the executive officer to take over as commanding officer as soon as the ship reached the shipyard to begin the big work time. Then, as the conversion was nearing completion and in time for any of the sea trials, a commander in rank would come aboard and relieve as commanding officer. The CO during FRAM, who was the former executive officer, would revert to that position. He would be the executive officer again.

A few days before Christmas 1964, Commander Arthur J. Languedoc came aboard and relieved Stu Landersman as commanding officer of USS Stickell (DD 888). Stu was once again executive officer of the ship. Clearly, Languedoc was not the confident competent officer in command that Stu had become accustomed to in destroyers and the new commanding officer made it clear that he would rely on Stu for a great deal more than would normally be expected of an executive officer.

The twenty-fourth day of December, the day before Christmas, often called Christmas Eve day, was the day the leaders of the Philly shipyard declared that it would be absolutely essential for USS Stickell to conduct her first sea trial. No other day would be considered. That meant an early morning underway, transit down-river, full power demonstration, a number of other tests and then the transit up the Delaware River. If everything went well with the tests the ship would be back at the shipyard by late afternoon of Christmas Eve Day.

But everything didn't go exactly well. A few of the tests had to be repeated. That took time and the delay resulted in the ship getting back to the shipyard in the dark of night on Christmas Eve. Commander Arthur J. Languedoc, who had never been underway in Stickell, was the commanding officer and it was clear that he had not been underway in a destroyer for some time and maybe not much before. Stu Landersman had been the youngest and most junior in rank of any officer commanding a destroyer but now he was the executive officer. It quickly became clear to the Stickell officers that the pilot who had taken them up the river was just for the river, not for docking. Also, this being Christmas Eve, it was understandable that the crews of the two tug boats always used to assist in docking were home preparing for the holiday. No docking pilot, no tugs, a CO with little to no experience and, oh yes, it was cold as Hell and windy, too.

Stickell was lying-to in the river, waiting to make her approach to her berth. The river pilot had indicated "no problem," he had docked a few merchant ships, and very soon it became apparent that this pilot did not understand the differences in power and tonnage between a Navy destroyer and a merchant ship. Typically, a merchant ship of forty thousand tons might have engine power of two thousand horsepower, whereas a Navy destroyer of twenty-two hundred tons would have forty thousand horsepower.

The pilot's first order was, "All engines ahead full." It took Stu Landersman less than a second to glance at the captain who nodded and Stu countermanded the order of the pilot with, "I have the conn. All engines stop." Captain Languedoc nodded again as the pilot sulked into the pilot house.

Stu had made a number of landings in his previous destroyer, Robert A. Owens, without tugs but none at night with off-setting cold wind. It was not a pretty landing but the aviators say, "Any landing that you can walk away from is a good landing." The Stickell men walked away from the ship that night, Christmas Eve 1964.

But again we're ahead of ourselves with the story of Stickell in the Philadelphia Naval Shipyard for FRAM conversion. Sea trials are at or near the end of the shipyard work. Let's go back to the beginning, the arrival at the yard for that preview, where the yard planners could do their jobs in preparation for the conversion.

One of the first orders of business for a new ship arriving in the shipyard for FRAM conversion was to find a place for the officers and crew to live as the ship would not be habitable. There would be some work to be done by ship's force on the ship but eating and sleeping had to be off-ship. The shipyard was adjacent to the Naval Station where there were barracks and mess hall for enlisted men from ships undergoing FRAM conversion. Officers could stay in the BOQ (Bachelor Officers Quarters) and use the officers club for meals.

Stu went to call on the senior commanding officer of the three destroyers that had been undergoing FRAM conversion already in the shipyard. That senior CO had made himself the czar of the FRAM ships in the shipyard and Stu was not well received. The lieutenant commander who had been executive officer of his destroyer and then taken command clearly did not think it appropriate for a mere lieutenant, as was Stu, to take command of a destroyer. The czar told Stu that there was no room for him and his people in the accommodations provided by the shipyard or the naval station and he offered no options. There was, "No room at the inn." Clearly, Stu would have to shift for himself, that is for his men and ship when they came back for the ten month FRAM conversion.

There was a popular television show about the Navy, well not the real Navy but some writers' idea about the Navy. It was called McHale's Navy. Anyone who has seen that show would understand how the good ship Stickell made it through FRAM conversion in the Philadelphia Naval Shipyard over the months of 1963-1964.

After being denied accommodations by the reigning czar, Stu met with those of the Stickell that he had selected to be with him for FRAM. He told them that they had been ostracized and they would have to make do for themselves. He had chosen the right men. A couple of days later a chief petty officer came to him and reported that he had found two barges that were not being used and had not been used for a long time. One was a berthing barge and the other was a work barge with machine shops.

Stu went to see the barges with some of the people that would be with him for the shipyard time. They learned that in the past these two barges had been used by diesel-electric submarines in the Philly shipyard for overhaul, but submarines hadn't come to this shipyard in some time so the barges were unused. The berthing facilities were not large enough for a destroyer's full crew but were just right for submarines which made them just right for the reduced size crew of a destroyer undergoing FRAM conversion. This would be ideal accommodation for Stickell, but the barges would need much work to be habitable and useable.

The berthing barge had two decks (floors). The lower deck had accommodations for ninety enlisted men including bunks, heads, washroom, showers and even a crew's lounge. Also on the first level was a galley and refrigeration space. The crew's lounge served as the mess hall. On the upper deck there were accommodations for officers with staterooms, wardroom and heads, washroom and showers.

The machine shop barge could be put to good use by ships force but also would require a lot of work. With these two barges Stickell would be independent of the shipyard for living accommodations and ships force work.

Sounds nice, doesn't it? Well, it really wasn't nice at all. Both barges had been neglected for years and needed considerable work, like major restoration, to be made useable. Many of the sinks and toilets were missing or broken. Most of the furniture and all of the galley equipment was missing. It would take a lot of work and finances to restore these barges to acceptable standards. How could all this be accomplished in time for the start of Stickell's shipyard period with no work force, no resources, no finances and no authorization?

Well, remember McHale's Navy? Sailors always find a way. There's a little known process that exists in the Navy, little known because it's slightly illegal, that is used by the most experienced Navy men in naval shipyards, by which sailors get unauthorized unfunded work done. All kinds of work. And this work is done by shipyard workers willingly to satisfy sailors. This process, this accomplishment of tasks by shipyard workers for sailors in ships is called "Kumshaw."

The word kumshaw is rumored to be a distortion of a Chinese word that meant getting something accomplished that was not authorized by giving something in return, like a form of bribery. Rumor had it that the word and the process originated with sailors serving in ships on the "China Station" prior to World War Two. On that station, sailors often had to obtain services without official authorization. In modern times in a naval shipyard an experienced sailor supplied with many pounds of coffee or sugar, or empty brass five inch cartridges, 22 caliber ammunition or empty fire extinguishers, or used mooring line or almost anything, can go into a shipyard shop, talk to the right man and get whatever the sailor needs. That's kumshaw and that's what the Stickell men either were or were soon to become experts in. Without any funding or authorization they could, and did restore those two neglected barges into comfortable living spaces and valuable work-shops. All by kumshaw like McHale's Navy.

This restoration of the barges was accomplished by a small cadre of Stickell men that were left behind in Philadelphia when the ship returned to Norfolk. Their task was to have the barges ready two months later when the ship returned for the long overhaul. They accomplished their mission without any authorization, funding or any other support, all off the record, kumshaw. All this was done with no knowledge or approval from the shipyard, the type commander or any other authority. McHale's Navy?

Another gimmick. One of the destroyers soon to finish FRAM at Philadelphia had been using two coin operated bottle vending machines during their shipyard time. These were not allowed aboard ship–bottles–empties–stocking–etc., so the CO was anxious to be rid of them before he departed the shipyard. Stu bought both machines for fifty dollars and established a ship's recreation fund. Those two machines made more money than the ship could spend on their recreation. Every time there was a charity drive of some sort by the Philadelphia Naval Shipyard, Stu would find out which activity had given the most and Stickell would give more. The Stickell crew didn't have to contribute any of their own money; soda bottle sales put up all that was needed. Shipyard workers kept the Stickell machines busy because a drink from those machines cost less than on the base.

Once each month there was a Stickell recreation day and the entire Stickell team went to a nearby athletic field for a cookout, beer, softball and horse-shoes all paid for by the bottle vending machines. When a sailor's father died in Kansas, flowers were sent, paid for by those same soda sales. If a sailor needed a loan, as so often sailors do, there were dollars available from soda bottle sales.

The soda bottles used in the machines were deposit bottles and so it was important to keep track of the used bottles. No matter how many bottles were lost Stickell didn't have to pay for lost deposits because the ship gave lunches to the soda truck drivers. McHale's Navy?

Who were these sailors of Stickell who had made those barges useable, were experts at kumshaw and accomplished all of the ships force work during the FRAM conversion? Well, there also is a story.

Months before the shipyard process began, ships scheduled for FRAM conversion received detailed descriptions of what was expected of them and what they could expect. Included in this information was a listing of the billets that would be maintained as the crew would be reduced from 320 to 40 enlisted men and of 25 officers only five would remain. That meant that only five officers and forty men would be ship's force for the shipyard time. Well, that was the plan for an ordinary FRAM conversion but Stickell was anything but ordinary. By manipulation of the personnel reporting process, Stu Landersman made arrangements not for forty but for sixty enlisted men to remain with the ship. Stu interviewed and selected the sixty so that every one was a volunteer for the shipyard process. The sixty were heavy with petty officers; 12 chiefs, 15 first class and most of the rest second and third class petty officers along with a dozen selected seamen. These were the men who took destroyer Stickell through FRAM conversion.

Arrival at the shipyard for the ten month conversion was immediately followed by a change of command ceremony in which Lieutenant Stu Landersman relieved Commander Tracey Wilder as Commanding Officer of USS Stickell (DDR 888). An all-hands ship's party followed at the nearby enlisted club in which Wilder said his good-bys to the crew that he had taken through a number of major fleet exercises, a Mediterranean deployment and the Cuban Quarantine. It was very well-said and there might have been a few wet eyes. The new CO followed with some words on hopes for the future.

As soon as the Stickell men had departed the ship for the party, shipyard workers with cutting torches began removal of everything above the main deck. That's right. Everything above the main deck was cut off, the entire deck-house, as the first step in the conversion of what had been a radar picket destroyer (DDR) to a straight-stick destroyer (DD).

The two Stickell barges remained moored outboard of their ship and the men lived comfortably in their berthing barge and each day did ships force work in their shops on the working barge.

Stu had had no contact with officers from the other ships in FRAM conversion until one day, a month into Stickell's shipyard time; the self-acclaimed czar came to call on Stu. He had looked over the work going on by Stickell sailors in their shops and he was very impressed with what Stickell had developed. He claimed that he had spoken to the representative of the type commander's staff and had been told that all of the ships in the shipyard for FRAM conversion were to share their resources. The lieutenant commander told Stu that the resources of the work barge should be shared by all of the destroyers in the Philly shipyard and that he, as the senior CO, would over-see the use of the shops in the barge.

Stu looked at the czar for a few seconds. "A few months ago when I was looking for a place for my men to live you told me to get lost. I went off on my own and my men created what you see here. Now I say to you, 'get lost.' There's no room for you here. Get the fuck off my barge."

The shipyard work on the conversion went well over the months that followed and, because of the workshops on the barge alongside the ship; ship's force work went even better. With the convenience and efficiency of the barges alongside the ship, the Stickell men didn't have to travel for meals, sleeping or even recreation. The conveniences of the barges together with a crew that became experts in that very special process of (remember?) kumshaw made the shipyard time easy and efficient. Oh yes, those kumshaw skills that had been so effective and valuable in preparing the barges did not stop with barges. That was only the beginning as the Stickell men made contacts all over the shipyard, with all of the shops and in all the months that followed there were countless informal accomplishments.

One kumshaw job that didn't go well involved the ship's motor whaleboat. All destroyers carried one and for the FRAM conversion Stickell's boat was scheduled for some repair and up-date by the shipyard. Routinely two Stickell men went to the boat shop to check on the progress of work on their boat. Ah-ha, what did they see at that shop? A number of brand new motor whaleboats sat on skids at the shipyard boat shop. Why not? The Stickell men arranged for their old boat to be put in place of one of the brand new boats and they moved a brand new motor whaleboat to their ship. It would have been the biggest kumshaw job of all. But unlike most of the smaller lesser material in the Navy, boats are carefully monitored.

Boats have serial numbers that are recorded and a couple of weeks later the shipyard discovered that a boat with a strange number was sitting on the skids that should be occupied by a boat with a different serial number. The loss was reported to the Naval Investigative Service and two agents spent time investigating. Stickell men knew nothing of this formal reported loss or the investigation that followed but the young commanding officer found out when the NIS men told him that his men very likely had stolen a Navy 26 foot motor whaleboat.

No, no, a boat like that couldn't have been stolen by hard working honest Stickell sailors. It must have been just a mix-up of serial numbers. His men wouldn't steal a boat, Stu explained to the agents and, after all, the new boat that the Stickell men were being accused of stealing had not left the shipyard so there really was no change of possession, no theft. Promptly the brand new whaleboat was returned to the shop where it came from. No legal or judicial action was taken as Stu and the sailors breathed a sigh of relief.

But the story of Stickell's motor whaleboat didn't end there. Stu told the two sailors to stay away from the boat shop for a month before they went to check on their original boat and they waited as told. When they went to look at their boat they made an amazing discovery and ran back to report to their CO. The shipyard boat shop supervisor had looked over the original Stickell whaleboat and decided that it wasn't worth repair so he had it surveyed (done away with) and substituted a brand new motor whaleboat for Stickell. Guess which new whaleboat Stickell ended up with. That's right, you guessed it. Stickell was given the very same motor whaleboat that they had taken without authorization a few months before.

The Stickell men that had been selected as ship's company for the long shipyard time in Philadelphia understood that this would be a "change of home port" in Navy terms and that entitled them to a full move of family and household. But as most of the men were more senior petty officers that meant that they had homes with families in the Norfolk area. As the original plan was for the ship to return to Norfolk after the conversion, all of the married men left their families in that area. It proved to be easy for them to spend the five day working week at Philadelphia and go home every weekend. The senior chief petty officer negotiated an agreement with their CO to work at least ten hours each day so that long weekend liberty started at eleven AM each Friday. It was a good life for what counted as "Sea Duty."

Stu Landersman was the only Stickell man who moved his family. Originally Martha elected to live in Norfolk for the months that Stu would be in Philadelphia as he would be home weekends until the ship returned to that home port. But as soon as it was announced that after the FRAM conversion Stickell's home port would be Newport, Martha sold the Norfolk house, had the furnishings put in storage and rented a nice furnished home in nearby New Jersey. It was the first of what would be many others in which Martha would sell their residence, pack-up the boys, travel to the area of Stu's new duty station and establish a new home.

Once a month Stu discussed the overall progress of the conversion with the Stickell officers and chiefs. Four, five, six months it all seemed to be going well and in the sixth month it looked like the shipyard work might be ahead of schedule. In the seventh month it was clear that the work was considerably ahead of schedule and so Stu reported to the type commander that Stickell would complete her conversion one month earlier than scheduled, in nine months instead of the scheduled ten months.

Remember though that "The best laid plans of mice and men—." Well, the Stickell plan that Stu had reported as finishing one month early needed to be adjusted and a month later Stu reported the adjustment to that one month earlier completion. Stickell would require two more weeks to complete the conversion, which would mean two weeks added to the one month reduction that had been previously announced. Still, it meant that Stickell would complete the shipyard conversion two weeks earlier than the originally scheduled time. No other FRAM conversion had been early, some needed extra time.

No response, no acknowledgement had been received for the report of one month reduction but an immediate abrupt question arrived from the type commander, abrupt enough to imply that Stu Landersman had done something very wrong to cause a two week delay in completion of the shipyard work. Remember from the earlier time following the Cuban Quarantine? This was the same section, the maintenance section of the COMCRUDESLANT staff.

At the end of the FRAM conversion with the new captain aboard, Stu was again executive officer. The officer and enlisted complement was increased to full operational destroyer numbers as the FRAM team moved off their convenient barge and back in their ship. The final shipyard work was completed and USS Stickell (DD-888) was made ready for sea.

On the day before the ship would leave to proceed to her new home port of Newport the captain was ashore and the executive officer, Stu Landersman was on board. A Navy chaplain came aboard and met with Stu in the wardroom. The chaplain explained that the Navy had a program that provided veterans with an option for burial at sea. The chaplain explained that he had very few opportunities to have this service performed because so few Navy ships from Philadelphia went into the deep water required for the burial service. The remains of this deceased Gunners Mate had been waiting for months.

On the wardroom table sat an urn with the remains and the chaplain gave Stu a small booklet that described the burial at sea service. Try as he might, Stu couldn't figure out a way to get out of this task and so finally the chaplain prevailed. Stickell would bury the Gunners Mate in deep Atlantic waters.

When the captain returned to the ship he shook his head at the burial at sea service Stu had committed them to and the captain said, "Okay Chaplain Stu, you got us into this, you conduct the service."

The next day when Stickell reached deep water the bosun's pipe trilled and the traditional word was passed, "Now hear this; all hands bury the dead," and the service commenced on the fantail. A squad of riflemen in immaculate dress blue uniforms stood at attention as the service was read. Three times a volley of shots were ordered as "Present" pause "Fire," but it didn't go just that way. The first volley went off all-together as expected but not the next two volleys. The rifles being used were military M-1s which are gas operated semi-automatic, which means that back-pressure from each firing cycles a round in place for the next firing. But for a ceremony such as this blank cartridges were being used and these cartridges did not give the back-pressure needed for the next round to be chambered. So the rifles had to be hand operated to put the next round in the firing chamber. After the first all-together round the next two rounds were like pop-corn as some sailors cycled rounds immediately and others had to see how it was done. Instead of two all-together, "bangs," it was, "pop, pop, pop."

The final part of the service was the spreading of the ashes. As the words were read, "Ashes to ashes," Stu tossed some of the Gunners Mate's ashes over the starboard side of the ship. The wind was hard on to the starboard side and that wind whipped the ashes back up and across the stern and all over the rifle squad in their immaculate dress blues.

Next was, "Dust to dust," and Stu reached out and down over the side with a little more of the ashes. But the wind would not be denied and it threw the Gunners Mate's ashes back over the rifle squad.

Last, and everyone knew what was coming, "So be it for all—etc," and Stu reached over and down as far as he could and released all of the remaining remains. The wind rose to the challenge and carried the remains of the Gunners Mate up the side of the ship, across the fantail and all over the rifle squad, white ashes on their immaculate dress blues and in their faces.

The ceremony over, as they wiped their smiling faces one of the riflemen quipped, "That Gunners Mate just wanted to be with his shipmates" and they all laughed.

More of McHale's Navy? Well, maybe that was the last of McHale's Navy because Stickell went to Newport, Rhode Island, then to Guantanamo Bay, Cuba for shakedown training.

On 25 May 1964, with orders to the U.S. Naval Academy, Stu departed USS Stickell after turning over duty as executive officer to Ian Donovan, who had been Operations Officer.

CHAPTER TWENTY SEVEN

UNITED STATES NAVAL ACADEMY
ANNAPOLIS, MARYLAND

1964–1966

In an early chapter you read of how I had used a manual from the Naval Academy to determine the academic program I would take in high school. At that time I developed an interest in the Navy and the Naval Academy but that same manual described the requirements for admission which included 20/20 eyesight. I didn't have 20/20 vision and didn't expect that there would be anything like a waiver, so to a 14 year old with no other sources of information the Naval Academy was not available to me. Too bad, because years later I found out that waivers existed and with all of my academic and extra-curricula activity, including honor graduate, eagle scout, Junior Achievement, class president, all-star basketball, and other sports and activities a waiver of correctable eyesight would probably have been granted.

Too late perhaps for entry from high school into the Naval Academy but here I was, 16 years later, a lieutenant-commander reporting for duty as Aide and Flag Secretary to the Superintendent of the Naval Academy.

There were very few officers on duty at the Naval Academy who were not graduates of the Naval Academy and I was one of them. More to that point; the Superintendent, a Naval Academy grad, had a number of other aides: chief-of staff, executive assistant, flag lieutenant and for special occasions there were two others who wore the "loafers loops" but I was the only aide who was not a "ring knocker;" a graduate of the Naval Academy.

The individual in charge of a civilian college or university is a President but at the service academies he is called the Superintendent and at the time I reported the Superintendent of the Naval Academy was a rear admiral. During the previous academic year, 1963-1964, the Superintendent, Rear Admiral Charles Kirkpatrick, was found to have heart problems and he went into immediate retirement. The Commandant of Midshipman at that time, Captain Charles S. Minter, had just been selected for promotion to the rank of rear admiral and so he was ordered into the Superintendent position.

Rear Admiral Minter was Superintendent of the Naval Academy when I reported to be his Aide and Flag Secretary in June 1964. The officer that I was to relieve in that position was Bill Bademan who, surprisingly, was from South Dakota. We had a good time talking about that state as we two claimed to be the largest concentration of South Dakota officers in the Navy.

Bill was very well organized and the turnover was made easy because of his professionalism. In an aide's position the job involves not only the professional and office work supporting the admiral but social matters in which the aide's wife is included. Bill Bademan explained all this to me and his wife detailed to Martha her duties assisting as hostess at so many social events at the Supe's house.

My tour of duty at the Naval Academy was scheduled for two years and that's what it was. The first year I served as Aide and Flag Secretary to Rear Admiral Minter. For me it was pretty much a learning time as I found myself in a job of which I knew very little, almost nothing compared to the shipboard jobs that I had previously held.

I remembered Roger Spreen from the DESLANT staff who knew so many slogans for so many situations. One was, "In a new job, find out who's in charge and give him what he wants." In this new job there was a Chief of Staff, a captain in rank, clearly senior to me but I could see that he was not concerned with the aides. Clearly it was the admiral who was "in charge" and so it was up to me to "give him what he wants."

I had a number of sit-downs with Admiral Minter as we discussed the duties of his Aide and Flag Secretary. Bill Bateman had prepared me well for this so it was easier than it sounds. I would handle all of the Supe's mail, prepare any responses, route any as appropriate, monitor finances for the various social events and share the hosting and escort duties with the Flag Lieutenant. So, I quickly understood that my primary duty was handling correspondence but in addition there would be the hosting and escort functions.

I soon learned that this was not an 8 to 5 job, five days a week. It was more like a seven to eleven job, six or seven days a week and my wife Martha would be involved in many if not most of the social activities.

For my eight year old son David the Naval Academy was a great big playground with about four thousand young men, midshipmen, looking after him. Mark was still too young to enjoy this playground. One day David came home and said he went to baseball practice with the midshipmen and carried Roger Staubach's bat. Another time he went out on the Severn River with the varsity eight-oared shell. Twenty years later, as a young officer in the Marine Corps, David found that his colonel had been one of that very crew, an oarsman in that shell on the Severn River.

The academic year ran from September to June, fall through spring, and in the fall and spring there were busy extracurricular events every Saturday. In the fall it centered around football and every Saturday in which there was a home game the Superintendent hosted about 50 guests for lunch and football, with the guests dining at his quarters, bussing to the Navy-Marine Corps Memorial Stadium and watching the game from the Superintendent's box in which there would be, of course, appropriate libation and finger food.

All this was timed to the minute. Lunch had to be finished at a precise time so that the busses could be loaded with departure at a precise time. The short trip from the Supe's residence to the stadium had been timed previously and a Marine Corps escort made sure the busses arrived at the unloading spot with just enough time to get all of the guests into the Superintendent's box and seated five minutes before kickoff.

Of course there were inevitable snags to this precise military planning and, just like real military planning, there were contingency plans to deal with these unforeseen events.

One Saturday the guests had all finished lunch and were being herded downstairs and into the busses when the Chief-of-Staff realized that one guest, the wife of a retired admiral, was in the ladies room and not in the bus.

He barked out an order, "Martha! Go in there and get Mrs. Jones out of there and onto the bus!"

Martha went into the ladies room and in a few seconds emerged without the woman. The Chief-of-Staff was angry but just before he could bark another order Martha cut him off. "Mrs. Jones is not going anywhere right now. You'll have to leave without her."

The CofS blinked and shifted to his contingency plan. "Martha, you stay with her until she's ready. There's a sedan with a Marine driver waiting. Take her to the stadium." Then, without missing a beat he turned to the bus driver and the Marine escort and barked, "Let's go!"

I was always impressed with the guests that the Supe hosted at the luncheons before the football games and at the many other social events at his quarters. Because of the proximity of the Naval Academy to the nation's capital there would be active duty and retired admirals, generals, politicians and celebrities with spouses at all of the events.

At a lunch before a football game the CofS barked at me, "It's time. Get those people out of the sun porch and into the busses."

On the sun porch was a long table that sat 17 people; eight on each side and one at the head and at this particular luncheon the person sitting at the head of the table was retired Admiral Arleigh Burke, former CNO and big time WW II hero. As I approached, Admiral Burke was in the midst of a sea story, "and the Japanese ships turned together as they—, "He stopped in mid-sentence and looked at me then turned to the others at his table. "When an aide approaches you have to stop what you're doing and get ready to do what he says." With that he looked at me with raised eyebrows.

"I'm very sorry to interrupt, Admiral, but it's time to get on the busses."

The admiral immediately stood with both arms extended upward. "Everybody up! It's time to get on the busses," and with that he took his wife's hand and they left the table.

Things didn't always go so smoothly. In the Supe's box at one football game we aides found that the lock on the inside of the door to the ladies room wasn't working, which meant that as a lady went in to use the room she couldn't secure it from a next would-be user. No problem, contingency plan, we had an aide's wife stand guard outside the ladies room at the door.

After a while, for some reason no one remembered, the wife standing ladies-room-door duty was called away. Inside the ladies room a guest wife was trying to deal with one of those female issues that we best not go into and she felt secure with a door guard at her door. Retired four star admiral Robert Carney had just gotten a drink at the small bar at the rear of the Supe's box and was on his way back to his seat. Along came a guest wife and just as she pulled open the ladies room door there was Admiral Carney whom she had not seen in some time and with whom she most definitely had to exchange pleasantries.

Admiral Carney stood agape, looking first at the newly arrived woman in front of him who was holding the ladies room door wide open while babbling away and then at the woman in the ladies room who was trying desperately to put herself in order. It was a very tense situation until the woman inside the ladies room was able to reach out, grab the door handle and slam the door shut.

The primary function of a flag secretary was to take care of the Supe's correspondence and this I learned to do in the first few weeks of duty at the Naval Academy. A typical day would see me arriving at my office at six or seven AM and the day's mail would either be on my desk or I would go to the mail room and pick-up all the mail addressed to the superintendent by his name. I would also include any other mail addressed to the Supe that I suspected might be of a personal nature but didn't use his name.

The Supe got about 20 or 30 items of mail in an average day and I would sort through them taking appropriate action. A few would be routed to another office in the Naval Academy. Some might go in to the Supe for information. Most needed a reply from the admiral himself and for these I would prepare his response. What does that mean?

There's an expression in the Navy used to tell young staff officers how to perform their duties regarding all forms of paper work; "Completed staff work." It means that if you are dealing with a problem of any kind, simple or complex, your presentation to the boss is to be a complete explanation of the situation along with the justified/recommended solution. In the world of paper-work it would be the solution or the response ready for signature.

Every piece of incoming correspondence that went in to the Supe would be accompanied by a response ready for signature. No roughs seeking comment or approval, no requests for background info or opinion, only a response ready for signature. Read this and sign, Admiral, that's completed staff work. It was the same for two years, for both admirals that I worked for.

Let me jump ahead into my second year at the naval academy, when I was flag sec to RADM Draper Kauffman. He had made it very clear to me that he wanted me to deal with every piece of correspondence that was directed to him, no matter the source or the subject, even if it was marked "Eyes Only" or anything like that. I understood and complied.

One morning the mail included a letter from Admiral Kauffman's mother. Okay, any subject or source, so I opened and read the letter. Nice, it was a mother writing to her son with family info and questions. I can handle this, I thought, and I wrote a two page response as if I were her son, was superintendent of the Naval Academy and I hadn't seen her in some time. Instead of ending with the usual "Sincerely" or "Yours truly" as most of what I prepared for the admiral, this one ended with "Love," and space for him to sign.

The letter went in to the admiral's in-box along with the rest of the day's mail and came out with "Draper" scribbled in the space that I had provided. Completed staff work even answering a letter from his mom.

Now that I've opened up my second year at the Naval Academy, let me go back for a moment for some brief comments to finish my first year, that of being aide and flag sec to RADM Minter. He was a real gentleman and very fine naval officer and it was a pleasure to serve as his aide. His wife was a perfect lady and hostess at the many social events. Martha and I learned a great deal from them and as we approached our second year we both felt confident that that we would be more than able to perform our duties with the new superintendent and his wife.

During the summer of 1965 I took some leave, a rarity for me, but the admin director at the Naval Academy explained to me that I had so many leave days "on the books" that I would soon loose some. It was like, "Use it or loose it," so Martha, our two boys and I rented a small cottage right on the ocean in Long Beach, North Carolina for two weeks.

What a great time we had! We could walk out our front door right onto the beach and a few more steps into the Atlantic Ocean.

One afternoon as I was sitting in a beach chair in the sand I saw some excitement about fifty yards up the beach. As I watched I could see a couple of people dragging something that might be a man from the surf. I ran up to that activity and saw that it was, in fact, a man and he was unconscious or worse as he lay on the sand. Six people stood there looking at the man and no one was doing anything about the situation. I got down and started to give mouth-to-mouth resuscitation.

A number of times I had gone through training for mouth-to-mouth resuscitation and the object of the treatment in every case was a dummy depicting an attractive girl or even a handsome man. But this was real life, no dummy and the object was a middle aged over-weight man. And the dummy used in training did not reveal everything it had eaten in the past hours. I won't go into what our real life patient had eaten but suffice to say that between mouth-to-mouths I would throw up into the sand and that continued until an emergency truck arrived and I was relieved of my effort. After washing off in the convenient nearby surf and as I walked back to the scene one of the on-lookers told me that he was a doctor and he could see that the man was dead when they pulled him from the water. Thanks Doc.

My second year at the U.S. Naval Academy; Aide and Flag Secretary to the Superintendent and the new Superintendent was Rear Admiral Draper Kauffman. I have to tell you the story of Draper Kauffman because his story is one of, and maybe the most dramatic of Navy biographies. I'll try to be brief.

Draper Kauffman graduated from the U.S. Naval Academy in 1936 in the midst of The Great Depression when only the top half of the graduates received commissions. Kauffman was not in the top half due to poor eye-sight so he went to work for a shipping company with offices in New York. As conditions in Europe developed toward war Kauffman became an advocate for the U.S. to join as an ally with France and England.

As war started in Europe he went to the French embassy in Washington and asked if there was some way he could serve. He was told to buy an ambulance and take it to France and there he could serve with his ambulance. He did so and when the Germans were threatening to over-run the Maginot Line he was heavily involved in evacuating French wounded. After being told this would be his last evacuation he insisted on one more trip and was captured by the Germans. The French awarded him the Croix de Guerre.

The Germans didn't want to be involved with an American prisoner so they offered Kauffman a deal; sign a pledge to no longer serve the French and we'll let you go. Kauffman signed, went to England and volunteered for the Royal (British) Navy.

Yes, the Royal Navy had just the thing for this graduate of the U.S. Naval Academy and French veteran; bomb disposal. Kauffman went through the British training and during the period of heavy German bombing in what was called "The Blitz," he disarmed a bomb in downtown London and received the King George V medal.

In 1940 he was able to get leave and visit home in the U.S. for Christmas. Kauffman's father was at that time a rear admiral in the U.S. Navy and the father convinced the son to leave the Royal Navy and return home to the U.S. Navy. The Brits released him and Draper Kauffman got his commission in the U.S. Navy. The main reason that the U.S. Navy wanted him was for his skill at bomb disposal which did not exist in the U.S. Navy.

Kauffman started a school for bomb disposal at Indian Head, Maryland. With the December 7th 1941 attack on Pearl Harbor an unexploded bomb was discovered in downtown Honolulu. Kauffman flew to Hawaii, disarmed the bomb and was awarded the Navy Cross. When there was a need for underwater demolition (Frogmen) Kauffman created that skill for the Navy and so was known as the father of EOD and UDT which later became SEALS. For his performance in beach clearing in the Pacific Island campaign he was awarded a second Navy Cross.

At the end of World War II Commander Kauffman was preparing to leave the Navy and return to civilian life. He was asked to stay in the Navy but he argued that he had never even had a tour of duty in a ship. How could he expect to compete for positions or promotions with Naval Academy classmates who had gone through the war? He was offered command of a destroyer with a very experienced executive officer. He took the offer, did very well, stayed in the Navy and was promoted to captain and then to rear admiral.

Draper Kauffman, a legend in his own time, came back to the U.S. Naval Academy as superintendent in 1965.

Most–almost all–general line officers of career status had made their way through the ranks and the years with specialization in surface warfare, aviation or submarines. There were a few other specialties but in 1965 they were not considered "career enhancing". Although Draper Kauffman was a Naval Academy graduate, he had not come through what anyone would consider to be a "career enhancing" background. But Kauffman had made his own way and to him it was all due to his ability as a leader.

To Kauffman, leadership was his most valuable asset and he considered that his mission as Superintendent was to convey his quality of leadership to the midshipmen of the Naval Academy.

Kauffman had relieved Minter as Superintendent's in the summer of 1965. Very soon after came football season and Navy's first game was at Penn State. Kauffman carried a bottle of champagne as he planned a post-game victory celebration in the locker room. Just before the game and just after the coach had given a pep-talk, Kauffman gave the Navy football team a pep-talk of his own. Remember, his strong suit was leadership and he was exercising it.

Well, Navy lost the football game to Penn State. The uncorked champagne went back to the Naval Academy along with a dejected Draper Kauffman. He sat at his desk shaking his head. "What did I do wrong? Did I say something wrong? I must have said something wrong or else we would have won that game."

I listened to him lament for a while and then offered, "Admiral, have you considered that maybe, just perhaps, that maybe Penn State had a better football team?"

He looked at me, tilted his head considering. "Yes, I did think of that but I knew that if I spoke to them, gave them the proper motivation, they could overcome even a better team. I knew that with proper leadership they would win that game, but I failed."

He failed. To Kauffman it was a matter of leadership; a good leader should be able to overcome any adversity and because of his failure to motivate, his failed leadership, Navy had lost that football game to Penn State.

Later that football season Navy played Notre Dame. The captain of the Navy team was Tom Lynch and by one of those twists of fate the captain of the Notre Dame football team was his brother Bob Lynch. Both were linebackers so they wouldn't be on the field at the same time. The sport press enjoyed this family association and in an interview their mother explained, "I had two sons; one for god and one for country."

Bob Lynch graduated from Notre Dame, played some professional football and then became a sports agent. Tom Lynch graduated from the Naval Academy, served his required time and then joined his brother as a sports agent. After a couple of years Tom decided he wanted to be back in the Navy. He was accepted and ordered as Executive Officer in USS BRONSTEIN, a DE in Destroyer Squadron Twenty Three. Guess who was commodore of that squadron? That's right, you guessed it. Me.

Peggy Kauffman, Draper's wife, was very active in all the events at the Naval Academy. A gracious hostess, she worked closely with the Social Secretary to ensure that the proper people were invited to the many social events. Peggy had a very close cousin, Barbara who was married to a first term congressman from Texas and that couple were often invited guests of the Superintendent at various events. We aides looked after all of the Supe's guests with much care and tenderness but Peggy's cousin and her congressman husband received special attention.

Usually, after a day or evening of busy social events Admiral Kauffman would ask his aides to stay a while, relax and have a drink so we could talk over the events. Often he would regale us with details of his storied past. On one such evening he told us that when his father was an admiral he had learned that an aide was, from that time on a part of the family, like a son to the admiral the aide served.

And being a part of that family lasted forever. So, we aides were and always would be part of his, Draper Kauffman's family.

The flag lieutenant spoke up. "So, Admiral, that means we're related to Peggy's cousin who's married to that congressman, right?"

Kauffman responded, "That's right; you aides are related to Congressman George Bush and his wife Barbara."

And so, ever since I was Aide and Flag Secretary to Rear Admiral Draper Kauffman, I and all my family have been and still are related to the George Bush family including two governors of states, two that served as President of the United States and a most popular wife of a president, Barbara Bush.

Back to my early time at the Naval Academy: The officer that had been ordered-in to fill the billet of Commandant of Midshipmen when Charles Minter moved up to be Superintendent was Captain Sheldon Kinney and this new Commandant had a career almost as dramatic as had the Superintendent. Let me give you a biographical sketch of Sheldon Kinney. Sheldon Kinney dropped out of high school in 1935, enlisted in the Navy and served aboard USS OMAHA and then as a signalman aboard USS NEW YORK. In 1937 he was selected from the fleet to attend the U.S. Naval Academy. He graduated with honors in 1941 and immediately went on sea duty as the U.S. was preparing for World War II.

He served aboard USS STURTEVANT on North Atlantic convoy duty and received the Navy and Marine Corps Medal for heroism for diving from his ship to rescue two downed aviators. Later, STURTEVANT was sunk and he survived by floating on a bag of coffee beans.

In 1943, Kinney took command of USS EDSALL and became the youngest commanding officer of a destroyer-type ship. After that, still a lieutenant, he commanded USS BRONSTEIN and received the Navy Cross for sinking five German U-boats in one continuous night battle. Later it was found that he had sunk three, disabled a fourth and the fifth one got away. Still, his three kills and one damaged were exceptional. In addition to the Navy Cross he received the Legion of Merit and his ship, BRONSTEIN, received the Presidential

Unit Citation, the highest of unit awards. Admiral Robert Carney, later CNO, described BRONSTEIN's fight that night as "the most concentrated and successful antisubmarine action by a U.S. Navy ship during World War II."

For the rest of WW II, Kinney served as the Anti-Submarine Warfare Officer on the staff of Commander Destroyers Atlantic. He then commanded USS LUDLOW and USS TAYLOR during the Korean War. He also commanded USS MITSCHER which has the distinction of being the Navy's first guided missile frigate and then he served on the staff of Commander, U.S. Naval Forces, Europe.

During the Vietnam War Kinney commanded USS MISSISSINEWA, Amphibious Squadron 12 and then Cruiser Destroyer Flotilla 11 in Operation Sea Dragon. His final command was as Commander Cruiser Destroyer Forces Pacific (COMCRUDESPAC).

He graduated in 1960 from the Naval War College and later received a Master of Science in International Affairs degree and a Juris Doctors degree from George Washington University. From 1963 to 1967 he was Commandant of Midshipmen of the U.S. Naval Academy which is where I met him.

In 1972 after 38 years of naval service Kinney retired and became president of SUNY Maritime College. He remained in that position until 1982 when he assisted in the founding of, and then presided over the International Maritime Organization of the United Nations at Malmo, Sweden. He also served as special adviser to the Secretary General of the IMO in London.

Kinney's other military decorations included the Legion of Merit (Combat V) with two Gold Stars, the Bronze Star (Combat V) and the Navy Commendation Medal. The Soviet Union awarded him the Order of the Patriotic War First Class and the Polish Government in Exile awarded him the Gold Cross of Merit for saving the Polish treasury.

There's another great story about Kinney taking the Polish gold treasury from England to the U.S. for safe keeping during WW II.

So there was I, a guy who had stumbled through college and then came from the amphibs into the real Navy, working closely with two true legends of the Navy. It doesn't get any better than that!

If you look back a few paragraphs into the bio of Sheldon Kinney you'll see that he had a Master of Science in International Affairs (MSIA) degree from George Washington University earned while he was at the Naval War College. That's the short story. The full story is that Kinney had been taking the "extra curricula" program offered by GWU when he was a student at the Naval War College but he became involved in a another separate program and so he was one course short of completing the GWU program when he graduated from the Naval War College. A number of years later, when he came to the Naval Academy he explored the possibility of completing the GWU program.

The pundits of GWU told him that if he could get a minimum of fifteen students to enroll, GWU would license a Naval Academy professor to teach one appropriate course and Kinney would get his MSIA degree. The other students that Kinney would recruit might, some day, be fortunate enough to be ordered to the Naval War College and there they would have one course already completed toward the MSIA degree.

I signed up for the course that Kinney had arranged and immediately learned that first I had to be accepted into the MSIA program and that involved a review of my college transcripts. Uh oh, not good. It took some time but just before the course at the Naval Academy was to begin I was notified that I had been accepted into the MSIA program on a "conditional" basis. Conditional meaning that only if I received a grade of A in this course could I be accepted into the program. And if I got that A and only then, it meant that I could complete the program and get a masters degree, when and if I were ever to go to the Naval War College. Many ifs.

I received a grade of A in the course; Organization and Function of the United Nations and my next duty assignment was to the Naval War College.

Shortly before I left the Naval Academy I went through a rough estimate with my secretary and we found that in my two years of duty as Aide and Flag Secretary I had prepared more than six thousand individual items of correspondence for the Superintendent and some of those were copied many times.

CHAPTER TWENTY EIGHT

U. S. NAVAL WAR COLLEGE
NEWPORT, RHODE ISLAND

1966–1967

A few lines from Chapter Six of that good
book; the novel Shellback:

*"—the real reason the Naval War College is in Newport goes back to
the days when the millionaires had their summer places here. You
know, the mansions on Bellevue Avenue?" Kim nodded. "They're
called cottages. Well, the millionaires left their wives and kids in the
cottages every summer and they went back to New York to spend the
hot summer being entertained by their mistresses. Meanwhile, back
at the ranch, or in this case the cottages in Newport, the wives tried
to outdo each other with elaborate parties. There being a shortage of
appropriate gentlemen for their parties, someone got the idea to invite
officers from the Navy ships that visited here. That worked nicely but
the ships weren't always here. So, the ladies pressured their husbands*

to pressure the Navy to see to it that there was an adequate supply of officers for their parties. Now, the husbands were having a great time avoiding the hot summer days in New York with their cool companions and they, the rich husbands, would do anything to keep their wives happy in Newport. So, the millionaires leaned on the Secretary of the Navy, a school for officers was started at Newport and a constant supply of stiff starched white uniforms was available for the gracious elegant lawn parties on Bellevue Avenue."

Well, remember a novel is fiction so that may not be the true origin of the Naval War College in Newport, Rhode Island, but it makes a good story.

The Navy had sent me to Newport duty three times before; first to OCS, then to the staff of COMDESLANT and then with a change of home port in STICKELL after the FRAM conversion, so I knew my way around that fair little city pretty well. More important, I had been married in that second Newport duty and so Martha had been with me for the DESLANT time. She knew the living/housing situation of Newport better than most and I had learned to leave that to her.

She found us a very nice brand new split-level house and we bought it with the expectation, or maybe just the hope that my next duty, after the one academic year at the Naval War College, would be in a ship home-ported in Newport. Remember, back when my time on the DESLANT/CRUDESLANT staff was drawing to the end, I was hoping for my next duty to be executive officer of a DEALEY class DE in Newport. I was a lieutenant then. Now, as a lieutenant commander I hoped to get command of one of those DEs. Buying a house for what might be only one academic year was a little risky but if command of a DE home-ported in Newport followed that could mean three years in that nice new split-level.

While we're talking about housing here, allow me to jump to the end of that academic year at the Naval War College: Toward the end of that school year I received my orders, not to command of a DE in Newport but to be executive officer of a DLG home-ported in Long Beach, California. Martha and I had not yet spoken of selling our house when I was approached by a classmate who had just received his orders to a Newport-based ship and he was interested in buying our house. That afternoon he and his wife came to look over the house and in a few minutes, while they were still looking, they announced that they wanted to buy it. We had to come up with a price right there on the spot. We did, they agreed and we were free to move to California.

The Naval War College offered two basic courses with each structured for particular ranks. As a lieutenant commander I was ordered to the Command and Staff Course. The other was the Naval Warfare Course which was for more senior officers like Navy captains and Marine colonels. Also, there was a course for foreign officers and a War Game Center.

The curriculum of the Command and Staff Course was very well formulated, very interesting and provided graduate level educational insight into the administration and operational matters of the Navy.

In addition, the Naval War College offered opportunity on a voluntary basis to earn a master's degree from George Washington University. To earn this masters degree a student had to complete either of the basic academic programs of the Naval War College and, in addition, pass four courses provided by GWU and write a thesis. Guess what? That's the very program I had joined in my previous duty at the Naval Academy, the one that Sheldon Kinney had coerced GWU into providing him with; the one course he needed to complete the program. So, having already been accepted in the graduate program and with one course completed (with a grade of A), I was now able to complete the program and receive the MSIA degree; Master of Science in International Affairs, heavy stuff for a guy that had struggled through colleges with more concern about basketball than academics.

In addition to the academics there was busy social activity at the Naval War College and Martha and I had always been active participants in the social activities of the various duty stations. In addition to the many get-to-gathers with the Command and Staff classmates, Martha and I volunteered to join in with "mixers" held by students of the Foreign Officers Course. At our first such party we noticed that a heavy-set gruff looking guy was by himself with drink in hand off to the side of the room while all the other foreign officers and their wives were in groups, in heavily animated conversation and hearty laughter.

Remember back in our early DESLANT party time when we were alone and I was ready to leave but Martha insisted that we join in and meet everyone? Well, here at this party we could see that this loner needed some encouragement. We went over to him, introduced ourselves, asked him this and that and forced the conversation. Little by little we learned that he was a Greek navy commander, his wife and children were to join him in Newport and he had rented a furnished house. He was very shy but Martha was able to get him to talk a little more as time wore on. Then it was time to leave. We said our goodbyes with much good wishes.

Scroll ahead one month. We received a very nice invitation for cocktails and dinner at the home of Commander and Mrs. Constantine Stamoulis. Constantine was a different man; outgoing, personable, charming and talkative, all this change because his wife and children were with him. Because we had sought him out and forced a small measure of hospitality upon him we were included in a number of social activities of the Foreign Officers Course after that. A number of years later I learned that Stamoulis had retired as a rear admiral of the Greek navy.

At another of the foreign officer's parties we got to know a commander from the Dominican Republic. He was very outgoing and talkative with a heavy Spanish accent, clearly the opposite of our Greek friend; he told continuous stories of his tiny country and navy. With a small group around him he described how a large portion of his nation had been wasteland, good for nothing and in such a small country they had to make use of everything they had. It was essential that they find a way to make this land productive, but how?

They found that the best people in the world at irrigation were the "you people" and the commander went on and on about how a group of "you people" had come to the Dominican Republic and in a short time they converted wasteland into productive farmland. On and on he went telling about these "you people" that had worked this miracle in his country. I listened to his description of what these "you people" had accomplished but could not understand who these experts in irrigation were until he made mention that in their own country they had turned the desert into farmland. The desert? Could he mean the Middle East? Could he be talking about Israelis?

When he stopped talking for a brief moment I asked, "Were these people Jews from Israel?"

He looked at me surprised that anyone hadn't understood. "Yes, that's what I've been saying, the "you people." To him they were the Jew people.

There was a requirement both in the basic Command and Staff Course and in the GWU masters degree program for a thesis and the same thesis would satisfy both programs. What to write about? I mulled over this for some time. Remember back in one of the early chapters of this tome I told about my uncle Moe Domes who had gone to Spain for the Spanish Civil War in the 1930s? I always had an interest, been curious about that conflict and so I decided that I would satisfy that interest and curiosity, as well as the thesis requirements, by writing about the Spanish Civil War.

My choice of subject matter was accepted by both programs and George Washington University arranged for a professor from Yale to be my proctor. He came to the Naval War College a number of times to discuss my project and when I finished he gave his blessing and I received credit for completing the thesis requirement for both programs.

My research for the thesis consisted of reading everything I could get my hands on concerning the Spanish war but the highlight of the bibliography was an interview with an actual veteran of that conflict. My Uncle Moe, Maurice Dumas in Spain, had always been very hesitant to talk about his time in Spain and just because I was writing a thesis didn't change his attitude. It was tough to get him to say much but he was impressed with what I had learned from my reading and he did give me some information. He knew or knew of most of the individuals that I had read of. He had participated in some of the key battles. He saw Ernest Hemmingway a few times "always drunk," and he knew of the heavy losses of the Abraham Lincoln and George Washington brigades so that the two international units were combined into one. He knew of the woman "La Paisionara" who chanted the battle cry, "They shall not pass."

The title of my thesis was "The Defeat of Communism in the Spanish Civil War" and the theory behind it was that there were three communist interests involved; Spanish, Soviet Union and International. All three were not defeated. Spanish communism definitely was defeated as Franco took over the country. The Soviet Union was pleased to be rid of many foreign intruders and to be the recipient of the Spanish gold treasury. International communism had demonstrated that they had wide support, could recruit all over the world and were willing to fight where-ever necessary.

My Yale proctor was "not sure" that he agreed with my theory of three communisms but he respected my analysis and condescended to give it more thought.

Toward the end of the school year the lieutenant commander detailer came to the Naval War College to discuss the next duty assignments with students. All had submitted their preferences some time before and now they would learn if they would get their choice or if the Navy wanted them somewhere else. I had asked for command of a DEALEY class DE home-ported in Newport and I knew I was qualified. For me it was a simple request. I had been "Qualified for command of destroyers" since my time in ROBERT A. OWENS, had command of STICKELL for almost a year during FRAM conversion and had twice served as her executive officer.

The detailer, as the representative of the Bureau of Naval Personnel, saw things differently; to him I had not had a full tour of duty as executive officer and time as CO during FRAM couldn't count. My qualification for command of destroyers put me in line for that duty but that would be offered to me later in my career. So, I would not be getting command of a DEALEY in Newport or anywhere else. As the detailer saw it, I would be going to a bigger ship to complete a full tour as executive officer.

What ship? Where? The detailer asked me for preferences. To that time all of my sea duty had been in the Atlantic, involved in the fringes of the Cold War. Now I could see an opportunity to get into the Pacific and the Viet Nam war so I asked for a combatant ship in the Pacific. The detailer had just the thing for me; executive officer of a DLG home-ported in Long Beach, California. The commanding officer was a captain in rank and the executive officer billet called for a commander. I was a lieutenant commander and would be in a commander billet. It sounded good. It sounded familiar. I remembered well that a few years ago as a lieutenant I went to a lieutenant commander billet in a destroyer and in this very meeting with the detailer I was told that some how that didn't count. Would this count? The detailer assured me that this would be a fine career assignment.

So, my next duty would be as executive officer of USS England (DLG-22) home-ported in Long Beach, California.

CHAPTER TWENTY NINE

THE BEST TOWN IN THAT
PART OF THE STATE

1967

A career Navy man gets transferred every few years and sometimes the transfer is from coast to coast across this great and great big country, like my transfer from the Naval War College in Newport, Rhode Island to a ship in Long Beach, California. The Navy takes care of the movement of household goods and the family can drive across the country and sometimes that drive is through Iowa.

Like most Navy transfers, this one took place during the summer and on a hot day on a long straight stretch of good highway through cornfields and hog pens the engine overheated. I slowed and coasted into the small Iowa town of Onawa, into the service station which was next to the diner, next to the motel on the three block long Main Street. I learned that my car radiator had a leak and I learned about Arnold.

"Best you and yer wife get a room at the motel. Marge and Charlie run the best motel in this part of the state and Arnold will fix your radiator tomorrow," advised the service station owner. Seems that Arnold had the only radiator repair shop in town or in any other town in this part of the state but Arnold wasn't working that day. Seems Arnold and his friends had been drinking late last night and Arnold was ill; diarrhea, so no radiators would be fixed today. A new radiator would have to come from Sioux City, cost a mint and take 3 to 5 days.

In our overheated car we crept to the motel and were welcomed by Marge and Charlie who expected us. "Oh don't worry. Arnold will fix your radiator tomorrow. He's got diarrhea today, drinking last night, but he'll be in the shop in the morning." Noting a Naval Academy plaque on the wall behind the desk, we learned that their son was a midshipman and Marge and Charlie learned that I was in the Navy. We were doubly welcomed into the best motel in that part of the state.

For dinner Marge sent us to the finest restaurant in that part of the state, tablecloths and all, middle of Main Street, where we had the best pork chops that one could get in that part of the state. Great pork chops! The owner, who was also the chef and his wife, who was also the waitress, both knew us as the Navy people with the radiator problem staying at the motel and told us, "Don't worry. Arnold will fix you up tomorrow morning. He's got diarrhea today. Out drinking last night. But he's the best radiator repair guy in this part of the state."

Next morning, early, we were sent by Marge to the diner for breakfast and were greeted with, "Oh, you're the Navy folks staying at the motel waiting for Arnold to fix your radiator, aren't you? Well, don't worry. Arnold was sick yesterday, diarrhea, out drinking, but he'll be at his shop this morning. He'll fix you up. He's the best radiator guy in this part of the state." There were at least a dozen customers in the diner and every one of them knew that we were the Navy couple from the motel waiting for Arnold, who had diarrhea, to fix our leaking radiator, and that we had pork chops last night at the fine place. A weathered farmer in bib overalls and tattered straw wide-brimmed hat told us that this diner had the best breakfasts in this part of the state.

In that diner we met his honor, the Mayor of Onawa, who ran a trucking business on the next street and knew that we were the Navy people staying at the motel waiting for Arnold to fix our radiator and that we had pork chops at the fine place last night. The Mayor told us that Onawa had the widest Main Street of any town in that part of the state and assured us that Arnold, who had diarrhea from drinking, was the best radiator repair man in this part of the state.

Arnold was at his shop right at eight and was expecting us; those Navy people from the motel who had pork chops at the fine place, were at the diner this morning and met the Mayor. Arnold fixed the radiator like new and we were on our way. It cost me less than I could have gotten it fixed anywhere else. Arnold surly is the best radiator repairman in that part of the state and maybe the entire state or anywhere else.

Just before we left his shop Arnold told us that he had been ill the day before, "diarrhea from too much drinking," he said, "But please don't tell anyone. I wouldn't want anyone in town to know."

Next time you're driving across this great country, across Iowa, be sure to stop in Onawa. You'll meet the finest people in what has to be the best town in that part of the state.

CHAPTER THIRTY

USS ENGLAND (DLG 22)

1967–1969

In September of 1967 Lieutenant Commander Stuart D. Landersman reported for duty as Executive Officer on board USS ENGLAND (DLG 22) at the ship's home port; Long Beach, California. At the time Stu reported to the ship the DLG designation stood for Guided Missile Frigate and USS ENGLAND was one of nine such ships of the LEAHY class. Originally, when the ships of that class were first commissioned, the DL portion of that class designation stood for Destroyer Leader but soon after DL was changed to Frigate by Secretary of the Navy directive. Still later, long after Stu Landersman had left the ship and had gone on to other duties, he was instrumental in a number of ship class designation changes that included the LEAHY class ships and USS ENGLAND became a Guided Missile Cruiser; CLG 22. Also, as part of the ship class designation changes that made some frigates into cruisers, destroyer escorts became frigates, but that's a story for later in this book.

Many people have assumed that USS ENGLAND (DLG 22) was named for the nation England but that was not so. USS ENGLAND (DLG 22) was the second ship named to honor Ensign John Charles England who was killed at Pearl Harbor December 7th 1941.

Ensign England was from the state of Arizona and was serving on board the battleship USS ARIZONA at the time of the attack.

The first USS ENGLAND (DE 635) was credited with sinking six Japanese submarines in May of 1944. At the commissioning of the second USS ENGLAND the Secretary of the Navy said, "There'll always be an England–in the U.S. Navy."

Sorry, Mister Secretary, but in later years when USS ENGLAND (CLG 22) was decommissioned there was no England in the U.S. Navy and there hasn't been one since.

Navy units; ships, boats and aircraft, performed a broad spectrum of operations during the Viet Nam conflict. In South Viet Nam there were specially built boats that operated in the maze of inland waterways and along the coast shallow draft Navy and Coast Guard ships interdicted junks. Just a little more off the coast destroyers and gun cruisers maintained the "gun line," providing naval gunfire support to troops ashore and interdicting Viet Cong. Further out in the Gulf of Tonkin were three SAR (Search and Rescue) stations and even further out were the aircraft carriers in Whiskey, Xray and Yankee stations. Cruisers and destroyers conducted periodic gun strikes against North Viet Nam often coordinated with air strikes.

Ships of the LEAHY Class, like USS ENGLAND, were known as "Double Enders" because they had Terrier missile launchers on their bow and stern. Clearly these were ships built for anti air warfare as their only guns were two twin 3 inch mounts, one mount on each side. Their anti air configuration included the most sophisticated up-to-date radars, fire control systems and combat information processing systems then available. That information processing system was called Naval Tactical Data System (NTDS).

These double enders were not at all suited for inshore or gun line operations but were ideal for duty in those three SAR stations. Why? Because those stations were more than search and rescue; they took turns performing the very complex function of monitoring the carrier aircraft that went in across the beach to Viet Nam and those returning, so that they could identify any "strangers" amid the returnees. That stranger just might be a North Viet Nam MIG attempting to attack an aircraft carrier on Yankee Station or a destroyer on the gun line.

How effective were those anti air defensive procedures? In all the years of the Viet Nam conflict no North Viet Nam aircraft ever went "feet wet" and survived. That means that any and every MIG that flew out over the Gulf of Tonkin was shot down; the pilot was killed, every one. Not many tried.

The SAR stations were named North SAR and South SAR, located in the Gulf of Tonkin as their name implies and between them was the third station with the unique moniker PIRAZ which stood for Positive Identification Radar Advisory Zone. The PIRAZ ship performed the aircraft accountability function backed up by the other two SAR ships and the three ships rotated the stations and the duties as each ship had the ability to perform both the PIRAZ and SAR duties.

U.S. Navy pilots were instructed that if their planes were damaged and they had to punch or bail out, to try to go feet wet, to get out over the Gulf of Tokin because in the Gulf were resources to recover them. That was the SAR function and on her previous just completed deployment USS ENGLAND had set the record for rescues. On the door to her Combat Information Center were painted 19 cartoon figures each depicting a pilot in the water with arm raised.

When Stu Landersman reported aboard USS ENGLAND in Long Beach the ship had recently returned from a six month deployment to the Viet Nam conflict. USS ENGLAND had operated in the three SAR stations including the PIRAZ function and the main objective of the ship now was to get ready to go again across the big pond and perform again the PIRAZ and SAR duties.

The commanding officer of USS ENGLAND was Captain Robert H. Ewing and he had received many kudos for the outstanding performance of the ship on her previous deployment. Commanding officers of DLGs were considered "front runners" in the highly competitive selection for promotion to rear admiral and so Bob Ewing was "looking good" for that selection.

The DLGs of that time were organized in destroyer squadrons, each serving as flagship for a destroyer squadron commander. It presented an awkward situation as both the ship's CO and the embarked squadron commander were senior captains in rank, both in their major command and yet one worked for or came under the other. Most of the time it worked well, but not always.

A change of command ceremony is when, as the name implies, an officer in command is relieved of that command by another officer. On board USS ENGLAND the squadron commander had just been relieved, the ceremony was over and the official guests were enjoying refreshment in the wardroom. It was almost time for the crew's mid-day meal and the galley was busy preparing lunch.

Suddenly the ship's general alarm sounded followed by, "Fire, fire, fire in the galley! All hands man your general quarters stations!"

The wardroom guests looked at each other in surprise and question. Stu stood in the center of the wardroom. "If I could have your attention please? There is a fire in the galley just below us. There's no cause for alarm but it would be best if all guests were to depart the ship now. Thank you." The guests all departed as did the former squadron commander and the brand new squadron commander with their families and the flotilla commander, a rear admiral in rank who had been the speaker at the change of command ceremony.

It would seem that a fire in the deep fat fryer in the ship's galley would be a manageable situation with limited damage but in this case the fryer was filled with cooking oil and the oil was burning; burning hot and fierce. It took all the fire fighting resources of the ship's damage control team including assistance from the DLG moored alongside to extinguish the fire.

It was then discovered that in the overhead immediately above the deep fat fryer was a major cable run that included 35 cables involved with almost every combat and information system of the ship. The galley fire had rendered the ship almost completely out of service so instead of a mere replacement and repair of some galley equipment the ship was in need of major repair and that meant time in the Long Beach Naval Shipyard, significant time.

During the shipyard time the commanding officer was relieved; Captain George A. Mitchell relieved Captain Robert H. Ewing. Stu as executive officer had gotten along very well with Ewing and that continued with Mitchell. Both captains were "front runners" who had previous command of destroyers and destroyer divisions. Both were Naval Academy grads who had gotten into the very end of World War II, then Korea and now Viet Nam.

As mentioned earlier, Bob Ewing had just completed a very successful deployment to the Viet Nam conflict with many rescues and kudos; good. Then there was a galley fire during the reception following the change of command of the squadron commander; not good.

There's a strange and informal policy in the Navy that borders on formality; the commanding officer of a ship is responsible for everything that happens in and to his ship and even to and by the men of his ship, on or off his ship. Now everyone knew that the captain had nothing to do with the deep fat fryer and certainly had nothing to do with the damage caused by the fire, but to have a fire during the squadron commander's change of command with the flotilla commander on board was not good.

In a few years that followed the USS ENGLAND galley fire four other DLGs of the same class with the same deep fat fryers had the same fires but Bob Ewing was not selected for promotion to rear admiral.

Repair of the galley and wiring damage took longer than expected and with the ship in the shipyard the type commander decided it was best to use that opportunity to upgrade some of the combat and information systems. That added more time and so USS ENGLAND came under a policy that required the ship to undergo Refresher Training before she could be returned to full operational employment.

Refresher training took place in San Diego and with completion of all shipyard work USS ENGLAND sailed south to that lovely city and moored to a buoy in the bay. As Captain Mitchell departed the ship by his gig (boat) to make his official call on the admiral, he told Stu that a pilot and two tugs would be at the ship at 1000 to move the ship to a pier at the naval station. At 0945 a tug arrived and made up to the bow. At 1000 the pilot had not arrived and at 1015 still no pilot. Stu recalled from college days a generally accepted rule that students would wait ten minutes for an instructor and 20 minutes for a professor but in this case, how long should one wait for a pilot? He waited the 20 minutes that a professor was entitled to, broke (undid) the mooring to the buoy and with one tug on the bow proceeded up the channel to the Naval Station.

Stu had made a number of landings in past ships and so this landing at the pier went fairly well in a twin-screw ship with a tug on the bow. When Captain Mitchell came on board he was surprised and pleased that Stu had not waited for the pilot and he commented that not many executive officers would have shown that much initiative.

For most of the history of the Navy the highest rank or rate of an enlisted man was Chief Petty Officer and sailors that reached that level were referred to simply as "Chief." With the combining of military services into the Defense Department following World War II it was found that the Army had two enlisted ranks or levels above what would be the highest of the Navy. The new Air Force, as an outgrowth of the Army had the same enlisted structure as the Army. All three had to be the same so it was determined that the Navy would create two higher enlisted levels. Thus were created the enlisted ranks or rates in the Navy as Senior Chief Petty Officer and Master Chief Petty Officer. They soon became called, "Senior" and "Master."

In USS ENGLAND the most senior of enlisted men was Master Chief Petty Officer James Moats. His specialty was misselman. He knew that he was the most senior and he also knew that there was nobody in or around this Navy that could tell him how to run his missile house. Ordinarily this would be very nice for a ship to have a real expert in charge of the "main battery" but USS ENGLAND was about to undergo refresher training in which a team of experts would come aboard and tell the ship's personnel how to run their ship.

Jay Hurlburt, the Weapons Officer, came to Stu with an idea and then the two of them went to the Captain. They proposed that in order for the missile division of their ship to get through refresher training with the least problems it would be best to send Master Chief Petty Officer James Moats on leave for the entire five weeks of refresher training.

Captain Mitchell thought it over for a few seconds then agreed. Moats went on leave, the ship sailed through refresher training and when Moats came back he changed everything in his missile house back to what it had been before refresher training.

With refresher training completed USS ENGLAND was ready to deploy to the Western Pacific (WESTPAC), to join the Seventh Fleet and to participate in the Viet Nam conflict. Most of the crew were the same men that had performed the duties of North SAR, South SAR and PIRAZ on the previous WESTPAC deployment and they were ready to do those functions again. They were not to be disappointed as those were the roles of the ship as soon as she reached the Gulf of Tonkin.

A couple of months before the deployment Stu had taken three days leave and with Martha went to Las Vegas for a rare vacation. They stayed at Caesars Palace, saw two nice shows, ate in fine restaurants and did a little gambling. Breaking even for the trip wasn't bad as long as a good time was had and the Landersmans had a very good time.

Two months into the deployment Stu realized that he still had some of the literature from that Las Vegas trip including the address of Caesars Palace. Why not, he thought? Why not give it a try?

Off went a letter on USS ENGLAND letterhead describing the ship, the deployment and the need for recreation. If Caesars Palace could spare some of those used decks of cards it would be much appreciated by the crew of this U.S. Navy warship currently operating in the Gulf of Tonkin.

A month later a large box, a carton arrived on the ship with much more than a few decks of cards. Caesars Palace had sent everything that would be needed for a Casino Night. Not only two dozen decks of cards but a roulette wheel, a dozen pairs if dice, table covers for black-jack, roulette and craps, visors and arm bands for dealers, gaming posters, chips, even Bingo and much more.

Along with what almost everyone learns about duty in a Navy ship, Stu had learned that U.S. Navy men will always surprise you with what they know and what they can do, even and especially when it comes to innovative non-regulation matters. In this case it only took a turnover of the gaming material carton to Master Chief Petty Officer Moats and soon there was a committee and a full Casino Night was planned. There were sailors that knew every game; dealers, croupiers and callers. The Supply Officer printed script so that for twenty dollars a player could get a hundred dollars of script as the maximum he could lose. Winners could turn in script for real money at the conclusion of the evening. It was agreed that any profit from the gaming would go to the ships recreation fund.

Like in all gaming there were only a few winners. Over-all the Casino Night made some money for the recreation fund but most important; USS ENGLAND sailors had a great time and could brag that they were the only ship that had a Casino Night right in the middle of the Gulf of Tonkin during the Viet Nam War.

Thank you Caesars Palace.

Little known, hell, totally unknown to anyone in the Navy, the State Department had, shortly after the Korean War, formed a program called "Sister City." In this program cities in the U.S. were matched with cities in Japan. The cities thus paired would communicate, exchange visits and share cultural memorabilia. Who knew?

Stu Landersman soon learned that George Mitchell, the commanding officer of USS ENGLAND was a native son of the city of Albuquerque, New Mexico. So, you might ask, what does that matter? It mattered to the deployment of USS ENGLAND because George Mitchell knew very well of this Sister City program, had participated in it in Albuquerque and had notified the mayor of Sasebo that a representative of their sister city would be visiting.

As USS ENGLAND approached her pier in the southern Japanese city of Sasebo the ship was welcomed as had few others. On the pier was the short stout mayor wearing his huge western ten-gallon cowboy hat, the entire city council, waving geisha girls and a musical combo. That started a series of social events all intended to welcome the son of their sister city.

After a three day visit that had been filled with Japanese social and cultural events it was time to depart. Just as in the arrival, the departure was a ceremonial send-off with mayor, city council and geisha girls bowing in the traditional style. Captain Mitchell stood on the starboard wing of the bridge clad in a beautiful Japanese kimono bowing as were those on the pier.

Then it was back to the Gulf of Tonkin, to North SAR station.

At 0430 in the dark of an early morning, surface search radar picked up three high speed contacts heading toward USS ENGLAND in North SAR station. The ship went to General Quarters while trying to identify the approaching contacts. The "shotgun," a destroyer paired with the DLG to provide naval gun support on the SAR station, moved between USS ENGLAND and the approaching boats.

In CIC, Operations Officer George Fitzgibbons exchanged some gibberish by radio with the boats then looked at the Captain. They nodded to each other and the Captain gave orders to stand down and be ready to receive the approaching boats alongside.

USS ENGLAND people learned that these were South Vietnamese attack boats conducting highly classified raids into North Vietnam on special missions to capture specific North Vietnam personnel. These boats had been instructed to approach ships on North SAR station only if they were in an emergency situation and these boats were indeed in trouble. So sensitive were these operations that in ships that were to serve on North SAR only the CO and one other officer were to know of these operations. USS ENGLAND remained at General Quarters the entire time these boats were alongside so as to limit the crew from seeing the boats and what went on.

In destroyer-type ships the only hospital-type facility is a closet-sized sick bay run by the ship's "Doc," a chief hospital corpsman cleared for independent duty. Little known by most destroyermen; the ship's mess deck, where the enlisted men eat is designated as the emergency battle dressing station. There were 20 tables in the mess deck and in an emergency situation each of these tables could be used for a patient. The ships on SAR stations in the Gulf of Tonkin each carried a doctor for just such rescue situations.

USS ENGLAND stretcher bearers carried 21 badly wounded Vietnamese from their boats to tables on the mess deck, putting one on the sick bay examining table. Doctor Ted Grandolfo functioned in a triage mode, seeking out and giving care to the most needy. Every table with every wounded patient had an IV suspended from the overhead. The doctor was assisted by the ship's chief corpsman and the chief corpsman from the shotgun destroyer. Five dead were placed in body bags.

Tiger Chang was commodore of the attack boats. He was walking with a bloody flesh wound on his shoulder and most significant; his left eye-ball was out of its eye socket, hanging just above his left cheek. The doctor determined that he could not replace the eye-ball so he fashioned a basket-like sling of moist bandage and adhesive tape that held the eye-ball in position. This was done with hope that a hospital facility might be able to save the eye. With his eye-ball in the sling and a bloody bandage on his shoulder, Tiger Chang kept moving among his wounded men giving them encouragement.

All the while these medical procedures were ongoing the three attack boats were moored to the fantail of USS ENGLAND where it was learned that the mission of these boats had been to bring back to Danang three specific prisoners. Clearly the boats had encountered significant opposition. They were severely shot-up and there were dead and wounded. The inboard boat, the one directly alongside USS ENGLAND was the flagship of the commodore; Tiger Chang. On that boat were three prisoners sitting on the deck with backs against a deck house. All three were bound, gagged and blindfolded. They didn't move or make a sound the entire time the boats were alongside. Sitting on the deck with their backs against a deck house directly across from the prisoners were three of Tiger Chang's men, each one holding an automatic weapon pointed directly at the prisoner in front of him. These guards also never moved or said a word, never took their eyes from their prisoner and kept their weapons pointed directly at their prisoner.

Aircraft carriers have small hospitals on board and with daylight helicopters from the carriers started to arrive and by 0900 the airlift of wounded was completed. Doctor Grandolfo had tried convincing Tiger Chang to go to the carrier and try to save that dangled eye but the commodore refused. Clearly, Tiger Chang wanted to be seen coming back into Danang, himself wounded, having successfully completed his mission despite suffering heavy losses.

In USS ENGLAND it was well past breakfast time, the crew had not eaten and they were still at a modified General Quarters. The mess deck was indeed a mess with lots of bloody dressings and IV remains. It had to be picked-up, hosed down, mopped up and disinfected before it could serve as a dining room. There was no breakfast in USS ENGLAND that day, maybe something closer to brunch.

As part of the normal daily routine in the ship, when it was quiet with no search or rescue at hand, the Captain liked to have a bridge game after dinner and it fell upon the executive officer to have three bridge players at the Captain's cabin each evening. Some times it was difficult to find three so Stu would be one of the three. Early on Stu had learned Doctor Grandolfo was a bridge player and could be relied upon as one of the three and Stu often joked that the doctor's most valuable contribution to the deployment was to be one of the bridge players for the Captain. Then along came Tiger Chang and his three boats that put the doctor in triage mode. Stu never again joked that Doctor Grandolfo was only on board to play bridge.

Remember back in her previous deployment USS ENGLAND had set the unofficial record for search and rescue with 18 pilots pulled from the drink? Well, on this deployment USS ENGLAND filled more than that on her mess deck with 21 and a few more walking wounded.

Must be some sort of record there, right?

CHAPTER THIRTY ONE

USS HEPBURN (DE 1055)

1969–1971

Napoleon said, "A man will give his life for a piece of ribbon," and military men have long known that among soldiers and sailors of all ranks and ages there is very little monetary reward for achievement, as is the common reward of the business world. In the military this is made up for by symbolic recognition such as a ribbon. Napoleon's awards are still used in the form of medals and ribbons for achievements which are acknowledged by the organization and recognized by its membership. A serviceman's chest often displays a colorful indication of significant accomplishment, achievement and participation. He has shed blood for that piece of purple ribbon.

In addition to medals and ribbons there are other honors, more subtle, that may be given to Navy personnel and among them is "Choice Duty Assignment." Not as apparent perhaps as a medal but it can be just as important to the individual and one such choice duty assignment is known as "New Construction."

Among sailormen it is considered an honor to be part of the first crew of a brand new ship; to be among those that put the ship in commission; to breathe life into the steel hull so that she can perform her mission as part of the United States Navy. Those that have that honor; those that put a Navy ship in commission are known forever after as "Plankowners" of that ship.

As Stu Landersman's time as executive officer of USS ENGLAND was drawing to a close he received orders to be the first commanding officer of a ship in "new construction." That ship would be USS HEPBURN (DE 1055) which was being built at Todd Shipyard in San Pedro, California. As the commissioning commanding officer, Stu would be the plankowner skipper of that ship. With the hull number 1055, HEPBURN would be the third ship of the Knox class as USS KNOX (DE 1052), being built in Seattle, would be the lead ship.

USS HEPBURN was to be named for Admiral Arthur J. Hepburn who had in 1938 headed a board that did a study and then made recommendations as to the need for naval facilities in the Pacific and Caribbean areas; naval facilities that would be needed in a major war. The Hepburn Board Report went to President Franklin D. Roosevelt and resulted in a massive expansion of shore facilities just before and during the early stages of World War II. With most new ships something like that would be all that anyone need know of the ship's namesake but not with USS HEPBURN.

Lieutenant George L. Custodi had been nearing completion of his one year tour of duty as an exchange officer with the (British) Royal Navy when he received orders back to the U.S. Navy to be part of the commissioning crew of HEPBURN. The British destroyer in which he served had just completed a round-the-world cruise and George was completing his time with the Brits. He was curious as to Admiral Hepburn's family name and soon learned that the admiral was a direct member of the Hepburn-Boswell family which had status in British heraldry. When George reported to the pre-commissioning detail of the new ship he brought to Stu Landersman the necessary information on how to obtain permission to adopt the Hepburn-Boswell family coat-of-arms as the USS HEPBURN logo.

Stu wrote a letter to the Lord Lyon King of Arms of England, Scotland and Wales. The letter explained that Stu was the prospective commanding officer of a U.S. Navy ship that would be named for Admiral Arthur J. Hepburn of the Hepburn-Boswell clan. It would be appropriate for the ship to have as its' plaque the family crest and Stu asked for permission to adopt that family crest for the ship's logo.

A month later came a response on impressive letterhead from the Lord Lyon King of Arms of England, Scotland and Wales. In bold hand-written scrawl the letter opened with:

Captain,

Nobody but nobody adopts a family coat of arms. You either have one or you don't. However, in your case I consider it appropriate that the Hepburn-Boswell family coat of arms be honored—.

And he went on to give permission for the ship to use, but not adopt, the coat-of-arms for its logo. Surely, no other U.S. Navy ship has ever had permission of the Lord Lyon King of Arms of England, Scotland and Wales for their ship's logo.

Lieutenant Commander Victor P. Peri was serving as Assistant Force Personnel Officer on the staff of Commander Cruiser Destroyer Force, U.S. Pacific Fleet when he knew that he would soon be receiving orders to sea duty. Vic knew the Navy personnel business better than most as he had been a Chief Personnelman as an enlisted man before he was commissioned. Rather than waiting for a "detailer" in Washington to determine his next duty, Vic was the kind of guy that would determine what he wanted and take steps to see that he got that duty. In this case Vic wanted to be executive officer of new construction, homeported in Long Beach or San Diego and with a commanding officer of his choice. He selected HEPBURN as the ship that met those requirements and he arranged orders as such.

In addition to arranging his own orders, Vic arranged the orders of every enlisted man who was ordered to HEPBURN, every one.

How could he do this? Well, his job as Assistant Force Personnel Officer put him in position to screen all enlisted distributions and one of his previous duties was at the Recruit Training Center (Boot Camp) in San Diego. When he learned that 40 men right from Boot Camp would be assigned to HEPBURN, Vic went to the Boot Camp, screened records and selected the 40 best for his ship. Vic Peri saw to it that all the enlisted men, not just the boots but all the enlisted men assigned to HEPBURN, the plankowners, were the cream of the fleet.

And the officers? Stu never learned who, "up there," was looking after him for assignment of officers. It might have been an extension of Vic Peri's influence on the staff of the type commander or it might have been Navy policy to send good people to new ships but whatever it was it had worked very well because the officers that reported for duty in HEPBURN, the plankowners, were the very best that Stu Landersman could have hoped for.

As the ship neared completion, while she was still the property of Todd Shipyard, it was necessary to test and to demonstrate her propulsion and ship control capabilities. This required a sea trial and as the ship was not yet a Navy ship she would be operated as would a merchant ship with licensed master, mates and engineers. Todd Shipyard had among their employees appropriately licensed personnel just for this purpose. Stu Landersman, as the prospective commanding officer was invited to be aboard for the sea trial. Also, a group of four congressional staff people came from Washington to observe the first underway trial of HEPBURN.

From the very beginning of the sea trial it was clear that the few shipyard people operating their ship had all they could do with full attention to that purpose and so it fell upon Stu to act as host of the congressional staffers, an easy task. Stu took them on an extended tour of the ship, explaining functions, describing various equipments and answering questions. They were easy to talk with.

When they had toured most of the below decks spaces and had worked their way up to the bridge and pilot house area Stu had almost run out of ship-tour information when one of the staffers asked a serious question. "Look, this ship has cost the government forty six million dollars and the Navy has contracted for twenty of them. That's a lot of money. Do you think that the ships are worth it? Is it money wasted or well-spent?"

Stu had dealt with similar issues before and so he was prepared. "Wasted or well-spent? Let's look at it this way; the money came to the government from taxpayers and when this ship is delivered to the Navy, Todd Shipyard will be paid forty six million dollars. Todd has paid almost half of that amount to workers, managers, executives and stockholders who will pay some of what they are paid to the government in income taxes.

"Every bit of steel, wire, pipe and paint that goes into this ship must be purchased by Todd from U.S. sources even if it could have been purchased overseas for less cost. If anything cannot be bought in the U.S. Todd has to prove it in order to get permission to buy foreign. What else is there? Every dollar of that forty six million is put back into the American economy. Wasted or well-spent? If we take delivery and then take her to sea and pull the plug, sink her, the American economy has benefited by recycling taxpayer money right back into the American economy and that benefit is even much more valuable because the U.S. now has a fighting ship for the next twenty years.

"Now tell me what's wrong with that reasoning."

The staffers looked at each other as one of them muttered, "I hadn't thought of it that way."

While Stu Landersman was serving in his previous duty as executive officer of USS ENGLAND he had become familiar with two very nice paintings that adorned a bulkhead in the wardroom of that ship. One painting showed USS ENGLAND underway in the quiet water of Long Beach Harbor while the other showed the ship at sea in heavy weather. Both indicated that the artist was Arthur Beaumont. How would one go about getting Arthur Beaumont to do a painting of HEPBURN?

Stu asked around and learned where Arthur Beaumont lived and soon a friendly relationship developed with the artist. About that same time an executive of Todd Shipyard notified Stu of a long-standing tradition in which the ship-builder presented the ship with a gift at the ship's commissioning ceremony. The Todd executive wanted to know if Stu had any idea of what that gift could be. Of course Stu had the answer.

A very nice gift from Todd Shipyard to USS HEPBURN at the time of her commissioning would be a painting of the ship by the artist Arthur Beaumont. The shipyard exec liked the idea and Stu put him in touch with the artist. A beautiful water color of HEPBURN underway in heavy sea-state was presented to the ship at the commissioning ceremony and that painting hung on the wardroom bulkhead for all the years of service that followed.

Before he did the painting Arthur Beaumont made frequent visits to the ship and he was on board for the second sea trial. He got to know his way around the ship and he knew a number of the people that would be serving in her. Stu joked that Beaumont was just like a plankowner and although Stu had been joking, the artist took it seriously. He asked Stu if he could be listed as part of the crew in the commissioning program.

USS HEPBURN (DE 1055) was commissioned at the Long Beach Naval Shipyard on 3 July 1969. The ceremony program was a very nice booklet that gave the shipbuilding background and details of the ceremony. On the cover of the program was a very accurate and colorful rendering of the ship's logo; the Hepburn-Boswell family coat of arms that had been approved for use, but not adopted, by the Lord Lyon King of Arms of England, Scotland and Wales.

U.S. Congressman Craig Hosmer gave the principal address. Carl M. Lippincott, General Manager of Todd Shipyards Corporation presented the ship with the Beaumont painting which caused the ceremony attendees to applaud and to utter appreciative oohs and aahs. In the center of each ceremony program was a removable black and white copy of the Arthur Beaumont painting of HEPBURN. In the program was a listing of the crew, all plankowners and under Operations Department, OI Division, one sailor listed was YNSA A. J. Beaumont.

A few months after the ship had been commissioned Stu received a letter from Arthur Beaumont describing how he had sent a bill for his painting to Todd Shipyard. As he had always done for other client/patrons, the bill listed the agreed upon purchase price for the painting, in this case one thousand dollars, plus fifty dollars for a "water wash."

The shipyard response was that they had not contracted for anything more than the thousand dollar painting and so had no intention to pay an additional fifty dollars. Beaumont explained to Stu that his process of painting a ship, and he had done more than a hundred of them, was to first do a sketch, a water color black-and-white that he called a water wash and from that he did the color painting. It was like a sketch for the artist to work from. No problem, he said, he would keep the water wash.

Stu saw a good opportunity. He wrote Beaumont that he would be more than happy to pay the fifty dollars for the water wash of HEPBURN. But Beaumont had the last word. No, Stu could not have the water wash for fifty dollars but he could have it for one dollar. And so Stu paid one dollar for an original Arthur Beaumont that he had framed and which hung on the wall of his every home for the rest of his life.

The Landersmans had been living in Huntington Beach from the time Stu had reported for duty in USS ENGLAND with her home port at Long Beach. Now, with orders as prospective commanding officer of HEPBURN which was being built in San Pedro and would be home-ported at Long Beach, the family could continue living in the same house. That would mean about four years in the same home, rare for the Landersmans.

The primary mission of ships identified as DE was anti-submarine warfare (ASW) but Navy ships very often, almost all the time, were used for missions other than their primary one. In the Viet-Nam conflict there was no ASW and so DE's were used in many of the same roles as were destroyers. The DE 1053 class, as example, carried one five inch gun mount that could be used for anti-surface, anti-air or shore bombardment. Not as effective perhaps as were multi-gun or missile equipped combatant ships but capable of performing some of the same missions.

Knowing that there would be no ASW for his ship in the Viet Nam conflict, Stu was determined to be part of the gun line; to participate in shore bombardment; to provide naval gunfire support to troops ashore. DE's were not required or expected to have the ability to provide the highest level of gunfire support but Stu was determined to achieve that qualification.

There were three levels of naval gunfire support. The first and most simple was targeting by visual or optical means; seeing the target, positioning the gun and firing at that target. The second level called for positioning of the ship by precise navigation, firing at a grid-target in response to direction from a spotter and adjusting fire as necessary to hit the target. That second level of naval gunfire support was considered to be the highest level that a DE could achieve. But not Stu Landersman.

The highest level of naval gunfire support was the third level; that which required a ship to answer a call-for-fire from a spotter ashore as in the second level but at night. The firing ship, in addition to providing destructive fire had to provide continuous illumination so that the spotter could observe the fall-of-shot and call for adjustment as necessary to hit the target. A multi-gun ship could have one gun or gun mount firing destructive fire while another gun or gun mount provided illumination fire. A ship with one gun would have to fire both destruct and illumination rounds from that single tube, positioning and adjusting as necessary for each. It had not been done before. If Stu had his way HEPBURN would be the first.

Many basketball teams, many coaches, had taught Stu Landersman how to put together a winning team often against the odds. Many meetings, many gunfire exercises, many more meetings and late one dark night off the Hawaiian gunnery range HEPBURN became the first single gun ship to achieve the full third level of naval gunfire support. The ship was still at General Quarters for the gunnery at 2100 (ten PM) as Stu got on the general announcing system and announced to the crew that HEPBURN had just done what no other single-gun ship had done before, "and just to show that it was no fluke we're going to do it again."

They fired the exercise again that night and again it was a success and the crew cheered as Stu announced, "Splice the main brace in Sick Bay." Late that night the HEPBURN crew lined up in the passageway outside Sick Bay and each received a shot of liquor from the Chief Hospital Corpsman.

Following is a letter that Stu Landersman wrote to the families and friends of HEPBURN crewmen:

USS HEPBURN (DE-1055)
FPO SAN FRANCISCO 96601
17 August 1970

Dear Families and Friends,
The past few months have been busy ones for your HEPBURN man. January found him sailing to the sunny climes of Hawaii on HEPBURN's second Shakedown Cruise. After our return to Long Beach we went into the shipyard for some minor modifications which are common in ships as new as ours. From the shipyard we were sent directly to San Diego for five demanding weeks of Shakedown Training designed to test not only the equipment aboard, but also the teamwork of the crew under all conceivable conditions. HEPBURN completed Shakedown Training and was welcomed into the operational fleet. Our division commander, Commander Destroyer Division 132, who was deployed with the other ships of our squadron off Viet Nam (alluding to the Black Cat symbol of our squadron) said, "It is with pride, we note that the black kitten we left behind has become in our absence and by herself a great cat. Welcome and WELL DONE."

Then after only a week in Long Beach to prepare, we set sail on the Pacific Fleet Midshipmen Cruise which annually serves as an operational training period for Naval Reserve Officer Training Cadets from colleges in the United States. Twenty-seven midshipmen came aboard for the six week cruise and offered a welcome addition to HEPBURN's working and social life. After a one day stop in San Francisco, HEPBURN proceeded to Monterey, California to celebrate the 4th of July and the local "Sloat Landing Festival" named in honor of the 19th Century naval officer who seized the area from Mexico. So while the other ten ships of the training squadron were in San Francisco, HEPBURN remained in Monterey until 6 July 1970. The ship was all dressed up for the occasion with brightly colored signal flags by day, and white dress ship lights at night stretched from "stem to stern."

We rejoined the task group and headed North, but were soon detached with the USS SOMERS to visit yet another exclusive port, but this time a familiar and favorite one–Vancouver, B.C. HEPBURN seems to enjoy real rapport with the citizens in this beautiful and friendly city–we had a total of about 5000 visitors aboard with an all time one-day record of 2500! We helped the Canadians celebrate their "Sea Festival" by contributing a drill team to their parade and illuminating our dress ship lights at night; in addition to hosting visitors on the popular guided tours already mentioned.

Leaving Vancouver, we rejoined the squadron for the long ten day transit to Hawaii. The last three days out of Pearl Harbor were spent in Hawaiian waters conducting exercises for midshipmen and crew training. We were all proud when HEPBURN became the first of her class to qualify fully for Naval Gunfire Support (providing artillery support for troops ashore). This involved firing a night exercise using alternately flares and explosive projectiles–a real juggling act with only the one gun, but it was carried off smartly. In addition, our midshipmen won first place in a squadron-wide gunnery competition.

After six sun-drenched days in Hawaii we were ready to head for home. The highlights of our return transit included a Fun Day involving intra-divisional competition in all kinds of activities such as tug-of-war, pie eating, and card playing. The competition was won by the Operations Communication Division. Fun Day also included a concert performed for the whole task group by the ship's rock group "The 1055 Revival." The concert was carried out by HEPBURN pulling alongside each ship in a special concert formation and serenading their crews gathered topside from our flight deck.

During this cruise, HEPBURN has made quite a name for herself as a ship that performs well and has a good time doing it.

I trust that the foregoing will serve to keep you abreast of the activities of your Navyman. He is doing a splendid job in preparing HEPBURN for deployment to the Western Pacific. He needs and deserves your continued support now more that ever. With so much dissent and protest in the nation your support of his efforts is most important. You can be proud of the fine work your HEPBURN man is doing.

Sincerely,

S. D. LANDERSMAN
Commander, U.S. Navy
Commanding Officer

Just as sailors give nick-names to their shipmates, so do they give nick-names to their ships. It would seem awkward for sailors in conversation to refer to their ship as HEPBURN; rather they would use a popular nick-name. Two very popular movie stars were Katherine Hepburn and Audrey Hepburn and the ship was named for Admiral Arthur J. Hepburn, so it seemed natural to the crew that their ship was Katherine, Audrey or Arthur. More common were the feminine names because Navy ships were always referred to in the feminine gender; as she or her.

In early February 1971, as the ship was preparing to deploy to the Western Pacific to be part of the Seventh Fleet and to participate in the Viet Nam conflict, Stu received a planning letter from the commander detailer in the Bureau of Naval Personnel. Stu would be relieved of command in May and ordered to the staff of Commander Seventh Fleet. He would relieve Bill Bademan on that staff. Wait a minute! Bill Bademan? Isn't he the same Bill Bademan that Stu had relieved back in 1960 on the DESLANT staff in Newport? Yes, same guy, and Stu knew that he would be relieving a guy very well organized, efficient and professional.

Commander Seventh Fleet and his staff were embarked in the cruiser USS OKLAHOMA CITY and that ship was home-ported in Yokosuka, Japan. That meant that when Stu returned from his WESTPAC deployment the Landersman family would move from their home in Huntington Beach to a new home in Japan.

Bill Bademan was the Surface Warfare Officer in the Operations section of the Seventh Fleet Staff and as such he had frequent dealings with CTF 75, the Surface Combatant Force Commander. When Bill found out that his relief would be Stu Landersman, the CO of HEPBURN, he decided that Stu should experience all of the roles or duties that surface combatant ships performed in the Seventh Fleet before Stu came to the new duty. Bill more or less took over the scheduling of HEPBURN and when he learned that HEPBURN, a single gun DE, had earned the full naval gunfire qualification, he saw to it that HEPBURN's first assignment in the Seventh Fleet would be on the gun line, firing naval gunfire support for troops ashore in South Viet Nam.

HEPBURN took station as directed by the gun line commander and established radio communication with the spotter ashore. Naval gunfire support was conducted by very precise terminology which was part of the gunfire exercises that led to qualification. The HEPBURN team was expert at it.

A "Call for Fire" from the spotter ashore! All the correct terminology and the phone talker on the bridge reported, "Ready to fire!"

Stu replied, "Your battery is released" and there was an immediate roar as the five inch 54 gun of USS HEPBURN fired the first of many rounds that followed.

That first gunfire blast was followed by, "Shot", then "Standby", as to alert the spotter that a round had been fired and then when he could expect the burst.

With that first shot, Stu realized that the goal he had set almost two years before had been realized; to take a ship from the builder's yard, put it through all the training, work-ups and qualifications, take it into combat and fire naval gunfire support. The gunfire mission continued. His very well-trained team would continue the mission without him and there were tears in his eyes as he slowly made his way to his seat on the starboard side of the pilot house.

Precedence of Navy messages is determined by the originator. Not just a matter of importance or rank of the originator, precedence of each message is determined by the need for action or response. The requirement to report an immediate threat like an incoming attack is given a higher precedence than a request for provision supply.

There were five levels of Navy message precedence when HEPBURN was serving on the gunline; Flash, Emergency, Operational Immediate, Routine and Deferred. The words themselves indicated the need for speed of response or action. Flash would be used for ongoing combat action while Emergency might indicate action very soon. Operational Immediate need not be associated with combat but, as the name implies, would be used when immediate action was required in any operation. Routine and Deferred speak for themselves.

HEPBURN had just completed her third day on the gunline when she received an Op Immediate message directing her to cease gunline duty, fuel and proceed south toward the Straight of Malacca, there to intercept a Soviet task group coming out of the Indian Ocean. HEPBURN was then to trail the group as it proceeded north through the South China Sea, past the ongoing action in Viet Nam and presumably enroute to their home port which could be either Vladivostok or Petropovlask. Navy people called those two Soviet Pacific Fleet ports Vlad and Petro.

With no oiler available, HEPBURN fueled to 103% from a supply ship, went toward the Malacca Strait and found a small Soviet task group in loose column formation creeping north at four knots. The group consisted of a destroyer of the KOTLIN class leading a minesweeper, a surfaced diesel electric submarine and a small oiler. HEPBURN took station on the starboard quarter of the formation and stayed with them as they transited through the South China Sea.

Long before the Viet Nam conflict aircraft carrier pilots had kept careful count of their landings on the flight decks of those ships and when a pilot reached one hundred landings he was forever after known as a "Centurion." Two hundred landings earned the title Double Centurion, three hundred was Triple Centurion and so forth. Ships firing on the gunline in Viet Nam had picked up on this so that a ship that fired a hundred rounds was a Centurion. Then they went double and triple as did the aviators.

HEPBURN had fired over three hundred rounds when she left the gunline and so the Triple Centurion gun barrel, normally a neat Navy haze grey was now charcoal color and pealing. Sometime during the first hundred rounds the barrel became so hot that the paint had burned and with the expected continuation of gunfire no effort was put towards scraping and painting. Now, having left the gunline the gunners had every intention of restoring their weapon to its usual handsome appearance.

Stu Landersman was in his chair on the starboard side of the pilot house when he saw the gunners mates about to start scraping the barrel of their five inch gun. "Whoa, hold it, don't scrape the barrel," he called down to the sailors and then sent the bridge messenger for the gunnery officer. Stu explained to Lieutenant Pete O'Conner that he wanted the Soviets we were tailing to see that HEPBURN's gun had very recently been used and used a lot. He wanted them to see that they were under surveillance by a very recent combat veteran, something he was sure they were not nor had been. Burned paint stayed on the gun barrel for all the time that HEPBURN was with the Soviet group.

Every morning HEPBURN exchanged pleasantries via flashing light and gave the KOTLIN range and bearing to each of his flock as without radar they scattered at night. Each report was received with a "Thank You."

One morning from HEPBURN; "It's a long trip to Petro at this speed," and the KOTLIN responded, "I'm going to Vlad." Those morning exchanges were included in reports made every four hours to higher authority.

Another day from HEPBURN; "This morning I have the pleasure to inform you that the U.S. astronauts have returned safely from the moon."

The KOTLIN came right back with, "Congratulations on your magnificent scientific achievement." All this was by flashing light; they were very good at it, fast in English.

HEPBURN sent, "Would you like me to send your congratulations to the astronauts?"

"Please do," from the Soviet ship, so that exchange was included in the next report.

Half way around the world in Poughkeepsie, NY, Stu's father was driving to work listening to the local radio station. The news included an item that USS HEPBURN, while on patrol in the South China Sea, met a Soviet destroyer and the Soviet ship asked that congratulations be sent to the astronauts. A call disclosed that the radio station had nothing more than that from a wire service. HEPBURN watched the Soviet ships in an aborted attempt at provisioning by high line; dried pigs were returned. Oh, hungry sailors! And refueling astern while almost dead in the water was not at all good seamanship, very clumsy. But as HEPBURN's rock band serenaded close alongside, the Soviet group commander asked for more and waved his appreciation.

HEPBURN stayed with the Soviets for ten days; through the South China Sea on that single fueling from the supply ship until relieved and arrived at Sasebo with 25% fuel on board, very low for a Navy ship. Remember, Bill Bademan had determined to see that Stu Landersman would experience all of the operations of a surface combatant ship in the Seventh Fleet and he continued that process. At Sasebo HEPBURN received orders to join with GRIDLEY, a DLG and escort that ship through the Sea of Japan and into the Sea of Okhosk. The patrol would be in support of a PARPRO operation which was a highly classified aviation surveillance mission across the Soviet Union.

The weather was bad, the sea was rough and it was cold in the Sea of Okhosk as the two ships worked their way closer to Soviet waters. From out of the north at high speed was first a radar contact then clearly visible was a beautiful Soviet guided missile cruiser. The Soviet ship closed the two American ships to a range of three miles and then commenced to circle them still at thirty knots. It was beautiful to behold; the huge ship pounding through rough seas at high speed as she circled GRIDLEY and HEPBURN. Beautiful it was, but wait, what happened?

The Soviet cruiser slowed, went dead-in-the-water and great vapors of steam came out of her stacks. Clearly, as ships' engineers called it, she had "lost the load" and the glamorous entry on to the scene was reduced to ineptness. It was very embarrassing for the Soviets as American admiration turned to laughter.

Shortly after that the PARPRO patrol ended and the two American ships turned and headed back to Sasebo.

Bill Bademan was true to his word; he continued to schedule HEPBURN, this time from Sasebo to Yokosuka for a brief port visit so that he could meet face-to-face with Stu Landersman and discuss some of the detail of the soon-to-be relief of his job on the Seventh Fleet staff. Those discussions went well. The evening before Stu was scheduled to depart Yokosuka he was having dinner at the officer's club and was surprised to see the commanding officers of two Knox Class frigates in the dining room. USS ROARK (DE 1053) and USS GRAY (DE 1054) had just arrived in WESTPAC and Yokosuka was their first stop. In a few days they would be enroute to the Gulf of Tonkin and the three frigate COs had a grand time discussing their ships' employment with the Seventh Fleet. Stu learned that Knox Class frigates now were not permitted to qualify for full day-night naval gunfire support. The only employment that these two new arrivals could expect was to escort carriers and serve as shotguns for the SAR ships.

Early the next morning HEPBURN was underway enroute to the Gulf of Tonkin. While transiting Yokosuka Harbor the channel took them past the pier area where ROARK and GRAY were moored. They were moored stern-to the dock, so that their bows were projected out into the harbor. Good seamanship. As HEPBURN glided past the two DE's Stu had an idea.

In rapid order Stu took the conn, ordered the signalman to raise GRAY and tell them that HEPBURN was coming alongside, directed the Bos'n to pass the word for the Supply Officer and notified the deck force that HEPBURN would be tying-up on her port side, stern-to the dock on the starboard side of GRAY. He then took a few moments to explain to the bridge watch that he was putting together a once-in-a-lifetime opportunity; three KNOX Class DE's with sequential hull numbers; 1053, 1054 and 1055 moored in Japan. The Supply Officer had a good camera and rounded up two crewmen also with good cameras and a harbor tug took the photographers to appropriate positions. Good pictures were taken and one of them was used many times in years that followed. If anyone looks carefully at that picture they could see that the mooring lines between GRAY and ROARK are doubled-up as would be appropriate but the lines between GRAY and HEPBURN are singled as in a temporary moor.

The picture of those three DEs tied up together in Yokosuka will be on the back cover of this book if I have my way.

Port Control in Yokosuka was not accustomed to have a routinely departing ship commandeer a tugboat and moor without permission. Stu didn't answer the angry radio calls demanding explanation until his operation was completed. Then he gave a brief apology as HEPBURN continued on her way.

In the Gulf of Tonkin HEPBURN served as shotgun for a South SAR ship and then was ordered to serve as plane guard for an aircraft carrier. Bill Bademan was still directing the schedule of HEPBURN and he knew it was time for Stu Landersman's relief. That change of command could easily be accomplished with transportation provided by an aircraft carrier.

Bill Sellers came aboard by helicopter from the carrier and after the ceremony Stu went to the carrier as the first leg in his complex path home to Huntington Beach, California.

Author's note:

You may have read back in an earlier chapter about how George Monroe and I hitch-hiked around the country in 1948. When I put that into this work-up I mentioned to my daughter-in-law Jil about that chapter. Jil was surprised that I put that whole summer adventure into one chapter; she insisted that I should write a book about it, not just a chapter.

Well, Jil was right, there surely was enough that summer for a book but I didn't think I had the time for another book. Now for this book I have taken on the task of writing a chapter of my time with the good ship USS HEPBURN and I must admit that, just like the hitch-hiking summer, there is more to the HEPBURN story than can be delivered in a chapter. It should be a book.

I apologize to all my great Plankowners and shipmates of HEPBURN for not acknowledging them by name in the chapter. It was a great adventure for me and my shipmates made it all possible. We did a lot of amazing things with that ship. No other ship of single engine, single screw and single gun did what we did. Soon after I left the ship the Type Commander directed that DEs would not serve on the gunline and they would not operate on one boiler as we had.

Later I learned that the leadership of the destroyer community had not been at all pleased with the DE 1052 Class. That class of ships had been imposed on them by money-savers in Washington. The ships were not supposed to be able to perform all destroyer duties. So as I was so proud of what we had done with HEPBURN, I couldn't understand the virtual silence or at best polite appreciation of the community leadership.

During my time in HEPBURN I received fitness reports from eight different reporting seniors. Rarely was I in company with my boss. Much of what I considered significant was not known by my reporting seniors who might be half a world away. That's the Navy system.

Still, I wouldn't have traded that duty for anything else. On a few occasions after I retired from the Navy someone would ask, "What was your favorite duty in the Navy?" and I would answer, "Commanding Officer of USS HEPBURN (DE 1055)."

CHAPTER THIRTY TWO

FROM DESTROYER ESCORT TO FRIGATE

1975

Destroyer Escort they were called, more commonly known as DE. The class of surface combatant ship originated in World War II, went through a number of name changes and stayed around as a class for at least 50 years but the DE was changed to FF and the classification that started as Destroyer Escort became Frigate. At the same time ships that had been known as Guided Missile Frigate became either cruisers or destroyers. Many people have claimed to be responsible for those changes but this is why and how it really happened and who caused it.

In 1941 a new class of small destroyer type ship joined the fleet. It was called DE for Destroyer Escort and during World War II U.S. shipyards built 561 of them. Many combatant ships were needed right away and DEs could be built in smaller shipyards, in less time and at less cost than destroyers. The DEs were intended to protect merchant ships from U-boat attack, as convoy escorts. They may have been slower, smaller, had less armament and lighter construction than destroyers but the DEs had some of the best anti submarine capabilities of their day.

World War II DEs were produced in classes named Edsall, Buckley, Bostwick, Rudderow and Butler, and many remained in service after the war. Some were converted to radar picket ships and amphibious light transports with new classes and hull numbers, and some were sold to foreign navies.

In the 1950s the DE classification name was changed from Destroyer Escort to Escort Vessel, then to Escort Ship and later to Ocean Escort but the DE designation remained as did the hull numbers. After World War II new classes of DE were built; Dealey, Courtney, Claud Jones, Bronstein, Garcia, and Knox all continuing the same hull number sequence. A new class was introduced, the Guided Missile Ocean Escort (DEG) Brooke Class, equipped with guided missiles for anti air protection with hull numbers one through six.

In 1975 the DE Ocean Escort designation was changed to FF Frigate so when the Oliver Hazard Perry Class Guided Missile Frigate joined the fleet it continued the Brooke Class hull numbers starting at FFG 7 and running to FFG 61 for the last ship of the class.

In 1969 Commander Stuart D. Landersman had the honor and good fortune to be Commanding Officer of the second ship of the Knox Class to be commissioned; plankowner skipper of USS Hepburn (DE 1055). The ship went through all the work-up, re-work and preparation of a new ship and deployed to the Western Pacific during the Viet Nam conflict. Stu completed his tour of duty in command of Hepburn in 1971 in the Gulf of Tonkin with orders to the staff of Commander Seventh Fleet.

As Surface Operations Officer from 1971 to 1973 Stu was responsible for the operational employment of surface combatant ships and having just come from command of a new DE he was the de facto staff action officer on matters related to that class of ship. While Vice Admiral James L. Holloway III, was Commander Seventh Fleet the seeds were planted that later grew to change the DE to FF;

Ocean Escort to Frigate and Guided Missile Frigate (DLG) to cruiser or destroyer.

As part of the regular morning staff briefing Stu Landersman gave the surface ship operations portion, laying out on a large vertical chart of the Seventh Fleet area and a separate Gulf of Tonkin and Viet Nam area chart, the positions and employments of Seventh Fleet ships. Often the admiral would question what a particular ship was doing and why or for how long and discussions would follow on tactics and other operational considerations. In addition to these briefings Stu had some other staff responsibilities that put him in conversations with the admiral more than he would have as a commander three levels below the admiral.

Vice Admiral Holloway questioned why DEs were in company with aircraft carriers and Stu explained that multi-gun destroyers were needed for naval gunfire support of troops ashore in South Viet Nam and for naval gunfire strikes against North Viet Nam and although single-gun DEs could be used for those gunfire missions if necessary, destroyers were better suited. That left the carrier escort duties to single-gun ships like DEs.

The Admiral explained that in Washington in his previous job he had to justify the Navy's budget before Congress which included defending against attacks on Navy requirements and costs by the other services. The Air Force in particular tried to attach all additional costs that they could associate with the aircraft carrier; to try and prove that the Navy was hiding what the Air Force claimed to be the much higher cost of an aircraft carrier. One of those Air Force claims focused on a Navy ship class, Ocean Escort or DE which the Air Force claimed existed only to provide protection for the aircraft carrier and as proof of that claim witness the employment of those ships in the ongoing conflict.

As the counter to that Air Force claim the Navy's position was that destroyers and DEs provided the carrier task group with an additional dimension of offensive power, they were much more than simply escorts for the carrier but with the "escort" word in that class name represented by the letter "E" it was difficult to argue.

Congress had authorized these ships to help fill a NATO perceived need for convoy escorts in case of the big war but the U.S. Navy used them almost interchangeably with destroyers for all "little war" operations. Still, a better class name should be found to do away with that "escort" word, it was misleading and it didn't reflect their real value.

Some of the NATO navies used FF for Frigate for their smaller destroyer type ships and in the old sailing ship navies use of frigates seemed more closely to parallel U.S. Navy employment of DEs. But at that time the U.S. Navy was using the Frigate name for another class of ship. DLG was called Guided Missile Frigate and if DE were to be Frigate then another classification name would have to be found for DLG. If DLG were changed to Guided Missile Cruiser it would free the Frigate name for DE, do away with the DLG designation and put the former DLG in a recognizable class.

With orders to the National War College Stu Landersman was making his detachment call on Vice Admiral Holloway when the admiral brought up the escort issue and reminded Stu to do something about it in the future. Neither of them knew at that time that Admiral Holloway's future duty would be Chief of Naval Operations and after War College Stu would again be on his staff in 1974.

The staff of the Chief of Naval Operations, known as the OPNAV staff is very large and as a brand new captain, head of the Surface Combatant Branch in the Surface Warfare Division of the Surface Warfare Directorate, Stu was four levels below the CNO. With deputies and executive assistants he counted at least nine people that would have to bless a piece of paper from him to the CNO, every one a hurdle to be overcome and if any one of those in the chop-chain chose to farm it out to a part of their staff the obstacles could be beyond count and the time beyond measure. There were heavy seas ahead.

Stu Landersman was new to Washington duty but he soon learned that the OPNAV staff consisted of two kinds of staff officers, originators and reviewers, the former being few and junior while the latter were many and senior. Reviewers were in two categories, fair and negative, the former few and the latter, opposing any change, many. All tended to claim authorship, ownership and bragging rights as the originator of any project they had chopped that was successful but only after it was signed out, while reserving denial of any association with failed projects. This made for a long and difficult process and many claimants of few successes.

An instruction promulgated by the Secretary of the Navy provided ship types and classes so that any change to a ship class would have to be accomplished by re-issue of that document. Stu re-wrote SECNAV Instruction 5030.1 attempting to offer as close to a smooth edition as he could. He prepared a forwarding letter from CNO to SECNAV, a briefing memo from the Deputy CNO for Surface Warfare to the Vice Chief of Naval Operations, another briefing memo from the Vice Chief to the CNO and still another memo from Stu to his immediate boss explaining what this was he was trying to do. All this went into an expandable correspondence folder that Stu delivered to the Deputy of the Surface Warfare Division. Completed staff work, every paper ready for signature. Every hatch covered. Water-tight. Every question anticipated and answered in the folder.

Every question? Not exactly. The package came back to Stu the next day scribbled up with many questions and changes and with, "Why are you doing this?" in big bold felt tip across his smooth memo. Stu had to start all over again. He wrote answers to the questions, made some of the changes to the SECNAV instruction (those that he perceived were legitimate), added two more briefing memos, re-wrote the explanation of why he was doing this and two days later when all the re-typing was done Stu marched down the hall to do battle with the Deputy.

As a responsible professional surface warfare officer and a Branch head in OPNAV, Stu Landersman felt that he should be able to accomplish a worthwhile task without the crutch of, "The CNO told me that he wanted this change." The project should be successful on its own merit if he could explain it properly. So he labored through, dealing with inertia against change, every level posing objections, asking questions, attempting irrelevant changes and after two months Stu was still re-writing and trying to work his way up the long chop-chain. Change in the Navy moves at the speed of a glacier and Stu had a hundred other projects going on but the DE to FF had become a personal challenge.

At Stu's level in the OPNAV staff he didn't have face-to-face contact with the Chief of Naval Operations but one day there was an accidental meeting. A four-star service chief walks the halls of the Pentagon accompanied by a crowd and always in a hurry between meetings. When Stu met the CNO the admiral stopped, exclaimed over meeting Stu, explained to the retinue that he was a Seventh Fleet shipmate and asked Stu how the escort change was doing. Stu told Admiral Holloway that it was in process but there was a long official path from him to the Chief of Naval Operations. The admiral could see that Stu was trying to get it done without the "CNO wants this" crutch as he looked at Stu and said, "Let me know if you need any help."

Stu came very close to seeking CNO help when his package reached the office of the Assistant Deputy CNO for Surface Warfare, a rear admiral who challenged the basic reason for the change and insisted that Stu had not made a strong enough case. Stu was up against a stone wall until one of the aides tipped him that the Assistant Deputy really didn't care about the DE to FF change but was only interested in the DLG to cruiser part of the package. The Assistant Deputy didn't want Mitschner and Farragut Class Guided Missile Frigate (DLG) to be cruisers so Stu changed the package to show those ships as Guided Missile Destroyer (DDG) and Leahy and Belknap Class DLG as Guided Missile Cruiser (CG). This kept Navy captains in command of 18 larger missile ships and commanders in 12 smaller ships.

Stu's secretary had re-typed the package sixteen times, she kept track as that was before word processing, and it went to the three-star Deputy CNO for Surface Warfare. A number of meetings, discussions, minor re-writes and a few more weeks and the package went to the Vice Chief of Naval Operations, then to the CNO where it was signed immediately and went to the Secretary of the Navy. A new SECNAV instruction was issued in 1975 as Stu Landersman had re-written it including Ocean Escort (DE and DEG) changed to Frigate (FF and FFG). The changes were made.

Over the years that followed there were informal and unsuccessful attempts to glamorize the simple Frigate classification as "Fleet Frigate" and "Fast Frigate" to match the double F, but the SECNAV instruction showed simply Frigate (FF) and Guided Missile Frigate (FFG).

Some analysts said that with the stroke of a pen the Secretary of the Navy had increased the Navy by 18 cruisers and Stu Landersman realized that the cruiser change was impressive, maybe even dramatic but getting rid of the escort word was the primary objective of that operation.

Author's note:

On 26 June 1998 Admiral James L. Holloway III, USN (Ret) read this piece and wrote, "I remember all of those events with remarkable clarity. You have captured it all in a very interesting summary."

CHAPTER THIRTY THREE

COMMANDER SEVENTH FLEET

1971–1973

I was at home in Huntington Beach, California. Martha had seen to it that this house had been sold. Except for a few items that would be shipped for us to Japan, all the furniture and furnishings, what the Navy called "household effects" would be put in storage as we would be provided all of that in our government provided housing in Japan.

I had orders to the staff of the Commander Seventh Fleet. The admiral and his staff were in USS Oklahoma City, a guided missile cruiser with home port Yokosuka, Japan. My family; Martha, David, Mark and I would be living on the U.S. Navy base at Yokosuka while I was serving on the COMSEVENTHFLT staff. The Navy travel office had made all arrangements for us to fly from Los Angeles to Japan. The date and time for our departure was all set and we would be met by a SEVENTHFLT staff host and hostess with sufficient transportation for us and luggage. Temporary lodging had been arranged until the more permanent quarters were ready. It was all very efficient.

Two weeks before we were to depart the U.S. I received a phone call that changed all the travel arrangements and timing. An agent at a government travel office in Washington wanted to know if, rather than for my family and me to fly to Japan, I would prefer to make the trip by passenger ship; cruise liner. Would Martha, the boys and I like that? You betcha!

The airline travel was cancelled. The Seventh Fleet staff host and hostess were notified of the change. We Landersmans were booked to sail from San Pedro (just outside of Los Angeles) on SS President Cleveland and instead of a twelve hour flight it was a fourteen day cruise with a half-day stop at Honolulu.

Who paid for this luxury? Well, it's complicated. The U.S. government paid for the cruise but in a round-about way. U.S. flag passenger ships could not compete with foreign flag liners and the U.S. shipping companies did not want to operate their ships at a loss. But U.S. war planning considered that these ships would be needed as troop carriers so the government paid U.S. shipping companies a subsidy to continue to operate passenger ships.

Some wise analyst came up with the idea that unused facilities on subsidized passenger ships could be used for government transportation. A procedure was put in place where two weeks before the scheduled departure of a U.S. flag passenger ship, that company would report vacancies to a Washington travel office. That office would scan planned government travel and if any matched the cruise line vacancies; Voila! The government would actually save money, the would-be costs of airline travel, by taking advantage of the unused accommodations in the subsidized passenger ship. So the Landersmans pleasure cruise to Japan actually saved the government money. (?)

The cruise to Japan was truly a pleasure for the Landersmans. We participated in all the activities and believe me there were many. As we left the ship in Yokohama the four of us agreed that when this tour of duty was over in two years, we wanted to go home this same way.

If I can be permitted to jump ahead with this narrative; two years later, when it was time to go back to the good ole' U.S., there were no more U.S. flag passenger ships receiving subsidies. We went home by air.

In 1971 the U.S. Navy operated four numbered fleets; two even numbered on the Atlantic side and two odd numbered on the Pacific side. The Seventh Fleet covered the Western Pacific which included Viet Nam waters, namely the Gulf of Tonkin and the Navy focus was on that Viet Nam war.

When time for me to leave USS Hepburn had been approaching, the detailer in BUPERS recommended to me that I should go to duty in Washington. It would be good for my career. But I told him that as long as there was a war going on that's where I should be. So duty on the Seventh Fleet staff as the Surface Warfare Officer in the Operations section of that staff sounded great to me and it proved to be so.

Most of the officers in the Operations section were naval aviators, almost all. John McMillan and I were the very few exceptions as we were surface warfare guys. If an aviator had a question about any Navy ship of any class, they would ask John or me. But if we asked one of them, say the F-4 guy, a question that happened to involve an A-3, we would be looked at with disgust and sent to the A-3 guy. Every one of these aviators had just come from previous duty as commanding officer of a squadron of the type aircraft that he represented on that staff and his squadron had just been involved in the Viet Nam war.

The Seventh Fleet was commanded by a vice admiral. One departed a couple of days after I reported to the staff; another was there for only a couple of months. Then came Vice Admiral James L. Holloway, III and he was one of the most impressive officers I ever served with. His father and his grandfather were admirals and later he was the Chief of Naval Operations. I served on his staff then, too.

Admiral Holloway changed the format of the regular morning staff briefing so that action officers rather than department heads gave their portion of the brief. It meant more individual briefings but it gave the admiral direct access to the action officers. For me it meant that I would brief the activities of the surface combatant ships every morning. Remember, Bill Bademan had seen to it that I experienced every (well, almost every) operation of destroyers and that was a great help in preparation of the brief and in understanding each operation.

One operation that Bill Bademan couldn't tell me about until I reported to the staff was the Anti-Infiltration Trawler Campaign. It was classified. He had been running it and so I inherited it from him. Before I go into any explanation of this operation I'd like you to read something I wrote sometime later. I think you will find it interesting.

The words jumped off the cover of the February 2008 Naval History magazine, "Exclusive! Secret Vietnam Sub Patrol Revealed," and the title of the article, "The Sculpin's Lost Mission", confirmed that I knew immediately what it was about.

As the Surface Operations Officer on the Seventh Fleet Staff in 1972 I was also the action officer of a highly classified long-time campaign directed at interdicting steel hulled infiltration trawlers that carried arms and ammunition from North Viet Nam to the Viet Cong in South Viet Nam. The anti-trawler campaign had been ongoing for years and U.S. success against these boats had been measured by turn-arounds; trawlers that changed course and went back to North Viet Nam rather than face destruction. This campaign was not connected with the better known but smaller scale operation directed against junks and sampans. These were steel hulled trawlers; much larger vessels that could carry much more arms. They came in versions of either 600 or 800 tons.

JCS rules of engagement allowed interdiction only when these steel hulled infiltration trawlers met nine specific criteria including attempting to penetrate Viet Nam waters. The at-sea detection, surveillance and tracking operations were under COMSEVENTHFLT, VADM James L. Holloway III at that time, and contacts were turned over to MACV only when they approached Viet Nam waters. The trawlers' cargos were vital to the Viet Cong and Sculpin's operation led to denial of arms that would have been used by the Viet Cong in the 1972 TET offensive. U.S. intelligence analysis had shown that a successful infiltration trawler delivery was always followed by Viet Cong offensive action.

It would be more definitive to destroy an infiltration trawler rather than just send them home and after trying with P-3, DD and DE resources we wanted a U.S. submarine, but the submarine force was engaged in Cold War operations that they considered more important than chasing trawlers. The Sculpin operation so accurately described by Admiral Larson was the climax of a long anti-infiltration trawler campaign. Sculpin's action led to termination of re-supply by that means and was one of the very few-maybe the only-combat actions by a submarine in the Viet Nam War.

Twenty years later I wanted to write the story of the Anti-Infiltration Trawler Campaign and called upon many potential sources to obtain documentation that I had either written or read; messages and reports that I had held in my hands, to give proof and credibility to what I could remember. Just as Admiral Larson found, all those documents had been destroyed.

The primary document that I sought was a highly classified (as was all) book-length report by the Pacific Fleet Intelligence Center that traced the history of the North Vietnamese Trawler Regiment and our own operations and compared U.S. intelligence analysis with that learned from the survivors of the steel hulled infiltration trawler that Harry Mathis and the Sculpin so successfully set-up for destruction. The South Vietnamese were very adept at extracting information from their enemy captives.

Much thanks to Admiral Larson for bringing the Sculpin's lost mission into the sunlight of naval history. Maybe now some reader can locate a hidden away copy of that lost U.S. intelligence report and the whole story can be told. Perhaps then Harry Mathis and the Sculpin crew can get the recognition and combat patrol pin they deserve.

That explains one of my duties on the Seventh Fleet staff. There were others.

From my time with HEPBURN on the gunline in South Viet Nam I knew that at times, not often, there were more ships waiting to provide naval gunfire support than could be used. I came up with an idea based on Clausewitz; "A defensive campaign cannot be successful unless it includes an offensive element." We were conducting a naval gunfire operation as part of the defense of South Viet Nam. If we used the destroyers that were not employed to form attack units, we could send them north of the DMZ and conduct naval gunfire strikes against North Viet Nam; an offensive element. These naval gunfire strikes would be coordinated with air strikes so that the ships would not be firing into air space of strike aircraft. It would add another dimension to our offensive efforts.

The naval gunfire strikes against North Viet Nam went very well and USS Oklahoma City, with Commander Seventh Fleet and his staff embarked participated in two such gun strikes. On the second such strike a North Vietnamese MIG was being tracked as it flew over land. The gunships conducting the attack, some of them with surface-to-air missiles as did Oklahoma City, knew that the Rules of Engagement prohibited firing at any enemy aircraft that was what the aviators called "feet dry;" flying over land. But if any MIG came out over the water, went "feet wet" they could be fired at. This MIG flew up and down the coast a couple of times and it looked like he wasn't intending to come out to sea. Suddenly he turned flying very low and fast, came across the beach and in an instant the MIG over-flew Oklahoma City. It was too quick and too short range for Oklahoma City to shoot. The MIG climbed steeply then descended at a sharp angle, leveled off and dropped a 500 pound bomb on the destroyer Higbee. The bomb hit Higbee well aft on the fantail, next to the after five inch gun mount. It penetrated the main deck and came to rest in the crew's after bunk space.

The gun mount captain ordered the mount cleared and the gun crew ran forward, clear of their gun mount. Down below in that after bunk space one sailor was in his bunk recovering from a malady as ordered by the ship's Doc. He saw and heard the bomb as it crashed through the overhead and came to rest in his compartment. In a second he was out of his bunk, out of the compartment and as he left the space he closed and sealed the water-tight door of the compartment. Good thing it was that he sealed that door because just as he departed the bunk room the 500 pound bomb exploded, destroying most of Higbee's stern including the propellers, rudders and the after gun mount. No one was injured and the ship was towed to Subic Bay where it was repaired. A couple of months later the good ship Higbee returned to the gunline just to show the world that the U.S. Navy had not lost a ship.

But just a minute! What about the MIG that dropped that bomb on Higbee? Well, that's a story, too. I was on the bridge of Oklahoma City for that gun strike. All the ships of our strike group were running at thirty knots. I saw the MIG come right over our ship flying very low and very fast. Along with the others on the bridge I saw it climb, then dive, drop a bomb on Higbee and climb again. As the MIG climbed there was a streak that followed it and then another streak followed the first one up, up and up. The first of those Terrier missile streaks hit the MIG. There was an explosion high in the sky and then another explosion as the second missile detonated among the debris. A DLG had been standing off just in case. Nice shooting! Remember, no MIG ever went feet wet and survived.

At a particular time in 1972 our intelligence people knew that there would be a huge offensive effort from the Viet Cong for their most important holiday; Tet. In preparation for what became known as the 1972 Tet Offensive every combatant ship was ordered to the gunline. There were no port visits for maintenance or liberty. That meant that there would be no reliefs for the Seventh Fleet ships so engaged.

I had come up with the "All hands on deck" procedure for the gunline and had written all the messages that directed the Surface Force Commander of the Seventh Fleet to carry that out. The immediate response from that force commander (a rear admiral) was, "Where are our reliefs?" The reply that I prepared was, "They're coming from San Diego and Pearl Harbor."

With that there were messages from COMSEVENTHFLT to his immediate superior CINCPACFLT asking that he lean on the destroyer force commander in San Diego to deploy immediately every ship that was ready. That was done and more than twenty destroyers were on their way to the Gulf of Tonkin, "from San Diego and Pearl Harbor."

Also, I reasoned that half way around the world in the Persian Gulf were two destroyers that really couldn't be doing anything more than showing the flag. Why not? I put together a message asking CINCPACFLT to request that the two Middle East Force destroyers be sent to the Seventh Fleet. All of us on the staff were surprised with the immediate response as those two ships were on their way to us. By the time they reached us the issue had been resolved but it was a nice effort anyway.

As it turned out, the destroyers on the gunline for the 1972 Tet Offensive were the most massive naval gunfire effort in naval history! Don't tell anybody but I put that together.

I read in an intelligence bulletin that the birthday of Ho Chi Min was approaching. That gave me an idea. It would seem logical that the Viet Cong leader would visit his "home town" on his birthday. There would be a big celebration and with him would be much of his immediate staff.

What if we hit that town with an ALFA strike from one of our carriers? We could take out the enemy's top leadership. First though, we had to locate that "home town."

I went to the Seventh Fleet staff intelligence officer, Commander Bobby Inman (You may recognize that name because some years later he was an admiral and the director of the CIA). Inman thought it was a good idea and he tasked his guys to find out the name of that home town and then locate it on a map. We agreed that not until we had all the details would we take this proposal to the admiral; completed staff work.

The intell guys found the name of the town and I worked with them searching for that town on a map of Viet Nam. We found the town. But wait! We found it again and then again. Yes, we found three towns in Viet Nam with the same name as the town in which Ho Chi Min was born. After conference with Bobby Inman I had to agree with him that accomplishment of the kill with collateral damage of one village might be acceptable but the collateral damage that would result in wiping out three villages? No way. We scrubbed my idea.

Let's see, another initiative that I was credited with was really my partner John McMillan's idea. It focused on the Thanh Hoa Bridge in North Viet Nam. Remember, John and I were surrounded by aviator staff officers, all with significant Viet Nam combat time. From them I learned that the Thanh Hoa Bridge was the single most important target in North Viet Nam for these aviators. It was the weak point in the main highway to the South and so it was important for the North Vietnamese to keep it useable so that they could send troops and supplies south.

Some analysts said that the Thanh Hoa Bridge was the most heavily protected target ever. Quite a statement, isn't it? But in support of that statement more of our aviators, Navy and Air Force were shot down trying to drop the Thanh Hoa Bridge than for any other target in North Viet Nam. It would be a real "feather in our cap" if we surface warfare guys could figure out a way to drop the Thanh Hoa Bridge.

The Seventh Fleet flagship, USS Oklahoma City carried the longest range surface-to-air guided missile in the Navy; Talos. That missile had a range of a little more than a hundred miles. The bridge was about fifty miles from the Gulf. The missile was almost an airplane by itself and even though most of its bulk was in its ram-jet propulsion system, it still carried a significant payload of explosives, enough to knock down a bridge. The Talos missile was designed to fly to and destroy aircraft that were being tracked by fire control radar. The big bird would fly to and hit the target that was being held, called "locked-on" by the radar. John McMillan and I thought it might be worth a try to use Talos on that bridge. Admiral Holloway told us that if we could drop the Thanh Hoa Bridge with a Talos missile we would be, "The most celebrated guests at the next Tail Hook convention."

So, if we wanted to hit the Thanh Hoa Bridge with a Talos missile we would first have to lock-on to the bridge with fire control radar and that radar required a clear path to the target. The bridge, of course, like most bridges spanned a river and like most rivers this one had over eons of time carved a path to the ocean or in this case to the Gulf of Tonkin. USS Oklahoma City took position off the mouth of the river while her fire control radar searched up the river valley for the bridge. No joy. The ship re-positioned. No joy. Again and again the guided missile cruiser re-positioned but was unable to find a clear path for the radar to lock-on to the bridge. Finally we gave up and so the Thanh Hoa Bridge was not knocked down by a Talos missile which was, after all, a surface-to-air missile. No Tail Hook for John and me.

Much later, I was in the midst of my portion of the regular morning briefing and I realized that it was the exact hour for the guns to go silent; the U.S. involvement in the Viet Nam War was ended. I continued with my briefing as if nothing had changed. In all the years that followed I have regretted that I had missed an historic moment. I wish that I had said something, anything to acknowledge that moment. I usually could ad lib, could "think on my feet" but I missed that opportunity to say something significant. Ah! Opportunity missed!

My next duty would be as a student at the National War College at Fort McNair in Washington, D.C.

Shortly before it was time for me to depart the Seventh Fleet staff with transfer to the National War College, I was asked by my boss, the Assistant Chief of Staff for Operations, Captain Bill Russell, to write a detailed summary of my accomplishments while on the staff. Captain Russell emphasized that I should not be shy, I should really "pour it on" because it would be used as the basis of an award recommendation for me.

This is what I wrote as I "poured it on" for Captain Russell:

From 1971 to 1973 Commander Stuart D. Landersman served as Surface Warfare Officer on the staff of Commander Seventh Fleet. As such he was responsible for Naval Gunfire, Infiltration Trawler operations, Surface Search and Rescue, Mobile Logistic Support forces, scientific and oil research ship protection, and many other programs involving surface ships.

He wrote the directives for and directed Seventh Fleet efforts against North Viet Nam steel hulled infiltration trawlers and was involved in turning back over twenty such trawlers and the destruction of one. These efforts denied vast quantities of supplies and arms that were sorely needed by Viet Cong forces in southern Republic of Viet Nam.

CDR Landersman was responsible for the preparation of directives that created Task Force 74 and sent that force into the Indian Ocean in response to the India-Pakistan War. He prepared directives that provided COMSEVENTHFLT guidance concerning U.S. Navy involvement with scientific and oil research ships. He has been active in directing the participation of SEVENTHFLT units in Search and Rescue Operations for fishing boats and merchant ships as well as Navy ships.

When the NVN invasion of RVN occurred on Easter Weekend 1972, CDR Landersman commenced a series of actions that led to the conduct of the greatest sustained naval gunfire effort in modern history. From ten to twenty-five naval gunfire ships were maintained continuously along the coast of Viet Nam for over nine months, firing over three quarters of a million rounds of ammunition in support of troops ashore. CDR Landersman was the Seventh Fleet staff officer responsible for this naval gunfire support.

In addition, CDR Landersman personally originated many ideas and programs like:

1. Request for USS Newport News from LANTFLT.
2. Positioning of a destroyer tender in Danang to expedite regunning and repairs.
3. Retention of various combatant and MLSF ships in Seventh fleet.
4. Provide backup NGFS ships for single gun 5 in/54 ships on the gunline.

5. Stand-down the PARPRO picket ships for operations in the Gulf of Tonkin and South China Sea.
6. Request for destroyers of MIDEASTFOR to augment SEVENTHFLT.
7. Request for Australian DDGs to augment SEVENTHFLT.
8. Created Red Dog Linebacker operations (naval gunfire strikes against North Viet Nam).
9. Recommended that rumor be planted in Washington that battleship USS New Jersey was being activated.
10. Advocated conduct of night or low visibility naval gunfire strikes for Linebacker ships.
11. Formed "Custom Tailor;" three cruiser gun strike at Hai Phong 10 May 1972.
12. Formed attempted Thanh Hoa Bridge naval Talos missile strike 14 April 1972.
13. Positioned ships for Hai Phong naval gunfire strike "Lions Den."
14. Alerted scientific research ships for possible retaliatory action by communist forces.
15. Utilization of DE 1033 Class ships on notification line in connection with Hai Phong mining.
16. Invited RVN to participate in notification line.

CDR Landersman has been instrumental in allocating naval gunfire ships to the gunline and his continuous efforts in this regard have provided COMUSMACV with the highest level of support. He has personally participated in over thirty Linebacker naval gunfire strikes against North Viet Nam and more that eighty days on the gunline. During these times CDR Landersman's ships have often been subjected to hostile fire.

CDR Landersman commanded USS Hepburn (DE 1055) in SEVENTHFLT during 1971. During that time Hepburn served in a broad variety of duties. She was the first ship of her class to serve of the gunline. For seven days she conducted close surveillance of a Soviet task group in the South China Sea. She participated in a

PARPRO Picket transit of the Sea of Japan and Sea of Okhosk. Under CDR Landersman, Hepburn was the first ship of her class to embark a UH-2 helo and detachment in combat. He has written a book on shiphandling the DE 1052 Class ship.

CDR Landersman has made most significant contributions to the readiness and combat effectiveness of the Seventh Fleet and he has given valuable advice to the commander of the Seventh Fleet.

Commander Stuart D. Landersman, U.S. Navy is highly recommended for the Legion of Merit with combat distinguishing device.

CHAPTER THIRTY FOUR

NATIONAL WAR COLLEGE
WASHINGTON, D.C.

1973–1974

The National War College is located in Washington, D.C. at Fort Lesley J. McNair. From the website of the school two mission statements can be found. The statements are generally consistent but deserve consideration.

Statement One: *The National War College mission is to educate future leaders of the Armed Forces, Department of State, and other civilian agencies for high-level policy, command and staff responsibilities by conducting a senior-level course of study in national security strategy.*

Statement Two: *The National War College mission is to prepare future leaders of the Armed Forces, State Department, and other civilian agencies for high-level policy, command, and staff responsibilities by conducting a senior-level course of study in national security strategy and national security policy.*

Notice that in Statement One the mission is to "educate" future leaders while in Statement Two the mission is to "prepare" future leaders. Perhaps to the academician education is the only means to prepare for higher responsibility but for the military there are some other means to prepare with "experience" as one of the most valuable.

Statement One describes the course of study as, "in national security strategy." while Statement Two describes the same course of study but adds, "and national security policy." So is policy included or not?

Description of the National War College student body and curriculum follows:

The curriculum emphasizes the joint and interagency perspective. Reflecting this emphasis, 59 percent of the student body is composed of equal representation from the land, air, and sea (including Marine and Coast Guard) Services. The remaining 41 percent are drawn from the Department of State and other federal departments and agencies, and international fellows from a number of foreign countries.

And another statement follows:

In furtherance of this mission, the College curriculum focuses on grand strategy–the integration of all elements of national power– as well as the theory and practice of war, fundamentals of strategic thinking for national security matters, the global security arena, the inter-agency decision-making process, contemporary military strategy, and joint and combined warfare. A fundamental strength of the College is its joint environment and approach. Students and faculty are drawn from all armed services and from civilian departments and agencies concerned with national security policies. The College program stresses "jointness" in military planning and operations and the interrelationship of domestic, foreign, and defense policies.

Commander Stu Landersman and his family moved from Japan back to the good ole' U.S.A. where Stu reported to the National War College and Martha did what Martha always did; found and bought a house. It was a beautiful house in Alexandria, Virginia, not far from Washington, D.C. and not far from the Pentagon. Most officers would have thought it risky to buy a house rather than rent when the tour of duty would be one year but Stu was pretty sure he would be assigned to his next duty in Washington so the Landersmans would probably be in that Alexandria home for three years. And that's the way it worked out.

At the National War College Stu was part of a student body of 150 military officers and people from a number of government departments. The military were lieutenant colonels and colonels, commanders and captains. Groups of four or five students, mixed military and civilian, were assigned to study rooms. Stu's study room had two Navy, one Army and one Air Force. The other Navy officer with Stu was Commander Les Palmer who Stu had known before.

If I can jump ahead to a few years later; Les Palmer was a Commodore (one star) at the Naval Academy and our Air Force room mate Tony McPeak was Chief of Staff of the U.S. Air Force. That's the way it was at the National War College; most were promoted including the civilians.

The academic program was very impressive with a faculty of highly credentialed and experienced professors. Also, being in Washington and just across the river from the Pentagon, the College could call upon key military and government people for their outstanding guest speaker program. All of the service chiefs, like the Chief of Naval Operations, came to speak as did the Chairman of the Joint Chiefs of Staff. Then there was the Secretary of Defense. Hold on! Yes, even the President of the United States came to speak at the National War College.

The Viet Nam War had ended the year before and our prisoners of war had been released. As an early step in returning some of the former POWs back into the military, seven of them were in the Class of 1974 at the National War College. All of the military students had been involved in Viet Nam and so there were many out-of-class questions and discussions especially with the very patient seven former POWs. The other students didn't realize the burden they were placing on these seven classmates.

At the request of the former POWs a special assembly was formed. On the stage were the seven former POWs. The audience was their classmates, faculty and students of the foreign officers' course. Each of the former POWs spoke for ten or fifteen minutes, telling the story of his capture, imprisonment and treatment. There was a question and answer period. When it was all-over the senior of the former POWs, Bill Lawrence, took the microphone and told the audience the reason for this assembly: The former POWs had been very patient in answering questions of classmates. They had told their stories. Now it was time to get on with the National War College program and treat the former POWs just like any other students. The audience cheered their classmates and after that they were treated just like everyone else.

One of the former POWs was John McCain and Stu Landersman got to know John pretty well. One morning over coffee Stu told John McCain that after most wars the U.S. public acknowledged their leaders by electing them to high office. But leaders of the Viet Nam War would not be so recognized as the public did not support that war. The public does, however, have great sympathy and support for the POWs and so there exists a path of popularity leading to politics for the POWs. John McCain listened carefully.

Who knows? Maybe it was Stu Landersman's comments that put John McCain into politics.

The academic program of the National War College included a number of class trips for the full 150 student body plus some faculty. At North Carolina the 82nd Airborne Division staged a mock battle highlighted by a massive parachute display that filled the sky with combat-ready soldiers. In New York City the class toured the United Nations building and spoke with the U.S. representative.

In the visit to Toronto, Canada the class was told in advance that they would meet and talk with the general heading all Canadian military; equivalent to the U.S. Chairman of the Joint Chiefs of Staff. As they had been told, the Canadian general singled out the U.S. Marine Corps officers in our group, shook hands with each and chatted; clearly he had great respect for U.S. Marines. The class had been told that a few years ago the Canadian general's son had been serving as a young officer in the Canadian armed forces. The son was able to put his commission on hold so that he could go to the United States and serve as an enlisted man in the U.S. Marine Corps. The son reasoned that he would be much more valuable as a military leader in Canada if he had combat experience. As a U.S. Marine he served with distinction in combat in Viet Nam and was killed in action. Rather then having ill feelings, the Canadian general had the greatest respect for the military in which his son had proudly served.

Early in the school year the students learned that one of the most important events in the National War College program, maybe the most valuable, were foreign trips; trips to various parts of the world where small groups of students, eight to twelve, would meet with key individuals and observe cultures. In the first month of school the students received explanations of the twelve different trips that would be available and each student filled out a preference form indicating his choice. Stu Landersman had listened carefully and selected Middle East–South Asia as his choice. His selection was approved and so over the months that followed, in addition to the regular academic program he attended courses focused on Middle East–South Asia history, modern conditions and conflicts.

A full chapter, maybe more, could easily be written about my National War College trip to the Middle East–South Asia but I'll try to condense it into something reasonable. It was a great trip, surely the highlight of my year at the National War College.

Now that I think about it; at the end of the trip I wrote a poem about the Middle East–South Asia trip and rather than trying to remember everything, I'm going to subject you, Dear Reader, to my poetic gesture from 1974.

MIDDLE EAST–SOUTH ASIA TRIP
          1974

C one forty one from McGuire,
If you wanna inquire,
From Andrews Air Base we started our trip.
Wheels up April twenty first,
Not long after quenched our thirst
And then landed on Rota's air strip.

Not for long were we there
Then off into the air
For the Holy Land our group then headed,
And then by that very night
After a day long flight,
In Tel Aviv, Israel was where we bedded.

In Israel's very sunny land
Orchards bloom from dry sand.
There is vitality and yes, there is youth.
Military is tough
On their enemy rough,
And an absence of what we call couth.

Golda Mier to us she spoke
And near tears did she evoke
From us men of U.S. military career.
She knows full well the score
And claims Rabin knows even more,
They will survive, above all it is clear.

Next land was nearby to the east,
Hospitality was great with much feast.
Hashemite Jordan sure looks ready for war.
There our fine army hosts

Just did the very most
And gave what we call "goat grab" galore.

Right hand you grab some meat,
While standing on your feet,
And a bunch of rice from underneath, too.
In sour goat milk it's cooked
And at our hosts we looked
As we rolled it all up into a goo.

Into your mouth next please do pop,
Even then you don't stop
Because more sour goat milk next do you drink.
It was sour and it stunk,
Worst thing I've ever drunk,
Meat, brains, even eyes; eat all don't stop to think.

Did party late last night
Now have an early flight.
We are all a good deal of sleep in need.
Bags in lobby sharp at six,
No breakfast time to fix,
C one forty one air crew serves good feed.

The far off Saudi land
Has oil and imports sand,
King says world problems are Zionists and Reds.
No eating pork or beef
And woe to any thief,
They stone adulteress and cut off hands and heads.

Face of Faisal the king
Is a mighty strange thing,
For it never changes its glassy stare.
No kind of female rights,

No short dresses or tights,
Are Saudi women allowed to wear.

Arab coffee you may taste
You will want to make it waste
To reject would be a real social blunder.
From a tiny common cup,
Please server don't fill it up.
Old king knows so little and we wonder.

India surely was very hot,
Had sacred cows yes a lot,
And many more people than it oughta.
There piles of cow dung dries
In sun with smell and flies.
Our doctor says, "Don't drink the water."

The building known as Taj
Sure is a true mirage,
Cause it's really much bigger than it looks.
Nine hours jammed in a bus,
Heat, flat tire, what a fuss!
Stay home friends, read about it in books.

Why U.N. proposed a motion
For the whole Indian Ocean,
To make of that body a peaceful zone,
Ustick asked of every speaker,
As those with runs grew weaker.
Bought beads not of ivory but of bone.

In all the military frame
It was just a Navy game,
For South Asia has not yet learned to fly.
So we talked powers at sea

And twas interesting to see
Our Air Force guys turn red and almost cry.

Next place was Pakistan.
On the bus we really ran
From Rawalpindi to the Islam City.
Did some carpet buying,
And heard Bhutto crying;
Of East Pakistan loss, oh what a pity.

Afghanistan is really very high,
Where mountains touch the sky,
And is close upon the Soviet Union border.
With Soviet relations good
As very well they should,
East–West are played in almost any order.

There some of us grew sick
And it is sure some trick
No matter what you, sir, may elsewhere hear,
To end your total life
Away from your dear wife
When suffering from classic acute diarrhea.

In rich Iran we saw
Crown jewels and the Shah,
And to the Twentieth Century we were returned.
"Oil prices," we were all crying,
Military hardware they were buying.
Admiral joined us and Celtic scores we learned.

Free time is never free,
Even midnight to hour three,
McPeak, Shalk, Merkel call late night staff meetings,
The old bazaar is closed

But then we are supposed
To shower, shave, dress make diplomatic greetings.

After flight of many mile
To Cairo on the Nile,
Saw the pyramids, sphinx and really had some fun.
U.S. embassy was very old
And twas there that we were told,
Arabs surprised Jews, crossed canal, used water gun.

Of Egypt's President Sadat,
I sure will kid you not,
The man was most relaxed and very cool.
With tea he quenched our thirst,
Said that Henry is the first
To come from us who is not just a fool.

Then we climbed into our plane
And flew to Madrid, Spain,
Enroute our home to arrive on twelfth of May.
The Africa trip crowd
Was waiting there and loud.
"Press on," Carpenter was oft heard to say.

Half a world we all saw
And viewed life rather raw,
Where most of the people struggle, live and die.
World's wonders, saw a few,
Six state leaders we talked to.
Mid East–South Asia; great trip, that's no lie.

So that's the story of my National War College trip to the Middle East–South Asia. Just in case you didn't get it from the poem; we visited eight countries; Israel, Jordan, Saudi Arabia, India, Pakistan, Afghanistan, Iran and Egypt. In six of those countries we had audiences with the head of state. One of our student-travelers was an air force doctor which was a very good thing because most of us got sick (In the poem I called it "the runs") and our doctor was able to provide medication.

As in the last line, "great trip."

CHAPTER THIRTY FIVE

CHIEF OF NAVAL OPERATIONS
WASHINGTON, D.C.

1974–1976

You may have read in an earlier chapter of this tome, I believe it was the chapter titled "From the DE to the FF," that I went from duty on the Seventh Fleet staff to the National War College. After that I went to the staff of the Chief of Naval Operations where, once again I served on Admiral Holloway's staff. With the Seventh Fleet he had been a vice admiral. Now as Chief of Naval Operations he was a full four star admiral.

I have borrowed a few paragraphs from that earlier chapter because they seemed to fit into this one. Please excuse my duplication.

The staff of the Chief of Naval Operations, known as the OPNAV staff, is very large and as a brand new captain, head of the Surface Combatant Branch in the Surface Warfare Division of the Surface Warfare Directorate, Stu was four levels below the CNO. With deputies and executive assistants, he counted at least nine people that would have to bless a piece of paper from him to the CNO, every one a hurdle to be overcome, and if any one of those in the chop-chain chose to farm it out to a part of their staff the obstacles could be beyond count and the time beyond measure. There were heavy seas ahead.

Stu Landersman was new to Washington duty but he soon learned that the OPNAV staff consisted of two kinds of staff officers, originators and reviewers, the former being few and junior while the latter were many and senior. Reviewers were in two categories, fair and negative, the former few and the latter, opposing any change, many. All tended to claim authorship, ownership and bragging rights as the originator of any project they had chopped that was successful, but only after it was signed out, while reserving denial of any association with failed projects. This made for a long and difficult process and many claimants of few successes.

Stu was considered a "Branch Head" which means that his immediate superior was a "Division Head," in this case the head of the Surface Warfare Directorate; Rear Admiral Roy Hoffman.

Hoffman was a gruff man; an unhappy man who seldom if ever smiled or had a good or friendly word for anyone. In their initial meeting Hoffman told Stu, in no uncertain terms, that all the captains that reported to him in his division were all captains that he had requested. Stu Landersman was the only exception. He hadn't asked for and did not know Stu and he didn't like having someone imposed on him.

What a way to start a new duty!

Some time later, when Stu looked back over his 30 year Navy career, he realized that the OPNAV staff was his only duty that was not in a ship or a school. There were other staffs but they were in ships. His Navy time was 18 years of sea duty, 10 years at schools and two years of shore duty in the Pentagon with OPNAV.

When Stu Landersman reported to OPNAV the others in the Surface Combatant Branch were two commanders; Bill DeHart and

Larry Lorden, LCDR Haig Alemian and Cathy Bassett, a secretary who took care of all of them. They were a fine group that had been doing the job of their branch very well and nobody could understand why the two commanders had not been selected for promotion to captain by the last Selection Board. That was the same Board that had just selected Stu Landersman. To make matters more uncomfortable, before those selections (or non-selections) of the Selection Board, both DeHart and Lorden had been higher on the commander list, that is senior to Stu Landersman. Now they found themselves working for a guy that had previously been junior to them. It could be an awkward situation.

Maybe nobody at the Surface Combatant Directorate could figure out why DeHart and Lorden had been passed over but as soon as Stu Landersman heard the story he knew the reason. Remember back to duty on the old DESLANT staff, where the Chief of Staff had just come back from serving on a selection board? That Chief of Staff had told of how destroyer officers were "killing their young" by writing mediocre fitness reports. From that brief Stu had learned to "pour it on" if you wanted to get an officer promoted and he had expanded on that.

In his first meeting with the two commanders Stu gave a great "locker room pep talk."
(Remember basketball pep talks?) Stu explained to the commanders that he knew how to write fitness reports better than anyone and if these two would stick with him they would be selected by the next board. The two commanders continued their good work and the next selection board selected both for promotion to captain.

Haig Alemian was a lieutenant commander who hoped to be promoted to commander before he left the staff then go to duty as commanding officer of a destroyer in the Atlantic fleet. He was one of the brightest and most capable officers Stu knew. He was promoted to commander as he served on the OPNAV staff and his next duty was in command of a destroyer in the Atlantic fleet. The story of Haig Alemian does not end there because while deployed with the

SIXTH Fleet in the Mediterranean he was very tragically killed in an automobile accident in Italy.

Cathy Bassett was an excellent secretary. You must realize that this was the time before everyone had and knew how to use computers with word processing, so everything that had to be typed was first written by hand and then that scrawl was given to a secretary/typist who had to decipher, edit and type the document without a misspelling, grammatical error or other mistake. Cathy Bassett was an expert at this and she did all the secretarial/typist work for Stu and the other three officers of the Surface Combatant Branch.

Cathy was a very heavy single young woman with pleasant features and nice personality. Heavy as used here is polite for grossly overweight. She had a problem with her social life because of that overweight as the only men that she could attract were not the kind of men she wanted to attract. The office and her association with the officers there were an important part of her life.

A few years later, after his OPNAV time, Stu Landersman stopped in to visit his former branch office and Cathy was still working there. But this was not the Cathy that Stu had known. She had gone through an intensive weight-reduction program, had a very nice figure and had done a lot with hair and cosmetics. She was good looking, confident and out-going and she told Stu that her social life was better than it ever had been. Good for Cathy!

Stu was very pleased that after about a year Rear Admiral Roy Hoffman was transferred to other duty. Who would replace him? Well, apparently there was no rear admiral readily available so an experienced Navy captain, Ed Field, shortly to retire, was temporarily placed in the job. To Stu, Ed Field was like a breath of fresh air. Although Stu had been able to satisfy Hoffman most of the time, it was always with a gruffness and growl. Remember, "I didn't ask for you!"

With Ed Field, Stu's life was completely changed. The new boss leaned on Stu, relied and confided in him. When it came time for fitness reports Ed Field wrote the most glowing report imaginable. He showed it to Stu and explained that he as a temporary and only a captain would not sign the report. It would go to one of the admirals for signature.

The next time that Stu Landersman saw his fitness report it was signed by an admiral but it was not the report that Ed Field had prepared and shown him. It was a run-of-the-mill fitness report typical of those that the long-ago chief of staff at DESLANT had cautioned about.

One more thing about fitness reports at OPNAV: Once, as time for captain's fitness reports approached, the leadership of the Navy's surface warfare in OPNAV decided that their section of the staff had not been appropriately represented by previous selections to rear admiral, so they made up their minds that one of their fifteen captains at the surface warfare section of OPNAV would be written up as the number one and all others would follow as some-what less than this paragon of achievement. The captain they selected to be their superman was actually a mediocre officer from their budget branch. He was written-up in the most glowing exaggerations and as could be expected was selected for promotion to rear admiral.

All the other captains from the surface warfare section of OPNAV including of course Stu Landersman received less-than-best fitness reports so that the leadership of the surface warfare section of OPNAV could boast of that one flag officer selection.

At home in Alexandria the Landersmans continued to live in the same house that they bought when Stu went to the National War College. Mark and David continued at the same schools. No one in the family knew why but for some reason Stu decided that it would be nice to have a Volkswagen convertible for driving to and from work. He scanned the newspaper want-ads for weeks before he found what he was looking for. A 1965 VW convertible was advertised for sale with only a very brief description and a phone number. Stu called the number; no answer. The next day he called again; no answer. A third try met with the same result. On the fourth telephone call a man answered. When Stu told him that he was calling about the VW advertised a few days ago the reply was, "Oh yes, thanks for the call but could you call back tomorrow? I'm very busy just now," and that ended the call.

Stu called again the next day and this time, finally, the guy was ready to talk about the car. He was very anxious to sell it as it hadn't been used in a number of months. As far as he knew it was in good shape and he would appreciate it if Stu would come and look at it. Stu got the address and made an appointment to look at the car. Hmm, Stu thought, the address was in a very nice residential section of Georgetown, sounds good.

With checkbook in his pocket, jumper cables and tow rope in the station wagon, Stu and David went to the Georgetown address. The VW convertible was in the garage, very dirty from long-time non-use and buried under cardboard boxes. All four tires were not exactly flat but were in dire need of air. Clearly, this was the car that Stu had in mind when he started his search. Somehow, before any negotiation concerning the VW, in pleasant conversation Stu learned that the owner was Timothy Wirth, a brand-new congressman from Colorado and this car had been used during his campaign as he traveled around his state. Now in Washington he had a full sized car and had no further use of the VW.

"So, how much do you want for the car?" Stu asked the congressman.

"Well, you can see that I have no further use for it. A few months ago my wife paid twenty-five dollars for a tune up and she would be upset if I didn't get at least that." He said with a laugh.

"Okay, I'll give you a hundred and twenty-five dollars."

"That's fine, take it away."

Stu and David were surprised that the bug started and ran. They limped slowly to a service station, inflated the tires and drove it home.

In all the years that followed, even years after that 1965 VW convertible was past fifty years old that car stayed in the Landersman family and was always referred to as "Timothy," after the congressman from whom it was purchased.

Let's go back to the Pentagon, to the OPNAV staff where a new rear admiral, Bob Morris relieved Ed Field as head of the Surface

Warfare Directorate, so Stu Landersman had a new boss. Stu found Morris to be good to work for, almost as good as was Ed Field and certainly much better than Roy Hoffman.

When he started this job Stu had been told by the Captain detailer that it would be for either two or three years. He had been in the job as head of the Surface Combatant Branch for almost two years and as he had not heard anything about moving on he assumed that he would be there for the three year stint.

One day Stu was called to Rear Admiral Morris's office. He was told that Captain Henry Mustin would be reporting in to their section of the OPNAV staff and would be assigned as head of the Surface Combatant Branch; Stu's present position. Stu would then be the assistant branch head under the position that he had held for almost two years. Stu could not help but recall his time in STICKELL where after being the commanding officer for nine months a new CO came aboard and Stu went back to being executive officer. That was a very unpleasant situation and Stu then vowed, "Never again," but in spite of that vow it was happening again.

Stu had met Hank Mustin before and although Mustin had a reputation for being hard to get along with Stu had not found him so. When Mustin came he explained to Stu that he understood the awkward position Stu was in and he hoped that they could work together. They did, they got along better than Stu had expected but Stu still figured it was time to move on.

Hank Mustin came from a family well known in the Navy. His father had been an admiral and his grandfather had been an admiral. There was a naval air station, Mustin Field. As an aide to the CNO, Hank Mustin had been one of the "sword bearers," close to Admiral Elmo Zumwalt and had been active in carrying out Zumwalt's "Z-Grams."

Stu went to see the Captain Detailer, John Tice, who had been the commanding officer of USS OKLAHOMA CITY when Stu was on the Seventh Fleet staff so they were like former shipmates. Stu had been on the bridge of Tice's ship in the Gulf of Tonkin when they were over-flown by the MIG. Tice listened patiently as Stu ranted and raged about being reduced to the role of assistant to the position that he had held for almost two years. Stu brought up his time in STICKELL when he went back to being executive officer and he claimed humiliation and embarrassment in dealing with the officers of what had been his branch.

Finally, Tice looked hard at Stu, "Are you finished?"

Stu nodded with, "Yes sir."

"Would Martha rather live in Norfolk or in San Diego?"

Stu was confused. "Does that really matter?"

Tice smiled. He was having a good time. "Yes it matters. I don't care about your OPNAV problem. I need you at sea. You can have either a cruiser or a DESRON in the Atlantic or the Pacific. Go home and talk it over with Martha and call me tomorrow."

The nicest choices of duty that Stu ever had. He did go home and talk it over with Martha. Also, he called his long time mentor Roger Spreen who asked, "Is there any doubt in your mind that you can command a ship?"

Stu replied, "No, I've already had command of two ships."

"Have you ever had command of a group of ships?"

"No, you know that."

"Then don't you think that it might be worthwhile even valuable to expand your command experience with a destroyer squadron?"

The next day Stu called John Tice and asked for a destroyer squadron with home port in San Diego and those were the orders he received.

CHAPTER THIRTY SIX

THE COMPOSITE WARRIOR

1976–1981

This chapter covers two duty assignments of Stu Landersman; Commander Destroyer Squadron Twenty Three and Commanding Officer, Tactical Training Group Pacific.

THE ORIGIN OF COMPOSITE WARFARE COMMANDER (CWC)

While serving as Commander in Chief, U.S. Pacific Fleet (CINCPACFLT) in the 1970's, Admiral Thomas Hayward turned the direction of the Pacific Fleet's war plans around from defending aircraft carriers to attacking the Soviet Fleet and the perimeters of the Soviet Union. He titled his strategic plan "Sea Strike" and stated, "I'm tired of being the High Value Target-we're going to be the High Value Attackers." Without such a strategic plan in the Pacific, the only other plan for employment of naval forces was a NATO based plan that moved all resources to the Atlantic. Hayward wanted a war plan that would keep his warfighting resources in the Pacific Fleet, and his agent in this project was an ebullient and forceful former diesel submarine officer, then CINCPACFLT's War Plans Officer, CAPT James M. Patton, PhD. Hayward and Patton recognized that the existing carrier battle group organization would not permit carrier task group commanders to react in a timely manner to air, submarine and surface threats that they would face in conducting direct attacks on the Soviets in the North Pacific. A new organization was needed within carrier task groups, an innovative command and control organization that would allow the carrier task group commander to focus his attention on the strike mission.

Commander Third Fleet (COMTHIRDFLT), as the tactical development agent for the Pacific Fleet was directed to develop a command and control concept for Sea Strike, one that would enable a massed carrier battle force to fight its way through Soviet air, submarine and surface threats and strike the Soviet Union in the North Pacific. The Composite Warfare Commander (CWC) concept of command and control was created to allow Pacific Fleet aircraft carriers to accomplish this mission. The CWC concept provided subordinate coordinators to deal with the major threats, freeing the carrier task group commander to concentrate on the primary strike mission. An important part of the Pacific Fleet plan was to use nuclear attack submarines (SSN) in integrated direct support and the command and control concept had to allow for this integration of submarines into the coordinated operations of the battle groups and battle force. CWC was the command and control concept created to allow Hayward's Pacific Fleet strategic plan, Sea Strike, to work.

THE SPOKESMAN FOR CWC

While serving as Commander Destroyer Squadron Twenty-Three and after as Commanding Officer, Tactical Training Group Pacific, Captain Stuart Landersman found himself spokesman for and salesman of the Composite Warfare Commander Concept that later became Navy Doctrine. Many Navy people thought that he had invented it, but the CWC Concept was created by Dr. Bernie Schniederman, a brilliant analyst who was working for a contractor and assigned to the Tactical Development and Evaluation (TAC D&E) section of the COMTHIRDFLT Staff under VADMs Jim Doyle, Sam Gravely, and Ed Waller in the 1970's. Dr. Schniederman reasoned that if the Navy was satisfied with putting all the anti air resources under a coordinator, that had been the practice for years, then why not put the resources of other warfare areas under similar coordinators? This would allow the Officer in Tactical Command (OTC), the carrier task group commander, to concentrate on carrying out strike warfare, the primary mission of the battle group.

Defense of the task group would be carried out by three principal subordinates; Anti Air Warfare Coordinator (AAWC), Anti Submarine Warfare Coordinator (ASWC) and Anti Surface Warfare Coordinator (ASUWC). These three principal subordinates would utilize resources of the task group as allocated by the Officer in Tactical Command (OTC). The OTC, called CWC, would watch over ongoing operations and intervene only if he did not agree with some action, a process called "Command by Negation." The three pillars of the CWC concept, the innovative command and control concept created for Sea Strike were: (1) Subordinate responsibility, (2) Command by negation and (3) Resource allocation.

THE ASWC

Captain Landersman's involvement with CWC began in late 1976 when, as a brand new destroyer squadron commander with all of his ships in overhaul, he was looking for some operational employment. The normal process for any fleet unit was to follow a schedule promulgated quarterly by the Fleet Commander in Chief. Every ship and unit commander had an employment schedule and the COMDESRON 23 schedule tasked the squadron commander with looking after ships undergoing major maintenance in shipyards. Having been involved in scheduling a number of times in previous duties, Landersman had developed a habit of checking often with the young scheduling officer on whatever staff he came under, just to see what was going on in the fleet. In this case he chatted with the Scheduling Officer on the staff of Commander Naval Surface Force, U.S. Pacific Fleet (COMNAVSURFPAC) and learned that there would soon be a major fleet exercise in which COMTHIRDFLT wanted to evaluate a new tactical concept. A new concept would exist in the form of a Tactical Note, called TACNOTE in the Navy's continuous process of acronyms.

COMTHIRDFLT TACNOTE 310-1-76 was titled "The Composite Warfare Commander Concept" often abbreviated as "CWC Concept" and sometimes merely "CWC" and the same title (CWC) was used as the title of the commander of the unit operating under the concept. The evaluation would require an Anti Submarine Warfare Coordinator, whatever that was, and as Landersman had been involved in a good deal of ASW previously he volunteered for the assignment. The Scheduling Officer made the appropriate modification to the COMDESRON 23 employment schedule and Landersman was assigned to participate in fleet exercise READIEX 3-77, 29 January to 4 February 1977. He had no idea what the Composite Warfare Commander Concept was and could only make a reasonable estimate of what an Anti Submarine Warfare Coordinator did.

The Commander Destroyer Squadron Twenty-Three (COMDESRON 23) staff consisted of some very fine officers:

LCDR George Cooper	Chief Staff Officer
LT John Martin	Operations Officer
LT Bill Carlson	Engineering Officer

Later the COMDESRON 23 staff changed as follows:

LCDR Tom Withey	Chief Staff Officer
LT Bo Scharnus	Operations Officer
LT Tom Byrnes	Engineering Officer
LT Matt Moran	Combat Systems Officer

John Martin knew more about CWC than anyone else along the San Diego waterfront at the time because he had actually read the TACNOTE, so John became leader of the effort to learn the concept.

Commander Carrier Group One (COMCARGRU ONE) was RADM Paul Speer, scheduled to be the Officer Conducting the Exercise (OCE) and the Officer in Tactical Command (OTC). He had been a recent classmate of Landersman at the first Senior Officers Ship Material Readiness Course in Idaho Falls. Landersman read the TACNOTE and called on RADM Speer and the two staffs started working in preparation for the exercise. Landersman soon learned that there were some others that had read the TACNOTE.

In preparation for that first exercise Landersman and his staff worked primarily with CDR Bill Stutzer, CDR John Brickner and CDR Paul Moses. Stutzer, the COMCARGRU ONE staff Anti Submarine Warfare Officer, had commanded a diesel electric submarine and Brickner, the Air Operations Officer, had commanded an F-4 fighter squadron. Stutzer knew all there was to know about submarines but had not been certified to be a Submarine Element Coordinator by COMSUBPAC. Brickner knew anti air warfare as he was one of the most experienced fighter pilots in the Navy with many Viet Nam combat missions. Paul Moses was the staff Surface Operations

Officer. Another that worked on that exercise planning was LCDR Wayne Perras, Intelligence Officer. All of the COMDESRON 23 staff and the COMCARGRU ONE staff studied and worked at how to make this CWC Concept work. They couldn't have realized it at the time but those same people would be working together on the development and promotion of CWC for the next four years, through Landersman's tour as COMDESRON 23 and his next duty assignment as Commanding Officer, Tactical Training Group Pacific.

In addressing one of the first problems, it was agreed that the best location for the ASWC would be in the aircraft carrier and Stutzer told Landersman that COMDESRON 23 and staff would be a part of the COMCARGRU ONE staff so that any and all communications would be from and to COMCARGRU ONE. Landersman objected to this, pointing out that the TACNOTE described the ASWC as a separate function. Stutzer insisted, pointing out that RADM Speer, his Chief of Staff and his Ops Officer all said that the squadron commander should be folded into the carrier group staff. After a few hours of disagreement Landersman told Stutzer that he wouldn't do the ASWC job as part of the carrier group staff and if they insisted on it being that way they could find someone else to do the job. Like a pouting kid Landersman started to pick up his toys to go home. He knew that as he had volunteered for the exercise, he could get the scheduling officer to change him back to looking after ships in overhaul. Stutzer stopped Landersman, went back to his seniors and COMDESRON 23 was permitted to participate on his own terms as a separate command.

Landersman worked with Stutzer, Brickner, Moses and Perras in a series of exercises in EASTPAC and WESTPAC over the next two years and the five of them were together at TACTRAGRUPAC after that. Often Stutzer and Landersman would reflect on how the development of CWC was determined with a threat to "pick up my toys and go home," because it determined that the subordinate warfare coordinators (later changed to commanders) would be separate commands. Landersman was always pleased that even after his insistence on a separate command policy, RADM Speer and the two rear admirals that followed him as COMCARGRU ONE (RADMs Stacer Holcomb and Bill Ramsey) welcomed COMDESRON 23 and staff on board the carrier, treated them socially as members of the COMCARGRU ONE staff and supported the CWC Concept.

During 1977 and 1978 as COMDESRON 23 and staff participated in 12 major fleet exercises, riding every Pacific Fleet carrier while performing as ASWC in most and on occasion serving as Anti Surface Warfare Coordinator, Anti Air Warfare Coordinator and Electronic Warfare Coordinator. By the end of his destroyer squadron command tour Landersman had served in almost every role in the CWC Concept, even as CWC of a small surface group. Most destroyer squadron commanders participated in 2 or 3 fleet exercises.

On 21 March 1978 Landersman met with RADM Bill Rowden on board the admiral's flagship, repair ship AJAX. Rowden had recently relieved RADM Carl Christoph as Commander Cruiser Destroyer Group Three (COMCRUDESGRU THREE) and Landersman had known Bill Rowden for years. Rowden had heard that COMDESRON 23 had been doing some very fine anti submarine warfare with carrier battle groups and he asked what was different to achieve this success. Landersman described how the CWC concept provided for an Anti Submarine Warfare Coordinator with resources and authority to act under a "command by negation" policy. As ASWC he had directed the movements and operations of all the ASW resources of the battle group, coordinating direct support submarines, maritime patrol aircraft, carrier ASW aircraft and helos, ships with towed arrays and ships with hull sonar. He had even used SOSUS and other intelligence when available. Even tactical fighter and attack aircraft were encouraged to report sightings. Utilization of all available resources was the key.

Rowden asked if the title "Coordinator" bothered Landersman and what did it mean. Landersman replied that he had never understood "Coordinator" and had acted as if in command of any and all resources allocated by the Officer in Tactical Command. He positioned the ships and aircraft and directed their movements, performing as would a "Commander."

"Then why don't we change it to Commander so that everyone will know what it means," asked Rowden?

Landersman agreed, RADM Bill Rowden made the recommendation to COMTHIRDFLT and the three principal warfare Coordinators became Commanders. More than just a title change, it clarified the status of the three principle subordinates under CWC as separate commands, each a commander of his warfare area.

COORDINATED BATTLE GROUP ASW

As a young officer Landersman had served as Operations Officer in USS Robert A. Owens (DDE-827), flagship of Destroyer Squadron Twenty Eight and later Thirty Six. Both squadrons consisted of eight DDEs, Escort Destroyers. The DDE was a full-sized destroyer configured primarily for anti submarine warfare with the latest sonar and weapons, not to be confused with the DE that was a smaller Destroyer Escort. For two years both destroyer squadrons served in hunter killer groups, HUK groups, whose mission was to locate a Soviet diesel electric submarine in the North Atlantic and hold it to exhaustion, until it was forced to surface from lack of battery or oxygen. Rather than defend a "high value unit" against submarines the HUK group went hunting for submarines. It was offensive ASW. From 1957 to 1959 the HUK Groups didn't find a Soviet submarine but some years later other Atlantic Fleet ASW units were successful in forcing a Soviet diesel electric submarine to the surface and earned the case of whiskey that had been offered as reward.

The primary ship of the HUK group was a World War II aircraft carrier equipped with ASW aircraft; S-2 Tracker aircraft and ASW helicopters. At sea the group would be augmented with land based P-2 maritime patrol aircraft. Most of the time one or two U.S. diesel electric submarines would be a part of the group to exercise as the opposition submarine. The group had little or no means of coordinating with these U.S. submarines. Sometimes the group included flying boats and a blimp with towed sonar array once joined. The HUK group was commanded by a rear admiral who was a carrier group commander and was embarked in the carrier screened by the eight destroyers. The Screen Commander was a destroyer squadron commander. The first of these post-World War II HUK groups was commanded by RADM John S. Thatch, a World War II hero, naval aviation legend as a fighter pilot and tactical innovator. Ask any fighter pilot about the "Thatch Weave."

In a typical practice scenario:

* aircraft some distance away from the carrier and destroyers gets contact (electronic intercept, magnetic anomaly, visual)

* manual plots maintained on the carrier and the destroyers provide an area of probability

* OTC directs Screen Commander to detach two destroyers from the screen as a Surface Attack Unit (SAU)

* SAU hustles to the area of probability and attempts to gain sonar contact

* contact held by destroyers and aircraft as long as possible

* confirmation obtained that any U.S. submarine was well clear

As Operations Officer in the flagship of the destroyer squadron commander Landersman was involved with every part of the HUK group process and learned the importance of:

- having all the right resources
- having good communications
- maintaining an accurate plot
- developing teamwork and coordination
- communicating with own submarine

- each element of the group knowing their role
- having someone in charge of the overall operation who knew what they were doing

In a typical pre-CWC carrier task group, a destroyer squadron commander would be assigned duty as Screen Commander and he would be responsible for the protection of the aircraft carrier using his eight destroyers. Sometimes he could augment his screen with close-in aircraft or helicopters but his authority was limited to the screening distance of the destroyers from the aircraft carrier, generally the visual horizon. CWC changed that. The traditional Screen Commander became ASWC and ASUWC with range extended to the limits of their resources, far distant from the carrier into offensive operations.

After READIEX 3-77, 29 January–4 February 1977, Landersman's first fleet exercise as ASWC, he saw that the CWC Concept established a coordinator that would serve as did the OTC of a HUK Group. Of course there were differences, mainly in that the ASWC could not direct the movement of the entire battle group. That was determined by the basic mission or objective of the battle group. Rather than roaming the seas searching for enemy submarines the ASWC conducted searches along the path and in the direction of intended movement of the battle group. The old HUK group had conducted offensive ASW and that flavor was carried over to the ASWC in the CWC Concept of the carrier task group. Offensive tactics were carried out far ahead of the battle group with P-3, S-3, SSN and TASS ships searching for enemy submarines long before the submarine could get in position to attack the carrier.

The comparison was the same for the other warfare areas. Under the CWC Concept each of the primary warfare coordinators (AAWC, ASWC, ASUWC) utilized the resources of the carrier battle group to accomplish their specific warfare area mission. The resources of the battle group were allocated by the CWC and re-allocated as tactical conditions changed. The warfare coordinators practiced sharing and change of primary operational control in coordination of resources.

As an example of sharing and change of primary control a missile ship would normally be allocated to and positioned by the AAWC. If the missile ship were to gain a sonar contact operational control of the ship would be passed to the ASWC. The missile ship would prosecute its sonar contact and would coordinate with ASW aircraft while still continuing to function as an AAW asset. When the ASW action was completed operational control of the missile ship would be returned to the AAWC. In another example, maritime patrol aircraft allocated to the ASWC could report surface contacts to the ASUWC. The CWC Concept emphasized the importance and value of teamwork and coordination. It took practice and training, it required good and extensive communications and it meant that there was no place for internal Navy community parochialism.

In <u>On War,</u> Clausewitz's fourteenth chapter, Economy of Effort is one of the most often stated but most commonly misunderstood portions of his work. To most modern military men it means to hold back a portion of the force or resource–don't use it all–keep some for later–economy. That interpretation shows that the user only saw the chapter name but didn't read the text. Because in Clausewitz's time economy had a different meaning–very different–and his chapter on Economy of Effort is the shortest in his book–two paragraphs on one page. In five minutes any one that reads it sees that he means, "—make sure that all forces are involved–always to ensure that no part of the whole force is idle." To Clausewitz economy meant ***use everything.*** Every part of the force must have a role. Don't waste anything, because not using an asset is wasteful, hence not economical. In coordinated battle group ASW under the CWC Concept, every resource of the battle group (that the ASWC could control or influence in any way) had a role.

Relationships between Navy communities were an important part of the CWC Concept. Success in any coordinated effort required the full support of each community represented in the battle group. The CWC Concept provided a Submarine Element Coordinator (SEC) and to conduct integrated direct support the SEC had to be approved and certified by COMSUBPAC. Within the submarine community there was established a standard and a process for this SEC certification and typically a submarine squadron commander would come aboard the carrier with a composite staff numbering almost as many as the CARGRU staff and with additional communications equipment. It allowed close coordination of direct support submarines and strong leadership for the full ASW effort.

The SSN was a very valuable addition to the battle group. It was the best all around ASW platform and could provide just as important service in anti surface warfare. But full effectiveness of this valuable asset could only be realized with good reliable two-way communications between the SSN and the battle group. There were many systems and processes in place that enabled the SEC, ASWC or CWC to contact the direct support submarine but none were reliable. Keyed sonar, Gertrude and practice depth charges, all of doubtful reliability at best were some existing systems. There were some new innovative systems using emerging technology tried by the battle groups but none provided consistent reliability. Coordinating with a submarine operating in integrated direct support became an art of blending all of the processes and systems. Full value of the SSN with the battle group required good communications and that was only achieved with experience in utilizing all available systems.

Communications was the most important factor in integrating the direct support submarine into the battle group. Landersman had first learned this with the HUK groups in 1957 when his bother-in-law was serving in the submarine that was assigned to the same HUK group. One day at sea the HUK group was holding sonar contact with a submarine as USS Robert A. Owens, Landersman's ship, was one of the destroyers circling the contact in "hold down" tactics. Every indication pointed to the probability that this was a submarine but the question was, "Was this the HUK group submarine or a stranger," a Soviet submarine? The screen commander, embarked in Owens, and the HUK group commander in the carrier tried every means they could think of to determine where their submarine was, to make sure they were not holding contact with their own submarine but their submarine would not answer any attempts to communicate. Finally, Landersman told the squadron commander about his brother-in-law being in their submarine and asked if he could try some informal and unofficial communications. The squadron commander granted permission.

By Gertrude (underwater acoustic telephone) Landersman spoke, "Now look, Tom, this is Stu and we have to know where you are. The commodore is very upset because we have to be sure that the contact we are holding is not you."

He went on and on emphasizing that they had to be certain about the contact they were holding and that their submarine was surely not being held by the HUK group. To confirm this the commodore wanted our submarine to release a flare. As they watched with wonder a flare came up right in the middle of the circling destroyers. The HUK group had been holding contact with their own submarine and that submarine had been sure he was well away from the HUK group with no destroyers pinging on him.

Long after, in port, Landersman learned that the submarine captain grilled Tom about his strange relative and only then released a flare. Before the flare clarified the situation there had been discussion on the Owens' bridge between commodore and captain as to whether they could get their submarine to come in and "take a look" at the stranger. The two most senior destroyer officers actually thought that their submarine had a Jules Verne-like picture window or porthole through which to observe underwater. Working with a submarine required effective communications and knowledge of submarines and they didn't have either in the HUK groups.

The Submarine Element Coordinator (SEC) brought knowledge and communications to the battle group. Having an SEC with the battle group was like having a kid on your little league team that could hit, throw, run and catch, but best of all, his father owned the sporting goods store. One such SEC was CAPT Jerry Holland, COMSUBRON ONE, who, in effect "wrote the book" on close integrated direct support submarines with carrier battle groups under the CWC Concept. At the time the submarine community wanted support for the SSN 688 Program and they got it because Jerry Holland, a true innovator, proved that submarines could operate in integrated direct support of carrier battle groups. Most analysts claimed that submarines could not function in close support but Holland proved it could be done.

No one completely solved the communications problem but Holland showed that it could be managed. Soon after, when the SSN 688 Class had been approved and were being built the submarine community decided that integrated direct support was not practical and withdrew submarines from carrier battle groups.

Years later, with the end of the Cold War, and with U.S. submarines looking for justification the same submarine community leadership rediscovered the value and methods of employing submarines in integrated direct support of carrier battle groups. In recent time Jerry Holland, a retired rear admiral, denies that the SSN 688 Class program drove the integrated direct support submarine operations of the 1970s. He claims it was motivated by desire to provide quality ASW capability to carrier battle groups in support of Sea Strike and he may be right.

Submarines were not the only community courted to participate in coordinated battle group ASW under CWC. Maritime Patrol Aircraft, P-3, were valuable additions to the extended ASW reach of the battle group and often Commander Patrol Wings, U.S. Pacific Fleet (COMPATWINGSPAC) would provide liaison officers to serve with the ASWC in the carrier. On board the carrier were ASW aircraft (S-3) and helicopters (H-3), part of the total ASW resources. It became normal practice for flight crews to brief and debrief with the ASWC before and after flights. After a number of fleet exercises as ASWC, COMDESRON 23 was very popular within Commander ASW Wings, U.S. Pacific Fleet (COMASWWINGSPAC). On 18 January 1979 CDR Don Baird relieved CDR Jim Durbin as Commanding Officer of VS-38, the Red Griffins, and the guest speaker was COMDESRON 23. Imagine, a black-shoe the speaker at a naval aviation squadron change of command ceremony!

Destroyer Squadron Twenty-Three is the most famous and the most highly decorated destroyer squadron in the world. The "Little Beaver" squadron of Arleigh Burke won two unit awards in World War II and under Pete Roane they earned a third for recovery of the Mayaguez and evacuation of Saigon in 1976. The squadron holds all three of the unit citations existing in the U.S. Navy; MUC, PUC and NUC. Landersman could, and often did brag of the squadron's notoriety because he had nothing to do with the fame or awards but shortly after he relieved Pete Roane on 16 October 1976 he realized that this was still a very special destroyer squadron. DESRON 23 was the ASW squadron of the Pacific Fleet.

U.S. SSNs were equipped with sensitive highly capable towed sonar arrays that gave them a fine capability in ASW. The SSN was, and still is, the best ASW platform. In the Pacific Fleet in 1976 three frigates were the only surface combatant ships carrying towed arrays, called TASS, SQR-15 and these innocuous little ships were by far the best ASW surface ships in the Pacific Fleet. These three little ships were the only true ASW ships in the Pacific Fleet because they were the only ships that could reach out far enough to do more than protect themselves, they could protect others and conduct offensive ASW with their TASS systems. But the full value of the TASS systems came only through coordination with aircraft. The TASS system had been made for strategic surveillance and when that role was no longer needed because of the SOSUS system, TASS became tactical and three systems were turned over to each Fleet. In both the Atlantic and Pacific the systems went into ships that were perceived to be the most expendable, the least capable, because the people making those decisions did not understand TASS capabilities. Three frigates in each fleet went from being the least capable to the most capable overnight except few people in either fleet knew how to use them, very few surface warfare officers, that is, but submariners did.

Two of the three Pacific Fleet TASS ships were in DESRON 23; USS Albert David (FF 1050) and USS Bronstein (FF 1037). In a battle group supported by direct support submarines that included a SEC like Jerry Holland the TASS ships were treated like integrated direct support submarines. Communicating with them was no problem and they often provided links to the SSN. It was natural then to allow the SEC control of the TASS ships as they complimented coordination between SSNs, P-3s and S-3s in the distant reach of ASW. As a tactical matter the ASWC overall effort became more offensive than defensive and focused on detection, localization and attack of an enemy submarine long before that submarine could attack the carrier. In all Fleet exercises game rules provided that the orange, or "enemy," submarine continue to penetrate and attack the carrier even if detected earlier and even if simulated attacks were conducted against him. Understanding this it became ASWC policy to conduct as many attacks as possible, often with a goal of fifty, on an orange submarine before the carrier was attacked.

In a major fleet exercise with full CWC and ASWC resources including multiple direct support submarines, P-3, S-3, H-3, TASS and other surface combatant ships it would often develop that an exercise submarine playing enemy would penetrate and launch a green flare signaling an attack on the carrier only to be met with, "Yeah, but we attacked you 50 times on your way in." LCDR Larry Seaquist, Commanding Officer of TASS ship Bronstein, wore a P-3 tie clasp with an explanation, "That's my primary weapon."

Among the very few surface warfare officers that knew anything about TASS was LT Matt Moran on the DESRON 23 Staff who had previous duty on a TASS ship. It was indeed fortunate that Moran came to the staff when he did as he was the first officer to fill the newly created Combat Systems Officer billet on a DESRON Staff, he was the only one knowledgeable in TASS and he came to a destroyer squadron with two of the TASS ships. Rarely did the Navy Manpower and Personnel Command perform with such foresight as it did in sending Matt Moran to the DESRON 23 staff. Moran worked closely with the Submarine Element Coordinator staff and ASWC staff and taught all of them how to utilize TASS in coordinated ASW operations.

Attacking the orange submarine far out meant positioning SSNs and TASS ships with VP support a hundred miles or more ahead of the carrier. This led to an ever-increasing search for more distance, more battle space, longer-range communications and it made the process offensive. Why not send the direct support submarine even farther ahead to a choke point that we have to transit in a few days? Why not send attack aircraft to destroy the enemy submarine before it gets underway? Why not ask for an Air Force strike before the enemy gets underway? Special Forces? Mine his harbor egress? What started out as defense of the carrier task group with the CWC Concept soon grew into an expansion of battle space and time as part of a Joint Task Force conducting offensive operations.

In one exercise the ASWC tasked the Air Wing to fly reconnaissance missions on the naval base so that the SEC could count missing submarines and determine how many would be used against the battle group. In another the Air Wing conducted simulated strike missions against potential enemy submarines not yet underway for the exercise.

Three baseball managers were sitting at a bar during the all-star break discussing how to keep Pete Rose from scoring. One told of positioning his fielders based on Rose's hitting patterns. Another told of studying pitch selection so that his pitchers wouldn't give Rose anything to hit. The third would concentrate on stopping Rose on the base paths. All three agreed that none of these tactics were likely to work. Down the bar sat a hockey coach who couldn't help overhearing and said, "Break his legs in the parking lot."

"Break his legs in the parking lot," became a tactical slogan at Tactical Training Group Pacific. It applied to all warfare areas not just ASW. Why try to shoot missiles out of the sky? Destroy the launching platform before it launches. Destroy the warehouse of missiles before they're placed on the launcher. Stop the purchase, shipment and importation of the weapon before it reaches a hostile enemy.

DESRON 23 was part of the Enterprise Battle Group under COMCARGRU ONE, RADM Stacer Holcomb, with his staff that COMDESRON 23 knew so well. The first phase of deployment to WESTPAC, the transit from San Diego to Pearl Harbor, was the major fleet exercise RIMPAC 78. COMDESRON 23 was in his familiar role as ASWC and the battle group included two submarines in integrated direct support and three in opposition. Harry Schrader, CO of the nuclear powered guided missile cruiser Long Beach was AAWC. Jim Hogg was ASUWC. Jerry Holland was SEC. In looking back on it years later Landersman thought that RIMPAC 78 was the finest of CWC demonstrations because the commanders were experienced in all warfare areas, they had all the proper resources and they functioned under a command by negation concept. They conducted great coordinated battle group operations in all the warfare areas.

Admiral Arleigh Burke visited his destroyer squadron in San Diego on 31 March 1978 just before the Little Beavers deployed to WESTPAC as part of the Enterprise Battle Group. A few months before, Landersman had expressed concern in a letter to Admiral Burke that the squadron was spending too much time in ASW. Also, that he had become identified as a specialist in ASW only because he was there at the right time and no one knew any better. Admiral Burke replied in a letter dated 8 November 1977:

"I wouldn't be too concerned about devoting most of your time to ASW. Not only is that of paramount importance, but the lessons you learn, the experiences you get, will be applicable to every other type of combat. Your explanation of how you became known as the expert in ASW is very similar to my good luck in being available for 'Up the Slot' duty years ago."

Admiral Burke's thought was what you learn in one warfare area applies to every other warfare area. In his next duty assignment Landersman would see how right Admiral Burke was.

TACTRAGRUPAC

In 1978, the CWC concept became Pacific Fleet doctrine as it had moved up the development ladder from a Third Fleet TACMEMO to CINCPACFLT TACNOTE 310-1-78. From VADM Sylvester Foley, COMSEVENTHFLT, who had been a classmate at SOSMRC in Idaho, Landersman learned that ADM Hayward wanted a new tactics school to be patterned after the Royal Navy Maritime Tactical School at HMS Dryad. ADM Hayward wanted a school to teach battle group tactics to senior officers. Foley suggested that Landersman leave his squadron in WESTPAC and fly west to go home, stopping in England to visit HMS Dryad but Landersman told him he'd prefer to stay with his ships. Later, with an opportunity to talk to Admiral Hayward Landersman expressed the thought that there really weren't any battle group tactics to teach but Hayward quickly assured him that he'd find some. Of course Hayward had his Pacific Fleet strategic strike plan, Sea Strike, in mind.

CDR John McMillan was the first officer to report in to COMTRAPAC to be a part of this new Brit-like activity that didn't as yet have a name, purpose, location or people. But that didn't bother McMillan, with whom Landersman had served years before on the staff of COMSEVENTHFLT. McMillan was one of the most organized, intelligent, dedicated and competent of persons and Landersman had specifically asked for him in this new duty because he knew that if something didn't exist and had to be created, John McMillan could do it. McMillan voluntarily gave up a chance to go to the Naval War College for this new assignment. He had a mind like a computer and a master's degree in computer systems management so he just made out a spread-sheet covering all the issues to be resolved and set about resolving them. After an analysis of the problem he found out where COMDESRON 23 was and journeyed to WESTPAC.

They met in Chinhae, Korea on board USS John Paul Jones (DDG-32) on 18 September 1978 and spent two days going over plans for this new training activity. McMillan had lots of questions:

What is the name of this activity?
What kind of facility will we have?
What are we to teach?
Who do we teach?
Who approves of what we teach?
Who do we work for?
What kind of, and how many staff or faculty will
we have?
When does the rest of this staff arrive?
Where do our billets come from?
When do we start?

One thing McMillan had resolved was where they would be located. COMTRAPAC had made space available in San Diego with cooperation of CAPT Bill Garcia, CO Fleet Combat Training Center Pacific. There was a classroom and some office space so that was a start. From ADM Hayward's staff Landersman had learned that the admiral wanted him to be titled Executive Director for Pacific Fleet Tactical Training so Landersman told McMillan that the name of the new organization would be Office of Executive Director for Pacific Fleet Tactical Training. McMillan said, "Okay, so we'll be an 'Office,'" and when Landersman reported to COMTRAPAC on 16 December 1978 that office was established.

They were to teach battle group tactics and as no one could figure out at the start what were battle group tactics, Landersman decided that they would teach the Composite Warfare Commander Doctrine as that was Pacific Fleet doctrine. They were a Pacific Fleet office and any tactics would have to be based on CWC command and control. So the Office of Executive Director for Pacific Fleet Tactical Training, later to be Tactical Training Group Pacific, started as a school to teach CWC to senior officers.

Later, among the "CNO Objectives" of ADM Hayward that was included as an initiative he had started as CINCPACFLT as, "Effective integration of air, surface and subsurface platforms into coordinated and tactically proficient battle groups." This would be accomplished through the CWC command and control doctrine. PACFLTTACTRA was built around CWC Doctrine.

The closest that Stu Landersman had to a career "mentor" was Roger Spreen, under whom Stu served three times. First, Commander Spreen was Operations Officer on the COMDESLANT staff in Newport, Rhode Island and Lieutenant Landersman was one of his assistants. Next, when Stu had command of Stickell, Captain Spreen was his destroyer division commander. When Landersman was going through pre-commissioning duty for Hepburn at Long Beach Naval Shipyard, Spreen, as Chief of Staff to COMCRUDESPAC, was once again Landersman's regular reporting senior. Spreen, who retired as a rear admiral a few years later after being head of naval ordnance, was an excellent person to work for and had an endless collection of sayings or expressions of leadership. Landersman tried to remember them all and follow the guidance that Spreen conveyed but there were too many sayings. He should have written them down. One that Landersman did remember and that had particular application to the formation of a new organization such as PACFLTTACTRA, later TACTRAGRUPAC, was, "The true leader surrounds him self with good people, listens to them and lets them perform."

Some of those from the COMCARGRU ONE Staff, those that developed CWC and made it work with the Enterprise Battle Group, came to help Landersman again at the new office. Bill Stutzer and John Brickner were great teammates from early CWC days. From the COMCRUDESGRU THREE Staff came Carl Stokes, H-3 pilot. In that "starting five" were Stutzer (submarines), Brickner (tacair), Stokes (ASW air), McMillan (surface) and Landersman. A little later came Digger Murray (A-3), Al Branch (P-3), Dallas Bethea (surface), Paul Moses (surface) and Wayne Perras (intelligence), the last two also from the COMCARGRU ONE staff.

Eighteen months later the Atlantic Fleet started a similar activity and their director wanted to be called "Commanding Officer" so Landersman agreed that if the new Atlantic Fleet activity would accept his Pacific Fleet three week course to start, he'd accept the change of name. On 1 June 1980 the Office of Executive Director for Pacific Fleet Tactical Training became Commanding Officer, Tactical Training Group Pacific and the three-week course that they had been teaching for 18 months remained. Title had been traded for curriculum. The Atlantic Fleet activity started with the new name a few days before the Pacific's title was changed so forever after TACTRAGRULANT has said they were first. A tactical error on Landersman's part.

The Atlantic counterpart was created by CINCLANTFLT after receiving numerous reports from his people who had attended the Pacific Fleet classes. At one time the San Diego activity had taught more flag officers from the Atlantic than Pacific.

Classes were made up of students from the various warfare communities. Although the school was established to teach flag officers, there wouldn't be enough of them to justify a full time staff, so personnel in or enroute to battle group jobs; staffs and ships filled classes. RADM Ed Carter was the first flag officer attendee as prospective COMCRUDESGRU THREE on 16 April 1979. This was significant for the new training activity, their first flag officer. Carter was tough and tactically knowledgeable but non-committal during the course. They didn't know how he felt about the course until the end of class critique and a letter he wrote to CINCPACFLT. Some of RADM Carter's comments:

> –the finest course which I have ever attended
> –one of the finest groups of professionals I have ever encountered in any activity
> –obviously experts
> –dedicated to and enthusiastic about their work
> –generate that same sense of enthusiasm in every member of the class

TACTRAGRUPAC gave special tactics courses at Pearl Harbor and to Air Force AWACS people in Seattle. John Brickner helped Top Gun get started at Miramar Naval Air Station. They gave a special flag officer short tactical course in San Diego.

The first civilian to attend a TACTRAGRUPAC course was Norman Polmar and he may be the only one ever. At one time TACTRAGRUPAC held a quota for a naval reserve officer that didn't show as LCDR John Lehman was appointed Secretary of the Navy. A couple of years later with the Strategic Studies Group Landersman had lunch with the Secretary and told him that he had been a no-show at TACTRAGRUPAC and Lehman apologized.

THE ADVOCATES

In the Pacific Fleet most officers, particularly flag officers, were supportive of CWC, understandably so because it was created in the Pacific Fleet by Dr. Bernie Schniederman at the Third Fleet Tac D&E shop under VADM Jim Doyle. Also, ADM Hayward supported CWC when he was CINCPACFLT and after he became CNO. VADM Sam Gravely had inherited the Tac D&E section as COMTHIRDFLT and he soon was a strong advocate and gave all battle group commanders and subordinate warfare coordinators freedom to develop CWC.

As a destroyer squadron commander Landersman had taken VADM Gravely's son on a training cruise (along with his son David) and Gravely was very supportive of Landersman's programs.

Hayward's deputy at CINCPACFLT, VADM Tom Bigley, had been as strong a supporter of CWC as any flag officer in the Pacific and so it was a great boost to the program when he became COMSECONDFLT in the Atlantic. Bigley was the first vice admiral to attend a course at PACFLTTACTRA. When he came to San Diego from Norfolk on 20 August 1979 he asked that his attendance not be advertised as he did not want his time taken up with calls or meetings with other flag officers and he used his time to study tactics. He did his homework and was an excellent attentive and active student, participating to the fullest and a roll model for other students. He liked the sobriquet "Stu's U," that was being used among Pacific Fleet officers for PACFLTTACTRA. Bigley's attendance of the Pacific Fleet course proved to be one of the most important steps in the Navy's acceptance of CWC.

Back in Norfolk after the course VADM Bigley preached CWC to his staff and subordinate commanders and was instrumental in convincing CINCLANTFLT of the value of a school such as TACTRAGRUPAC. He had Landersman come to Norfolk and introduce CWC to the Second Fleet staff and subordinate commanders.

Most of the carrier group and cruiser-destroyer group commanders in the Pacific supported CWC. They were anxious to see it work in the fleet exercises each conducted. At the time only carrier-group commanders, naval aviators all, were allowed to command carrier task groups in the Pacific. No cruiser-destroyer group commanders (surface warfare officers all) were allowed to command carrier task groups or to embark in aircraft carriers for any reason. Particularly supportive of CWC in the early days were carrier group commanders RADMs Paul Peck, Paul Speer, Stacer Holcomb, Tom Brown, Sylvester Foley, Bill Ramsey and Hunt Hardesty, all naval aviators. Cruiser-destroyer group commanders had less to do with CWC because they were denied access to carrier battle groups. Still, most of them were supportive.

RADM Ed Briggs, COMCRUDESGRU THREE, was particularly anxious to be involved in CWC and negotiated his way into a major carrier battle group exercise by volunteering to be ASUWC in a cruiser. It was the only time anyone more senior in rank than a captain performed that role. In most major fleet exercises in which Landersman was ASWC he would also serve as ASUWC, keeping the functions as separate as was reasonable, so it was good to have someone else fill the ASUWC job.

RADM Boot Hill had been COMTRAPAC when the new tactics school started. He gave strong support and then moved on to the staff of CNO where he continued the support. He had Landersman come to Washington to talk CWC to the OPNAV staff. Landersman also went to the Third Fleet Staff at Pearl Harbor, Second Fleet Staff in Norfolk, Sixth Fleet Staff in Naples and Seventh Fleet Staff in

Yokosuka. So during his first year as Executive Director for Pacific Fleet Tactical Training Landersman talked CWC with all four numbered fleet commanders. He was directed by CINCPACFLT, then ADM Sylvester Foley, to go to the Naval War College in Newport and tell the Operations Department how to teach tactics, a rather sensitive assignment. Imagine, telling the Naval War College how to teach naval tactics! Landersman was received with more grace than he could have expected.

Support for CWC Doctrine was based on parochial internal Navy objectives. The Navy aviation community saw that CWC Doctrine provided full support of all resources to the Carrier Task Group, later called Carrier Battle Group, and focused all attention on accomplishment of the aircraft carrier attack mission which was the objective of ADM Hayward's strategic plan for the Pacific Fleet. Flag officers of aircraft carrier background, the "tail hookers," were strong supporters of CWC Doctrine and in that time only naval aviation flag officers commanded carrier task groups in the Pacific Fleet. In the Atlantic, black-shoe rear admirals were allowed to command carrier task groups but only until they arrived in the Mediterranean or other potential hot spot where aviators took command. The maritime patrol aviation community saw that CWC Doctrine provided a role for them in carrier operations. The naval aviation community was united in strong support of CWC Doctrine.

Among surface warfare officers Landersman pointed out that most of the time the three principal warfare area coordinators (AAWC, ASUWC and ASUWC) were surface warfare officers, each operating under a command by negation policy that allowed the coordinator more freedom to act than in any other command arrangement. So, he reasoned, surface warfare officers were really running the battle group.

A number of years later naval aviators figured out that surface warfare officers really controlled all the assets of the battle group including most of the aircraft in the air wing. And by 1985 black-shoe rear admirals (cruiser destroyer group commanders) in the Pacific as well as the Atlantic fleets were allowed to embark in carriers and to command carrier battle groups. That would never do to the most parochial naval aviators so CWC doctrine was changed to create a Strike Warfare Commander, a new commander equal to the three principal warfare commanders of the original CWC doctrine. This impressive new title and function would always be given to CAG, the Carrier Air Wing Commander. Also, ASWC and ASUWC were combined into one warfare area commander.

Remember, one of the primary reasons for the origin of CWC doctrine was to release the OTC from the burdens of defending the carrier so that he could concentrate on conducting the primary strike mission. Now, with creation of a Strike Warfare Commander the CWC had only to sit back and command by negation, having turned over even the primary strike mission to a subordinate. And besides, it increased the importance of CAG making that billet stronger for promotion. But probably the most important reason for creation of the Strike Warfare Commander under CWC was that by 1985 black-shoe admirals were allowed to command carrier battle groups even in the Pacific, and having CAG in control of all aircraft in the carrier kept aviation assets under a naval aviator even if the battle group commander was a surface warfare officer.

The submarine community saw the CWC Doctrine as a means to justify force levels, to justify the 688 Class, to help accomplish the Pacific Fleet strategy and as a process of retaining operational control of their submarines even in battle group tactical employment. Also, it exposed the submarine community to carrier task group operations about which they previously had very little opportunity to learn. Perhaps in the future a submarine flag officer might command a carrier group if he had served as CO of an SSN in integrated direct support, attended TACTRAGRUPAC and then served as a Submarine Element Coordinator. It did happen years later when a dolphin-wearing rear admiral commanded a carrier battle group in the Mediterranean. The submarine community was united in strong support of CWC Doctrine.

The surface warfare community of the Navy was divided. Within the surface warfare community are officers with primarily cruiser-destroyer background, the majority of whose sea duty has been with carrier task groups. Most of these had accepted the aviator-only command of the battle group situation and had established positions of responsibility in the anti-air and anti-surface roles of the carrier task groups. These officers saw CWC doctrine as a formal policy that placed them in command positions within the carrier battle group, responsible and with authority for performing the various warfare roles using the resources of the carrier task group. Most of the surface warfare cruiser-destroyer community supported CWC Doctrine. But the surface warfare community also included officers with primary involvement in amphibious warfare.

THE OPPOSITION

Early in his Navy career Landersman learned from Roger Spreen that the first thing you did in a new job is to find out who you work for, who's in charge. The second thing to do was to determine what had to be done, what's the mission and third; identify the enemy. Admiral Hayward, as CINPACFLT and then as CNO clearly was in charge and he had directed Landersman to promote CWC and so Landersman knew that the job was to promote, sell and teach that concept, to have it accepted as Navy doctrine. So, next he had to identify the enemy. Where was the opposition? They were numerous but because of the high level support of Admiral Hayward and obvious support of the many other flag officers, it was not good politics for any officer to demonstrate overt opposition. The opposition was subtle, covert, making it much more difficult to deal with.

A large segment of the surface warfare community was based on amphibious warfare. Established and hard learned policy from World War II, amphibious operations required that the Commander, Amphibious Task Force (CATF) has authority over allocation and tasking of all resources of the force. Amphibious warfare doctrine held that allocation of aircraft from the decks of aircraft carriers must be subject to requirements of the amphibious operation as first priority.

There had long been–and still exists–a controversy over whether the aircraft carrier belongs to the commander of an independent carrier task group or if that carrier group and aircraft carrier are subordinate to the commander of the amphibious task force. As the CWC concept became doctrine in the Pacific Fleet and moved towards becoming Navy doctrine, those officers whose interests were in amphibious warfare saw CWC doctrine as a threat and opposed it. These amphibious warfare oriented surface warfare officers based their opposition on the need to have close control of all resources for accomplishment of the primary amphibious warfare mission. It was a controversy based on two opposing valid, dedicated and conscientious beliefs.

The controversy over allocation of resources was not resolved and may never be resolved. CWC doctrine gives allocation authority to a battle group commander in support of his strike mission. Amphibious Warfare doctrine gives allocation authority to an amphibious task force commander in support of his amphibious operation.

VADM Lee Baggett was COMNAVSURFPAC. He attended one day of the special three day flag officers course at PACFLTTACTRA. His Chief of Staff, Captain Bob Hoffman attended a briefing on the CWC Concept and went away mumbling that it was nothing but a program intended to eliminate the surface warfare community from the most important naval operations. He conveyed this to VADM Baggett who added the opinion that real professional naval officers didn't have to be taught battle group tactics, these were procedures learned in the progression of increasingly responsible jobs at sea leading up to ship command.

Baggett's view was that any officer that had completed a successful ship command could step into the AAWC, ASWC and ASUWC roles. He felt that it didn't take special training and CWC was nothing new, it was one of the options offered in ATP-1 for command and control of Navy task groups.

Opposition to CWC by the admiral and chief of staff quite naturally spread to the COMNAVSURFPAC staff. Quotas for surface warfare officers went unfilled and the more senior students failed to show up or were permitted in their orders to leave before the course ended. CWC meant little to some of the senior surface warfare leaders because their rear admirals were not allowed to command carrier battle groups in the Pacific. From the very beginning, the aviation community and the submarine community gave very strong support to CWC and to PACFLTTACTRA but not the surface warfare community. There were individual supporters, like Carter, Briggs, Schrader, Hogg and Rowden but amphibious commanders and many of the top surface warfare community opposed it.

PROTECTION

Introducing a change, new system or new concept into the Navy is like introducing social change into a society. It is very difficult to change cultural procedures. It meets with obstacles. This applies to military innovation as well as civilian and business. Senior people that have succeeded in a culture, in a structured society, who have risen to top leadership positions tend to oppose innovations that would change the structure of that culture or society. The leader at the top of an organizational ladder does not want to see the ladder rungs changed. And these leaders are inclined to focus personal dislike on those that would change the culture or structure in which the leaders have succeeded and in which they are comfortable. If the inventor is out of reach the messenger gets shot. The innovator and the advocate make enemies.

If an innovator is to be successful in winning acceptance of his product he must overcome obstacles. He must persevere, even use guile and deception. He must be a salesman, a product champion, an advocate. The innovator needs tenacity and determination if he is to succeed and he needs protection. Protection may be in various forms but, to be practical, in the Navy it means that the innovator must have a mentor, an individual of sufficient rank or position to overcome opposition. And the mentor must demonstrate that protection.

As CO TACTRAGRUPAC Landersman had been promoting the acceptance of CWC in the Atlantic and Mediterranean as well as in the Pacific when the CNO came to visit him in San Diego. Only a few days before he had received a call from the CNO's aide telling that ADM Hayward would be coming to see him on 6 December 1979. The CNO would be arriving by air at NAS North Island, wanted to come directly to TACTRAGRUPAC and return directly to NAS North Island and depart.

Landersman met the CNO's plane at the VIP landing site, took him by car to the boat landing, by barge (borrowed from COMTRAPAC) to the NTC Kidd Club landing and by car to TACTRAGRUPAC. After ADM Hayward toured the facility they reversed the travel arrangements and the CNO flew away. Landersman and Admiral Hayward talked about tactical training that day.

During his tour of TACTRAGRUPAC that day Admiral Hayward asked to see the War Game Center. Landersman showed him a classroom with magnetic ships and blackboard and the CNO expressed surprise. Landersman told him this was how it was done at the Royal Navy Maritime Tactical School and that it was very popular and successful here at TACTRAGRUPAC. He had no desire to change it. Later, after the CNO had returned to Washington his staff started the process that led to creation of a magnificent sophisticated war game system for TACTRAGRUPAC, a system that developed after Landersman was gone.

Landersman didn't understand why ADM Hayward had come to San Diego just to see TACTRAGRUPAC until some months later when one of the CNO's staff explained that the admiral had thought it best to demonstrate support, to give protection and to provide some clout. Surely, every flag officer in San Diego and in the Pacific Fleet knew that the CNO had gone to San Diego and visited only TACTRAGRUPAC.

THE HAYWARD STORY

When the Enterprise Battle Group reached Pearl Harbor at the end of RIMPAC 78 Landersman was told to call on ADM Hayward, CINCPACFLT. In the absence of ADM Hayward he talked with the Deputy CINCPACFLT, VADM Tom Bigley, who explained that after deployment and for his next duty ADM Hayward wanted Landersman to start a school in San Diego that would teach battle group tactics to senior officers. They discussed what was meant by battle group tactics, where it would be taught and who would attend. Later when Landersman spoke with Admiral Hayward he was told more about the school; that it was to be patterned after the Royal Navy Maritime Tactical School at HMS Dryad and Landersman became the Executive Director for Pacific Fleet Tactical Training which became Tactical Training Group Pacific. During Landersman's time at TACTRAGRUPAC ADM Hayward became Chief of Naval Operations.

Nearing completion of his time as CO TACTRAGRUPAC and having failed selection for promotion three times Landersman's retirement request was approved for 1 June 1981 and he had accepted civilian employment to commence immediately upon his retirement.

At 1530 Pacific time on 29 May 1981 Landersman was at home on leave, laying floor tile in the master bathroom of his home in Rancho Bernardo, San Diego when his wife answered the phone.

"It's for you."

"Look at me!" He showed her his hands covered with plaster-like adhesive. "I can't come to the phone. Can't you take a message?"

"I think you'd better take this call. The Chief of Naval Operations wants to talk to you."

Landersman took the phone.

ADM Hayward explained that he was starting a Strategic Studies Group at the Naval War College in Newport, Rhode Island and he wanted Landersman to be a part of it. Landersman explained that he was set to retire in two weeks and the CNO said that could be taken care of. Landersman accepted the offer, his retirement orders were cancelled and replaced with orders to Newport and he served for the next year as a CNO Fellow with the first Strategic Studies Group under Bob Murray former Under Secretary of the Navy.

As the year at Newport drew to a close Landersman had again submitted a request for retirement, it had been approved and he had orders to retire on 1 October 1982. He had accepted a civilian employment position with the Johns Hopkins University Applied Physics Laboratory in Laurel, Maryland. ADM Hayward offered a Chair of Naval Tactics that was to be created at the Naval War College. It was a very tempting offer and Landersman was flattered. He pointed out that he had orders to retire, had reached the mandatory 30 years to retire and had a civilian job. The admiral told him that the orders could be cancelled, he could be allowed to remain on active duty after 30 years and, if it would be any consolation, they would both be making the same amount of money if he stayed in the Navy. (Landersman knew that pay of senior military officers at that time was limited by a congressional imposed pay cap under which a four star admiral received the same pay as a Navy captain with over 26 years service.) As tempting as was the offer, Landersman very respectfully declined, retired from the Navy and went to work as a civilian.

Twelve years later, with both of them retired, Landersman met Admiral Hayward at a U.S. Naval Institute function. He had given up the duties that he wanted to start TACTRAGRUPAC for Hayward in 1979 and withdrew his retirement to serve on Hayward's first Strategic Studies Group in 1981. Landersman walked up to Hayward, held out his hand and said, "Admiral, good evening. Stu Landersman."

With a grin and a gleam in his eye ADM Hayward gripped his hand, shook it and replied, "Oh yes, Landersman, the guy that turned me down on the tactics chair at the Naval War College."

SUMMARY

The Composite Warfare Commander Doctrine of command and control for carrier battle groups was created during the Cold War to support U.S. Pacific Fleet and then Navy strategy. CWC was necessary at that time. With the breakup of the Soviet Union, U.S. military strategy changed but the focus has remained on the carrier battle group as the primary response to crises, contingencies and limited intensity conflicts. A modified CWC doctrine is still used in the battle groups.

CWC was created so that the officer commanding the carrier task group could concentrate on accomplishment of his primary mission; strike warfare, leaving defense of the battle group to subordinates. Changes to the doctrine have given the primary mission to the Carrier Air Wing commander who also controls all aircraft and it has combined two of the warfare area commanders. The three pillars of the original CWC doctrine; subordinate responsibility, resource allocation and command by negation remain but responsibility for mission accomplishment lies somewhere between the flag officer commanding the battle group and the air wing commander. Allocation of aircraft for any mission is still the responsibility of the CWC but seems to be in the hands of the air wing commander. Command by negation is still the function of the battle group commander.

The anti submarine warfare function of the carrier battle group has been downgraded, replaced by Undersea Warfare which is not the same thing and many of the systems that enabled offensive ASW have been eliminated. The anti submarine and anti surface positions have been combined and now resembles the old Screen Commander. Both creation of the Strike Warfare Commander and melding anti submarine and anti surface have had one major effect on carrier battle group operations. Now, with the changed CWC doctrine naval aviators are in complete control of all aircraft from the flight deck of the carrier.

The controversy concerning control of carrier aircraft between the carrier battle group and the amphibious commander is still unresolved, complicated further by joint task force considerations. On the very positive side, submarines routinely operate with carrier battle groups.

Battle group effectiveness is still dependent on effective command and control and Composite Warfare Commander Doctrine is still in use with emphasis on complete coordination and cooperation of all naval warfare communities. Those in command positions and their staffs of carrier battle groups are today's Composite Warriors.

CHAPTER THIRTY SEVEN

A FLAGSHIP MOMENT

1976

USS John Paul Jones (DDG-32) was the flagship of Destroyer Squadron 23 and so Stu Landersman spent most of his time in that ship, that is when he was not in the aircraft carrier that the squadron was escorting. Stu got to know all the officers in John Paul Jones. They were a very good group. One was a brand new ensign, right out of the Naval Academy, who showed great promise. His name was Dave Crisalli.

The Secretary of the Navy Guest Cruise Program was a program in which civilians would be invited to visit and cruise in Navy ships to observe operations and meet Navy men. The program could be used by those who understood it to visit a particular ship at a time of their choosing and Dave Crisalli's father arranged a SECNAV guest cruise in the ship in which his son was serving. Stu felt that it was a pleasure to have Dave's father aboard.

After his cruise David Crisalli (Dave's father) wrote a thank-you note to the Secretary of the Navy. That note follows as written by David Crisalli.

In June of 1976, while the nation was celebrating its bicentennial, my son graduated from the United States Naval Academy. He reported to his first ship in December of that year and went to sea. In 1977, I was privileged to sail with him on a cruise to the central Pacific as a guest aboard his destroyer for a month. This was quite a thrill for me as I had not been at sea aboard a warship since my own experiences as a radioman and gunner in torpedo planes during World War II. His ship, the U.S.S. John Paul Jones (DDG-32), was the flag ship for DESRON 23 (Destroyer Squadron 23). This same squadron had become quite famous during World War II under the daring command of a man named Captain Arleigh Burke. In the years after the war, Admiral Burke eventually became the first Chief of Naval Operations. As the flag ship, the present squadron Commodore, Captain Stu Landersman, was embarked aboard the Jones. During my cruise with the ship, I came to know the Commodore very well. After much additional training, my son qualified as a Surface Warfare officer in April of 1978, just prior to the start of a 10 month deployment to the western Pacific. The Commodore invited me to the ceremony to see my son receive his Surface Warfare insignia. Since I had been a goldsmith for longer than I cared to remember, I told him that, rather than pinning on one of the standard brass insignia, I would like to make the insignia for my son out of gold. The Commodore was pleased and kept both my invitation and the gold insignia a secret. He also had one other surprise waiting for all of us. On the day of the ceremony, it was not Commodore Landersman who presented my son with his insignia, but his surprise guest of honor, now long retired but still very feisty, Admiral Arleigh Burke. The Admiral pinned my son's insignia on his uniform and he wore it proudly until he retired 20 years later. However, all through his career in the Navy, people would stop and ask what was different about his Surface Warfare pin. He would tell his story and I would get a call to make a special insignia for someone else. And so it began, and we have been making insignia and insignia jewelry ever since.

David Crisalli

CHAPTER THIRTY EIGHT

STRATEGIC STUDIES GROUP

1981-1982

Nearing completion of his time as Commanding Officer, Tactical Training Group Pacific and having failed selection for promotion, Stu Landersman's retirement request was approved for 1 June 1981 and he had accepted civilian employment to commence immediately upon his retirement.

Admiral Thomas Heywood, the Chief of Naval Operations called Stu.

The CNO wanted Stu to be a CNO Fellow with the first Strategic Studies Group. After a day of consideration and discussion with Martha, Stu accepted the offer. His retirement orders were cancelled and replaced with orders to Newport and he served for the next year as a CNO Fellow with the first Strategic Studies Group.

Mr. Robert Murray had been the Under Secretary of the Navy when he accepted the newly created position of Director of the Strategic Studies Group which would be at the Naval War College.

He and his wife moved from the Washington, D.C. area to Newport, Rhode Island.

At the Naval War College Bob Murray met with the eight officers; six Navy and two Marine Corps and he immediately became a close associate, sympathetic advocate and loyal confident of the members of the first Strategic Studies Group. He gave his full support to their program and his very recent status as Under Secretary of the Navy provided the group with ready access everywhere in the military. His presence and often just his name opened doors and made travel easy and there was much travel and many high ranking, influential and authoritative people to see.

As their Director, Bob Murray led the group with a loose rein recognizing that their professionalism carried a dedication and thoroughness that required very little, if any, overt direction.

In the first few weeks the SSG developed a plan to gather and review the war plans of the various fleet and theater commanders. This, they hoped would give them the overall plan for the employment of U.S. naval forces in a NATO-Warsaw Pact war and tying together these plans would provide a picture of how the Navy and Marine Corps would fight what could be called World War III. To obtain these plans a series of trips were planned, trips to each major command wherever located in the world, to brief that commander on the project and to gather his views. It was an energetic program and the travels had to be accomplished promptly because the information thus collected had to be assembled and analyzed by the SSG back at the Naval War College. But that was to be only the start as the group then intended the most ambitious of projects. They would, after analysis of the existing plans, formulate one coherent and comprehensive plan to be called "The Naval Strategy" that would be presented to the Chief of Naval Operations, modified if necessary and then with his approval, taken to those same commanders around the world and briefed to them.

Early on Bob Murray had gotten to know all eight members of the Strategic Studies Group very well and they knew him, trusted him and treated him as if he were one of them. They had traveled together, eaten and had drinks together and there were often stunts and harmless "con" jobs played during their travels. Once Murray found that the airline people had been told that he was a U.S. Senator on a familiarization trip to Japan, another time he was Vice President of the American Medical Association enroute to a symposium on herpes. On a plane to Rome he was a representative of the America's Cup Committee of the New York Yacht Club on the way to talk with Italian financiers about the next challenge series. In all of these and others he was "set up" without knowing how, why or as what by his team of the SSG and always the first he would know was when approached by a stranger who discussed or questioned his views on a peculiar issue, but it was not all play.

They developed a Naval Strategy and their lives were filled with operation orders, operation plans, logistic plans, contingency plans, charts, maps, graphs and interview notes.

One day Bob Murray asked Stu about what had been his previous duty as CO of TACTRAGRUPAC, what it was and what it did. "Almost everywhere we go Navy officers comment to you about TACTRAGRUPAC. Tell me about it, please."

Stu described the Tactical Training Group Pacific, which he had started as the first commanding officer. He described that he had been asked by Admiral Hayward, Commander in Chief, U.S. Pacific Fleet to start a school in San Diego similar to the Royal Navy's Maritime Tactical School near Portsmouth, England. "Go over there, visit the British school and get whatever paperwork they'll give you. Then give us a school like it but modified so as to be best for us." That was the CINCPACFLT's guidance, along with, "We need a school to teach battle group tactics to our battle group commanders."

Stu explained to Bob Murray that he had been selected for this role by CINCPACFLT because the admiral had heard so much about his accomplishments as a destroyer squadron commander in fleet exercises involving carrier battle groups. The admiral had promised and delivered Stu's choice of four officers with which to start the new school. The four officers he had asked for all had experience on a battle group commander's staff.

They had formed a very successful training activity, teaching admirals and officers going to admirals' staffs, ships' commanding officers and other officers going to key operational jobs as TACTRAGRUPAC quickly became recognized as the authority in battle group tactics. A year and a half later the Atlantic Fleet started a similar school.

"So you see, wherever we go and talk to Navy people someone there, often the admiral, has been to my course," summarized Stu.

"They've been students of yours?" continued Bob Murray.

"Yes."

"You've taught battle group commanders how to fight their battle groups. The admirals of the Navy, at sea, learned their tactics from you." The statements were partial questions, partial summaries.

"Well, not all the admirals and not all the tactics. A lot of them knew a lot of tactics before TACTRAGRUPAC and it wasn't just me. I had a great team of real experts y'know."

"But a lot of them didn't know much tactics before you and your team taught them." Murray wouldn't let go.

"Let's say some of them needed some refreshing of their memories."

"Why aren't you an admiral?" asked Murray.

Stu hesitated. "You know the system. You were the Under Secretary of the Navy. It's a complicated process. Not many make it. Why haven't I been selected? I don't know. It's complicated. What do you want me to say? 'I'm incompetent.' 'I don't know the right people.' 'I haven't had the right jobs.' Take your pick. We don't get a report card, y'know."

Murray pursued it further. "You know better than that. You've been in the right places, you've had the right duties, you know the politics and you must have some idea as to why you haven't been selected. I'd like to hear why and I have a real reason for knowing, not just curiosity."

"Tell me your reason and maybe I'll tell you why," responded Stu.

"I want this Strategic Studies Group to attract the best the Navy has to offer. If the guys here get selected for flag it helps get the best officers for subsequent years. Don't you agree? Doesn't it add prestige to the organization?"

"Well, flag selection will surely attract those seeking future flag selection and it would add to the prestige."

"Why were you not selected?" insisted Murray.

"There are probably a lot of reasons and I don't know them all." Stu's vague response didn't satisfy Murray so he tried a new approach.

"What do I have to do, what can I do, to get the eligible guys of this SSG selected? You, to start with. I've gotten to know you real well these past months and I know that you should be an admiral. You're a fine leader. Everyone respects you. You're sensitive, demanding, intelligent, practical and everything else. You're one of the finest officers I've come across. So tell me."

Stu went through an explanation of the selection process, not the legal or formal procedures well known to Murray but the real world practical process. "Selection by a flag board is by community; aviators, submariners and surface ship guys. Even with the few specialties you have to be 'in' with your own community, one of their very own super achievers. There are a few jobs in the Navy, specific billets from which selection probability is very high, almost certain. Commandant of Midshipmen at the Naval Academy, Executive Assistant to the Secretary of the Navy or to CNO are examples. A few other billets have a reasonable chance of selection such as some of the other executive assistants to senior appointees and four stars. From most captain billets, and I mean most, no one has ever been or probably never will be selected for flag. A captain ordered into one of these simply will not make flag rank. He knows it. The detailer knows it. Everyone knows it. Legally he's still in the running but practically he's not going to be selected. In defense of this seemingly inequitable situation, the guys sent to those high and highest billets are super achievers. They've done it all and done it right so selection is not from the entire population of legally eligible captains, it's from among those who are in, or who have been in, those few right jobs. Then it gets to support within one's own community.

"In my case I've had some of the right jobs and done them well. I've commanded two destroyers and a DESRON with all the right operations. I've served in the Surface Warfare section, OP03, in Washington. So, I have all the right tickets for the surface warfare community but I spent my most valuable promotion time, which is right after my DESRON, teaching carrier battle group tactics. That's not first line surface warfare community. Maybe it should be, but that's academic. The community promotes.

"I've told our SSG guys that this duty here cannot be looked upon as being away from their community. Each of them reports to 02, 03, or 05 whenever they're in Washington to maintain clearly that loyalty line to their community." Murray knew that 02, 03, 05 were the sections of the CNO staff responsible for submarine, surface warfare and aviation respectively.

"Now, we have two others in the SSG eligible for promotion this year, Sam Leeds and Dan Wolkensdorfer. You should talk to them for sure, but I can tell you this; both are aviators and both have excellent chances for selection. Dan is VP," Navy abbreviation for land based maritime patrol aircraft, "and Sam is VF," Navy for carrier based fighter aircraft. "In aviation, selection gets into sub-communities. Dan is a super achiever candidate of the VP sub-community and Sam is the same among the fighters. With the right help they could both make it this year."

"What kind of help?" asked Murray.

"I'd suggest that you write to the sub-community leader of each, explain your position here, point out that you feel responsible for this particular guy's career because this is a new and unknown organization and ask him for a recommendation as to what you can do or whom you should contact to ensure that this 'hot prospect' remains competitive. Your letter will flatter the guy that gets it and he'll be in sympathy with you for looking after a guy from his community but most of all, if you pick the right sub-community leader, you've already influenced him toward selection if he ends up on the board."

"Gee, that's brilliant! Can I do it for all three, or would a phone call be better?" asked Murray.

"No, no. No phone call. That's too easily forgotten. The written word is more valuable."

"And how about you, can I do it for all three of you?"

"Well, I'm a tougher case than the other two. You can try. It can't hurt."

"I'd like to try for the three of you. Could you rough out a letter for me and maybe suggest whom they should go to?" asked Murray.

Stu Landersman smiled and thought of the administrative process of "completed staff work" to which he had always adhered. Bob Murray soon had three smooth letters ready for signature and mailing. Sam Leeds and Dan Wolkensdorfer had readily agreed that it was a smart move and three letters went out as Stu had recommended and prepared.

Dan Wolkensdorfer was selected for promotion to the one star flag rank of Commodore but Sam Leeds and Stu Landersman were not selected.

As the year at Newport drew to a close Stu Landersman had again submitted a request for retirement. It had been approved and he had orders to retire on 1 October 1982.

Admiral Hayward was still not finished with Stu and he offered a Chair of Naval Tactics that was to be created at the Naval War College. It was a very tempting offer and Landersman was flattered. He pointed out to the admiral that he had orders to retire, had reached the mandatory 30 years to retire and had a civilian job. The admiral told him that the orders could be cancelled, he could be allowed to remain on active duty past 30 years and, if it would be any consolation, they would both be making the same amount of money if he stayed in the Navy. Landersman knew that pay of senior military officers at that time was limited by a congressional imposed pay cap under which a four star admiral received the same pay as a Navy captain with over 26 years service.

As tempting as was the offer, Landersman very respectfully declined, retired from the Navy and went to work as a civilian. He had accepted an employment position with the Johns Hopkins University Applied Physics Laboratory in Laurel, Maryland.

CHAPTER THIRTY NINE

NO GOLD STAR

1982

Except for Naval Academy graduates, junior officers seldom thought of possibilities for promotion or achievement of high rank. Every ensign expected to become a lieutenant (junior grade), it was almost automatic. Most planned to be out of the Navy and hard at work in some civilian employment making lots of money long before they would have been considered for promotion to the rank of lieutenant.

Making lieutenant was a little more challenging but the general view was that anyone who had been an officer of the deck and qualified for fleet operations would be promoted. Actually, it took a little more than that but it was pretty much that way for seagoing junior officers and going to sea for the first years was the normal pattern. Those that spent their early years in some cushy shore job, which may have been all their years on active duty for some reservists, were usually not surprised when they were not promoted to lieutenant.

Lieutenants spent about half of their time at sea and the other half ashore. It was common for a young lieutenant to do a two year tour as department head in a ship, then two years at Post Graduate School, then to a staff and then be ready to make lieutenant commander.

Executive Officer of a ship might follow then staff, schools, other staffs and then promotion to commander and command of a Navy ship. Commanding Officer, Captain of the ship was the position most sought after, considered the ultimate achievement of seagoing officers. But not all officers were seagoing at the commander level. Many had specialized in fields of naval service that didn't accommodate tours of sea duty and these found their niche in positions ashore and found paths to promotion away from the ocean.

All commanders were career minded and each focused on what he saw as the best path for himself, the best path to selection for promotion to the rank of captain. Each studied promotion statistics and would hypothetically insert themselves into previous years' selection results, trying to determine their probability of selection or probability of being passed over. As time approached to be looked at by a selection board, eligible commanders would hear about previous results with wonder. They would hope that they were one of the top performers, that it showed in their fitness reports and that a past commanding officer was on the board.

Usually about 20% of eligible commanders were selected for promotion to captain and the 80% that failed to be selected pretty much knew before the board's results were made public or even before the board met. A fellow could lay out his fitness reports and project as to their impression on the board. There weren't many surprises but the unexpected always attracted more attention so to the uninitiated the process of Navy promotion was and still is an amazing stress.

One saying was, "The day the captain's list is made public, half of those on the list drop out of competition and two years later half of those others drop out." If correct, it means that of 100 named to be promoted to the rank of captain, 50 immediately no longer aspire to be promoted higher and two years later only 25 of that year group are still trying for promotion. Five of those original 100 might eventually be promoted to flag rank so statistically it would appear that only 5% of captains are promoted to rear admiral. But like so many other statistics, these are misleading because only about 25% of captains are still trying and if 5 of those are promoted, that would represent a 20% probability of selection.

As graduation speaker at Surface Warfare Officers School I was introduced as "Mr. Tactics." John Nyquist, later vice admiral and head of the surface warfare community, referred to me as "The Navy's leading tactician." Friend Captain Sam Pearlman said I was the Navy's "Tactical Maven." Others called me a "tactical guru" and Tactical Training Group Pacific was called, "Stu's U." Bob Murray, Director of the Strategic Studies Group and former Under Secretary of the Navy said I should be an admiral and asked me what he could do to make that happen. Rear Admiral Hoss Miller, my Group Commander when I was COMDESRON 23 told me I should be and would be an admiral, as did Rear Admiral Jerry Thomas, COMTRAPAC when I was CO TACTRAGRUPAC. Both of these rear admirals were on flag selection boards that did not select me.

As COMDESRON 23 I served as ASWC with the Enterprise Battle Group under COMCARGRU ONE in the major fleet exercise RIMPAC 78. The exercise was conducted as the first phase of the transit to WESTPAC for the battle group's deployment. I was in my familiar role as ASWC and the battle group included two submarines in integrated direct support and three in opposition. Harry Schrader, CO of the nuclear powered guided missile cruiser Long Beach was AAWC. Jim Hogg was ASUWC. Jerry Holland was SEC. The exercise was a huge success especially in ASW and COMTHIRDFLT and CINCPACFLT had high praise at the critique in Pearl Harbor. As the exercise had focused on ASW and I had been ASWC, I received a great deal of attention and very nice compliments from many senior officers. RIMPAC 78 was the finest of the CWC demonstrations because the commanders were experienced in all warfare areas and we had all the proper resources. Further evidence of the caliber of commanders in that exercise came years later when every officer that had filled a major CWC role; every commander and coordinator plus the carrier CO, XO and air wing commander were selected for flag rank. Every one, that is, but one. The one that was not selected was the one that had been the most successful in the warfare area of primary focus for the exercise. There was no gold star for the ASWC; Stu Landersman.

Admiral Hayward, as CINCPACFLT and later as Chief of Naval Operations personally selected me for two of my most valuable duty assignments and offered me a third. Vice Admiral Sylvester "Bob" Foley, COMSEVENTHFLT when I deployed as COMDESRON 23 and was later CINCPACFLT when I was on the Strategic Studies Group said that the coordinated ASW I conducted was the best he had ever seen and he put that in a concurrent fitness report. Foley sent me to discuss ASW with the Taiwan CNO, announcing me as, "The leading ASW expert in the U.S. Navy." With the Strategic Studies Group I told the others to visit their community leader (OP O-2, 0-3, 0-5) every time we went to Washington because promotion came from one's own community not from parochialism. Years later Admiral Bill Owens said that it was the most valuable advice any one had given him. But it was not for me; it was too late.

My own feelings were that I never expected to make flag rank. I considered myself very fortunate to have had the opportunities to serve as I had done and was very pleased to be a captain. I could not help, though, but compare my accomplishments with those of my peers and it did appear to me that if selection were based on accomplishment, I stood a good chance of being selected for flag rank. I knew that I was at least as good as any of them. More important, if selection were to be based on potential for future Navy contribution, that I could do more as a flag officer than most of them. Do more, that is, in development of improved procedures and tactics. Also, I knew that I had done more to coordinate the various warfare communities than anyone else. As it turned out, that elimination of parochialism and bringing together the warfare communities in tactical battle group operations as a team effort, as valuable as it was to the Navy, was my downfall. It was surface warfare parochialism that caused me to be passed over.

You don't get a report card or a transcript to review or a letter from the academic board of review explaining why you didn't graduate.

You just see a flag selection list without your name each year until you reach thirty years and then you retire. Flag officers that serve on flag selection boards do not tell "how it went," even to friends afterward. So one never knows why. One can only surmise and take solace in having had a wonderful 30 year career, a great trip, a great adventure with reward in having given valuable service alongside the best of people in the best of causes and in being respected by those one respected.

One day late in my time with the Strategic Studies Group I was visiting in the Pentagon, sitting next to the desk and talking to Captain Pete Corr, Executive Assistant to VADM Carl Trost. Admiral Trost, a submarine officer, had just recently been on the flag selection board. Suddenly he came out of his office walking quickly toward his deputy's office, saw me and waved with a grin and a greeting, "Hi Stu." Another two steps and Trost stopped, looked straight ahead as if in thought for a few seconds, then turned and faced me. "The trouble with the surface warfare community is that they're too parochial," Trost stated. Then he turned and continued his walk. Pete Corr and I looked at each other, shrugged and smiled knowing that Trost meant something concerning flag selection but ethics limited him to that tiny fragment. It was the only comment from a senior officer as to why I was not selected, but those few innocent words told me. Clearly my own community, the surface warfare community, did not share my passion for non-parochial operations. The aviation and submarine communities thought I was great but promotion comes from your own community just as I had told the members of the Strategic Studies Group.

CHAPTER FORTY

STU'S NAVY DUTIES

The Full Career

Officer Candidate School, Newport, RI Student 4 mos.   1953

USS LST 542, Little Creek, VA First Lt & Gunnery Off   1953-1954

USS LST 1153 (TALBOT COUNTY), Little Creek, VA
First Lt & Gunnery Off, Supply Off   1954-1956

Inactive Naval Reserve ~ 4 mos. Nov 56 to Feb 57   1956-1957

USS ROBERT A. OWENS (DDE 827), Norfolk, VA Gun Off, 1957-1959
Ops Off

USNPGS, Monterey, CA Student General Line School   1959-1960

COMDESLANT and COMCRUDESLANT staff, Newport, RI
Asst Ops & Plans Off On board destroyer tender USS YOSEMITE 1960-1962

USS STICKELL (DDR 888) (DD 888), Norfolk, VA, Philadelphia, PA, Newport, RI XO/CO   1962-1964

US Naval Academy, Annapolis, MD Flag Sec & Aide to Supt.   1964-1966

Naval War College, Command and Staff School, Newport, RI Student   1966-1967

USS ENGLAND (DLG 22), Long Beach, CA XO   1967-1969

USS HEPBURN (DE 1055), Long Beach, CA CO   1969-1971

COMSEVENTHFLT staff, Yokosuka, Japan Surface Warfare Off On board cruiser USS OKLAHOMA CITY   1971-1973

National War College, Washington, DC Student   1973-1974

OPNAV staff, Pentagon, Washington, DC Surface Comb Branch Head   1974-1976

COMDESRON 23, San Diego, CA Commodore   1976-1978

PACFLTTACTRA and TACTRAGRUPAC, San Diego, CA CO/Director   1978-1981

Naval War College, Strategic Studies Group, Newport, RI CNO Fellow   1981-1982

CHAPTER FORTY ONE

RETIREMENT

1982

Most career people in the Navy retire after twenty years of service. Twenty year retirement gives them one-half of their basic pay for the rest of their lives. Not bad but not enough to live on especially if the retiree has a family to support. So most, almost all twenty-year retirees seek employment as a civilian. In addition to their Navy pension retirees have access to base facilities such as shopping at exchanges and commissaries, recreation facilities and social activities. One of the most valuable benefits to the retiree and his or her family is health care.

Some career Navy people stay in service longer than twenty years. Some stay the maximum; thirty years and in those cases retirees receive three-quarters of their basic pay. Some can live on that thirty-year pension but most seek employment to augment that income.

Roger Spreen, who gave Stu Landersman valuable career guidance through most of Stu's Navy time, had philosophy regarding career length. He said that most officers should plan on retiring after twenty years and with that plan in mind they should arrange their last duty as preparation for the employment that they would seek in retirement. Spreen's plan allowed exceptions to the twenty-year retirement only if the officer planned for and had a good chance of being selected for flag (admiral) rank. For most it would be difficult to judge their own flag potential but some were willing to take that chance.

As he approached the twenty-year time Stu Landersman knew the Spreen retirement philosophy and had great respect and appreciation of career guidance of the past. But Stu felt that he represented a different situation then the Spreen philosophy was directed toward. Stu was enjoying his Navy service and was looking forward to increased responsibility. Martha, too, was enjoying Navy life. So Stu stayed in the Navy past the twenty year point and finally ended up with thirty years of naval service. Well, not really thirty years, he was actually two months short of thirty years but it always sounded easier to answer inquiries on length of service with thirty years rather than explain twenty-nine years and ten months.

When Stu was serving as Commanding Officer of Tactical Training Group Pacific he was passed over for flag selection and prepared to retire. A phone call from a former shipmate sent Stu to interview with Boeing in Seattle; nice offer but Stu and Martha decided against it. Another call came from a retired admiral that Stu had worked for and Stu went to Laurel, Maryland to interview with the Johns Hopkins University Applied Physics Laboratory. All sounded good and Stu accepted employment with that lab.

Then came another phone call. This one was from the Chief of Naval Operations offering a position with the first Strategic Studies Group at the Naval War College in Newport, Rhode Island. Stu couldn't refuse the CNO so his orders to retire were cancelled and the Landersmans went back to Newport.

JHU APL was very understanding and told Stu that there would be a place for him when he later retired. And that's the way it worked out. After a year with the Strategic Studies Group Stu retired from the Navy, Martha and he moved to Maryland and Stu went to work at JHU APL.

CHAPTER FORTY TWO

JOHNS HOPKINS UNIVERSITY
APPLIED PHYSICS LABORATORY

1983-2003

There's an over-used expression, call it "hackneyed" that goes something like, "As war clouds gathered—"and then the story would go on to describe the preparations or the romance that occurred just prior to a war. Hackneyed it might be but it would best describe timing of the origin of the Johns Hopkins University Applied Physics Laboratory. From now on let's refer to that lab by its commonly used abbreviation; JHU APL.

As war clouds gathered in Europe in the late 1930s and then the war began in 1939, it had come to the attention of U.S. Navy leadership that among all the navies of the world only the German navy had what was called a "proximity fuse" for their gun projectiles. Few U.S. Navy men had heard of it. Most didn't know what a proximity fuse was.

The fuse is what detonates a projectile. Ideally, a projectile fired from a Navy gun would fly to a target and detonate (explode) at the precise moment that would cause the most damage to the target. If the target was enemy troops in an open area then the firing ship would want the detonation to occur just overhead of the troops so that the fragments of the projectile (shrapnel) would hit the most enemy personnel. If the target was a light structure the firing ship would want the projectile to penetrate and then detonate inside where it would cause the most damage.

Timing of the detonation was very important for this type of naval gunfire and projectiles used for this would be fitted with mechanical time fuses. The mechanical time fuse was very similar to a self-winding watch that was set to detonate the projectile by a very precise clock-like process.

Hard targets such as a warship would require a projectile that could penetrate armor and then detonate so the armor piercing projectile had to have a sharp very hard nose. The fuse, then, could not be in the nose, it had to be in the base of the projectile.

There were three types of Navy gun projectiles; mechanical time fuse (MTF), armor piercing (AP) and point detonating (COMMON) that were in use in most of the world's navies. As what would be World War II approached (As war clouds gathered) it was clear to U.S. Navy leadership that one of the major considerations in any future war would be dealing with enemy aircraft. Could MTF, AP or COMMON projectiles be used against attack aircraft? Certainly not AP or COMMON. Maybe MTF but it would be very difficult to get a hit on a fast maneuvering aircraft that would require rapidly changing timing. There would be very low probability of hit with timing the detonation so as to scatter shrapnel near the target. A better projectile was needed; a projectile that would detonate when it was near the target; that is in close "proximity" to the target.

Perhaps a more clear understanding of the problem might be found with a comparison of duck or pheasant hunting with trying to shoot down an aircraft. The hunter does not use a rifle in bird hunting, he uses a shot gun. His probability of hitting a bird with a bullet would be very low. To increase his probability of getting a hit, his shot gun puts out a large pattern of pellets, any one or a few of which could bring down the bird. Similarly, a projectile with a proximity fuse would detonate in the vicinity of the enemy bird, filling the air with dangerous pellets.

Navy officers involved with Research and Development went to nearby Johns Hopkins University and explained their problem. The Applied Physics Laboratory was established and two years later a proximity fuse was developed for Navy gun projectiles. World War II had just started and a major part of the nation's electronics industry produced proximity fuses for the nation's military. The fuse name had become "variable time" and was abbreviated as VT.

The VT fuse carried miniaturized radar that was energized when the projectile was fired. If the radar were to detect a target it would initiate a sequence that would detonate the projectile spreading shrapnel with the expectation that some of that shrapnel would hit the enemy aircraft. The VT fuse made gunnery against air targets much more effective.

As World War II came to an end, JHU APL prepared to close shop but the Navy had other plans for the lab. Guided missiles were catching attention and the Navy tasked the lab to develop surface-to-air missiles.

In Stu Landersman's Navy time the surface Navy was equipped with three different surface-to-air guided missiles that had been developed by JHU APL. They were called "The Three T's" for Talos, Terrier and Tartar. Talos was the longest range, was the largest and was only installed in the largest surface ships, like converted World War II cruisers. Terrier was installed in surface combatant ships that were larger than destroyers and smaller than the WWII cruisers, like DLGs. Tartar was the surface-to-air missile system for destroyers and DEs.

Even though Stu had been designated and was best known as an ASW sub-specialist, he had served in or with all of the Three T missile systems and was also designated as an AAW sub-specialist.

This appealed to the leaders of JHU APL and Stu was hired after a pleasant day of interviews.

Martha did what Martha had always done in their Navy time; she found a beautiful house in Columbia, Maryland close to the lab and that was the Landersmans home as Stu worked at JHU APL.

Years later, like when Stu struggled to put together this memoir that you are struggling to read (Thank you!) he put together two lists; one of bad decisions and failures in his life and one of good decisions and successes in his life. He couldn't remember them all for either list but one of the good decisions, well certainly one of the best decisions that he made was to go to work for JHU APL.

I had been at The Lab in Maryland for two years when my son Mark had the tragic death of his wife. I explain that in a later chapter *My Two Sons*. Martha and I talked it over at great length and decided that it would be best for us to move to the San Diego area so that we could be closer to Mark and be able to help him in any way that we could.

When I told my bosses at The Lab of my problem and that I would have to leave, Dick Hunt the Department Director told me to wait a few days before we made that official. He spoke with Rear Admiral Wayne Meyer, director of the AEGIS program and Meyer said that he needed The Lab to have a representative in San Diego. The first AEGIS ships would be joining the Pacific Fleet in just a couple of months and he needed someone there to answer questions and to alert him to any problems. I had known Wayne Meyer for some time and he told Dick Hunt that he couldn't think of anyone better suited to be his representative in San Diego than Stu Landersman.

So instead of leaving employment of JHU APL, The Lab moved Martha and me with all household goods (just like a Navy move) to San Diego. They even moved my boat; Miss Sadie B. Oh yeah, I received a pay raise and an additional pay for living away from The

Lab. They even rented a car for me to use. I told you earlier in this writing that accepting employment at JHU APL was one of my life's best decisions and this was just another example of that.

Where could I have an office? The Lab was prepared to pay the expenses of renting an office and hiring a secretary. I went to see Ned Roberts the Chief of Staff of Commander Naval Surface Force Pacific at the Amphib Base in Coronado. Ned had been a class-mate of mine at National War College. He took me in to see his boss Rear Admiral Harry Schrader whom I had known for years. They both thought that it would be great to have me on their staff.

The admiral asked, "You mean to tell me that I can have you on my staff and it won't even cost me anything?

I replied, "Only a little office space."

He turned to his Chief of Staff, "Fix him up."

So I became the JHU APL representative on the staff of COMNAVSURPAC. Rear Admiral Meyer had told me that his requirements of me would certainly not be all-time-consuming and that he was sure that I would find ways to be of value to that staff. Of course he was right because over the following years I kept busy with SURFPAC projects while JHU APL and Wayne Meyer's people were always very satisfied.

I had been working at The Lab in Maryland for two years when Mark's tragedy led to the move to San Diego. Well, I say San Diego but my office was really in Coronado and Martha made our home in Rancho Bernardo. We still owned our home there, it had been rented and the tenant was ready to move out as we needed to move in. Very convenient.

My major accomplishment during my first six years with SURFPAC was to procure a shiphandling simulator for the Pacific Fleet. You'll read about that later. And when some admirals in the Atlantic learned of that simulator, I was asked to come to Norfolk and get a shiphandling simulator for the Atlantic Fleet. So Martha and I rented our Rancho Bernardo house again, had The Lab move us to Norfolk and I found a position for myself with the CINCLANTFLT staff. Martha, as she had done so many times before, bought a beautiful house for us. Now I was the JHU APL Representative on the CINCLANTFLT staff.

Remember when I went to San Diego I found an office because I knew the chief of staff and the admiral at SURFPAC? Well this time in Norfolk the Commander-in-Chief Atlantic Fleet was Admiral Bud Flanagan who as a lieutenant commander had command of USS BRONSTEIN in DESRON 23 when I was his squadron commander. I called on him, he made a big fuss at seeing me, we told sea stories and he told his aides that I had an open door to see him anytime and to see that I got anything I needed. Nice start.

I was well situated on the CINCLANTFLT staff as I started the process that, remember, took me six years to get a simulator in San Diego. It soon became apparent that this Atlantic Fleet project could better be accomplished through the type commander rather than the fleet CINC, so I transferred myself to the staff of COMNAVSURFLANT. There, yes, I knew the chief of staff and the admiral, they welcomed me and I went to work to get a shiphandling simulator in Norfolk.

Am I a slow learner or fast learner? Take your choice. It took me six years to get a shiphandling simulator in San Diego and three years to get one in Norfolk. But with that accomplished I made plans to return to San Diego.

All this time, all these years, I was employed by JHU APL and I kept my bosses informed of what I was doing and what was going on in the fleet with a monthly written newsletter and a visit. The chief of staff and the admiral at SURFPAC said that they would be very pleased to have me back; my former office was still available. Martha sold our lovely Norfolk house and The Lab moved us to San Diego. Well, not really San Diego but as before, back into our Rancho Bernardo home. Again, our tenant had just vacated.

I worked for JHU APL for 20 years, most of it in San Diego. While I was with JHU APL I went through training and passed the tests to become a licensed Master Mariner but never sailed with my license. The Lab had encouraged me to get the license. The license did come in handy later when I worked at ship handling simulators training young naval officers for ten years. By then Martha and I were living in Coronado, California.

Soon after I retired from the Navy I learned of a NATO program that provided for each NATO country to have Convoy Commodores in case of war. I went through that program and participated in two exercises at sea, one in the Atlantic and one in the Indian Ocean. In addition to being a U.S. Convoy Commodore, I went through the various programs and became a Convoy Commodore in the Royal (British) Navy, the Canadian Navy and the Australian Navy. JHU APL was very tolerant, even encouraged my participation in the Convoy Commodore program.

In 2003 I retired from JHU APL. Soon after I went to work, well, part time work at the shiphandling simulator that I had been instrumental in creating. I had given up my position as JHU APL representative on the COMNAVSURFPAC staff and just before I left I was awarded the Meritorious Public Service Award. Very nice.

CHAPTER FORTY THREE

CORONADO CAYS

1998

The west side of San Diego Bay in southern California is formed by the small city of Coronado. Three sides of Coronado are water; the Pacific Ocean on the west side and San Diego Bay on the north and east sides. To the south lies a strip of what was a sand bar that has been built up over the years into what is now called the Silver Strand which provides the basis of a divided highway. This Silver Strand highway provides Coronado with a land bridge which was its only connection to the California mainland until a beautiful suspension bridge was built across San Diego Bay. That bridge now links the cities of Coronado and San Diego.

Along the sides of the Silver Strand, landfills have provided areas of state and federal properties that have separated a residential area from the rest of the City of Coronado.

Originally a pig farm then a city dump, a group of imaginative businessmen converted the dump into the upscale tax producing residential community of Coronado Cays, the Cays name reflecting a Caribbean theme. It includes some 1200 homes mostly on the water and most with their own boat docks. Coronado Cays consists of ten villages; four are two or three bedroom condominiums, four are attached homes and two of the villages are large individual multi-million dollar homes.

Home owners and residents in Coronado Cays come from all parts of the country and include many retirees, many vacationers, some dual home owners and a few still employed in the San Diego area. A significant number of The Cays residents are retired military like Stu Landersman, a retired Navy captain who lives in a condominium in Antigua Village.

How did the Landersmans come to Coronado Cays? Well, remember that when JHU APL moved Stu to San Diego they also moved his boat. The Landersmans were living in Rancho Bernardo and Miss Sadie B was home ported in the Chula Vista Marina, about 30 miles away. Martha and Stu spent many weekends on their boat cruising San Diego Bay or just enjoying their boat in the marina or at anchor.

Martha was looking across the Bay. She pointed and asked Stu, "What's that group of houses over there?"

"I think that's called Coronado Cays. I was there once to pick-up Moe Peele for the trip back to Idaho Falls. It looked like a lot of nice houses."

"Why don't we go over there and take a look?" Martha was always interested in "nice houses."

Miss Sadie B carried them across the bay and they went up and down the water ways of Coronado Cays. Martha didn't say much at the time but later she confessed that during that first Cays boat tour she made up her mind; Coronado Cays would be their next home. She sold the Rancho Bernardo home and bought a condo in Antigua Village. It included a boat dock for Miss Sadie B.

The Landersmans lived in that condo for many years; longer than they had ever lived in any place before.

Antigua Village consists of 108 condominium units; half on ground level and half one floor above. Each unit has its own boat dock and its own two car garage. Each village in The Cays is represented by an elected member of the homeowner's association board of directors and you guessed it; Stu Landersman was elected to that board three times; three terms of two years each. In one of those six years he served as president of the board.

One day Martha said to Stu, "Why do I have to travel to the waterfront or to Lowe's Hotel to get breakfast. We should have a breakfast cart or some place here in the Cays where a person can get a cup of coffee and a pastry in the morning. You're president of the HOA; can't you arrange something like that?"

Stu thought for a moment. "You know, that's a good idea. I'm gonna look into that."

Most mornings Stu visited with Larry Peterson, General Manager of Coronado Cays to discuss issues before the Board of Directors. In his next meeting Stu brought up Martha's suggestion. Larry smiled, "That's a great idea and I know just the person to give us that."

It took two months for Hanan Martha to get city permits and for her husband "T" to build the facility and then there was a fine coffee cart in Coronado Cays. Actually it was a bit more than a "cart." The Calypso Cafe was more like an outdoor snack bar but all of the components were on wheels so it qualified as a "cart." Martha was very pleased.

The Calypso Café was the favorite eating establishment of the Landersman's for all of the years that followed, especially when Hanan and T did away with their cart, moved into the adjacent building and The Calypso Cafe became a real restaurant.

The Landersmans were not the only ones that enjoyed The Calypso Café. Most of the residents of The Cays found it convenient and enjoyable with very good food, excellent service and even entertainment. One group that made The Calypso Café their club house was the Weezers and Geezers (Their spelling).

The Weezers and Geezers were a tennis group. Fifteen to twenty-five men aged from sixties to eighties played tennis weekday mornings in The Cays from seven to eight-thirty. There were a few younger players. After tennis most of them would assemble at The Calypso

Café for breakfast or just coffee and lots of talk. The group had been written about in local journals.

Stu was not a tennis player but he and a couple of others of the proper age were tolerated as social members of the group and were allowed to meet with the real Weezers and Geezers. Their meeting place was under the canopy of what had been the original coffee cart of The Calypso Café.

The Weezers and Geezers were an interesting group. There were doctors, lawyers, military men of all services, business men of many businesses, engineers, professors, teachers, police men, salesmen, insurance men, investment men and many others, even an Indian Chief. They came from all parts of the country and some other countries. One thing that they had in common was that whatever their field, they had achieved some measure of success or they wouldn't be in Coronado Cays.

For years Stu had tried to get the Weezers and Geezers to write a book. He suggested that each guy would write a chapter of his life and what had brought him to The Cays. Each time that Stu brought it up he would be met with blank stares. No one wanted to write their story even though almost everyone could and would tell his story to the coffee-mates. A few suggested that Stu interview each and, "Write the damn thing yourself!" Another book that will never be written.

You'll read about the Coronado Cays Lighthouse in a later chapter. The project started in one of those morning meetings with Larry Peterson, the General Manager. With little more than a vague idea Stu brought it up. "Why couldn't we have a lighthouse on the southern end of Grand Caribe Island?"

Larry thought it was a great idea and they spent some considerable time discussing it.

The Unified Port District of San Diego controlled all waterfront properties around San Diego Bay so to put up any structure, like a lighthouse, would require their permission. The proper path to The Port was through the City of Coronado and the official route for a request of The City would originate with the Coronado Cays Homeowners Association.

Stu spoke with the mayor of Coronado and three members of the city council; they were all for a lighthouse in The Cays. He spoke with the Commissioner of The Port and there, too, was strong support. All that was needed was a request from the Coronado Cays Homeowners Association and Stu was a member of the Board of Directors.

Not so easy! A few homeowners were able to influence the Board to delay. Stu shifted the title from Coronado Cays Lighthouse to Navy SEAL Memorial Lighthouse and had over 350 supporting signatures when he was informed that the SEAL high command would not allow that title. The lighthouse was torn down before it was put up. There would be no lighthouse in Coronado Cays.

A beautiful January day in 2010; Martha and Stu were having breakfast at a table in the patio area near The Calypso Café. That morning and most of the previous day's afternoon and evening Martha had talked about nothing but what Stu should do after she was gone; how he should live his life, not to spend months in mourning, which ladies he should take to dinner and where. In spite of Stu's insistence that she stop, Martha continued.

Breakfast finished, Stu started slowly to walk away waiting for Martha to catch-up. Martha passed away that morning at The Calypso Café just like that (snap your fingers), just like she knew it would happen. And it happened at The Calypso Café which came into being because six months earlier Martha had asked for just such a place in Coronado Cays.

A few months after Martha passed away, Stu was sitting with Don Patrick at the very same table at which he had been sitting with Martha that January morning. A very nice lady walking her little white dog came by and stopped to chat with Don Patrick. They knew each other from the Coronado Cays Yacht Club. Don introduced Betty Schulman.

"Why haven't I seen you at the yacht club?" Betty asked Stu.

"Probably because I'm not a member," Stu answered with a laugh.

"Well, I'd like to take you to dinner tonight at the yacht club and you can pick me up at six." She gave Stu her address and walked away with her little white dog.

Betty and Stu dated too many times to count over the years that followed and whenever asked how they met Stu would answer, "She picked me up at The Calypso Café."

One evening Betty and Stu met a new couple at the Yacht Club. In the exchange of pleasantries the husband asked, "How long have you been married?"

Betty promptly answered, "Ninety-eight years."

Of course the new couple was surprised. "How can that be?"

Betty responded, "Stu was married fifty-five years and I was married forty-three years. We're not married, just dating."

CHAPTER FORTY FOUR

I AM A CONVOY COMMODORE

1983

In 1983, a few months after I retired from the Navy, Martha and I were living in Maryland close to my place of employment; Johns Hopkins University Applied Physics Laboratory. A phone call came from Rear Admiral Warren Hamm. I had served with him years before on the DESLANT staff in Newport, Rhode Island and hadn't seen him in some time. I knew that he was serving as the Deputy Director of the Military Sealift Command. We exchanged pleasantries, asked of each others' family and then he got to the real purpose of the call.

"Stu, have you ever heard of the Convoy Commodore Program?"

I thought for a couple of seconds. "No I can't say that I have."

"Well, you should find out about it because it's just the thing for you."

"How do I find out about it?"

"I'm going to send you a letter inviting you into this program and if you would like to know more about it the letter will tell you how to get the details. As I said, it's just the thing for you."

I went into the program, participated in a number of at-sea exercises and wrote an article that was published in the Naval Institute Proceedings. After I became a Convoy Commodore in the U.S. Navy, I became a Convoy Commodore in the British, Canadian and Australian navies. I taught convoy procedures in all three navies and wrote a book on modern convoy procedures.

What follows in this chapter is the article that appeared in the June 1986 issue of the Proceedings; "I am a Convoy Commodore."

It was Friday the 13th when my convoy of nine ships was attacked by aircraft and surface combatant ships. We had departed Iceland three days before. The Canadian destroyers did their best to provide protection but the enemy's forces were too many. Murmansk run? World War II? No, it was September 1985 and the occasion was a large NATO exercise; Ocean Safari 85. The convoy consisted of Free World merchant ships and the enemy's forces were British ships and aircraft simulating a strong opposition.

On that day, as the weather worsened into a full North Atlantic storm, I was the Convoy Commodore. We were between Ireland and Scotland enroute to southern England. The convoy was visited by a Krivak class destroyer and an intelligence ship. They were real Soviets. The five British Canberras approaching us were simulating Soviet attack aircraft. Buccaneer aircraft flew low in the role of surface-to-surface missiles and Nimrod aircraft circled overhead in a surveillance mode. All day we received air raid warnings from the Canadian officer in tactical command but we could not do much maneuvering because of heavy seas. Two of the ships in the convoy could not keep up and had to steer their own courses for ship safety and to make bare steerageway. This slowed the entire convoy. The two ships dropped back all night in spite of my efforts to keep the ships of the convoy together. We remained in communication and gradually, during the next day or so, were able to form up-arriving at Portsmouth, England as scheduled on 18 September.

This was not my first experience as a convoy commodore. I had served with most of these same ships in a run from Boston to Iceland the previous week and a year and a half earlier I had been convoy commodore during an exercise in the Indian Ocean.

In 1982 when I retired from the Navy I thought that going to sea was over for me. I had spent 18 of my 30 years in the Navy at sea. I had commanded a frigate, a destroyer and a destroyer squadron and enjoyed every moment of it. So I was pleased to receive the letter inviting me to join the convoy commodore program even though I had known nothing of it before.

Retired Navy captains and admirals are selected annually for training as convoy commodores. These retirees have had recent tactical command at sea and meet certain other age and health criteria. This selection process also includes recently retired reserve admirals and captains. Those selectees who want to attend the convoy commodore course and accept mobilization assignments receive orders to a two-week training course at either the Fleet Antisubmarine Warfare Training Center Atlantic in Norfolk or Pacific in San Diego. In the event of a war or national emergency the officers who successfully complete the course and qualify as convoy commodores could be called to active naval service with their retired rank to command merchant ship convoys.

The training topics addressed by convoy commodores include:

- U. S. civil direction and naval control of shipping

- Merchant ship characteristics

- Control of shipping communications systems

- Convoy planning, including routing, organization, sailing and forming

- The threat to convoys
- Convoy at-sea operations, including communications, maneuvering, emergency procedures and protection

The course is taught by regular Navy instructors at the antisubmarine warfare schools often with some naval reserve assistance. Guest speakers cover the history and advantages of convoys, merchant ship characteristics and convoy commodore experiences. These courses are open to British and Canadian students as well as to naval reserve officers from convoy commodore staff units and Naval Control of Shipping units. The course I attended in August-September 1983 in San Diego consisted of seven retired Navy captains, 19 naval reserve officers, and one Canadian reserve officer.

Although there are about 125 convoy commodores in the United States, most of them have nothing more to do with the program after completing the course. There is no follow-up or required refresher program and there are very few at-sea training opportunities. Only about 20 convoy commodores have had a chance to go to sea and practice. I have been one of the fortunate few. Besides three at-sea convoys, I have participated in additional events involved with naval control and protection of merchant shipping.

Of all the retired naval officers I have asked only those few involved in the convoy commodore program have any association with a mobilization task. I have been unable to find another program that provides for mobilization or emergency use of retired Navy line officers. The Navy is busy trying to train Naval Reserve officers to augment major staffs for crisis situations but apparently has little use for retired officers who have spent years of duty on those very staffs and years commanding major subordinate activities.

In October 1983 I was invited by the Commander Military Sealift Command to serve as convoy commodore in a Rainbow Reef exercise at Diego Garcia in the Indian Ocean. The exercise was scheduled for February 1984 preceded by a weekend of refresher training at San Diego. Weekend training is common in the convoy commodore and Naval Control of Shipping programs because the staffs are manned by naval reserve personnel and preparing for an exercise becomes their weekend training.

The Rainbow Reef exercise was a marvelous experience. Just getting to Diego Garcia is a challenge. Starting in Baltimore I flew by commercial airline to Norfolk where I boarded a military aircraft. After a five-hour wait the C-141 departed for Europe then diverted to McGuire Air Force Base in New Jersey. Six hours later, on a different C-141, we departed again for Europe. After stops of two-to-four hours at Torrejon, Spain; Sigonella, Sicily and Nairobi, Kenya we arrived at Diego Garcia, some 40 hours in elapsed time after my Baltimore departure.

Diego Garcia is an atoll in the north central Indian Ocean owned by the British and leased to the United States. It is about 15 miles long and 7 miles wide. The enclosed lagoon provides an excellent anchorage for about 14 merchant ships of the Maritime Prepositioning Program, formerly known as the Near-Term Prepositioned Force. These ships are loaded with heavy equipment which could be used to support a large-scale military operation. They go to sea at least once a month under their own squadron commander and practice formation steaming which makes them the most experienced merchant ships in the world in convoy procedures. Four times a year these at-sea exercises are made available to the Naval Control of Shipping Organization and labeled Rainbow Reef. A convoy commodore and naval reserve staff, and a Naval Control of Shipping officer and staff conduct these exercises. The ships' masters and mates are familiar with the signals, formations and procedures and do not hesitate to inform the convoy commodore of an incorrect move. It is a challenge for the convoy commodore and staff and a fine opportunity to learn how to control a group of merchant ships at sea. As all convoy commodores have a background of Navy ship experience, the first lesson to be learned is that these are not Navy ships and the difference between Navy and merchant ships is not trivial.

The weather was fine throughout this exercise. The ships steamed with no problems in the various formations and maneuvers. It was a valuable learning experience.

After the exercise, the briefing I gave the Commander Military Sealift Command was well received and generated an interest in other convoy activities. My briefing generally covered convoy procedures, the prepositioned ships at Diego Garcia and my specific Rainbow

Reef exercise. But questions usually centered on naval protection, which is a separate but related subject. So I did some research on that and since adjusting my briefing to include naval protection of merchant shipping I have lectured at many naval reserve units and addressed classes taught at Navy schools.

On 8 May 1984 I lectured at the Master Mariners Readiness Training Course. This was the first of its kind, a one week pilot course at the U. S. Merchant Marine Academy, Kings Point, New York for 12 working merchant ship masters. The course provided specialized training in naval requirements for maneuvering in convoy, routing procedures, rescue and assistance, underway replenishment, reactivation of mothballed ships and military communications. The course was sponsored by the Maritime Administration. That pilot course has since been given to U.S. merchant ship masters a number of times.

On 13 February 1986, I gave another lecture in the same course at Kings Point. My report and briefings led to an invitation to participate as a Chief of Naval Operations representative on the formal audit of the Convoy Commodore and Staff Officer Course taught by the Fleet Antisubmarine Warfare Training centers. This gave me an opportunity to include in this course some of the lessons I had learned from my experiences and from the discussions which always followed my lectures.

The Naval Sea Systems Command (NAVSEA) had a project which included considerations of various combat systems for naval protection of shipping. My involvement in the convoy commodore program and extension into naval protection of merchant shipping provided the basis from which I developed a scenario that included various requirements for and means of protecting merchant ships in wartime. I contributed the scenario to the NAVSEA project.

During 1984 the Royal Navy extended an invitation to the U.S. Navy to send a convoy commodore to the British course at HMS Vernon in Portsmouth, England. The British wanted a U.S. convoy commodore with experience in a Rainbow Reef exercise to provide a mutually beneficial dialogue. When asked, I leaped at the opportunity.

Convoy commodore training in the Royal Navy is not as extensive or intensive as it is in the U.S. Navy. The Royal Navy course is three-and-a-half days in duration as compared to ten classroom days in the U.S. Navy. Within the short time available the Royal Navy course is able to cover only the basic elements of how to run a convoy. The U. S. Navy course includes much more of the background, threat, organization and procedures of convoys. The Royal Navy course is taught at the Maritime Trade Faculty by a staff of five officers dedicated to teaching naval control of shipping and convoy procedures. There is no similar organization in the U.S. Navy, where naval control of shipping and convoy procedures are taught as additional tasks by the Fleet Antisubmarine Warfare Training Centers. The U.S. Navy piggybacks naval control of shipping on antisubmarine warfare instructors who take the time for preparation and classes "out of hide," including many weekends. The Royal Navy has dedicated people for this purpose.

A weekend of refresher training for the convoy portion of Ocean Safari 85 was held in Norfolk, Virginia on 3-4 August. It was an excellent opportunity to review the details of convoying with people who would be involved in the Boston-to-Iceland-to-England convoys.

The exercise started in Boston with a pre-sail convoy conference on 28 August. There were about 60 people at the pre-sail convoy conference hosted by the Naval Control of Shipping officer at a Coast Guard facility. Masters, chief mates and radio officers of the convoy ships, the officer in tactical command and his staff, representatives of each escort ship, representatives of associated staffs and the convoy commodore and vice commodore with their staffs listened to presentations on mine countermeasures, communications, departure procedures, enroute operations and arrival instructions. The convoy we were forming would sail from Boston to Iceland. At Iceland another convoy would be formed to sail to southern England.

As convoy commodore I gave a short talk on the various formations and maneuvers we would use and some internal convoy communications procedures. NATO's Commander Standing Naval Force Atlantic, who would be officer in tactical command for the departure from Boston and the first day under way, gave a briefing on the anticipated threat to the convoy and his intentions regarding protection. The at-sea schedule called for Commander Canadian Fleet with his ships to take over as officer in tactical command on our second day at sea. A representative of the Canadian command gave us some information on protection procedures and his commodore's intentions. The conference followed a formal agenda, as taught in the schools and in the naval control of shipping doctrine.

Weather, which later proved to be the most important of considerations, was not covered in the conference. Immediately after the conference we went to our merchant ships and got under way. We formed up in a column and followed the minesweepers out of Boston Harbor through channels swept through simulated minefields.

At sea I formed the convoy in a circular formation, then into rectangular, diamond and various other configurations. Gradually the formations and maneuvers became more complex and the merchant ships' crews became more familiar with formation steaming. We practiced zig zagging and changing stations as well as basic station keeping in formation.

Probably the most important consideration for a convoy commodore and staff is patience. With a group of Navy destroyers at sea, tactical signals are executed quickly and the ships hustle to their stations at high speed. With merchant ships in a convoy the signals must be put out slowly, with time to look up the meaning and determine the proper action. Then the signal is executed followed by a slow process of adjustment. This can be frustrating for Navy people but understanding the ship control procedures of merchant ships leads to patience and appreciation for the problems of maneuvering these ships.

The next day Commander Canadian Fleet took over as officer in tactical command and the Canadian ships became the escort force for the next 21 days of the exercise. The other NATO forces departed to meet requirements elsewhere. The weather was fine when we departed Boston, but in a few days it started to deteriorate. Along the Grand Banks off Newfoundland we had to divert toward the east to avoid icebergs. As we transited from Nova Scotia past Newfoundland, land-based aircraft flying from Canada made simulated air attacks on the convoy. U.S. carrier based aircraft from the Navy battle group several hundred miles to the southeast often over flew the convoy.

We practiced emergency turns and evaded an exercise submarine. However, by the fourth day the sea conditions were so bad that the small ships had difficulty maneuvering. High winds and heavy seas forced the convoy to slow and to steer courses into the seas. I felt fortunate to be embarked in a large comfortable merchant ship which rode well even in heavy seas. At night the smallest merchant ship dropped back and the officer in tactical command and I decided to keep the convoy together rather than declare the small ship a straggler. The convoy made only about two knots good until the weather improved.

Three separate storms hit the convoy before we reached Iceland. Each time the smallest ship dropped astern, the convoy slowed to a crawl and we hung on until the weather improved. The convoy experienced sea state 6, Beaufort scale 9, in each of the storms. Seas were 30 to 40 feet with wind speeds up to 60 knots and the master of the smallest merchant ship reported 50 degree rolls.

Two serious medical problems developed during our transit to Iceland. A crewman in one merchant ship came down with a severe case of pneumonia and later a crewman in another ship developed acute appendicitis. Each had to be removed from his ship by helicopter. The pneumonia patient was in critical condition and was treated by the doctor on board a Canadian Armed Forces ship. The appendicitis case was put on board a destroyer for an increased speed run toward the north and then a long range helicopter trip to a hospital at Iceland. Both crewmen survived because of outstanding attention by Canadians.

On 7 September during a period of decent weather I was at lunch when the bridge called to report a Soviet surveillance aircraft. I bolted up five levels of ladders in time to see a Soviet Bear just below the cloud layer. The Bear circled the convoy and disappeared into the overcast sky.

For two periods of 24 hours each I turned the convoy commodore duties over to the Canadian vice commodore to give him and his staff the experience of running the convoy. It also gave my staff and me a little more rest. I knew that on the next convoy, from Iceland to England, I would be vice commodore and I hoped the convoy commodore would reciprocate.

The convoy had consisted of four ships when we departed Boston and the next day Commander Canadian Fleet brought an underway replenishment ship with him. A few days later two large merchant ships joined and the next day another, so that there were eight ships in the convoy as we arrived at Iceland on 9 September. We entered a fjord at Hvalfjordhur with the last ship anchoring just before midnight. The port information book included little about the fjord. Of 41 detailed headings grouped under general information, logistics, port facilities and navigational information, 29 were covered by "information not available." It was interesting that according to the port information book Hvalfjordhur was pronounced "kwoffewda." The next question was how do you pronounce "kwoffewda?"

At Iceland the next morning we met in a steel building near a fuel pier for the "hot wash up" meeting of the Boston-to-Iceland convoy. After discussing the convoy and what could have been improved we took a short break and reassembled for the pre-sail conference of the Iceland-to-England convoy. The same ships participated along with a small Norwegian freighter, bringing the total to nine ships. They carried the flags of the United States, Canada, Great Britain, Germany and now Norway. Similar to the pre-sail conference at Boston the Iceland meeting followed a formal agenda according to doctrine. A Canadian commodore took over as convoy commodore and I became vice commodore. After the pre-sail conference we departed Hvalfjordhur under gray skies, met our Canadian escorts and formed the convoy enroute to southern England.

Again, we exercised convoy fundamentals including various random formations. The weather was nice the first few days and there were no exercise attacks from our simulated enemy.

I suppose I have always been a little superstitious, but that did not come to mind when the convoy commodore duties were turned over to me on Friday the 13th. However, as I mentioned earlier, a Soviet destroyer visited the convoy along with a Soviet intelligence ship and waves of British aircraft conducted simulated attacks on the convoy. By 14 September the weather was similar to the storms we encountered enroute to Iceland. The small Norwegian ship had serious problems keeping station in heavy weather. Again the convoy had to slow, making little to no speed and wait for better weather. We considered detaching the two smallest and slowest ships to proceed south through the Irish Sea while the remainder of the convoy kept to the prescribed track west of Ireland. However, because it was judged more important to stay together we all rode out the storm.

Again, I was fortunate to be in a large comfortable ship. Tonnage is misleading but the merchant ship I rode was about the size of an Iowa class battleship. However, while the Iowa carries a crew of about 1,500 men, 26 personnel ran my merchant ship.

On our final day at sea, as the convoy entered the southwest approaches to the English Channel (which the British call "Swapps"), British and Dutch ships and British aircraft and submarines conducted simulated attacks on the convoy. Later, in heavy fog the Canadian officer in tactical command passed control of the convoy to British minesweepers which guided us through safe channels to anchorage areas off Portsmouth, England. Boating was difficult in the heavy chop and it was after midnight when my staff and I arrived at the hot-wash-up meeting ashore at Bincleaves, Portsmouth Harbor.

The hot-wash-up meeting marked the end of a long rough transit for the convoy ships and so the gathering took on a festive air. British, American, Canadian, German and Norwegian seagoing officers enjoyed the refreshments provided by the Royal Navy.

There is always paperwork associated with fleet exercises and Ocean Safari 85 was no exception. I submitted a report to the NATO command and another to the U.S. Navy, making some recommendations to improve convoy procedures:

In World Wars I and II, convoys used various visual methods as primary tactical communications, including flashing lights, colored lights, signal flags and shapes. Since World War II the bridge-to-bridge very high frequency (VHF) voice radio has become the primary means of communicating among merchant ships, just as truckers use the citizens band radio on our highways. The visual signals became secondary systems. Because modern merchant ships are so large and need dispersal as a means of protection we have separated the ships from the former few hundred yards to the current few miles. This increased distance among ships plus the obstructed views, scarcity of personnel and lack of familiarity with visual methods have made all visual means of communications impractical.

We now have a usable primary system; the VHF voice radio but no secondary means of tactical communications. The VHF voice radio is easy for an enemy to exploit. Often we encounter interference from other ships or fishermen. The VHF voice radio should be relegated to a secondary status and new technology should provide a primary tactical communications system for convoys. The new system might be electromagnetic or laser. It could be digital, burst transmission or data stream. It should have a low probability of intercept and should be portable.

Past convoys and convoy exercises have used the broad front rectangular formations developed during World Wars I and II. The threat then was the diesel-electric submarine, which generally used a tactic of positioning ahead of the convoy, letting the convoy run over her submerged position and firing torpedoes as the target merchant ships passed. The broad front rectangular formation was designed to minimize the targets presented to the submarine. Today's threat submarine has much more endurance and mobility and more sophisticated torpedoes.

Merchant ships today are larger, faster, less maneuverable and must be spaced further apart. New formations have been developed which are more flexible, provide better protection and allow more maneuverability. These new formations should become part of our convoy doctrine.

Existing doctrine learned in World Wars I and II provides for forming convoys as slow, medium or fast based on the merchant ships' declared speeds. There are other important factors, such as the ships' capability to proceed in heavy weather. Some ships have to make more speed because of engine type or the need to maintain control. The grouping of ships in a convoy should take these considerations into account.

Masters and mates are not familiar with convoy procedures and cannot be expected to be. In Ocean Safari 85 each merchant ship had a naval liaison officer (NLO) provided by his country, which proved very valuable. In many cases masters and mates do not pass along information on convoy procedures and have language problems. The NLO can provide the necessary information to help the mates on watch. A pool of NLOs should be established. They probably should be naval reservists and perhaps they could be members of convoy commodore staff units to provide officers to go on board merchant ships in convoy. There should be one such officer per ship, familiar with convoy procedures and equipped with the portable communications system recommended earlier.

The Boston-Iceland-United Kingdom convoys in Ocean Safari 85 received excellent escort services, primarily from the Canadians. The U.S. Navy has apparently abrogated its basic task of protecting the sea lines of communication. The U.S Navy doctrine is outdated and the Navy does not practice protection of merchant shipping nor is it taught at schools. The commanding officer of a Navy destroyer or frigate could very well find himself as officer in tactical command of a convoy, a role for which he is not prepared and for which he has no documentation or background on which to rely. The Navy should recognize the importance of naval protection of shipping, organize for it, dedicate resources and train in and develop procedures for modem naval protection of shipping. This should include convoying as well as other means of protection.

My other recommendations included considerations of maneuvering a convoy under conditions of restrictive electronic emissions, the function of preparing the sailing folders for each ship, pre-exercise in-port training and the equipment needed by a convoy commodore and staff at sea.

As one of the most active retired officers in the convoy commodore program, I have become an experienced convoy commodore. It is not a crowded field. Perhaps we will never need convoy commodores in a real global conflict, I certainly hope not, but in case we do the program deserves the best we can give it. Thousands of retired Navy people could provide worthwhile experience to the active forces in a crisis. There should be more programs that make use of the background and experience of these retired personnel.

CHAPTER FORTY FIVE

THE CORONADO CAYS LIGHTHOUSE

2010

Residents of Coronado Cays, the residential marina community of 1200 homes located five miles south of the Coronado City Hall, want to build a Caribbean replica lighthouse on a lonely sand spit at the south end of the Cays. The Cays community was built with a Caribbean theme and is separated from the rest of the City of Coronado by federal and state properties.

Cays residents want to have a full size replica of a Caribbean lighthouse, standing alone on the southern end of South Grand Caribe Island in Coronado Cays. That south end of the island would be named "Coronado Cays Point" and the lighthouse "Coronado Cays Lighthouse." The Coronado Cays Lighthouse would not be a navigation aid but would be the lighthouse deepest in the southwest corner of the United States. Also it would highlight the maritime background of Coronado Cays and the City of Coronado.

A number of years ago a group of Coronado Cays homeowners thought that the southern end of the long sandy overgrown spit of

South Grand Caribe Island, on the San Diego Bay side of the Cays, should be marked with a lighthouse. In fact, if a lighthouse were to be placed anywhere in Coronado Cays or in the City of Coronado, the southern end of Grand Caribe Island is the only ideal location. A lighthouse must be near waters edge on a lonely point or crag, a spit or shelf or cliff-top, away from buildings, streets, wires or traffic.

Lighthouses have personalities as loners and they do not mix with others. As the theme of Coronado Cays is Caribbean, all ten villages and every street carries a Caribbean name, it is appropriate that the lighthouse should be Caribbean. Could they find a lighthouse that could be moved from the Caribbean to Coronado, with permissions, method and means? An internet search revealed over a hundred Caribbean lighthouses, almost all too tall, many of peculiar shape and most made of brick, stone and mortar, making them undesirable and/ or too difficult to move; many and most but not all. One lighthouse was found that was the right size, classic shape, not in use and made of cast iron panels which could be taken apart and moved; the St. Johns Lighthouse. Just right!

Inquiry to the U.S. Counselor Agent in St. Johns, the capital city of the Caribbean nation Antigua and Barbuda, brought the following response:

> *I would be more than happy to personally assist you in your endeavor. I am closely acquainted with the Prime Minister of Antigua & Barbuda, The Hon. Baldwin Spencer and will contact him with your request. I have often felt the St. John's Lighthouse deserved a distinguished home capable of providing the restoration it so desperately needs as well as the ability to provide continuous maintenance.*
>
> *As a Native Californian and a repeat visitor to Coronado, I will do my best to ensure you are provided the opportunity to see your project to*

fruition. I believe Coronado would be an honorable home for our beloved St. John's Lighthouse. I will contact you again with further information very soon.

Coronado Cays Lighthouse advocates were very pleased with the positive response and offer of assistance from the U.S. Counselor Agent. Yet there were some points touched on briefly in the response that raised some eyebrows; "providing the restoration it so desperately needs" and "continuous maintenance," which were not anticipated in the original concept. Would they be taking on more than they expected or wanted? A Coronado Cays homeowner went to St. Johns and inspected the lighthouse.

The St. Johns Lighthouse is over a hundred years old. It was never completed and put into service so what would have been the light enclosure has been left open, exposing the internals of the cast iron panel structure to continuous tropical rain in a salt water environment. In short the lighthouse is rusting away, falling apart, impractical for relocation and even if it could be moved it would be a continuous maintenance nightmare.

But all is not lost! From pictures and descriptions a professional architect has produced renderings which can be used to construct a full sized replica of the St. Johns Lighthouse and the program is proceeding in that direction. The owner of a construction company has volunteered to build it of modern low maintenance materials. Without any solicitation of funding, about a dozen people have offered financial contributions. The Coronado Cays Lighthouse will be of no cost to Cays homeowners, Coronado taxpayers or the Unified Port District of San Diego.

A project in process, a replica Caribbean lighthouse to be found only in Coronado; the Coronado Cays Lighthouse.

The Coronado Cays Lighthouse was never built.

The preceding couple of pages represent some of the early propaganda used to promote the project and it looked like there would be a lighthouse in Coronado Cays. Approval would be needed from the Unified Port District of San Diego and the director of The Port told Stu Landersman that it was a great idea. The mayor of Coronado was waiting anxiously to give his favorable endorsement. As a first step in the approval process a request would have to originate with the Coronado Cays Homeowners Association.

There were 1200 homes in Coronado Cays. A group of five people representing three homes in Coronado Cays objected to having a lighthouse on the southern tip of Grand Caribe Island. They claimed that a lighthouse would interfere with their view of the landscape and seascape.

Stu went to the eastern end of Kingston Court for the best view of the island and measured what would be the width of the lighthouse across 180 degrees of view. He found that the lighthouse would occupy less than one percent of the visage. Better put; the lighthouse would take up less than one degree of the 180 degrees of horizontal view and most important; a lighthouse on the southern end of Grand Caribe Island would be a great improvement over the barren eroding strip. Still the few were able to influence the many and the Homeowners Board of Directors hesitated to go forward with the lighthouse request.

Much later Stu would learn that those few who objected really were not concerned with the lighthouse blocking their landscape view. That was just a meaningless excuse that they used. What they were really concerned about was that the lighthouse would attract and bring into Coronado Cays an undesirable element of society, people who should not be in Coronado Cays. Some of these people just might see that homes in the Cays would be very lucrative burglary targets. The objectors knew that this, their real concern would not go over so well; they might be considered "snobs." It certainly wouldn't go over well because that's exactly what they really were; "snobs."

Coronado Cays is part of the City of Coronado but is separated from the rest of the city by state and federal properties. Among these properties is the home base of U.S. Navy SEALS. Much of the training; the swimming done by the SEALS is done in San Diego Bay and at times a SEAL unit swims to the Cays, enjoys some refreshment and rest and then swims back to their base. So it was not unusual for fifteen or twenty frogmen to come ashore, hose off and come to the Calypso Cafe for breakfast.

The Calypso Café was the regular morning breakfast spot for Stu Landersman and he enjoyed talking with the SEALS. One such morning Stu was having coffee with a SEAL team commander and Stu described how he was trying to get approval for the lighthouse.

The SEAL commander showed great interest. "Look, we're neighbors here on the strand; SEALS and The Cays. If there were a lighthouse here in The Cays, why couldn't it be a memorial to your neighbors the SEALS, honoring those who have been killed in action, a SEAL Memorial Lighthouse?"

That gave Stu an idea. How could anyone object to a SEAL Memorial Lighthouse? With that he could overcome the very few objections and the Homeowners Board of Directors could go forward to the city and the port, where approvals were waiting.

Stu started a campaign for the SEAL Memorial Lighthouse. Volunteers circulated petitions and very soon over 350 of the 1200 homes had signed and the volunteers were still gathering signatures when a letter arrived from the SEAL headquarters in Florida. Stu opened the letter expecting a "thank you" with nice words of appreciation. What a disappointment!

In a few harsh words the commander of all SEALS directed Stu to stop immediately any attempt to use the SEAL name for a lighthouse or in any other way. He was prepared to take legal action if necessary.

"Shot down" best explains what happened to Stu Landersman and his lighthouse project. He sat down with his close few and discussed the situation. All agreed that they had gone so far down the road with the SEAL Memorial thing that they couldn't just change it back to Coronado Cays Lighthouse. They had put all their effort into the SEALS and now they couldn't just change it. Don Patrick returned the more than $50,000 that he had collected from donors. Petitions were turned in. Posters were taken down.

Stu explained to the Homeowners Board that the lighthouse issue was dead. The five who had opposed the lighthouse just gloated as snobs do.

So ends the tale of the Coronado Cays Lighthouse and the SEAL Memorial Lighthouse.

CHAPTER FORTY SIX

SHIPHANDLING SIMULATOR

1986

One day I was at the San Diego Naval Station (Navy people called it Thirty-Second Street) and I watched a ship changing berths as a pilot with two tugs moved the ship, a very common procedure. What made this move special for me was that this ship changing berths was USS HEPBURN (FF 1055).

As I stood there watching I could not help but reminisce, to think back about the great times I had in that ship, the great people, combat on the gun line, Sea of Okhosk, South China Sea, so much else over fifteen years ago, even Pentagon duty with changing DE to FF. I thought back and remembered and wondered. I wondered where those people were and how life was treating them. I thought about the shiphandling that I had done and tried to teach others and I wondered about how much if any shiphandling any of them had done after our time together.

From that moment on, after watching HEPBURN shifting berths through the many years that followed, shiphandling was my primary project. I had learned early in my Navy time that the best way to learn how to handle a ship was to actually handle a ship. Oh sure, a novice had to watch it being done, talk it over and read the standard texts but just like in aviation, after appropriate preparation and instruction you had to "solo", you had to do it yourself.

In my earliest Navy time in the LSTs there were four OOD watch-standers so we all had opportunity to learn ship handling. In destroyers there were more officers and I saw that you had to hustle to get those opportunities. In R.A. OWENS the captain made me OOD for Special Sea and Anchor Detail so I had many shiphandling opportunities. When I had command of HEPBURN (1969-1971) I did a lot of shiphandling myself and I focused training on my department heads. But that was all ancient history in 1986. Where were we now? Were young officers learning to handle their ships? I asked around.

A number of officers that recently had command of destroyers were proud to tell me that on their ship, "The junior officers did all the shiphandling." Looking into this further I found that with twenty or so junior officers in a ship, that usually meant that each had two or three shiphandling opportunities, certainly not enough to develop any skill and especially when those few shiphandling experiences were acting as a parrot, just repeating orders from a more experienced officer or a pilot. It didn't end there because I also learned that upon taking command of a destroyer most officers had little more then that minimal shiphandling training that junior officers received in his ship. They were products of the same system.

In 1977 when I was a DESRON commander involved in the development of coordinated ASW procedures I had visited naval air stations where P-3 and S-3 aviation squadrons called home. At these air stations I saw the simulators that were important parts of aviator training. When I lectured on convoy procedures at the U.S. Merchant Marine Academy, Kings Point, New York, I saw a shiphandling simulator used in the training of cadets in handling merchant ships. I heard of and then visited other shiphandling simulators run by maritime unions in training merchant mariners in Maryland and Florida. I found that there was a shiphandling simulator company that had tried to interest the U.S. Navy but could not find anyone who took an interest.

The largest aviation simulation company in the world was Flight Safety International with home office at LaGuardia Field, New York. They had aviation simulators all over the world and in the U.S. at key airports. A few years before I came on the scene FSI had organized a branch which introduced shiphandling simulators to the merchant shipping industry. That extension of FSI was named Marine Safety International and having established themselves with merchant shipping they had tried to interest the Navy.

MSI ran the shiphandling simulator at Kings Point and when I visited there I had opportunity to talk with the MSI people who had tried in vain to obtain Navy interest.

Well, I told them, I was Navy and they had my interest.

It took me a long time, six years is a long time, but I finally was successful in getting the Navy shiphandling simulation.

Let's have a brief outline of Navy shiphandling simulation:

LOCATIONS: The original contract was arranged for a shiphandling simulator facility in San Diego. It took six years from my idea to the first ship using the facility. Soon after, I moved to Norfolk to give the Atlantic Fleet a simulator facility. That took him me three years. Both simulators were established with separate competitively bid contracts and both were awarded to Marine Safety International. A few years later MSI was awarded a contract to put simulators in Everett, Pearl Harbor, Mayport, Yokosuka and Sasebo.

SHIPS MODELED: Every U.S. Navy ship class was accurately modeled; every ship class from the newest aircraft carriers to the smallest patrol craft. By accurately modeled is meant that every ship responded to environmentals and performed exactly as that particular class ship would react under the given conditions. The bow image as viewed from the pilot house or bridge wing was exactly that which would be seen in each ship. Most simulators used a generic or common ship operating under established conditions. Aviation simulators were for one type aircraft. These shiphandling simulators could replicate every U.S. Navy ship with accurate visual and performance.

PORTS MODELED: Every port used by the U.S. Navy in the U.S. or in any part of the world was accurately modeled with landscape, navigation aids, currents and berthing. From Norfolk to San Diego, Puget Sound to Key West, Yokosuka, Japan to Naples, Italy and all those between, every port was accurately modeled.

FIDELITY: Every ship model was programmed to respond accurately to all the various sea conditions; wind, current, bottom and side effect, Bernoulli Effect, etc. The ship models would roll, pitch, surge, yaw, rise and fall as would a real ship in the various conditions of sea state. Early in the contract process I wanted to have actual mechanical movement of the pilot house but when I learned it would more than double the cost of the simulator I had to settle for movement conveyed with the visual scene. Even with that some students would feel the effects of "mal de mer."

ENVIRONMENTALS: The simulators could present any night or day tones based on time of day with any sun and cloud effects. The sun would be in position based on time of day programmed and would move accordingly. There could be any degree and variation of rain, snow, sleet or hail. The most commonly used environmental considerations in shiphandling were wind and current and these could be applied as might be expected in any port, any berth, any time and to any ship.

TRAFFIC SHIPS: Up to 50 traffic ships were available. The simulator user could select any number, any type, in any traffic or rules-of-the-road situation. Traffic ships might be container ships, fishing boats, sampans, tankers, tugs, other Navy ships, private yachts or sailboats and these could be placed and programmed to provide challenging situations or innocent passage.

SUPPORT SHIPS: Tugs were provided as would be available in each port. The various ports have various type tugs and the simulation provided the type tugs that would be used in each port. Just as various type ships perform differently, so would the various type tugs perform and the shiphandling simulation accurately programmed the type of tugs that would be available in each port.

COMMUNICATIONS: Bridge-to-bridge voice radio and internal ship communications were "played" by the computer operator. Some operators would use accents to provide realism to the simulation such as the mate on a Japanese container ship responding to a crossing situation.

STUDENTS: The primary purpose of shiphandling simulation was to train Navy ships' officers. Programs were established for officers based on their level of experience; basic, intermediate or advanced. The original intent of shiphandling simulation was to prepare the student for the real and most important shiphandling training that could only be done on the ship. It soon evolved into a situation where the officers rarely (if ever) did any real shiphandling as commanding officers considered the simulator as adequate training.
In the early contracts for San Diego, when the facility was not in use by the Navy, the contractor was allowed to train licensed merchant mariners and the simulator facility was certified by the Coast Guard. Later, as use of the simulator by the Navy increased there was no time for merchant mariners.

INSTRUCTORS: The early contracts provided that instructors would be retired Navy captains with at least two ship commands. Later that was eased somewhat with a single command and a merchant ship master. But just a minute! Here we are talking about instructors when there were no instructors in the early contracted simulators. They were called facilitators. Why? Because in the early contracts every effort was made to keep the Fleet's shiphandling simulation away from the Navy training establishment. CNET it was called, for Chief of Naval Education and Training in Orlando, Florida. I had very carefully avoided any association with CNET when I established Tactical Training Group Pacific in 1978 and was convinced that success of TACTRAGRUPAC was due in large part because of my deliberate steps to be free of CNET. Now, in starting Navy shiphandling simulation I was determined to once again avoid the Navy training establishment. I did so with the funding, which came from the Pacific Fleet's operating budget and the careful avoidance of training and education terminology in the contracting process. Instructors were called facilitators. Classrooms were learning feedback centers. Curriculum was programs. It worked for a number of years until CNET finally got into the contracts for shiphandling simulation but I was not in the process by then.

At the Surface Warfare Officers School in Newport, Rhode Island, lieutenants were used as instructors and these had about the same level of shiphandling experience and ability as some of the students at the San Diego facility.

CURRICULUM: All common Navy shiphandling events such as getting underway from alongside a pier and mooring to a pier under all conditions of wind, current, day and night were programmed. The shiphandling simulator could replicate transit in or out of any of the ports programmed. Formation steaming and going alongside an oiler for refueling were available programs. All of these and more could be exercised with any Navy class ship. Before any of these simulator exercises a preparation session would be held in the learning feedback center at which the facilitator would explain the program. After the event the class would once more assemble in the learning feedback center for critique.

Among the more popular formal 40 hour training courses that were available were Bridge Resource Management (BRM) and Basic Shiphandling (BSH).

And here is a more detailed description of Navy shiphandling simulation:

Each shiphandling simulator facility includes at least one Full Mission Bridge simulator, a classroom and the current version of the shipboard simulator. At the two largest fleet concentration areas of Norfolk and San Diego there is an additional Full Mission Bridge simulator and a Bridge Wing Simulator.

The Full Mission Bridge Simulator is a full-sized stand-up and walk-around replica of a Navy ship's bridge and pilot house with projected on screen large-scale video display providing realistic, animated and responsive seascape. Classrooms equipped with projection and playback are used for critique of shiphandling evolutions, seminars and courses of instruction related to shiphandling, safe navigation and collision and grounding avoidance.

The shiphandling simulators at all of the fleet concentration areas are capable of simulating a broad spectrum of Navy shipboard bridge operational situations including open ocean maneuvering and advanced maneuvering in restricted waterways for safe navigation and collision avoidance. These simulators are capable of providing a realistic environment for the development and maintenance of proficiency in basic, intermediate and advanced levels of shiphandling skills:

Naval shiphandling training is currently being conducted in state-of-the-art simulators that are owned and maintained by the Navy. A contractor provides instructional and scheduling services using retired Navy and Coast Guard officers who have significant at-sea and command experience.

Exercise scenarios can be provided at the basic, intermediate and advanced levels and with a full spectrum of environmental conditions such as varying daylight from bright to dark, any sea-state, wind and current. Every Navy ship class is an accurate hydrodynamic model in the shiphandling simulator, responding to six degrees freedom of motion, with Bernoulli and Venturi effects, bottom and bank effects, turning, accelerating and stopping as does each class of Navy ship.

Even with the fine realism of full mission bridge shiphandling simulators and highly experienced instructors, nothing is as good, or as realistic as handling an actual ship. Simulators come close and offer more opportunities, and once the students have mastered handling a ship in a simulator they are ready to handle a real ship and to become real mariners.

Bridge Resource Management Course (BRM Course).

Derived from international and U.S. Coast Guard approved courses, this course is modified for Navy applicability. Analyzes Navy maritime collisions and groundings, reviews teamwork considerations and factors in sound decision making. Provides skills necessary to increase effectiveness of teamwork of the ship's bridge watchstanding team in reducing probability of collisions and groundings. Provides students with opportunity to apply teamwork principles in the shiphandling simulator.

Basic Shiphandling Course (BSH Course)

The Basic Shiphandling Course (BSH) is a five day course of instruction consisting of about 10 hours of classroom and 30 hours of shiphandling simulator exercises. This course is intended for the inexperienced Navy novice seeking qualification as Officer of the Deck and Surface Warfare Officer. The course covers the very basic principles of shiphandling utilized in controlling the movement and positioning a basic Navy destroyer type ship.

And why not finish this chapter with a little nautical poetry:

THOSE OLD SAILORS AT THE SHIPHANDLING SIMULATOR

You may talk rough seas and rudder
When you're home with kids and mudder
And tugs and pilot take y' out a port,

But when it comes to stress
You'll truly ship finesse
And you'll bless the time y'had in simuludder.

For its sim, sim, sim,
Not with mischief use the sim,
'Cause when time comes you'll need it
And be glad that you did heed it,
That teacher been there, done that, bet on him.

Now in Nado's sunny clime,
Where y' put dozen years time,
A'servin' in the Pac Fleet percolator,
Of all projects y' done
There stands out special one;
Twas Pac Fleet shiphandling simulator.

For its sim, sim, sim,
You hydrodynamic modeled ship sim,
Right full rudder, engine flank,
You can take it to the bank,
You'll be doin' UNREP daylight or dim.

Now I shant forget the night,
With all lights aburnin' bright,
That I cleared an oiler in Tonkin Sea.
Twas then to my surprise
A carrier did suddenly arise
In sight ahead, I barely there could see.

Without sim, sim, sim,
Had no training then in ships sim.
All back full, rudder hard,
Held breath, drew lucky card
And missed the beast with margin only slim.

Then I'll meet those from the sim
In that place dead sailors swim
Where its watch and watch with no lib.
On the foc'sle they'll be squattin,
Tellin' tales exaggerated and rotten
And I'll learn still more as sim guys ad-lib.

CHAPTER FORTY SEVEN

TIME AND WIND

2002

The following is not fiction. It really happened just that way. On March 2, 2002 Carol and Bill McClennan were with Martha and me aboard our boat, Miss Sadie B as we went for a lunch across San Diego Bay from where we lived in Coronado Cays. Bill and Carol were our upstairs neighbors. I wrote this just after the event and the local newspaper wanted the full story but they insisted on having the names of all the people involved, even those of the capsized sailboat. The owner of that boat was very embarrassed and didn't want his name made public so there was no newspaper story. Fran Farley and I exchanged these by email and a couple of weeks later our two couples had a nice dinner together.

Gleaming in the sun, the bright orange life jacket bobbed slightly as it floated lightly on the calm harbor water. With only a slight wind it moved very little as the twenty-six foot boat drew near. Coasting slowly with his engine in gear but at idle, Stu allowed his boat to slow into the wind and when almost alongside turned right, across the wind. He had spotted the jacket in the middle of the inner harbor and with no other boats or people interested, had headed towards it.

"See, just like a 'man overboard' recovery. If you get upwind of the guy in the water you can let the boat drift down on the guy and make it easy to pick him up."

"Yeah," Bill replied, "but this life jacket can move with the wind even more than your boat."

"Maybe, but the boat cuts off the wind when we're alongside and the boat still gets the effect of the wind. The jacket doesn't."

"Looks like you're right, Captain." Bill reached out with the boat hook and expertly swung the dripping life jacket into the afterdeck, tossing it on top of two blue fenders. "There, a little bit of harbor clean-up is a good thing."

They all laughed and Bill's wife Carol said, "And we're just in time to use the wind and recover a nice life jacket."

"Now we have another life jacket to put away," Martha said as she looked at her husband. "Why are we going over here, Stu?"

"Just want to take a look at a boat that used to be over here, to see if it's still here."

The boat continued across the inner harbor area of Chula Vista Marina, circled around and headed west, past the breakwater into San Diego Bay. They followed the channel north and waved to the few fishermen along the pier.

Miss Sadie B. had departed Coronado Cays about three hours earlier, just before high tide, and because of the added depth of water Stu had decided to go straight across the south bay. He had made the trip from home to Chula Vista and back many times, even in the dark of night, but had always gone around. Water depth was less than 3 feet in some spots of the south bay at mean low water and Stu always had gone north from the Cays channel to deep water, then east across the bay to Chula Vista channel. It took more time to go that way rather than straight across, but it was safer. Time was seldom important to a retired guy, or in this case two retired couples, just taking a boat ride instead of driving to lunch.

They had a light lunch at the little café in the Marina, joked with the snappy waitress, chatted with a live-aboard who opened the gate for them, and took their time. They had lots of time. And the wind was very light, not enough to be concerned. Stu had put Miss Sadie B into an available slip near Bob's On the Bay seafood restaurant. He had turned sharply at the last second, away from a slip directly ahead where Bill, Carol and Martha thought he was heading, into a narrower one on the right, expertly twisting his single inboard/outboard to slide into the berth.

"Why here? Bill asked for the three of them.

"It's the wind," Stu answered. "Wind makes all the difference. Even with this very light wind, if it's still the same when we leave, we can back out into it and turn around."

Sure enough, after almost an hour and a half of time for lunch the light wind was the same and Stu backed neatly out of the slip, twisted around and headed for the breakwater that marked the inner harbor. Miss Sadie B headed north in the Chula Vista channel to red day-marker 16 near the South Bay Boat Yard, and turned left to cross the south bay directly to Coronado Cays. Stu had decided that the tide was still near high, so that there would be plenty of water to go straight across. Still, because of his concern for the water depth, Stu kept his eyes on the depth finder.

Only a few boats were out in the south bay. Over to the right a guy stood fishing in a fifteen-foot outboard, a mile or so away. A sailboat to the left loafed along heading southward. Nothing to interfere with Miss Sadie B's transit across the bay as she proceeded at about ten knots, cautious of the water depth. Martha and Carol chatted about family and friends, Bill and Stu about boating and business, Stu's eyes never far from the depth gauge. Fine, at least seven and a half feet. Plenty of water. Plenty of time. Very little wind. A nice outing, Beautiful day.

"Hey! That boat's in trouble," Bill pointed toward the left, toward where the loafing sailboat had been a few seconds ago. No longer a boat sailing, it was over at least ninety degrees on the side, mast and sail in the water, keel exposed. "They need help!" Miss Sadie B turned hard left and headed for the capsized vessel.

"Where did this wind come from?" Stu found them heading into at least ten miles per hour of wind and with Miss Sadie B increasing speed from 10 to 15 it made for almost 25 miles per hour of relative wind.

Slowing as they approached, the four in Miss Sadie B called out what they saw.

"Looks like two people in the water."

"There's one still in the boat, hanging on."

"Looks like three total."

"They don't see us yet."

Stu sounded the horn a number of times as they approached and slowed.

"The guy on the keel is waving," someone offered.

Stu shared his thought, "I think he wants us to pull his boat upright with a line. See, he's waving away from the keel."

Bill's view was, "No, he's pointing away from the boat, to our left." Bill was right because as they slowly drew closer they could hear the man on the keel shouting, "Get her! Save her! Out there!" over and over again. They looked in the direction he indicated and Bill shouted, "There's someone in the water! Right there." Stu followed Bill's extended arm.

Carol saw what Bill pointed at, "It's a child." Martha thought it was a woman. Bill agreed. It looked like a child at first to Stu, a small pale face under the water, short blond hair, eyes opened, arms extended, very little movement. Then Stu saw that it was a woman and her face came out and back in of the water, very pale, staring eyes, maybe comatose, but then a movement, a gasp. She was alive! She gasped again. A man from the capsized boat had thrown a life jacket but the same wind that blew the boat away from her carried the life jacket further from the woman.

They were heading directly into that same wind and Stu slowed Miss Sadie B almost to a stop as they drew alongside with the woman to starboard. Bill was leaning over the side with a boat hook as Stu turned sharply to the right, across the wind. With the wind on the port side of the boat and the woman on the starboard side, the wind eased the boat gently toward the woman, within easy reach of the boat hook. But the woman wasn't responsive. She was just under the water and Bill couldn't reach her. He nudged her hand with the boat hook. She grabbed the boat hook and held on as Bill brought her to the stern, to the swim platform. Stu cut the engine and went back to help Bill, who was trying to pull the woman out of the water onto the platform. Not an easy task.

Not easy is an understatement. Bill certainly couldn't lift the woman out of the water by himself and even with Stu the two of them struggled to get a grip, to plant their feet, to not injure the woman as they literally dragged her sideways onto the swim platform. She still had a solid grip on the boat hook as Stu pried it from her hand.

The woman was ashen in color, cold to the touch, gasping and moaning and couldn't move herself. She was about 150 pounds of weight but not dead, fortunately, as Bill and Stu struggled to get her up off the swim platform, over the teak rail and onto the afterdeck. But they couldn't. They reassured her, talked with her, asked if she was cold (she said no), wrapped her in a blanket and decided that she would have to remain lying on the swim platform until more help arrived.

The capsized sailboat had righted itself and the other three passengers were safely on that boat.

Leaving the woman under the care of Bill and Carol, with Martha passing blankets and supplies from the cabin, Stu went to the VHF Marine Band Radio. He was panting from exertion and shaking from 70+ age nerves as he picked up the handset on channel 16.

"Coast Guard San Diego, Coast Guard San Diego, this is vessel Miss Sadie B, Miss Sadie B, I have an emergency situation to report. I am in South Bay about 1000 yards west of Chula Vista Marina. A sailboat has capsized and I have recovered a woman from the water. She is barely conscious. Probably suffering from hypothermia. I have her out of the water on my swim platform but cannot lift her over the rail into my boat. I need assistance. Over."

"Miss Sadie B this is Coast Guard San Diego. Full copy. Standby. Out."

A few seconds later the Coast Guard called to report help on the way and asked for a description of Miss Sadie B for identification and verification of location. Stu then realized that they had drifted west so that Coronado Cays was closer than Chula Vista. He made that report.

"Miss Sadie B this is Lowe's Marina. A rigid inflatable in on the way to you," and as they looked in the direction of Lowe's Resort Hotel the inflatable was in sight, bone in it's teeth, heading straight for them. In a matter of seconds the soft bulky round gray side of the Lowe's boat cushioned alongside Miss Sadie B's swim platform. Bill, Stu and the Lowe's guy slid, edged, pushed and pulled the woman from the swim platform into the inflatable and she was off, headed to Lowe's Marina.

They could hear the inflatable reporting, "Lowe's this is Rubber Ducky. I have the woman on board, heading to you. She's conscious but probably suffering from hypothermia and is in need of medical help."

At Lowe's Marina Mrs. Fran Farley received the medical attention she needed. An ambulance with paramedics arrived as did a Harbor Patrol boat and a Coast Guard boat. There seemed to be about 20 care providers in the marina as the foursome of Miss Sadie B came in to retrieve their blanket. Apparently, every one of those coastees, cops and care-givers had to make their own report, and all agreed that a few moments more, a little more time in the water, and Mrs. Farley (age 65+) wouldn't have made it. Stu had the opportunity to whisper to a barely conscious Mrs. Farley amid all the attendants, "See, I told you help was on the way and that you would be fine. Now you're in the hands of these experts and they'll take good care of you." She smiled and thanked him.

Using the time and the wind to pick up a life jacket was preparation for a life saving. Taking time for an extended lunch put them in the place they were needed. The wind put them alongside. Now it was time for Miss Sadie B to take her foursome home.

CHAPTER FORTY EIGHT

GUNS OF THE IRONCLADS

2002

They are the wrong guns. The two 11-inch smooth bore Dahlgren guns of USS Monitor retrieved from the deep off Cape Hatteras during the summer of 2002 are not the guns intended by her designer and builder.

John Ericsson had contracted to build a Union ship to stop the Confederate ironclad CSS Virginia. To accomplish this Ericsson knew that his Monitor had to be armed with guns capable of sending shot through at least four inches of iron plate mounted over heavy wood planking. The guns that Monitor carried into battle in April 1862 were not those that Ericsson intended. The guns of Monitor were not capable of carrying out the mission for which the Navy had contracted. They were the wrong guns.

CSS Virginia also went into that famous battle with the wrong guns. Lieutenant John Mercer Brooke designed and had built special guns with armor piercing projectiles for use against ironclad ships and Chief Naval Constructor John Luke Porter intended these armaments for the Confederate ship, but Brooke's armaments were not on board when Virginia battled Monitor.

The guns of both ironclads were the wrong guns.

THE CONFLICT

To most of the public and historians the most famous naval engagement of the American Civil War is known as a conflict of iron, steam, smoke and gunfire between the Monitor and the Merrimack on placid Chesapeake Bay. Actually, when the two ships met on March 9th, 1862 what had been the USS Merrimack had been salvaged, rebuilt and renamed CSS Virginia by the Confederacy. So it was a heralded battle between USS Monitor and CSS Virginia in Hampton Roads that caught the attention of the world and demonstrated the obsolescence of wooden sailing ships. Still, much of the news media at the time referred to the Confederate ironclad by her original name, Merrimack, sometimes spelled Merrimac.

Prior to the American Civil War the most common measure and comparison of fighting ships was by number of guns. The number of guns was often spoken of as part of the name. Among the 18 Union warships at Hampton Roads in the early spring of 1862 were the 24 gun sloop USS Cumberland, 50 gun frigate USS Congress and USS Minnesota, flagship of the North Atlantic Blockading Squadron, a 44 gun frigate. The number of guns was a measure of firepower, so it was natural that when CSS Virginia engaged the Union fleet in Hampton Roads, March 8th and 9th 1862, tacticians would focus on the number of guns of those ships. USS Cumberland's 24 guns should have been dominant over CSS Virginia rated at ten guns, and Virginia's ten guns would be clearly superior to USS Monitor's two guns, but steam driven ironclad ships with newly developed guns and ammunition changed that reasoning.

The battle of the Monitor and the Virginia marked the first meeting of two steam driven ironclad warships in combat, two innovations in naval science. After that battle an observer from the London Times wrote, "There is not now a ship in the English navy—that it would not be madness to trust to an engagement with that little Monitor."

That first battle of steam propelled ironclads also demonstrated that smooth bore guns with traditional shot were things of the past, that battle with armored ships required rifled guns and armor piercing projectiles. In that first battle the guns of the ironclads were not capable of firing a projectile that could penetrate the armor of those ships. Both ships were truly naval innovations but with traditional guns; guns that were ineffective against heavy armor.

More than a century ago the U.S. Navy, uncertain about what it needed for a specific mission, invited proposals for a new innovative ship. Secretary of the Navy Gideon Welles didn't know what the new ship should look like, how it should be constructed, propelled or manned, or what weapons it should carry, but a ship was needed to deal with the Confederate steam ironclad ram, CSS Virginia. He placed an advertisement in a New York newspaper asking that shipbuilders submit proposals for a ship that could stop the Confederate ironclad. Industry responded, an innovative proposal was approved and USS Monitor was built. But then the Navy balked at the ordnance installation proposed by the designer. Lesser guns and ammunition were mounted in USS Monitor, and by one of those strange coincidences of history, CSS Virginia also was not equipped with the guns and ammunition intended by her designers. So when the two ships met in that most historic naval battle, the guns of both ironclads were not what they should have been.

THE VIRGINIA GUNS

USS Merrimac's sunken and burned hulk had been towed into dry-dock at Gosport Shipyard, in Portsmouth, Virginia in June 1861 and converted by the Confederates into the ironclad CSS Virginia. At

Gosport, Confederate Chief Naval Constructor John Luke Porter was in charge of the project and Lieutenant John Mercer Brooke, was project director on the staff of the Confederate Secretary of the Navy in Richmond, Virginia. Both Porter and Brooke claimed to be in charge of and responsible for creation of the ironclad steam battery ram CSS Virginia.

In ordnance and armor tests conducted at Jamestown Island, Virginia, Lieutenant Brooke determined that the best configuration for the shielded battery would be four inch thick iron plate over 24 inch thick oak planking formed into a 35 degree inclination of the shield. Ten gun ports were fitted; one forward, one aft and four on each side.

Porter and Brooke agreed on the number of guns but disagreed on the types, finally compromising to provide eight 9-inch Dahlgren smoothbore guns salvaged from the original USS Merrimac arranged four on each side. These were the most common guns then used in major combatant ships and Dahlgren had copied these guns from the previous century British "Long Nine," also called "32 pounder," as it fired a round iron ball of that weight. This shot was very effective against wooden ships but could not penetrate iron plate backed by oak.

Two 7-inch pivot rifles, one forward and one aft, were designed by Brooke to be used against ironclads with special wrought iron shot; steel pointed solid cylindrical projectiles that could pierce iron plate, also designed by Brooke. These two 7-inch guns were heavily reinforced around the breech with three-inch steel hoops shrunk on. Later Porter and Brooke agreed to include two 6.4-inch guns of the same make in place of two of the 9-inch smooth bore side guns, but they didn't have time to complete the ordnance outfitting before the ship went into combat.

When the time came to place guns aboard CSS Virginia Commodore Franklin Buchanan was at Gosport eager to take his ship into battle and break the Federal blockade. To accomplish this CSS Virginia had to engage the North Atlantic Blockading Squadron in nearby Hampton Roads and Buchanan was confident that the

Union squadron could not stop his ironclad's ram and guns from destroying wooden Union ships.

Buchanan knew the Union Navy very well. Only a few months before he had been the senior captain of the U.S. Navy and in command of the Washington Navy Yard, certain soon to be a flag officer until he resigned his commission in protest over the use of federal troops to quell draft riots in Baltimore. Later, his request for reinstatement with his previous rank was denied as the Secretary of the Navy questioned Buchanan's loyalty. Angered by this affront to his honor, Buchanan joined the Confederate States Navy where he received the flag officer status he had been denied in the U.S. Navy. He was the most senior naval officer to change sides in the Civil War and became the senior ranking officer of the Confederate Navy.

After breaking the blockade and after further fitting out, the Confederate commodore planned to steam his ironclad up Chesapeake Bay and attack Washington. Buchanan also was aware that the Federals had been building a steam driven ironclad at New York specifically with the objective of stopping CSS Virginia, but he did not know when the Union ironclad would arrive in Hampton Roads or if it would be capable of stopping his ship. It was clear to the Confederate commodore that his best chance of breaking the blockade was to attack the Federal ships in Hampton Roads before the Union ironclad was on the scene. Buchanan was therefore very anxious to get underway from Gosport, so anxious that despite the appeals for more time from Porter, Brooke and the shipyard commander, he ordered the shipyard workers off his ship before it was fully outfitted with the new innovative guns and ammunition.

CSS Virginia steamed down the Elizabeth River to do battle with the Union fleet on March 8th 1862. CSS Virginia departed Gosport without the full ordnance configuration intended by her designers and builders for use against ironclad ships, but Buchanan knew no Union ironclad was in Chesapeake Bay and he had every reason to believe that he could destroy the blockade. He considered the ram as his primary weapon against the wooden ships that he expected to meet.

A personal notebook was kept by Confederate Constructor Porter, a journal that his family has not made public. This diary by the responsible ship designer and builder, written on-scene and unprejudiced by developments nor warped by time provides a most credible source of information. Facts from this diary come to us through historian Dr. Alan Flanders, who has done the most detailed and accurate research on Merrimac/Virginia, including access to the private Porter diary. Flanders writes:

"According to the Constructor only six guns of the Virginia's battery were aboard ship the first day of action and ammunition had not arrived that would have placed the Brooke rifles at the bow and stern in total operational efficiency. So, the effectiveness of the Virginia's battery was severely limited. On the first day of battle, the battery was four cannons, plus two poorly supplied Brooke rifles."

No other source document specifically addresses CSS Virginia's ordnance configuration on March 8th, which would have been Porter's "first day of action." As CSS Virginia did not return to Gosport until the evening of March 9th, her ordnance outfit would have remained so for the March 9th engagement with USS Monitor. This lack of guns is substantiated by an entry in another journal, one that has been made public, in which Porter states that four of the ports had no guns in them.

Official Records of the Union and Confederate Navies in the War of the Rebellion, Series II, Vol I, the most common source of historians, shows CSS Virginia's battery on March 11th 1862 as simply, "10 guns." March 11th was three days *after* CSS Virginia's engagements with Cumberland and Congress, two days *after* CSS Virginia's famous battle with Monitor and two days *after* CSS Virginia had returned to Gosport shipyard where the additional armament was installed. Official Records, the most widely used source by historians, does not give the armament that existed on the March 8th and 9th combat actions of CSS Virginia. Official Records does not give the battery that existed in CSS Virginia when the Confederate ironclad destroyed USS Cumberland and USS Congress or when the ship fought her famous engagement with USS Monitor. Most historians have used this ten-gun configuration, but Porter's personal diary and his journal give CSS Virginia's ordnance configuration during those battles as six guns. Statements and reports written years later by principals of the battle likely relied on Official Records and designer intentions rather than what was actually on board.

It is unlikely that Porter's diary is wrong, as no contemporary original source conflicts with his statement of six guns. All other sources that mention the number of guns were written long after the actions from memories warped by time, influenced by political considerations and distorted by self-serving intentions.

Constructor Porter's use of "poorly supplied Brooke rifles," from his private diary refers to lack of armor piercing projectiles, supported by a statement in his public journal, "As we did not expect to encounter any ironclads, she was only provided with shells for all guns, rifled and smooth bore. The Brooke experimental shot was not on board." His expression, "only provided with shells, "indicates there was no solid or armor piercing shot on board.

Lieutenant Catesby ap Roger Jones, Executive Officer of CSS Virginia who took command after Commodore Franklin Buchanan was wounded on March 8th, confirms the lack of armor piercing projectiles in his report, "We had no solid shot." According to Chief Engineer H. Ashton Ramsay, "If we had known we were to meet her (USS Monitor) we would at least have been supplied with solid shot for our rifled guns." CSS Virginia did not have ammunition with which to fight an ironclad when she departed Gosport on March 8th, 1862 or when she met USS Monitor the next day.

Less firepower mattered little on the first day of combat, March 8th, when CSS Virginia sunk USS Cumberland and USS Congress and forced USS Minnesota and USS Roanoke aground, but the next day against USS Monitor more firepower and better ammunition might well have made a difference. This becomes more significant considering CSS Virginia's battery had been further reduced by USS Cumberland.

Upon getting underway from Gosport, Buchanan announced that he would make straight for and ram USS Cumberland because that ship had a new rifled gun that could penetrate four inches of iron; a single stern mounted 6-inch rifled gun on pivot firing 70 pound shot, plus one 10-inch smooth bore and twenty two 9-inch smoothbores.

CSS Virginia's first shot at USS Cumberland tore into the Union ship killing and wounding many men. After delivering a critical ram, Virginia stood starboard to starboard with the sinking Cumberland, exchanging deadly broadsides. At very close range, Cumberland fired three direct broadsides of eleven 9-inch guns, each firing 80 pound solid shot against the armored shield of Virginia. Most of the shot bounced harmlessly away, but not all. Some tore away iron plates and crushed heavy oak planking but none penetrated the casemate. Two of Virginia's 9-inch Dahlgren smoothbores on the starboard side were damaged, one shot off near the trunnion and another broken off obliquely, about 18 inches from the muzzle. Two Virginia crewmen were killed and nineteen wounded.

Damage to two guns of CSS Virginia on March 8th is confirmed by Commodore Buchanan's after action report, "The muzzle of one of them was soon shot away—," and another gun, "The muzzle of their gun was struck by a shell from the enemy, which broke off a piece of the gun." According to Lieutenant Catesby Jones, in charge of the gun deck at that time, "Our after nine-inch gun was loaded and ready for firing, when its muzzle was struck by a shell, which broke it off and fired the gun. Another gun also had its muzzle shot off." Also on the gun deck was Midshipman Littlepage who reported, "The broadside fired by the Cumberland just as the Merrimac rammed her cut one of the Merrimac's guns off at the trunnions, the muzzle off another."

CSS Virginia had departed Gosport on March 8th not with ten guns as had been planned but with only six. She lost two of these guns on her starboard side in the March 8th engagement with USS Cumberland. Despite this reduction in firepower, CSS Virginia went on to destroy Cumberland with a combination of gunfire and ram, damaging her own bow and losing her 1500 pound cast iron ram in the process. The Confederate ironclad, using gunfire, then forced

USS Congress to surrender and left that Union ship aground and burning. Over 300 Union men had been killed.

As Congress lay burning near shore she struck her colors but Union soldiers on the beach continued rifle fire. Buchanan, irate over this violation of combat ethics (firing in support of a ship that had struck) climbed out of his protective armored shell and exchanged rifle fire with the Union troops ashore. A Union bullet seriously wounded the Confederate commodore, who was removed from his ship that night and he later lost his leg.

As she retired to anchorage under protection of Confederate guns at Sewell's Point with Commodore Buchanan seriously wounded and soon to be removed, CSS Virginia had an effective battery of four guns; two 7-inch Brooke pivot rifles, one forward and one aft, and two 9-inch Dahlgren smoothbores fixed on the port side.

During the night of March 8th at anchor CSS Virginia evacuated her dead and wounded including Commodore Buchanan. Catesby Jones took command and probably wanted to shift one fixed 9-inch Dahlgren, weighing over five tons, from port to starboard, but there is no record or indication that this was attempted. The lack of effective guns on one side is supported in Catesby Jones' report of his battle with USS Monitor, "She once took a position for a short time where we could not bring a gun to bear on her." With the only two guns on her starboard side rendered ineffective by USS Cumberland, CSS Virginia had a major ordnance blind spot.

The morning of March 9th CSS Virginia, unprepared to fight an ironclad and somewhat handicapped, went into battle against the newly arrived USS Monitor. CSS Virginia had started with six guns but now two of those guns were ineffective. She had no ram, no gun port shutters, no shot for use against ironclads, was leaking in the bow and had lost her commodore-captain. Chief Engineer Ramsay wrote that CSS Virginia's return to Gosport on March 9th, after the battle with USS Monitor, was prompted among other reasons, by need to get solid shot and to have, "—the guns whose muzzles had been shot away replaced."

THE MONITOR GUNS

The guns of USS Monitor is a story closely attached to the ship's designer and builder, Captain John Ericsson. Born and educated in Sweden, Ericsson had gained experience and reputation as an innovative engineer in England when he met Robert F. Stockton of New Jersey. Stockton commissioned Ericsson to construct a ship and later arranged for Ericsson to come to the U.S. and assist him in the design and construction of USS Princeton. The first warship with screw propeller and below-deck engines, Princeton had many innovations including two 12-inch guns, the largest in the U.S. fleet of 1843.

Stockton designed one 12-inch gun, "The Peacemaker", and Ericsson brought the other, "The Oregon", from England where he had designed it and had it built. Stockton's Peacemaker was the largest mass of iron ever forged in the United States, much larger and heavier than Ericsson's gun of the same bore.

On February 28th 1844, Stockton in USS Princeton conducted a demonstration cruise on the Potomac River for President Tyler, members of the cabinet, members of both houses of Congress, ranking military and their families. Ericsson was not on board. As a final gun demonstration of the day, for entertainment of the guests, Stockton had his Peacemaker fired. The gun burst, killing and wounding twenty people. Among the dead were the Secretary of the Navy, Secretary of State and close family friends of the President. Even though Stockton's gun had exploded and Ericsson had not been on board, Stockton was cleared of responsibility by shifting blame to Ericsson.

Years later, in 1861, the U.S. Navy was desperate to produce a ship that could deal with the Confederate ironclad CSS Virginia being built at the Gosport Shipyard in Virginia. With very strong support of Cornelius Scranton Bushnell and endorsement by Secretary of the Navy Gideon Welles, President Lincoln approved and Ericsson was commissioned to design and build USS Monitor at New York.

Although Ericsson got his way on most of the ship building controversies and the ship was delivered on time, there was a controversy over armament that Ericsson did not win. USS Monitor was to be fitted with two large guns inside an innovative rotating turret. In his original design, endorsed by Welles and approved by Lincoln, Ericsson intended to use 15-inch guns that he would have built. Seeing that would take too much time, he changed his plans to use two 12-inch Oregon guns that could send solid projectiles through four and a half inches of iron. But the stigma of the 1844 USS Princeton gun disaster still hung over Ericsson, even though it was Stockton's Peacemaker that had exploded, and the Navy's ordnance director, Captain John A. Dahlgren, insisted that two 11-inch Dahlgren smoothbores be used and those with only one-half of their regular powder charge. USS Monitor did not have the ordnance configuration intended by her designer and Ericsson knew that 11-inch Dahlgrens with half powder could not penetrate 4-inch iron plate.

THE BATTLE OF IRONCLADS

The first battle of ironclads took place in Hampton Roads between USS Monitor and CSS Virginia on March 9th 1862. Neither ship was able to inflict serious damage on the other, gunshot from each glancing off the other with little effect. Between the ironclads it was a tactical draw, but still, the objective of CSS Virginia was to break the Union blockade and that was not accomplished, while the objective of USS Monitor was to stop the Confederate ironclad from breaking the blockade and that was accomplished.

Given another day or two without Monitor's presence, Virginia most likely would have destroyed enough of the Union fleet to render the blockade ineffective. Without the Union blockade, England and France might have allied with the Confederacy, Washington and

New York could have been shelled and the Civil War might have had a different ending.

CSS Virginia kept most of the North Atlantic Blockading Squadron in Hampton Roads waiting for the Confederate ironclad to come out of Gosport Shipyard for another attempt to break the blockade. So much of the Union fleet was involved with CSS Virginia that insufficient ships were available for blockade duty elsewhere and there were not enough ships to support the Union army in the Peninsula Campaign. As she lay at Gosport, with two ventures into the upper Roads and James River, CSS Virginia contributed to the failure of the Union's Peninsula Campaign and weakened the blockade. With full armament on March 8th and 9th she might have done even more.

The battle of the ironclads could have been different, too, if Ericsson's bigger guns had been used by USS Monitor or if full powder charges had been used in her Dahlgrens. With 12-inch guns USS Monitor might have destroyed CSS Virginia on March 9th, the Peninsula Campaign would have had strong naval gunfire support and transportation, leading to the fall of Richmond and the Union blockade would have been more effective. The Civil War might have been shortened. On the other hand, with heavier guns Monitor would have been even less sea-worthy on the open ocean, the cause of her ultimate demise, and she might have foundered on her original and difficult transit from New York to Chesapeake Bay.

AFTER THE BATTLE

Following her battle with USS Monitor, CSS Virginia returned to Gosport Shipyard where considerable improvements were made, including additional armament, as indicated by the battery configurations from <u>Official Records.</u> She didn't do battle with an ironclad in that full armament.

Later, rather than have her fall into Union hands, CSS Virginia was scuttled and destroyed by her Captain Josiah Tattnall and crew at Craney Island, across the Elizabeth River from Norfolk, Virginia on May 11th 1862. Prior to that destruction some of her crewmen, including Confederate Marines of Company C, had removed a few of her guns at Gosport and taken them to Fort Darling, seven miles below Richmond on Drewry's Bluff on the south side of the James River. Most likely they took those guns of lighter weight.

After a march of 22 miles from Craney Island to Suffolk, some of CSS Virginia's crew went by train to Richmond, then boat to Drewry's Bluff. There they might have been joined by the two 7-inch Brooke rifles or the two 6.4-inch Brooke rifles removed at Gosport and some of the guns of CSS Virginia may have had another chance at Union ironclads.

At Drewry's Bluff on May 15th 1862, former CSS Virginia sailors and marines participated in the defense of Richmond and Confederate guns were effective in stopping Union ironclads, including USS Monitor, on the James River. From heights overlooking the river Confederate guns fired on the Union ships that had been stopped by obstructions. The only ship capable of elevating guns to take the bluffs under fire, ironclad USS Galena anchored to engage the artillery batteries and Confederate fire focused on her.

High velocity grazing enfilade fire impacted on USS Galena, the effectiveness of each round amplified by the force of gravity and impacting on the ship in a near-vertical trajectory, particularly devastating to horizontal decks with light armor. USS Galena was so heavily damaged that she had to be towed to Gosport, then in Union hands, where she was later converted into a wooden gunboat. Cornelius Scranton Bushnell, who had been instrumental in gaining approval for Ericsson's Monitor, had built ironclad Galena for the Union Navy. Perhaps CSS Virginia's guns and the armor piercing projectiles designed by Lieutenant Brooke for use against Union ironclads proved themselves after all.

GUNS OF THE IRONCLADS

Both of the famous ironclad ships, USS Monitor and CSS Virginia, were handicapped by lesser ordnance than intended by designers; Monitor had guns of smaller caliber and reduced powder charge, Virginia had fewer guns than intended and no armor piercing projectiles.

Some of CSS Virginia's guns were used at Drewry's Bluff while others are buried under landfill of Craney Island across the Elizabeth River from Norfolk, Virginia.

The two 11-inch Dahlgren smoothbore guns of USS Monitor rested in deep water off Cape Hatteras, where the Union ironclad ship sunk during a stormy passage on December 31st 1862. After 140 years the Monitor guns were brought to the surface by an expedition of Navy salvage divers working with underwater archaeologists from the National Oceanic and Atmospheric Administration. After a long electrolyte bath to curtail further deterioration, the guns are now displayed in the Monitor Center at the Mariners' Museum in Newport News, Virginia.

The guns of both of the most famous ironclad ships, the wrong guns of both ships, rest in peace within ten miles of each other and of their famous battle scene.

BIBLIOGRAPHY:

Baxter, James Phinney, 3rd, The Introduction of the Ironclad Warship, Harvard Univ. Press, Cambridge, Mass, 1933

Catesby ap Roger Jones, The "Virginia," The First Confederate Ironclad, Formerly the United States Steam Frigate "Merrimac." A Narrative of her Services by Catesby ap R. Jones, Her Executive and Ordnance Officer and Commander, in Her fight With the "Monitor.", New York, October 8th, 1874.

Clancy, Paul, "The Monitor Mission," The Virginian-Pilot, Norfolk, VA, July 21-23, 2002.

Daley, R. W., How the Merrimac Won, The Strategic Story of the CSS Virginia, Cromwell Co., NY, 1957.

Donnelly, Ralph W., The Confederate States Marine Corps: The Rebel Leathernecks, White Mane Publishing Co., Shippensburg, PA, 1989.

Flanders, Alan, "Craney Island last resting place of the Virginia," The Compass, pg 14, The Virginian-Pilot, Norfolk, VA, May 9, 1996.

Flanders, Alan B., The Merrimac, The Story of the Conversion of the USS Merrimac into the Confederate Ironclad Warship, CSS Virginia, Portsmouth Naval Shipyard Museum, Portsmouth, VA, 1982.

Jones, Rev. J. William, Southern Historical Society Papers, Volume XIII, Richmond, VA, 1885.

Mokin, Arthur, Ironclad, The Monitor and the Merrimack, Presidio Press, Novato, CA, 1991.

Official Records of the Union and Confederate Navies in the War of the Rebellion, Secretary of the Navy, Washington, D.C., Series II, Vol I, 1921.

O'Neil, Charles, Radm, USN(Ret), "Engagement Between the Cumberland and Merrimack," U.S. Naval Institute Proceedings, U.S. Naval Institute, Annapolis, MD, June 1922.

Porter, John L., CSS Virginia (Merrimac), Story of Her Construction, Battles Etc., Portsmouth Naval Shipyard Museum, Portsmouth, VA, 1874.

Porter, John W. H., A Record of Events in Norfolk County, Virginia, from April 19th, 1861, to May 10th, 1862, etc., W. A. Fiske, printer, Norfolk, VA, 1892.

Wells, Tom Henderson, The Confederate Navy-a study in organization, Univ. of Alabama Press, University, AL, 1971.

Wright, Gen Marcus J., LaBree, Col Benjamin, Bay, James P., Official and Illustrated War Record, Commissioner of War Dept., Washington, D.C., 1899.

CHAPTER FORTY NINE

ABOUT "GUNS OF THE IRONCLADS"

2002

*"Guns of the Ironclads" is the best thing that I have
ever written but I was never able to get it published.
Maybe someone else can. You're welcome to try.*

In the previous chapter you read *Guns of the Ironclads* which I wrote
in 2002 while I was serving as a docent at the Hampton Roads Naval
Museum. That gave me access to the other museums and libraries in
the area including the Portsmouth Naval Shipyard Museum as well as
discussions with a number of Civil War historians. Dr. Alan Flanders
had done extensive research on the conversion of the remains of
USS Merrimack into CSS Virginia and he arranged for me to have
entree to the library vault of the Portsmouth Naval Shipyard Museum.

   In 2006 I submitted *Guns of the Ironclads* to a number of
publishers. One of the editors wrote in the rejection letter:

"The key point you make–the Virginia lacked her full complement of guns–is indeed controversial. Unfortunately it's not based on credible, verifiable evidence. Historians who read your article could not consult Porter's notebook but would be forced to take your word and Mr. Flanders' word about its existence and content. Moreover, your bibliography lists only a newspaper article written by Flanders."

At the Portsmouth Naval Shipyard Museum I had sat at a small table in the vault under constant view of a museum staffer. I was not permitted to scan the shelves or touch any of the musty books, all more than a century old. The museum staffer, wearing plastic gloves, removed the book I had asked for from the shelf, placed the book on the table in front of me and turned to the page that I had requested. I read directly from a journal hand written by Confederate Chief Naval Constructor John Luke Porter and I took notes careful not to touch the sacred tome. This was credible verifiable evidence. Historians that make arrangements could visit that same museum. This was primary source material.

The Porter journal was included in the bibliography.

Dr. Flanders had read this years before and he had also read the private Porter diary that keyed him to the armament that existed on board the Virginia on March 8th 1862. From these prime sources, supported by recorded statements of others on the scene, we can be assured that CSS Virginia got underway from Gosport Shipyard not with the ten guns shown in all later dramatic art works but with only six guns and without armor piercing shot. Also, it is clear that two of those six guns were damaged beyond use by USS Cumberland the day before the famous battle with USS Monitor.

The most commonly used reference, Official Records of the Union and Confederate Navies in the War of the Rebellion, is indeed very accurate and lists Virginia's armament as ten guns, but that list is noted as armament as of March 11th, three days after the famous battles, when the ship had returned to Gosport Shipyard. <u>Official Records</u> does not give the armament before March 11th.

Primary source material shows that CSS Virginia departed Gosport Shipyard on March 8th with six guns and that two of those six guns were destroyed by USS Cumberland. The following day, March 9th, when CSS Virginia did battle with USS Monitor, CSS Virginia had only four operational guns.

Guns of the Ironclads explains the armament that was actually on board CSS Virginia and USS Monitor at the time the two ironclads met. They were not the guns intended by the designer/builder of either ship. They are not the guns shown in every painting of the famous battle.

Please keep in mind that this was written in 2005. Much has changed since then but, unfortunately much remains the same.

CHAPTER FIFTY

VERY FEW ARE CAPABLE MARINERS

2005

"It is by no means enough that an officer of the navy should be a capable mariner. He must be that, of course, but also a great deal more. He should be as well a gentleman of liberal education, refined manners, punctilious courtesy, and the nicest sense of personal honor."

That statement attributed to John Paul Jones has served as a guiding tenet of the U.S. Navy since its origin. If Jones could stand near the helm of one of his navy's warships today, the "Father of the Navy" would turn over in his crypt, for an evaluation of Navy officers would show that very few are capable mariners. Many have liberal educations, all have decent manners, are courteous and honorable, but as to meeting the initial and most important requirement; very few officers of the U.S. Navy are capable mariners.

For more than 50 years the primary text used by the U.S. Navy for learning the basic requirements of the capable mariner has been Crenshaw's <u>Naval Shiphandling.</u> The book supports John Paul Jones' statement by describing demonstrated ability to control the movements of a Navy warship as essential to a career officer's reputation, professionalism and promotion. What may have been so in Jones' time through Crenshaw's first edition in the 1950's does not apply in a 21st Century Navy where shiphandling has little or no bearing on career success. While Crenshaw wrote about showing off professional skill and the importance of earning respect as a capable mariner, many of today's ship captains complete a full tour without demonstrating that they can handle their ships.

The 2005 Naval Institute Press text, Barber's <u>Naval Shiphandler's Guide</u>, starts with a quote of Thucydides, 404 B.C.

> "Their want of practice will make them unskillful and the want of skill timid. Maritime skill, unlike skills of other kinds, is not to be cultivated by the way or at chance times."

Thucydides is better known for "A collision at sea can ruin your entire day," and both of his quotes show the age-old consideration as to the importance of maritime skill. Barber confirms this by stating that for as long as there have been navies, shiphandling has been one of the most important professional skills and that shiphandling is a source of pride and personal satisfaction. Not so in the U.S. Navy today.

For more than 50 years, through many revisions and variations, the Fitness Report used by the Navy carried seamanship as one of the important blocks evaluated by the reporting senior. Today, as an indication of the evolutionary movement away from the importance of shiphandling, seamanship is not included in the most recent Fitness Report and Counseling Record and the recently announced program, XO/CO Fleet-Up will result in shorter tours for commanding officers, making those officers available for what are apparently more important staff jobs ashore.

Opportunities for officers to develop shiphandling skills in ships have been reduced and Barber points out that the most important and valuable advancement in this training has been the introduction of shiphandling simulators, valuable aids in learning the art and science of shiphandling.

SHIPHANDLING SIMULATORS

The first full mission bridge shiphandling simulator was made available for U.S. Navy use at the Surface Warfare Officers School (SWOS) in Newport, R.I. in 1986, twenty years after merchant ships had been using similar training systems and over 75 years after aviators had made flight simulation a formal part of their training and qualification programs.

Before the SWOS use of a shiphandling simulator, Navy officers had to learn how to operate ships by hands-on or on-the-job training, given rare opportunities in real ships. With the introduction of shiphandling simulation at SWOS, followed by Navy contracted simulation for the Pacific Fleet at San Diego, California in 1993 and for the Atlantic Fleet at Norfolk, Virginia in 1998, most Navy shiphandling training has been at these facilities. Fewer ships, lower operational tempos and more officers on board along with (depending on the commanding officer) less interest, different operating patterns and greater emphasis on caution have resulted in fewer opportunities for young officers actually to learn to drive their ships, and shiphandling simulators with experienced instructors at major Navy bases have become the primary means of learning shiphandling.

Aviation training is a prime example of the need, value and proper use of simulation, where after receiving instruction from a very experienced pilot in a flight simulator, the student-pilot learns to be an aviator by actually flying under instruction by a very experienced pilot in a real airplane. After he earns his gold wings the young pilot then commences really to learn by logging hours of actual "stick time" flying his type of aircraft. Then, even after accumulating hundreds of hours, pilots return periodically to flight simulators where, again, very experienced flyers put them through further training.

Not so in the surface Navy where young officers qualify as Officer of the Deck and earn the Surface Warfare Officer (SWO) badge by demonstrating a few basic and simplistic processes and most often never again handle a ship in close seamanship situations. Whereas the aviator goes through rigorous training, demonstrates that he can fly, earns his wings and then accumulates many hours of flight time before he is considered a capable pilot, the surface warfare officer does minimal preparation, converts prompting into orders without understanding why, earns his SWO badge and may not drive again until he is given command of a warship.

The shiphandling simulator training facilities available for the Navy in San Diego and Norfolk are commercially owned and operated, each under a separate contract awarded through competitive government procurement process and meeting rigid specifications. Each contract specifies that Facilitator/Instructors must be former Navy or Coast Guard ship commanding officers with at least two sea commands and 10 years of sea duty, or licensed master mariners. Most have had more than the required commands and sea time, all have experience in actual close shiphandling with various ship types and additional experience instructing in shiphandling simulators. These instructors are clearly well qualified and experienced to teach shiphandling to Navy officers; basic, intermediate or advanced. Not only has simulator utilization become an important part of Navy shiphandling training, shiphandling simulator facilities are now virtually the only place for Navy officers to learn to be capable mariners.

But even though contractor owned and operated shiphandling simulators with highly experienced instructors represent a challenging and economical place for Navy officers to learn shiphandling, these simulators are going away. At Newport, SWOS has terminated the contracted simulator and instructor services, opting instead to use home-made arcade type games first with junior officer instructors and later with some of the same instructors from the contracted service. The most powerful Navy in the world uses third-rate shiphandling simulators that do not meet international standards established by the International Maritime Organization and the instructors used by SWOS are far less experienced than has been specified and provided through over 15 years of contracted shiphandling simulator services at San Diego and Norfolk.

With the Newport high quality contracted shiphandling simulator services gone, the Navy has already notified the Pacific Fleet facility in San Diego that their contract will not be renewed and the simulator contract for the Atlantic Fleet at Norfolk has only a short time remaining with no Navy plans for renewal.

QUALIFICATIONS

There are about 300 commissioned vessels of the United States Navy today and some are commanded and operated by competent, professional and confident officers who would meet the highest international standards that ensure safety of life at sea. These standards have been established by international conventions to which the United States has not only agreed, but has been in the forefront of promoting, urging and encouraging application to world shipping.

Even though those that operate "government vessels" are not required to meet these international standards as are masters and mates of commercial or merchant ships of the world, still some U.S. Navy ship captains and officers meet those standards. Some, but very few, for very few U.S. Navy ship captains or ship officers are capable mariners, qualified by international convention and national law, experienced by requisite in-job time-at-sea or have confidence that comes only by practiced seamanship evolutions. Very few could qualify for and pass the dozen examinations of a licensed master mariner and these U.S. Navy officers command and operate the most expensive, sophisticated and valuable war-fighting vessels in the world. Valiant and capable combatants they might be, let us hope so, but professional mariners they are not.

"Navigation, Seamanship and Shiphandling Training Requirements Document" issued by the CNO Surface Warfare Directorate 15 June 2002 states that this document "is consistent with the specifications and requirements of the *1995 Convention on Standards of Training, Certification and Watchkeeping (STCW) for Seafarers,* which came into full force on February 2002, and the US Code of Federal Regulations, Chapter 46." The document also states, "Additionally, though warships are exempted from the STCW requirements, as a Party to the Convention the U.S. had agreed that 'persons serving on board such ships (will) meet the requirements of the Convention so far as is reasonable and practical.'"

One of the key provisions of the STCW Code is the requirement that seamanship, navigation and shiphandling competencies be demonstrated, evaluated and documented, and although this is recognized and repeated in the Training Requirements Document, the CNO Surface Warfare Directorate of the U.S. Navy has not complied with this agreement.

COMPETENCE

Navy officers' ability as mariners is tried every time a U.S. Navy ship gets underway, operates at sea or comes into port. In practice today almost every port departure, entry and pier landing is done by civilian ship's pilot using tugs, as Navy ships use "valet parking" in their own home ports as well as in distant ports of the world.

Most U.S. Navy ship captains are "sea buoy to sea buoy" operators, but also they know little of accepted practice at sea, where merchant mariners have learned that a gray hull with U.S. flag is a dangerous amateur bully that does not understand or follow accepted safe maritime practice. Most U.S. Navy ships are not equipped with internationally certified and required systems such as Automatic Identification System (AIS), Electronic Chart and Information Display System (ECDIS) and Automatic Radar Plotting Aid (ARPA). Few Navy ships use proper VHF bridge-to-bridge voice radio procedure. Navy ships are not equipped, and the people operating those ships are not in compliance, with international conventions and U.S. national laws that apply to every merchant vessel, even though years ago the CNO Surface Warfare Directorate stated that the Navy would meet those standards "so far as is reasonable and practical."

Only a few U.S. Navy ship captains are competent in basic shiphandling and seamanship, are confident in getting their ship underway, operating at sea and bringing their ship into port, anchor, buoy or pier. Most have little or no experience with mooring lines, anchors, mooring buoys or controlling their own use of tugs. When they were junior officers most of their captains did not let them do it and now they don't allow their officers the repetitive opportunities necessary to achieve genuine capability. After accomplishing the minimal seamanship experiences leading to award of the SWO badge, senior officers of today do no more shiphandling, leaving that to other brand new ensigns who "parrot" someone more experienced, like a pilot, so that the ensign thinks he or she is "shiphandling."

While every U.S. Navy commanding officer is quick to say that in his or her ship "the junior officers do all the shiphandling," closer investigation reveals that few if any junior officers actually receive any real level of experience, that most is by ensigns parroting and award of the SWO badge means the end of shiphandling opportunity. This is directly opposite to the award of Navy wings of gold that start aviators on their serious flying careers. All aviators agree that real flying is learned after earning their wings, but after earning the Surface Warfare Officer badge, most SWOs don't conn a ship again until getting command and then, remember, the junior officers do all the shiphandling.

Making a landing by putting a ship alongside a pier is only one shiphandling evolution, often the most demanding, but using that as a measure of experience an informal poll revealed that upon taking first command most COs had previously made about four landings, most in different class ships, most more than eight years before and most parroting someone else. A mariner does not learn to put a ship alongside the pier in four parroting tries and some COs have never actually handled a ship making a pier landing, not even once. With this minimal to void experience level commanding officers are entrusted with powerful, expensive and sophisticated vessels that operate in heavily-trafficked professional sea-going environments, and these COs are also expected to train junior officers in the seamanship skills that most COs do not possess.

PLANS

Present plans call for the Navy to terminate the contracted shiphandling simulator services that have provided virtually the only really valuable shiphandling training for over 15 years. Instead of this high quality training, the Navy is buying (not leasing) shiphandling simulator systems from a foreign source, without appropriate software, ship models or scenarios, without defined maintenance commitments, without instructor qualification specifications and without any concept of curriculum or use, all with the announced intent to save money. All of this will result in far less quality training at far greater overall "real" cost. Soon, the Navy will own shiphandling simulators and will then have to determine what to do with them.

The Navy plans to put desk-top and helmet simulator devices on board ships so that young officers can learn shiphandling at their desks in off-duty hours using self-paced programs. It will be far less effective than the shore based contracted simulators with highly experienced instructors because shiphandling cannot be taught without capable mariners as instructors. Surely it will cost less and just as surely it will be far less effective. Reading a shiphandling book would cost even less.

With Navy plans for these cost-less programs, including SWOS use of arcade game simulation the Navy will re-learn the old adage, "You get what you pay for," but in this case the Navy will end up paying more for less quality training. Overall, the situation shows lack of Navy understanding as to the real costs and benefits involved in providing high quality training in shiphandling as aviation learned long ago.

REAL COSTS

Prior to the contracted shiphandling simulator training services in Newport, San Diego and Norfolk, the Navy purchased simulators for training LCAC (Landing Craft Air Cushion) crews at Amphibious Bases at Little Creek, Virginia and Coronado, California at a cost of $27 million. These training systems are government owned and are operated by a contractor for a per year cost with instructors experienced in that one craft. Consideration of initial cost amortized over the life of the simulator, maintenance, upgrades and operating costs with usage time shows that the LCAC simulator costs the equivalent of more than $1500 per hour for training 4 crewmen in this single craft system.

At every major Naval Air Station high technology realistic flight simulators provide valuable training to naval aviators with experienced instructors. Including initial costs, amortization and operating expenses the cost of this training comes to about $4000 per hour for one aviator in one type aircraft.

Navy accounting procedures for LCAC and aviation simulators disregard the sunk costs of procurement and modernization, and consider only annual operating costs as these come out of another budget pocket and do not reflect the "real costs."

In 1993, when the Navy contracted for shiphandling simulator training services for the Pacific Fleet at San Diego there were no purchase or start-up costs for the government. The contractor bore all capital investment and initial costs and the Navy has paid and still does pay an hourly rate for scheduled hours. Up to 15 personnel can be trained at a time, in any ship class and in any port or scenario, with accurate hydrodynamic ship models operating in any environmental conditions. The most highly qualified and experienced facilitator/instructors provide a level of training that cannot be equaled and the cost of this shiphandling simulator training to the Navy is about $600 per hour.

The comparisons are clear; $600 per hour for training 15 ship personnel in any Navy ship class with experienced instructors; $1500 per hour for training 4 crewmen in one LCAC craft with experienced instructors; $4000 per hour for training one aviator in one aircraft with experienced instructors; or millions of dollars to purchase shore based simulators and desktop and head-mounted devices with limited ship and scenario modeling, some to go aboard ships for self-paced programs of questionable value with inexperienced instructors; and bargain priced arcade games ashore.

In simulation the highest value of training comes with realism, the more realistic the simulator, the more valuable the training, and realism is expensive. Aircraft simulation is expensive because it must have realism; actual cockpit motion and accurate smooth visual display. The LCAC simulator is actually an aircraft simulator with deck motion that's why it cost so much.

Shiphandling simulators at Newport, San Diego and Norfolk use simulated deck motion. It's not as realistic as aviation simulation, but the hourly rate at these shiphandling simulator facilities includes two complete simulators properly staffed, so that two separate scenarios or separate ships can be operated at the same time or two ships can be operated together in the same scenario at the one hourly rate.

The contracted shiphandling simulator services that have been provided to the Navy for the past 15 years are truly a training bargain. Every other comparable training service costs more and/or delivers less. One surface force commander years ago said, "If we prevent one accident it will more than pay for 10 years of shiphandling simulator use."

FUTURE

In most navies of the world (U.S. exempted) and in every merchant maritime service in the world (U.S. included) ships' officers are either Deck or Engineering. Only in the U.S. Navy is an officer expected/required to be capable of both responsibilities. Yet in the training and preparation of officers for shipboard duty, leading eventually to command, time allotted toward learning to be a capable mariner is less than one-tenth of that devoted to combat systems and engineering. Perhaps the future U.S. Navy is moving toward following the lessons of the world's maritime services and will soon operate ships with separate Deck and Engineering officers of the Navy.

Today, logistic support ships that used to be commissioned vessels of the U.S. Navy are operated by the Military Sealift Command with licensed civilian masters, mates and crews. Those ships that provide the essential underway replenishment services, the "Beans, Bullets and Black Oil" that keeps Navy ships operating at sea are not operated by Navy officers and enlisted personnel but by civilians qualified by license, experience and training.

A fleet of over 100 ships that support all parts of the U.S. military is operated or contracted by the Military Sealift Command with qualified civilians. This includes two hospital ships, each actually a complete military hospital that is positioned on board a vessel so that the hospital can be moved to where needed, that are moved by qualified civilians.

USS Blue Ridge is a former amphibious warfare ship reconfigured and serving as flagship of Commander, Seventh Fleet in the Western Pacific and Indian Oceans. Blue Ridge carries a complete command center with necessary communications, processing, displays and hotel facilities positioned on board a ship operated by qualified civilians.

Perhaps the Navy might choose to have deck and engineering watches stood by merchant marine personnel who would do nothing but stand those watches. They would remain with the ship and not have to rotate or participate in recurrent training. Consider the reduction and savings in training dollars that could ensue. In the process of Sea Swap, where today's Navy crews exchange in a deployed ship; those personnel standing deck and engineering watches would not have to be swapped. There would be further savings in training money because officers would not have to practice in simulators or study that portion of the Professional Qualification Standards among other savings. Productivity would increase because the licensed merchant mariner would be familiar with the ship and not have to go through a learning process every two years.

The current process of MSC operated ships has been successful, so why not continue the trend toward disinterest in seamanship, navigation and ship handling and move further toward utilization of licensed merchant mariners, allowing professional career Navy officers to focus on combat systems?

Is that what we want?

SUMMARY

In 2005 the U.S. Navy took steps to lessen the importance of seamanship, navigation and shiphandling as evidenced by fitness reports, XO/CO Fleet-Up, training, career and promotion emphasis. Also, there is a clear trend toward more Navy ships being turned over to licensed civilian operation. Could this lead the Navy from today's "valet parking" and "sea-buoy to sea-buoy operating" to the next logical step; "chauffeured driving?"

If valet parking, sea-buoy to sea-buoy operations and chauffeured driving is not in the future, *and it shouldn't be*, the Navy must establish a clearly defined program with the objective of producing capable mariners using internationally certified shiphandling simulators and curricula with qualified, certified and experienced instructors. If not, a future Navy may see warships operated by full time civilian masters and mates who will drive ships to the scene of action so that combat systems can perform. If this occurs John Paul Jones might roll over in his crypt as his Navy would recognize that it is, indeed, expecting too much that an officer of the U.S. Navy should be a capable mariner.

Addendum to Chapter Fifty Two

CAPABLE MARINERS EXPLANATION

To understand the statement that "Very few are capable mariners," referring to officers of the U.S. Navy, we must first agree on what is meant by "capable mariners," then we must find a means of assessment, of measuring that capability. If it is determined that the statement is incorrect, that most officers of the Navy are capable mariners, then the existing and planned programs can be continued with confidence that future Navy ships will be operated by fully qualified and experienced personnel. But if we determine, or if there is a question, that very few officers of the U.S. Navy are capable mariners it may be worthwhile to look back and see how the Navy arrived in this predicament so that measures can be developed and instituted to change, if change is desired.

THE MEANING

Dictionary definitions offer that a mariner is a person who directs or assists in the navigation of a ship, or any person employed in a ship, a sailor, a seaman. Capable means having fitness or ability, able, efficient or competent. Considering the origin of the John Paul Jones statement that, "It is not enough that an officer of the Navy should be a capable mariner," we can be reasonably sure Jones meant that an officer should have competence, ability and be efficient in the navigation of the ship for which he is responsible. In our context, navigation has a number of connotations all pertaining to the science and art of taking actions and utilizing processes involved with directing the movement of a ship. Navigation covers everything from the broad scope of utilization of science, technology and judgment over a wide expanse to the detailed direction of movement in narrow situations; from planning and conducting an ocean transit to putting the ship alongside a pier.

Shiphandling is the most common Navy term for close-in navigation, for directing the ship in pier landing or getting underway, in anchoring, mooring to a buoy, transiting a harbor or going alongside another ship for underway replenishment. All of these require direction of the movement and positioning of a ship along with the practice of seamanship including use of electronic and mechanical aids and judgment of distance, time and speed called "Seaman's Eye," with mooring lines, anchor chain and deck tackle.

The title of the Navy's new program, "Navigation, Seamanship and Shiphandling," covers the intent of John Paul Jones' statement, as the program seeks to develop ships' officers with competence, efficiency and ability into "competent mariners."

THE ASSESSMENT

Naval Shiphandler's Guide, Captain James Alden Barber, USN (Ret.), Naval Institute Press, Annapolis, MD, 2005, states, "The most important and valuable advancement in shiphandling training has been the introduction of shiphandling simulators." Barber goes on to explain that the training provided by these simulators is essential for the safe operation of Navy ships. But the shiphandling simulator facilities for Fleet use were not established for teaching ships' officers how to handle the ships in which they served, they were established to provide ships' officers with opportunities to maintain, enhance and improve the skills they already had.

The first shiphandling simulator facility for Navy use was made available At Surface Warfare Officers School as part of the regular curriculum to teach shiphandling to officers ordered to duty in Navy ships. Throughout the process of obtaining contracted shiphandling simulator facilities in San Diego and Norfolk the implication was avoided that officers actually serving in ships had to learn shiphandling. Every effort was made to convey the image that those officers serving in and responsible for Navy ships were fully capable of safe navigation (that they were "capable mariners") and the shiphandling facilities in San Diego and Norfolk were for those officers to maintain that fine ability.

The concept for use at the first of the Fleet shiphandling facilities (in San Diego) was for a ship to request scheduled time in the facility, intended as a 20 hour segment called a Shiphandling Availability. During this time the commanding officer of the ship could use the full facility (2 simulators, 2 learning feedback centers and full staff) in any manner that he determined was best for his ship. It was envisioned that the CO would take his officers to the simulator facility, give lectures and demonstrate, then allow his officers to handle the ship in a simulator and he would critique. Each simulator was staffed with a Computer Operator and a Facilitator. Technicians and Software Programmers were available. The entire facility could be used as the ship's CO desired, including using the Facilitator for scenario description, preparation explanation, instruction and/or critique.

Specifications published for the original contract carefully avoided the training connotation. Facilitators were so named to avoid the "training" implication associated with Instructors and the classrooms were called Learning Feedback Centers. The Facilitator's function was to make the facility available for the ship, to facilitate its use and to explain the scenario, not to teach unless specifically requested by the ship. Every effort was made to avoid the sense of teaching officers to do the jobs they were required to be capable of as they were already serving in positions of responsibility.

After the first few ships used the shiphandling facility fewer COs participated. Some showed up for brief appearances to show interest. Very few gave instruction, observed performance or offered critique. Soon it became apparent that the shiphandling facility would not be used as the force commander originally intended, that more often COs had nothing to do with the use of the facility. Ships sent junior officers as instructors with more juniors as students to learn shiphandling and more often asked for the Facilitator to lecture, coach, prompt and critique; to teach. Facilitators by contract became instructors in practice.

The shiphandling facility intended as an opportunity for ships officers to maintain and to hone their skills evolved into a schoolhouse for brand new ensigns and the magnificent shiphandling simulators with accurate hydrodynamic models, all environmentals, all ship classes, all scenarios in full mission capability–as required by Navy specifications-were used for the most basic training. The most advanced shiphandling simulator systems of their time evolved into the "kindergarten" of Navy shiphandling training.

Few department head level officers utilize the shiphandling simulators, fewer executive officers and even fewer COs show up at the facility. About ten percent of COs demonstrate any interest in shiphandling by making an appearance when the junior officers of their ship are learning shiphandling and of those COs that do show up half of them clearly know little of navigation, seamanship and shiphandling.

Junior officer shiphandling opportunity in Navy ships is inversely proportionate to the size of the ship; the larger the ship the fewer shiphandling opportunities. Small ships provide more shiphandling opportunities for junior officers and at the shiphandling simulators it is very apparent that real shiphandling is learned by junior officers serving in Oliver Hazard Perry Class frigates. Patrol Craft personnel, junior officers as well as enlisted personnel actually handle their small ships in close seamanship evolutions. In aircraft carriers and other large ships harbor pilots are used for all close shiphandling; valet parking. Some former Navy ships; logistic support and fleet flagship, have been turned over to civilian ship handlers; chauffeured driving.

CHAPTER FIFTY ONE

CAPABLE MARINERS EXPLAINED

2006

The preceding chapter, "Very Few Are Capable Mariners' was originally an article that Captain Stuart D. Landersman, U.S.N. (Ret) submitted to the U.S. Naval Institute for publication. The article had been accepted and was to be included in a special supplement to the Proceedings. Originally planned for March 2006, the supplement slipped to April and then was planned for May. Finally, the whole project of which "Very Few Are Capable Mariners" was to be a part was cancelled so the article never saw the light of day.

If the article had been published by the Naval Institute it would have been heavily edited, there was no way to avoid it, but it was the very strong hope of the writer that the message would not be lost. What you have is the unedited version of "Very Few Are Capable Mariners" containing the full message; that our Navy is going in the wrong direction and we must do something about it. If not, pretty soon there wouldn't be any shiphandlers in the most powerful Navy in the world and maybe there would be more collisions.

Mr. John O'Brien, Director of Publications, U.S. Naval Institute reported the following to Stu Landersman in a March 7, 2006 e-mail:

The supplement is not running due to a profound lack of sponsor support from Sim/Train vendors. Too bad the community needs to pay more attention here and Proceedings should be shaping the discussion.

That said, we are attempting to construct an "Annual Contractor Review" that would run as a part 2 to the Proceedings Annual Review of the Sea Services in May. I'd beg your patience as I would like to open one section of this piece, if successful, with your article.

If you have a better dance partner I certainly understand. Otherwise, I'd ask for a few more weeks to see if the contractor review will work.

As you can see, the Institute needed support from simulator and training vendors. More important; if "Very Few Are Capable Mariners" had been published maybe the U.S. Navy would have done something about it and maybe a collision or two could have been avoided.

Or maybe the Navy didn't want "Very Few Are Capable Mariners" to be published.

If "Very Few Are Capable Mariners" had been published, readers and critics might well have asked about the writer, "Who is this guy who claims to know so much about the Navy's shiphandling capability?

This is that guy:

"Very Few Are Capable Mariners" is based on information from numerous highly qualified and experienced shiphandling simulator instructors; observations, interviews, evaluations and estimates of more than 1000 officers of all ranks and experience levels serving in Navy ships. As was required by contract specifications, each of these instructors (facilitators) was a former Navy or Coast Guard ship commanding officer with at least two sea commands and 10 years of sea duty. Most had more than the required commands and sea time, all had experience in actual close shiphandling with various ship types. Stu Landersman had been directly associated with Navy ship personnel for over 50 years, as had many of the shiphandling instructors.

Captain Stuart D. Landersman, USN (Ret) served 30 years as a surface warfare officer, commanded a DE, DD and a destroyer squadron. His service included 30 months of participation in the Viet Nam conflict and duty on the COMSEVENTHFLT and OPNAV staffs. He was an aide to the Superintendent of the Naval Academy and attended the Naval Postgraduate School, Naval War College and National War College. He was the first CO of Tactical Training Group Pacific and was a fellow in the first Strategic Studies Group. He has a Masters degree in international affairs from George Washington University and has written 12 magazine articles and a book on Navy shiphandling.

Following Navy retirement Captain Landersman was a Fleet Representative with Johns Hopkins University Applied Physics Laboratory for 19 years, serving on the staffs of COMNAVSURFPAC, COMNAVSURFLANT and CINCLANTFLT. During this time he also served as a Convoy Commodore, participating in numerous at-sea exercises with merchant ships and writing a number of tactical documents. Also, he was instrumental in the procurement of shiphandling simulator services for Navy use.

Since retirement from JHU APL Captain Landersman has been associated with a contractor teaching shiphandling, bridge resource management and security courses to Navy and merchant ship personnel. He has a Masters license and is a certified USCG instructor.

CHAPTER FIFTY TWO

ANTISUBMARINE WARFARE
PAST AND FUTURE

2004

Submarine warfare is centuries old, with countless untried concepts and proposals long before the first underwater mission was actually undertaken. In the American Revolutionary War, September 1776, a small submersible called *Turtle* attempted to attach an explosive charge to *HMS Eagle*. There was no formal type warfare or tactics to deal with this threat but the operation failed due to inability of the weapon delivery system. More than two hundred years later, when the undersea vessel has developed into a major warfare system and revolutionized naval warfare, all navies continue to search for a means to counter the submarine threat.

World War I saw the introduction of many new weapons and forms of warfare including unrestricted submarine warfare, in which German U-boats destroyed large numbers of Allied and neutral merchant ships. Great Britain would not survive unless a means could be found for reducing losses to submarine attacks in the North Atlantic. On April 6, 1917 the United States declared war on Germany and immediately the British asked for assistance in dealing with the U-boats. Within days help was on the way and on May 4, 1917 six U.S. destroyers arrived in Queenstown, Ireland with the historic announcement, "We are ready now." The U.S. warships were ready for operations against German submarines; patrol duty, protection and escort of merchant shipping. To counter this newest form of naval action, unrestricted submarine warfare, another new form of warfare was required; antisubmarine warfare, which became better known by its acronym; ASW.

The primary combat system of the time used against submarines was the destroyer, a small multi-purpose naval combatant ship; fast, maneuverable, heavily armed (for its size) and lightly armored. Destroyers carried guns and torpedoes for use in surface engagements and depth charges, nicknamed "ash cans," as the primary weapon in this battle against submarines.

World War I ASW was conducted by destroyers using visual sightings of surfaced submarines or periscopes, naval gunfire and ash can weapons. Submarines of the time were small ships with a unique capability to go underwater for short periods of time, spending most of their time on the surface where they were most vulnerable. Often submarines attacked their prey on the surface with a deck gun, using their underwater capability to get in position and/or escape. Sometimes they would take position on the surface ahead of a target, submerge and maneuver as necessary to be in position to attack with torpedoes or surface and use their gun. As submarines were surfaced most of their time, the most common tactic against them was for the destroyer to use guns on a surfaced submarine. If the submarine submerged, the destroyer would close the visually observed point where the surfaced submarine went under water, judge the movement and attack the estimated position with depth charges. Visual contact on the surface was the most common and reliable detection. ASW was, in 1917, at best a less than marginal capability that provided protection only close to the destroyer.

The idea of detecting underwater vessels by listening for sounds and with reflected acoustic energy had been proposed before World War I and a group of British scientists, the Anti-Submarine Detection Investigation Committee, authorized development of a practical echolocation system in June 1917. The system took its name from the committee, ASDIC, but was too late to play a role in World War I. Later, when the U.S. Navy developed a similar system, it became known as SONAR, from Sound Navigation Ranging.

Indicative of the effectiveness (or ineffectiveness) of World War I ASW; 900,000 tons of Allied shipping were lost to U-boats in May 1917, a month before the first American destroyers came to aid the British. Six months later, in November 1917, with more than 75 U.S. Navy destroyers helping the British and with a shift to the convoy system, loses to U-boats were 300,000 tons. During the full U.S. participation in World War I, American destroyers sunk only one German U-boat and lost one destroyer to enemy submarines.

By the beginning of World War II in 1939, higher numbers of more capable German U-boats presented an even greater menace to the British, whose ASW capability had improved with sonar and better weapons. With the U.S. entry in 1941, ASW was still dependent on destroyer-type ships but with improved sonar. Later, Allied ASW included the introduction of radar at sea, for submarine detection on the ocean surface. While sonar and radar were among the most significant ASW developments in World War II, visual detection continued to be the most reliable means of detection. New ahead-thrown weapons such as hedge-hogs were developed and the ash cans that were still rolled over the stern could also be projected a short distance and even laid in patterns.

The introduction of aviation into World War II ASW was another of the most significant developments in combating the submarine threat. After the fall of France in 1940, the Germans built bombproof concrete submarine facilities at five ports on the French coast and massive Allied bombing attacks had little effect on U-boats operating from these protected ports. Later in the war, the strategic bombing effort yielded significant results where U-boats used ports with no concrete pens in the Mediterranean, Baltic and North Seas. Allied strategic bombing of submarines in ports destroyed forty-one German U-boats.

At sea, land based maritime patrol aircraft, sea planes and blimps turned around the battle of the North Atlantic and reversed U-boat successes. Late in the war escort carriers gave air support for convoy protection and Hunter-Killer groups searched the seas for U-boats. Antisubmarine torpedoes were developed. Destroyers were no longer alone in the battle against submarines. ASW had become a form of warfare that included other Navy resources and the need was increased for more training, better tactics and improved command and control procedures. By the end of World War II, the combined effects of strategic bombing, intelligence and coordinated naval operations had produced effective protection for convoys and other high value units at sea. U-boats, previously hunters, were being hunted at sea.

Hunter-Killer groups represented a major change in the strategic concept of dealing with the submarine threat. Pure defensive mentality gave way to a new campaign concept in which all fleet resources were used under the same command structure including defense of the aircraft carrier and offensive actions to search out and attack enemy submarines rather than wait in a protective screen.

Following World War II in the Cold War the U.S. Navy faced potentially a much more dangerous submarine threat from the Soviet Union than had been faced in World Wars I or II; a communist threat with the largest submarine fleet ever and with the impending introduction of nuclear powered submarines. The U.S. Navy focused on ASW with the development of new ships, submarines, aircraft, detection systems, weapons, communications, tactics and command with great emphasis on training in coordination, so that all resources could be brought to bear effectively against Soviet submarines. Flag level ASW operational commanders were established in the Atlantic and Pacific. The Navy built on successes of late World War II with Hunter Killer groups, forming Task Group Alfa in 1959 followed by Bravo and Charlie. Each HUK group consisted of an ASW aircraft carrier, ASW air wing including helicopters and fixed wing, and eight-ship destroyer squadron, and was supported by U.S. submarines, land based maritime patrol aircraft and national level intelligence.

The mission of these new HUK-like groups was to demonstrate ASW capability by seeking out Soviet submarines and holding them to exhaustion, forcing them to surface. Separate from the Hunter-Killer operations, U.S. Navy submarines developed a dramatic capability to joust with Soviet submarines in undersea contests of advanced technology and nerve.

In the 20 years 1960-1980 the U.S. Navy developed the best ASW capability the world had ever seen with strategic surveillance systems, long range aircraft, hunter-killer like carrier battle groups and with U.S. submarines proving to be the most effective platforms; fortuitous timing as the Soviets presented the biggest submarine threat. With the introduction of nuclear power, submarines no longer spent most of their time on the surface and far from its origins as a duel between destroyer and U-boat; ASW was now a major strategic contest including national resources.

With the break-up of the Soviet Union and end of the Cold War, potential hostiles to the U.S. did not include significant submarine threats and the U.S. Navy deemphasized antisubmarine warfare, even changing the name to undersea warfare. The Atlantic and Pacific ASW Force commands were disestablished and the magnificent nuclear attack submarine ASW capability was reduced in number and span of operations. ASW mission systems were removed from many surface combatant ships and ASW aircraft were reduced, some eliminated. A century of continuous improvement in warfare against undersea vessels reversed and the high level of ASW capability ebbed away as the tide, no longer perceived as necessary.

On September 15, 2003 the Chief of Naval Operations announced a small step in an attempt to improve ASW capability now viewed as essential to support joint warfare operations.

1. BATTLESPACE CONTROL OF THE NEAR LAND ENVIRONMENT IS ESSENTIAL TO THE NAVY'S

ABILITY TO ENSURE PROMPT ACCESS FOR JOINT FORCES MOVING FROM THE SEA TO OBJECTIVES INLAND. OUR FUTURE ANTI-SUBMARINE WARFARE (ASW) EFFECTIVENESS IN THIS CRITICAL AREA DEMANDS MORE THAN JUST NEW TECHNOLOGIES AND NEW IDEAS. IT REQUIRES A DEDICATED FOCUS ON INTEGRATING ADVANCED NETWORKS AND SENSORS, NEW OPERATING CONCEPTS AND FLEET ASW TRAINING.

2. IN REF A, THE FLEET WAS TASKED TO DEVELOP A STRATEGY TO IMPROVE ASW READINESS AND CAPABILITY IN THE NEAR AND MID-TERM. AS JUST ONE OF THE FIRST STEPS IDENTIFIED IN THAT STRATEGY, FLEET ASW COMMAND (FASWC) WILL BE ESTABLISHED TO SET THE STANDARD FOR INTEGRATED ASW OPERATIONS AND TRAINING. FASWC›S MISSION WILL BE PHASED IN INCREMENTALLY AND WILL FOCUS ON FIVE ASW AREAS APPLICABLE TO ALL WARFARE COMMUNITIES AND DISCIPLINES. THESE AREAS INCLUDE:

A. FOSTERING HIGH PERFORMANCE IN INTEGRATED ASW OPERATIONS THROUGH QUALITY INTEGRATED FLEET ASW TRAINING.

B. ASSESSING INTEGRATED ASW PERFORMANCE AT THE THEATER, GROUP AND INDIVIDUAL SHIP, SUBMARINE AND AVIATION SQUADRON LEVEL AND COORDINATING OPPOSITION EXERCISE FORCES.

C. COORDINATING (WITH NPDC AND TYPE COMMANDERS) INDIVIDUAL STUDENT ASW TRAINING AND QUALIFICATION IMPROVEMENTS AND DEVELOPMENT OF INTEGRATED ASW TRAINING RESOURCES.

D. PROMOTING RAPID DELIVERY OF SELECTED NEW ASW TECHNOLOGIES AND TRAINING

AND DEVELOPMENT OF INTEGRATED ASW INNOVATIONS.

E.   IMPROVING THEATER USW CAPABILITY.

3.   THE COMMANDER, FASWC IS EXPECTED TO BE A FLAG OFFICER AND WILL REPORT TO COMMANDER, U.S. FLEET FORCES COMMAND (CFFC) AS AN ECHELON III COMMANDER. FASWC WILL BE ESTABLISHED ON 1 JANUARY 2004 AND COMMANDER, U.S. PACIFIC FLEET (CPF) WILL BE THE EXECUTIVE AGENT FOR FASWC'S INITIAL CREATION AND OPERATIONS. ASW RESOURCE SPONSORS, PROGRAM MANAGERS, LABS, TRAINING ORGANIZATIONS, AND OPERATIONAL AND TACTICAL DEVELOPMENT COMMANDS WILL COLLABORATE AND COORDINATE WITH FASWC TO COLLECTIVELY IMPROVE OUR ASW CAPABILITIES. CFFC WILL ANNOUNCE THE IMPLEMENTATION ORGANIZATION, ISSUE DETAILED GUIDANCE, AND PROMULGATE A POAM TO ESTABLISH FASWC PRIOR TO 1 OCT 2003.

4.   INTEGRATED ASW IS OUR IMMEDIATE AND EXCITING FUTURE. WE ARE ON THE CUSP OF REVOLUTIONARY CHANGES IN UNDERSEA TECHNOLOGIES ABOVE, BELOW AND ON THE SEA. BY SPEARHEADING THE RAPID INSERTION OF THESE TECHNOLOGIES INTO OUR CONCEPT OF OPERATIONS AND OUR TRAINING, TACTICS, AND PROCEDURES, FASWC WILL HELP MOVE US SMARTLY TOWARD A NEW LEVEL OF USW PREEMINENCE.

Creation of a new command, Fleet Anti Submarine Warfare Command (FASWC) on April 8, 2004 was a small but important step toward regaining the capability of some 30 years before, with hope for moving smartly toward a new level of undersea warfare preeminence. If "integrated ASW is our immediate and exciting future," there are lessons from years ago that would be well to recall. It was found then and would apply in 2004 that to be effective integrated ASW needs:

1. Understanding of integration and coordination.
2. An operational commander with knowledge and control of all resources.
3. Communications.
4. Dedicated participation of all ASW resources.
5. Time to develop procedures and tactics and to conduct realistic exercises.

The various communities of the Navy had for years separately pursued their ASW mission. Destroyers, submarines, land based maritime patrol aircraft and ship based aircraft had to be taught the meaning of integration and the benefits of coordination. It did not come easily. Each community had to understand and be convinced of the synergistic benefits of integration and coordination; that they were not in competition with the other ASW communities, they were team-mates.

Senior officers had been successful in their communities but had little involvement with others. An officer in command of an integrated group or force had to know the capabilities and limitations of all resources and, just as important, he had to know the capabilities of enemy submarines. These people did not exist. They had to learn before the integrated unit could be effective.

Navy communities had developed their own individual procedures but for effective integrated and coordinated ASW they had to be able to work together. Communications linking all resources with the commander was one of the most important ingredients of effective integrated coordinated ASW. It didn't exist. It had to be created.

A menu of all ASW resources would include ships, aircraft, and submarines but also intelligence, communications, attack aircraft, Special Forces, surveillance systems, satellites and a host of others. From this long list the integrated ASW commander must have dedicated resources with which to develop, train and exercise. His force composition must be consistent so that procedures and tactics can continually improve rather than require periodic start-over with new participants. The Navy rotates ships, aircraft and submarines with little continuity. To be effective an integrated ASW force must build on what it learns and changing personnel and unit participation denies improvement.

It takes time to develop procedures, tactics and coordination in integrated ASW. Molding ships, aircraft and submarines that have not operated together into an effective team is a challenge. The integrated ASW unit must be given time with dedicated resources for development and exercises at sea and in port.

Integrated fleet ASW is not enough. Effective ASW must include offensive actions. The span of control of this new ASW command appears to fall short. Its authority to integrate all resources is vague. FASWC is established by the Chief of Naval Operations, and so is limited to Navy resources in the five "ASW areas," focusing on "fleet ASW," while modern and future ASW must include more than the "fleet." Inclusion of "theater" shows a broader area consideration but still is limited as a Navy command would not include joint or national resources.

For almost a hundred years, since the Allies of World War I saw the need for undersea detection and formed the ASDIC committee, navies have focused on defensive detection and attack of submarines operating underwater. That Navy mind-set of defensive ASW limited to search, detection and attack of submerged submarines must be changed. It must be expanded to include offensive actions that can be utilized against the submarine; surfaced or submerged, prior to or during a campaign, far from, near or in an objective area.

Antisubmarine Warfare and Undersea Warfare are not synonymous as ASW is not limited to actions beneath the sea. The submarine, even nuclear powered, is still most vulnerable on the surface, which might be departing, entering or in-port. Next, the submarine is almost as vulnerable when in transit. Once in his chosen operating area the submarine owns his element and becomes a most lethal foe with every advantage in his favor. Modern and future

ASW cannot be limited to at-sea, under sea, Navy-only or even in-theater operations. To be effective, ASW must include resources from diplomacy to depth charge.

Senior career military officers attend senior service colleges, war colleges tailored for each individual service and defense requirements. These graduate level educational institutions have differences in curriculum but all try to bring together the best sources of information and theories on warfare. One text used by all of these academic institutions is On War by Carl von Clausewitz, assembled from his notes written 1816 to 1830. The flyleaf of the most common English edition explains, "On War constitutes the most significant attempt in Western history to understand war, both in its internal dynamics and as an instrument of policy. Since the work's first appearance in 1832 it has been read throughout the world, and has stimulated and influenced generations of soldiers, statesmen, and intellectuals—."

The key is "stimulated and influenced," as Clausewitz has been studied at military institutions for over a hundred years, with supporters as well as detractors. Some see On War as a virtual bible of warfare and just as the Holy Bible is interpreted by various perceptions, so is Clausewitz. Other military theorists studied and compared at the service war colleges include General Baron de Jomini, a contemporary of Clausewitz and Julian S. Corbett, published in 1918. These and some others disagree with Clausewitz on some matters but all fully agree that war is an extension of politics and that attack or offensive action must be part of defense. The name Clausewitz is synonymous with the study of warfare and he is perhaps best known for the often repeated view that war is an extension of the bargaining table.

Clausewitz's work is eight books of six to thirty chapters. Book Six is the longest and in Chapter One under The Concept of Defense, Clausewitz offers that if we are waging a defensive campaign "we must return the enemy's blows". Jomini agrees that defense "must always be supplemented by attack." Corbett writes that "counter attack is the soul of defense." All use "must" regarding inclusion of offensive action in an effective defensive campaign. It is not a matter of choice.

According to Clausewitz, "The defensive form of war is not a simple shield, but a shield made up of well-directed blows." Regarding classic fortress defense Corbett offers, "Men know that sooner or later the place must fall unless by counter attack on the enemy's siege works or communications they can cripple his power of attack."

Clausewitz would agree with the Hunter-Killer mentality used in an ASW campaign strategy in which a major part of a defending force seeks out and attacks an opponent. But Clausewitz would be disappointed with the short scope of ASW actions against submarines, limiting operations to Navy units at sea pinging and listening in an area chosen by the enemy, omitting the full extent of resources.

Congressional staff members of the House Armed Services Committee visiting the Viet Nam area in 1972 received briefings on board USS Oklahoma City, flagship of Commander Seventh Fleet. After a detailed presentation by Vice Admiral James L. Holloway, III, later Chief of Naval Operations, a staffer asked, "How are you going to defend your carriers against the Styx missile?" The question reflected concern following the October 1967 sinking of the Israeli destroyer Elath by Egyptian high speed boat attack using a Soviet furnished surface-to-surface missile.

Admiral Holloway hesitated only a moment before explaining that defending a carrier against the Styx missile starts far away and a long time before any at-sea incident. It starts as intelligence and state department functions. Upon learning that the Soviet Union is considering transfer of these weapons to North Viet Nam, our state department uses their influence to dissuade the Soviets from this course of action. Failing in this, we try to keep track of the movements so that we know when and where the weapons are located. If allowed, we try to interdict the transport of the weapons. If we have not stopped the weapons from reaching our area of operations we try to learn of the storage facilities and if rules of engagement allow we try to destroy the weapons. Holloway went on to describe how similar procedures would be used regarding the high speed boats that would carry and launch the missiles. He described how his Seventh Fleet used all assets to locate, identify and destroy the missiles and boats long before they could be used against our carriers. He described the disruption of training and destruction of logistic support, so that an enemy would have a great deal of trouble mounting a credible confident attack.

Holloway explained that if we fail in all these pre-engagement procedures, which was very possible and which he believed to be the basis of the staffer's question, we have resources available and in position to deal with high speed boats closing our carriers and with the missiles that they may be able to launch. He explained that there were ships and aircraft to detect, identify and destroy the boats before the missiles could be launched and to detect, identify and destroy the Styx missiles in flight. It took a lot of resources for this shield to be effective and those resources were available and well trained. Holloway cautioned not to think that this action against approaching boats and in-flight missiles was our only defense. It was a very important part of a defensive system that started long before any action, a continuous process of many layers, much time and considerable space, and included offensive actions and our full national resources.

What Holloway described for the congressional staff was right out of Clausewitz; from extension of the bargaining table to the use of attack in a defensive campaign; the defensive form of war, "not a simple shield, but a shield made up of well-directed blows." Even today, the question asked by the congressional staffer could be altered to, "How are you going to defend (Blank 1) against (Blank 2)," and Holloway's explanation would be appropriate and similar whatever was substituted for Blank 1 and Blank 2. "How are you going to defend your joint task force against enemy submarines?" Read Clausewitz. Follow Holloway's explanation.

Some years later the Pacific Fleet tactical training school converted Holloway's explanation of defense into an anecdote:

Three baseball managers were sitting at a bar during the all-star break discussing how to keep Pete Rose from scoring. One told of positioning his fielders based on Rose's hitting patterns. Another told of studying pitch selection so that his pitchers wouldn't give Rose anything to hit. The third would concentrate on stopping Rose on the base paths. All three agreed that none of these tactics were likely to work. Down the bar sat a hockey coach who couldn't help overhearing and said, "Break his legs in the parking lot."

"Break his legs in the parking lot," became a tactical slogan and like Holloway's explanation it applied to all warfare areas not just defending against a particular weapon. Why try to shoot missiles out of the sky? Destroy the launching platform before it launches. Disrupt the training and maintenance. Destroy the fuel supply and the warehouse of missiles before they're placed on the launcher. Stop the purchase, shipment and importation of the weapon system before it reaches a potential hostile.

German concrete submarine pens provided protected safe parking lots for submarines in World War II, but when exposed in uncovered ports Allied strategic bombing exploited their vulnerability and damaged or destroyed 41 U-boats, breaking their legs in the parking lot.

Admiral Sandy Woodward of the Royal Navy told that in April of 1982 the British were preparing to sail a flotilla to re-take the Falkland Islands from Argentina. Military leaders asked Prime Minister Margaret Thatcher for permission to strike diesel electric submarines alongside the pier at their naval base in Argentina, before those submarines could get underway and interdict British shipping. Thatcher listened carefully and asked questions but finally denied authority to conduct the strike because she felt that to the rest of the world it would be perceived as spreading the conflict beyond the immediate area of operations in the Falklands. The Argentine submarines got underway but only one reached the area of operations and that submarine had numerous opportunities to torpedo key British ships but couldn't launch an attack due to internal technical problems.

British antisubmarine forces conducted over a hundred attacks on what proved to be false contacts while the Argentine submarine was never under attack. But for Argentine incompetence the British could have lost a number of primary ships and perhaps the conflict. British military leaders knew that the best way to deal with the submarine threat was to destroy it by air attack before it could be dangerous to them, to "break his legs in the parking lot." It was the duty of the British military leaders to propose the most effective military plan and the decision not to strike targets in Argentina was political. Denied pre-emptive strike permission, they had to deal with the threat under conditions more favorable to the enemy submarine, and only the chance of enemy failure worked in their favor, just as the *Turtle* was unable to deliver its weapon in 1776.

Antisubmarine warfare is a defensive campaign that must be carried out in accordance with the best experience and teachings using the full extent of national resources. Effective ASW cannot be limited to defensive naval operations against a submerged enemy in an objective area where the submarine has every advantage. Clausewitz explains that a defensive campaign must consist of a shield and well directed blows. Screening ships and aircraft can form a shield as attacks are carried out by aircraft, submarines, special forces and sabotage. The U.S. must negotiate for cooperation, identify the "parking lots" and if necessary go there and "break their legs" before an enemy submarine can get underway or reach an objective area. To be effective, ASW must cover the full extent of time and distance with diplomacy, intelligence, negotiation, surveillance, interdiction, coordination, offense, detection, intercept and attack.

Experience shows clearly that in a contest limited to destroyer versus submarine the submarine wins. Coordinating the addition of aircraft, submarines and multiple ships might even the odds. Extending battle space and time with the full spectrum of national resources, including offensive actions reaching out to stop the submarine before it materializes into an unmanageable menace is the most effective dimension and is essential for modern and future antisubmarine warfare.

In about a half-century antisubmarine warfare moved from ASDIC and ash cans to towed arrays and torpedoes. In the half-century that has followed, ASW must advance to include politics and parking lots.

CHAPTER FIFTY THREE

MORE ON THE OFFENSIVE
ELEMENT OF DEFENSE

2008

There are so many examples of the Clausewitz lesson that tells us that a successful defensive campaign must be accompanied by an offensive element! I couldn't put all of them into the previous chapter so I've added this chapter to include just a few more.

The game of chess originated in India in the 6th century where its early name meant "four divisions of the military" which were; infantry, cavalry, elephants and chariots. These are represented respectively today as pawn, knight, bishop and rook. These pieces are used to protect the monarch and to attack and capture or destroy the opponent's king.

Chess originated as a war game requiring strategy and tactics directed at defending while attacking. The chess game follows real war, but without destruction, violence and bloodshed of combat, in that vital property and personnel must be protected while at the same time aggressive offensive action must be directed against the enemy. The game cannot be won by using all assets to protect the king as a powerful shield alone cannot bring success. Winning demands that an effective defense must be accompanied by offensive thrusts against the enemy.

Chess is but a game of strategy and tactics, as are competitive games from checkers to football, and in all such games the principle of war applies; victory cannot be achieved by defense alone. The campaign must include offensive action.

The Great Wall of China did not keep the Mongol and Manchu hordes from China during the 6th through the 16th Centuries and the Maginot Line did not stop Germans from invading France in World War II.

Army, Navy, Air Force and Marine Corps each have a war college tailored for its individual service requirements and the Defense Department conducts a National Defense University, all of which bring together all sources of information for study. There are considerable differences in curriculum at these institutions but there are some commonalities. One text used by all of these service institutions is On War by Carl von Clausewitz. In The Concept of Defense Clausewitz offers, "If we are really waging war, we must return the enemy's blows; and these offensive acts in a defensive war come under the heading of 'defense.'"

Also according to Clausewitz, "The defensive form of war is not a simple shield, but a shield made up of well-directed blows."

Other military theorists studied at the service war colleges include General Baron de Jomini, a contemporary of Clausewitz, and Julian S. Corbett, published in 1918. These and some others all fully agree that war is an extension of politics and that attack or offensive action must be part of defense.

Jomini agrees that defense, "must always be supplemented by attack" and Corbett writes that, "Counter attack is the soul of defense." All insist that inclusion of offensive action is necessary in an effective defensive campaign. It is not a matter of choice.

Regarding classic fortress defense Corbett offers, "Men know that sooner or later their place must fall unless by counter attack on the enemy's siege works or communications they can cripple his power of attack."

"Break his legs in the parking lot," became a Navy tactical slogan and like Holloway's explanation to the congressional group it applied to all warfare areas, not just defending against a particular weapon. Why try to shoot missiles out of the sky? Destroy the launching platform before it launches. Disrupt the training and maintenance. Destroy the fuel supply and the warehouse of missiles before they're placed on the launcher. Stop the purchase, shipment, and importation of the weapon system before it reaches a potential hostile.

Football fans chant, "Dee-fense. Dee-fense," as their team fights to stop the attacking enemy force in the final two minutes of a close game. Fans know that no defense can be successful with all eleven players forming a wall and every fan takes for granted that almost half of their defensive team must attack the enemy, knock down pass receivers, get in their backfield, sack the quarterback, and/or tackle the ball carrier. A major part of "Dee-fense" must be offensive and every fan knows that the best defense is a good offense.

Texians and Tajanos in the Alamo made a feeble offensive thrust against Santa Anna's army in February 1836 and after that it was only a matter of time before the old mission fell. The Japanese attacking Wake Island in December 1941 first eliminated 8 of the 12 Wildcat fighter aircraft that could have been used against them and with the remaining four wildcats the first assault was repulsed. The second Japanese assault destroyed the remaining defending aircraft and, without any means of offensive action, the island fell. In both of these cases defense without offensive action could not succeed.

From chess and checkers to the China Wall, Clausewitz through Corbett, Holloway and hockey, Woodward and Wake Island, and football, Jomini, the Alamo and Maginot Line, the message is clear; a defensive campaign can be successful only when accompanied by an aggressive effective offense. The War on Terrorism is a defensive campaign being carried out in accordance with the best experience and teachings.

Clausewitz explains that a defensive campaign must consist of a shield and well directed blows. Homeland defense is the shield, being made stronger by continuous improvements keeping terrorists off-balance, forcing them to look for softer targets. Well directed blows are being carried out in areas identified as providing refuge for terrorists. There are others providing terrorist havens and the U.S. must identify each "parking lot," go there and "break his legs" before the terrorist can strike.

That's breaking his legs in the parking lot. That's the offensive element of defense.

CHAPTER FIFTY FOUR

WHAT'S A KURD?

2002

Every day news from and about Middle East struggles tells the public about ISIS, Syria, Iran and Iraq. Recently there has been mention of another group; Kurds, and with the Kurds there is always mention of the Pesh Merga. News media tells us that the U.S. has tried to get weapons to the Kurds, to the Pesh Merga, but the Iraqi government has delayed or blocked this process. Why this blockage? Years of disagreement, distrust and conflict between Kurds and Iraqis.

At the beginning of the 21st century, from inside Iraq came word that a powerful ethnic minority of largely Sunni Moslems called Kurds would field an army of a hundred thousand to support any U.N. or U.S. military action to oust the Iraqi dictator Saddam Hussein. The U.S. State Department hosted meetings of Kurdish leaders to discuss this support. These Kurds had experienced severe repression at the hands of Saddam Hussein and they were very anxious to be rid of the dictator and gain their freedom. Kurds had long sought freedom.

After the Kurds supported Iran in the long Iran-Iraq war of 1980, Saddam Hussein retaliated, razing villages and attacking peasants with chemical weapons. The Kurds again rebelled after the first Gulf War only to be severely crushed by Iraqi troops. Approximately 2 million Kurds fled to Iran. To protect about five million Kurds still living in northern Iraq, the United States created a safe haven for them by establishing a "no-fly" zone north of the 36th parallel inside Iraq.

We must ask ourselves who and what are these Kurds and what is Pesh Merga?

The answers are in a long story that starts far back in history.

Solomon, the ancient Hebrew king, was very wise and powerful. When he found that the magical spirits called jinn were causing too much mischief and too many problems, he expelled 500 of them from his kingdom and exiled them to the Zagros Mountains. These jinn first went to Europe, traveling on their magic carpets to the area now known as Germany, took 500 blond virgin brides and then settled in what became known as Kurdistan. Jinn is what we know as jinni, or genie; a magical creature that gives three wishes if anyone rubs the lamp or bottle to release him. King Solomon's expulsion of jinn is Kurdish legend that explains their origin.

Thousands of years later Kurds, living in the harsh Zagros Mountains straddling the borders of Turkey, Syria, Iraq, Iran, and Armenia (formerly part of the Soviet Union), call their land Kurdistan for "Land of the Kurds", but it is not theirs. It is the land of those five host nations, and the problems of Kurds today are the same as for centuries; Kurds living in areas controlled by others. The Kurds have tried to set up independent states in Iran, Iraq, and Turkey, but their efforts have been crushed every time. Their struggle for autonomy, sovereignty, independence or recognition is one of the longest and saddest–of stories. If their jinn forefathers would grant the Kurds but one wish, surely it would be for creation of a Kurdish state.

Over a period of 3000 years before Christ the area called Kurdistan was controlled by Persians, Babylonians, Sumerians, Amorites, Kassites, Assyrians, Medes and Greeks. After Christ's time came Romans, Arabs that converted all to Islam, Mongols, Turks and Persians again.

Around the time of Christ, Kurdistan was part of the Persian Empire and the people were followers of the Zoroastrian religion. Persian and Zoroastrian legend both tell of three priests that traveled west from Urmia, in what is now northern Iran. The priests were astrologers, interpreters of dreams, givers of omens and they were searching for a prophet or redeemer. They followed a bright star and are known today as the three wise men, the magi, who came to Bethlehem at the birth of Christ. They were Kurds.

During the Crusades, Saladin was the most successful and famous leader of Islam, leading the Moslem reconquest of Jerusalem in 1187 AD. Salah al Din Yusuf ibn Ayyubi, known to his Muslim contemporaries as al Nasir, "The Victorious", and to an admiring Europe as Saladin. Saladin is the most famous single figure in the history of the Crusades, even better known than his Christian foe Richard the Lionhearted. Saladin was a Kurd but his leadership did nothing for Kurdish independence.

The beginning of the 20th Century found Kurds living a nomadic life herding sheep and goats throughout the Mesopotamian plains and the highlands of Turky and Iran, generally known as Kurdistan, but divided between the Ottoman and Persian Empires. Their language was spoken, rarely written, in two principal dialects similar to Persian but related to European. Some looked like Arabs and others were fair skinned with light hair. Up to that time Kurds had never had their own country but they were a distinct ethnic group, existing under their own feudal process with tribal leaders and serfs. After centuries of alien occupation they had absorbed and reshaped cultures from all that had occupied and passed through. When they were not fighting outsiders they fought other ethnic groups in the area; Armenians and Assyrians, or they fought among themselves. Kurds have seldom been united.

World War I, the Great War (1914-1918), gave Kurds an opportunity for autonomy. Ottoman Turkey joined Germany as the principal Central Powers against the Allies led by Great Britain and

France. Persia was sympathetic to the Central Powers. By siding with the Allies, Kurds expected to be rewarded with independence as part of an Allied victory. After the war Woodrow Wilson's Fourteen Points included a statement that sizable ethnic minorities of the Turkish Empire would get their own states. This was a direct reference to Kurds, Armenians and Assyrians. Wilson's points never went into effect.

1919 saw the breakup of the Ottoman Empire as a result of the Great War, with Mustafa Kemal Ataturk establishing the Republic of Turkey. The 1920 Treaty of Sevres included the guaranteed establishment of a Kurdish state within one year, but it was rejected by Kemal and replaced with the Treaty of Lausanne in 1923. The new treaty made no mention of Kurds and they received even harsher treatment from the new Turkish government. Great Britain saw to it that the oil rich areas of Kurdistan didn't fall to Turkey, creating Iraq to ensure Arab control of that resource and British control over Arabs. The breakup of the Ottoman Empire created a number of new nation-states, but not a separate Kurdistan. Kurds, no longer free to roam, were forced to abandon their seasonal migrations and traditional ways. The Kurds had joined the winners of World War I but gained nothing.

During World War II (1939-1945) Iran was sympathetic to Germany and troops from the Soviet Union moved into western Iran to ensure continued Allied access to oil. Kurds had supported the Allies and after the war in 1946 a Kurdish nation, the Republic of Mahabad, was established in what had been the Iranian portion of Kurdistan. As soon as Soviet troops departed Iranian troops eliminated the new republic. For almost a year a Kurdish republic had existed but, again, Kurds had backed winners and gained nothing.

A Kurdish hero of the 1946 Mahabad Republic was General Mulla Mustafa Barzani, who fought the Iranians until forced to retreat into the Soviet Union. In 1958 he brought his army back to Iraq following the coup that put Abdel Karim Qassem in power. Qassem promised to share political and economic power with the Kurds but by 1961 Iraq was in chaos with socialists fighting nationalists. Barzani's army, grown into the "Pesh Merga" (Death Facers) fought against Qassem for nine years. At first the Kurds were united but unity was brief. The Kurdish Democratic Party of Barzani wanted the old feudal systems but New Left socialists split from this party led by Jalal Talabani.

But now we finally know the meaning and origin of Pesh Merga, the Death Facers, as active today as they were in the middle of the previous century. Time has little meaning in the Middle East as sons take over leadership from fathers.

In 1970 the Kurds of Iraq signed a fifteen-article peace agreement with the new Baathist leader, Saddam Hussein. The agreement included a census to be taken in northern Iraq to determine areas with Kurdish majority. Those areas would be given self-government. Before a census could be taken Iraqis began deporting Kurds from the north into areas of southern Iraq inhabited by Shiite Muslims. If continued, this would have balanced the minorities so that there would be no self-government. No census was taken.

Shortly before the fall of the Shah of Iran, Iraq began a campaign to remove all Kurds from the Iraq-Iran border. All Kurdish villages within 25 kilometers of the border were burned and villagers were driven away. Hundreds fled into Iran where they were attacked by Iranian military forces. In 1974 the Shah of Iran encouraged Kurds of Iraq to start fighting again because of Saddam Hussein's failure to keep his word. When the Shah was overthrown and replaced by Ayatollah Khomeini, the Kurds were left on their own again and Barzani's army escaped along with refugees into Iran.

In the U.S. a report by the Pike Committee to Congress on the role of the CIA in covert actions included a brief reference to Kurds as an "ethnic insurgent group." This report said the U.S. and the Shah of Iran encouraged Kurds to begin their 1974 revolution in Iraq because Iran wanted to harass the Baathist regime. The Pike report called it a "cynical enterprise," leaving 3 million Kurds in Iraq plus 200 thousand Kurdish refugees in Iran without support.

In their recent struggles Kurds have searched for and accepted assistance or promises of aid from any source including the U.S., the Shah and even Israel, further alienating Muslims and Arab nationalists.

Mustafa Barzani died in 1979 and his son, Massoud, gathered up his father's army in Iran and led them back into Iraq. Talabani had continued the fight and was a wanted man by Saddam Hussein, with a price on his head. During the long Iran-Iraq War both sides at various times courted and fought the Kurds and in 1988 as the Iran-Iraq War ended the Kurds were despised by the governments of Iraq and Iran, as well as by Turkish leadership.

When the U.S. led coalition opposed Iraq over the invasion of Kuwait, Kurds saw another opportunity. They cooperated with the coalition, but when the short war ended Kurds were left to face Saddam Hussein's surviving army again. This time there was a considerable focus of international public attention. By May 1991 Kurd fortunes seemed to be turning as Saddam Hussein had embraced Talabani, promising autonomy again. Even with the common goal of independent statehood, the 20 million Kurds in various countries were hardly unified. From 1994 to 1998 two Iraqi Kurd factions; the Kurdistan Democratic Party led by Massoud Barzani, and the Patriotic Union of Kurdistan led by Jalal Talabani, fought a bloody war for power over northern Iraq. In September of 1998 the two sides agreed to a power-sharing arrangement.

Ayatollah Khomeini of Iran had declared Kurds to be agents of Satan and sent a military force after them and Iran's present government has not changed that view. Saddam Hussein of Iraq had fought them including the use of chemical weapons and promised autonomy again. Turkey, since Mustafa Kemal Ataturk, has maintained a policy of nonrecognition, stating that there are no Kurds, or Armenians, or Assyrians, only Turks. Within that policy all ethnic groups are outlawed.

Turkey does not want more Kurdish refugees from Iraq, particularly with about 20 percent of Turkey's population Kurdish, the largest of Turkish minorities. Syria has few Kurds. The former Soviet Union had absorbed Kurds as a small minority in the Soviet Socialist Republics of Armenia and Azerbaijan, with ongoing fighting between those republics. These host countries all consider Kurds to be a problem, and all do not want to see an autonomous Kurdistan formed across their borders as each would have to deal with their own Kurdish populations' desires to become part of that republic.

Kurdish autonomy in Iraq, even if it would have come about as a U.S. reward for cooperation, would not have been enough. Kurds of at least four other states would have insisted on joining, and those other states would not have allowed such secession or breaking-away of their territory, including the close U.S. ally Turkey. This, once again, would have placed the Kurds in the same dilemma they have faced for centuries; siding with a winner and gaining nothing.

For centuries the Kurds have sought their own nation but achieving Kurdish autonomy will take much more than all three wishes the jinn can offer.

CHAPTER FIFTY FIVE

ANOTHER GREAT WHITE FLEET

1999

Following is an article I wrote that was published in
the Naval Institute Proceedings February 1999.

February 1999 is the 90th anniversary of the return of the Great White
Fleet from its epic voyage around the world, a perfect time to look at
the journey's reasons, benefits, and lessons and to start planning for a
similar voyage early in the 21st century.

At the beginning of the 19th century, the young U.S. Navy had
been reduced to "Mr. Jefferson's Navy," a handful of lightly armed
sloops incapable of opposing ships-of-the-line or the frigates that
England and France were operating in U.S. waters. Without an
effective Navy, the young United States was forced to pay tribute in
the Mediterranean, and in large part, Impressment—the seizure of
crewmen from U.S. ships for service in the Royal Navy—led to the
War of 1812.

A century later, President Theodore Roosevelt showed that the United States was a world power by sending his fleet around the world. "A proper armament is the surest guarantee of peace," he said, and the U.S. Navy went on to become the most powerful in the world.

On 16 December 1907 Rear Admiral Robley D. "Fighting Bob" Evans, Commander-in-Chief of the U.S. Fleet, the Navy's senior officer and a veteran of the Civil War and Spanish-American War, stood on the flag bridge of the USS CONNECTICUT leading a column of 16 battleships from Hampton Roads, Virginia, out to the Atlantic Ocean. He was taking the fleet from the Atlantic around the southern part of South America to the Pacific, in the first leg of what would later be known as the 'round-the-world cruise by the Great White Fleet. As the ships steamed by the presidential yacht MAYFLOWER, the President waved his hat as the band played "The Girl I Left Behind Me."

This was Roosevelt's fleet. More than anyone, he was responsible for its creation. As Assistant Secretary of the Navy, then as Vice President and President, he had fought and lobbied for legislation to build a world-class Navy. At the start of his presidential administration, the U.S. Navy ranked fifth in the world, largely because of Roosevelt's previous efforts in the Navy Department. When he left the presidency seven-and-a-half years later, the U.S. Navy was second only to the British Royal Navy.

Some critics and politicians were concerned that shifting the fleet to the Pacific would leave the U.S. East Coast vulnerable and undefended. This encouraged legislation for the construction of new warships and also demonstrated the value of a canal across the Isthmus of Panama, another Roosevelt project then under construction. When asked how the Navy would pay for fuel to bring the fleet back to the Atlantic, Roosevelt suggested that if Congress wanted the fleet back on the East Coast, it could appropriate funds for fuel. Although the fleet's voyage to California was all that had been announced publicly, Roosevelt had a much longer trip in mind.

The British Royal Navy, while still the largest in the world, was being reduced in the early 20th century. As part of that reduction,

British ships no longer maintained a continuous presence in the Pacific and Indian oceans. This and the rapid rise of Japan as a world power caused Asian discomfort and European economic concern. Lessening of British influence in the Pacific left the area vulnerable to Japanese exploitation. By moving the U.S. fleet to California, Roosevelt wanted to demonstrate that the United States could influence events in the Pacific and that it had the resources and the will to use them. Even so, many critics doubted this resolve and the prospect that the fleet could influence events in the Western Pacific—or anywhere else.

Another of Roosevelt's purposes was to impress on the American people, and the world, that the U.S. fleet could operate in any ocean, and that its presence was not an indication of hostility. Roosevelt directed the movement of the fleet without consultation with his Cabinet or Congress.

The fleet stopped at Trinidad, Brazil, Chile, Peru, and Mexico before arriving in San Diego. At every port, coal was the major consideration, as it would be for the entire voyage. The ships burned a great deal of fuel and required frequent replenishment. Huge crowds everywhere it stopped received the fleet warmly.

San Francisco welcomed the 16 battleships on 6 May 1908. Newspapers reported that more than a million people came to see the fleet, making it the greatest movement of people the Pacific coast had ever seen, for the greatest display of naval strength ever to be assembled in the West. The cruiser force had been operating in the Pacific and was at San Francisco to welcome the battleships.

The city opened its arms to the sailors of the Great White Fleet. It also had to welcome a large number of animals because wherever they had visited, sailors were given pets as mascots; pigs, goats, monkeys, cats, dogs, birds and especially bears, Teddy Bears, in honor of President Roosevelt. While in San Francisco, Evans retired, turning over command of the U.S. Fleet to Rear Admiral Charles M. Thomas, who retired a week later, placing Rear Admiral Charles S. Sperry in command.

From Washington came an announcement that the President had ordered the fleet to return to the Atlantic by way of the Indian Ocean and the Mediterranean Sea—essentially by going around the world. These ships comprised the most powerful naval force ever to make such a voyage. Some critics and naval analysts declared that it could not be done, because available coal was insufficient, the ships would break down, and the men could not take it. But Roosevelt's battle fleet did embark, showing the flag and reinforcing that the United States was no longer just an energetic former colony; it was a major power, able to influence events anywhere in the world. Roosevelt was aware that officials of other leading navies, including the British, did not believe that their fleets could go around the world, and even more they doubted that a U.S. fleet could do so.

After leaving San Francisco, the fleet stopped at Hawaii, New Zealand, and Australia. Because the British Royal Navy had left the Pacific and Indian Oceans, the people of New Zealand and Australia felt abandoned, particularly with what they perceived as a growing Japanese threat. They welcomed the presence of a powerful U.S. fleet in the Western Pacific.

Japan had been rising rapidly from a backward, distant, archaic country to becoming a world power. Because of this, Roosevelt as well as his critics were concerned with how Japan would receive the fleet, how the battleship sailors would behave and how diplomatic events would unfold.

The visit could not have been more successful, from every aspect. Even the Japanese Emperor himself greeted the visitors and received them with warmth, hospitality and appreciation. It was high achievement, a worthy cause, and the Great White Fleet had dared to accomplish what cold and timid critics had doubted. All this was particularly satisfying to Roosevelt, especially since he had been the first American to be awarded the Nobel Peace Prize in 1906 for having a direct involvement with ending the Russo-Japanese War.

After visiting China, the fleet assembled at Manila Bay in the Philippines in November and conducted annual gunnery battle practice. It then departed on 1 December 1908, flying "homeward bound" pennants more than 200 feet long. The fleet stopped at Ceylon as it crossed the Indian Ocean and then transited the Red Sea and the Suez Canal. In the Mediterranean Sea some of the ships helped with disaster relief following an earthquake in Italy before assembling at Gibraltar.

The supply ship sent a message with arrival plans from Rear Admiral Sperry to a radio station on Fire Island, New York. A milestone event in communications, this message was transmitted from a ship at sea, over 2,000 miles, received at a shore station and acknowledged, allowing authorities in the United States to make plans for the return of the Great White Fleet. Radio communication was in its infancy between 1907 and 1909, and the Navy was trying to solve problems of radio transmitter power, antennae length and frequency selection for long-distance high-frequency use. U.S. Army Signal Corps personnel embarked for the voyage were helping with radio communications.

Four additional battleships and five cruisers joined the fleet at sea, 1,000 miles from home. On Washington's Birthday, 22 February 1909, in spite of rain, huge crowds lined the shores of Hampton Roads as 20 battleships, 5 cruisers, and 3 supply ships steamed majestically through the channel. Each ship fired a 21-gun salute while passing the MAYFLOWER; a simultaneous 21-gun salute by all ships followed. President Roosevelt, in the last few days of his presidency, was moved deeply, and in later years he evaluated this as one of his greatest achievements and the most important service he had rendered to world peace.

The ships remained at Hampton Roads long enough to send contingents of sailors to march in President William Howard Taft's inaugural parade in Washington, then returned to their home ports. Soon after, the ships' scrollwork was removed, their masts replaced with lattice works, their white paint covered with gray. After steaming more than 42,000 miles in 14 months, the Great White Fleet had come to an end. But it represented the beginning of a new century of naval development. This is still the most powerful fleet ever to circumnavigate the globe.

Over the past 90 years, the United States has fought in two world wars and has used military and naval force in more than 300 crises, contingencies and conflicts influencing events all over the world and evolving into the most powerful nation with the most powerful Navy.

As the 21st century begins, it not only is appropriate, but essential, that the United States send a battle fleet around the world again. It should be called Theodore Roosevelt's Fleet, after the President who recognized Thomas Jefferson's mistake, corrected it, displayed the strength of the United States to the world and led the way to greatness. A new great fleet—Theodore Roosevelt's Fleet—of aircraft carriers, cruisers, submarines, destroyers, and amphibious warfare ships with embarked Marines should open the 21st century by showing U.S. strength and resolve with a voyage around the world.

CHAPTER FIFTY SIX

COMMERCIAL ATHLETES ARE
UNDERPAID ENTERTAINERS

1998

Kevin Brown signed a seven year contract for $105 million and the sports world is shocked. Why? Ball players are entertainers and top entertainers make more than $15 million a year. Oprah and Madonna each make more than the entire payroll of a baseball team. Garth Brooks and Neil Diamond each make more than Kevin Brown, Mike Piazza and Bernie Williams combined.

When Harry Wright organized the first all-salaried baseball team in 1869 it meant more than just paying players. The Cincinnati Red Stockings represented a significant change from a game that had been played for the amusement of players to a game of players paid for entertaining an audience. It was a shift from amateur recreation to entertainment. Ball players became entertainers and there was then and is now no reason for the pay of a baseball or football entertainer to differ from that of any other entertainer, whether it is on stage, screen, circus, opera or field.

Entertainers demonstrate a talent, be it physical coordination, agility, voice or ability to act like someone else, and all require practice and application. Athlete, actor, acrobat, magician or musician; each receives compensation for display of a skill to the public and the amount of his or her pay is determined by how much that public is willing to provide.

In a crossword puzzle, a three letter word for *profession* might be *vow* because from the Latin *professio,* which meant a public declaration or oath, the English word *profess* has been developed along with the misused term *professional.* From the original meaning, *professional* applies only to those who take an oath, such as doctors, judges, clergy and military, who vow to uphold, defend and heal. But *professional* has been distorted to cover those engaged in any activity as a means of livelihood or for financial gain, a person with a business or occupation or anyone who receives pay. Clearly this is not the original Latin meaning but it is the abused Americana use.

The most abused of the term *professional* relates to athletes that make a vague agreement (they call it contract) to play (they call it work) for a specific organization (they call it team), and there's an implication of conformance with rules, but there is no oath or vow, as the so-called professional athlete is in the game for money. There are no professional athletes, only commercial athletes, and the commercial athlete is an entertainer.

The true amateur performs for his own enjoyment, as the word comes from the Latin *amator* for lover. Even today an amateur engages in an activity for his or her own pleasure, their love of the game, the personal challenge, rather than financial benefit. So if an athlete is not playing for love of the game he's not an amateur, and if he doesn't take an oath he's not a professional. He is a commercial athlete, an entertainer.

Huge amounts being paid to commercial athletes are not disproportionate to compensation pocketed by other entertainers. The basis of public revulsion over multi-millions going to ball players is disparity over pay versus contribution. But why single out ball players for criticism when society chooses to pay an inverse proportion in so many other livelihoods?

The President of the United States is not paid as much as a fast wide receiver. A brain surgeon does not make as much as a good relief pitcher. A lawyer takes away more money from one civil suit than another is paid for a year's service as a judge and a cosmetic surgeon charges more for a face-lift than an emergency room doctor gets for saving a life. The fireman who risks his life to save someone in a blazing home and the policeman who protects citizens from dangerous criminals are paid far less than the anchor-person who reads the news to us on TV. We entrust our children's education and development to teachers paid less than bartenders, which is consistent as we, as a society, spend more on alcohol than education.

In our society and the economy that makes it run, pay is neither proportionate to responsibility, nor to authority, nor humane contribution. By measure of compensation, Americans place more importance on amusement and the satisfaction they get from watching or listening to an entertainer, than health or security. We are more willing to pay millions to a crooner or catcher than to a surgeon or senator.

So who pays these commercial athlete entertainers? Back in 1927 when the New York Yankees signed Babe Ruth for an unprecedented $100,000, players' salaries came from the gate or out of the owner's pocket. The fan that went to a game paid the players. That's changed. Now more money comes from television, television revenue comes from advertising and advertising money is derived from public buying.

The baseball fan that buys a ticket to watch a game contributes only a portion of the multi-million dollar salaries paid by his favorite team. A million paying customers at twenty dollars a seat brings in twenty million dollars, not enough to pay the typical top five players on one team $5 million each, to say nothing of the nineteen other lower salaried ball players and other costs of that one team.

And what about that expression, "comes out of the owner's pocket?" Nonsense! Not a single major franchise in any sport is owned by a person who plans, expects or needs to make an annual income from that franchise. Every owner has made and is still making his or her fortune in some other very lucrative enterprise and owning a major franchise is a hobby, a tax write-off and/or a safe investment. On occasion the public hears of impressive annual losses that are really voluntary rejections of payout on investment and tailored pay-in of excess profit by the owners from their other successful businesses for tax write-off. Don't pity the poor owner who more than makes up for carefully controlled losses when he sells a $90 million team five years later for $500 million.

Going to a game is truly a bargain where live commercial athletes perform, entertainers whose salaries are being paid by those who buy products and may not even be at the game or watching on TV, but paying so that others can see millionaires frolic. Drink Budweiser and pay a players salary. Buy a Ford and a player receives a part of the money. Don't buy the advertised product and someone else pays the player you enjoy watching.

But don't blame Kevin Brown for accepting $105 million to play baseball because he's not the highest paid entertainer and in our distorted economic culture he's worth it. Disparity in pay exists in every occupation and society would be well served by changing the contradiction of compensation paid for service rendered. As long as entertainers are paid more than those who perform vital functions, we teach our children a clear lesson that entertainment is the highest contribution to a self-indulgent society.

How many fathers have just recently encouraged their sons to work on that fast ball?

CHAPTER FIFTY SEVEN

TONS AND BARRELS

As kids we learned a lot of weights and measures. Twelve inches in a foot, three feet to a yard, sixteen ounces in the pound, four quarts make a gallon. There were many of them and they became part of our language and our thought process. We could see twelve inches in a foot because that was the ruler the teacher wielded. Milk came in quart bottles, butter in one pound blocks and we knew that the walk to school was two miles. These measures had meaning for us.

I can remember a ton of coal, which was delivered by truck and tray through the basement window into the coal bin and I knew that there were 2000 pounds of coal in that ton.

As children mature they learn some harsh realities of life. Santa Claus, the Easter Bunny and the Tooth Fairy take on different meanings. But changing the meaning of those solid fixed "laws" of weights and measures is heresy! We learn that our familiar pound has different meaning in systems called avoirdupois, troy and apothecaries in addition to a British money system.

Our quart is used for U.S. dry, U.S. liquid and British Imperial capacity systems, which bothers us when we find that Canadians get about five of our quarts in a gallon of their gasoline while we get only four quarts in our gallon. Certainly a unit as solid as the ton cannot be subjected to meanings other than those 2000 loyal U.S. pounds, or can it?

The two most popular means of describing the size of a ship are length and tonnage. A 1052 Class Frigate is 438 feet long, a battleship 860 feet. The re-flagged tanker TOWNSEND is 350 meters long. The aircraft carrier ENTERPRISE is 1040 feet long. We can understand that. We know what length means. A football field is 100 yards or 300 feet long, at least in the U.S. and between the goal lines. Of course the football field is actually longer if you count the end zones and even more if you are in Canada, but then the ships' lengths are different at the waterline than at the main deck.

The other popular means of referring to the size of ships is by tonnage. We learned as kids that the ton consisted of 2000 pounds but some how that meaning doesn't quite fit in every case.

Since ancient times seamen had known the importance of a ship's cargo carrying capacity. The length of a ship was not measure enough even with the breadth and depth. In the thirteenth century a system of measuring a ship's capacity was started by referring to the number of wine barrels which could be carried in a ship. These barrels or casks were called tuns and were standardized in England during the fifteenth century as holding 252 gallons, occupying about 57 cubic feet, and weighing 2240 pounds. Probably it held about 33 cubic feet of wine and the 2240 pounds included the weight of the cask. Taxes and other fees were based on this tun which later was changed to ton even though we pronounce it still as if it were tun. If you have wondered about the traditional connection between the sailor and his drink note that even hundreds of years ago his ship was measured in terms of capacity for wine.

By the fifteenth century there was considerable confusion as to the meaning of tun. It represented space occupied as 57 cubic feet and with weight as 2240 pounds. This confusion has not lessened over the years and today's ton is even more difficult to understand than was the medieval tun. The basic confusion still centers on whether we mean weight or volume.

With a little research we can find a number of meanings for ton. Each meaning is clear by itself but the general use of the word ton can cause confusion.

Short Ton: The short ton is that good old American two thousand pounder that we learned about in grade school. It is a unit of weight avoirdupois. We got it from the British but they don't use it anymore.

Long Ton: The long ton is 2240 pounds of weight avoirdupois. It is used in Great Britain and a lot of the rest of the world. It came from that old tun of wine, remember, which took up 57 cubic feet and carried about 252 gallons. It so happens that 35 cubic feet of seawater, which weighs an average of 64 pounds per cubic foot, weighs 2240 pounds.

Metric Ton: The metric ton is a unit of mass or weight in that other system to which we are supposed to be converting. It consists of a million grams or a thousand kilograms, which approximates 1.1 short tons. We are not going to discuss the metric system in this paper, but after seven hundred years of confusion with tun and ton, using weight and volume, I wonder what metric will add to the problem.

Tun: Remember the old wine tun? It was a cask or barrel which carried 252 gallons of wine which occupied 57 cubic feet and weighed 2240 pounds. It was a measure of both weight and volume. If a ship happened to carry a cargo other than wine an immediate problem developed. The cargo had a different weight but occupied the same volume. Do we tax based on the equivalent weight of tuns or on the number of tuns by volume?

Register Ton: Now we're getting into some modern applications. As became evident in the tun days, it was more important to know the space which was available for cargo in a ship than the weight of the cargo. A complete set of rules was established for ship designers to determine the volume of the ship's hull in cubic feet. This gross volume is divided by 100 cubic feet and the result is called the gross register tonnage. This figure is adjusted to allow for non-earning space by subtracting space for machinery, passengers, ballast and some others, at the rate of 100 cubic feet to one register ton to give us the net register tonnage of the ship. The register ton is a unit of volume equal to 100 cubic feet. It is generally used for taxes and fees for merchant or cargo carrying ships. The tanker TOWNSEND, for example, is a ship of 160,010 gross registered tons. TOWNSEND has 16,001,000 cubic feet of total space in her hull.

Displacement Ton: A body immersed in a liquid is buoyed up by a force equal to the weight of liquid displaced. Archimedes taught us that. Displacement is the weight of water displaced by a ship. It is measured in those long tons the British use which weigh 2240 pounds. The displacement ton is a unit of weight which happens to occupy 35 cubic feet. This assumes that a cubic foot of sea water weighs about 64 pounds. The displacement of a ship is the weight of the ship and can be expressed as empty, full load or standard. When the cargo carrying capacity of a ship is not important, the size of that ship is generally given as displacement. The displacement of a SPRUANCE Class destroyer is 7000 tons.

Deadweight Ton: Since World War II merchant ships have increased in size dramatically. This has brought into use the term deadweight tonnage. Deadweight tonnage is the cargo carrying ability of a ship expressed as weight. It is the difference between the displacement of a ship loaded and the displacement of the ship empty. Deadweight tonnage is the weight of the cargo measured in those British long tons of displacement which are 35 cubic feet of seawater. Lloyds Register of Ships uses a Summer Deadweight ton measurement and specifies the load to the maximum summer load line. The tanker MIDDLETON is 290,085 deadweight tons. A tanker's capacity is often given in another measure; barrels.

Measurement Ton, Shipping Ton: As if we didn't have enough meanings of ton there are still more. Usually measurement or shipping ton refers to a volume measure of 40 cubic feet.

Freight Ton. The freight ton is a slightly different twist in meanings. It is a unit of volume for a particular freight that weighs one ton. It varies with the type of freight. A ton of timber might be 40 cubic feet, while a ton of wheat might be 20 bushels. Freight ton is a volume measure of a long ton by weight of cargo. Sometimes it is called Weight Ton.

TEU: One of the newest measures of cargo carrying capacity of merchant ships is the TEU, which stands for Twenty Equivalent Unit. Okay, it's not a ton or tun but it is a measure of cargo. The TEU refers to a container box 8 feet by 8 feet by 20 feet. The number of these containers which can be carried on a container ship is the TEU measure of that ship. A merchant ship might carry 1750 TEU.

Now that we have explored some of the uses of the term ton let's go back to that old container, the tun. It was originally a cask or barrel for carrying wine and when the British standardized it in the fifteenth century it became one of the first fixed measures of a barrel; 252 gallons. Apparently that size barrel didn't suit the wine industry because another standard barrel for wine has come into use at 31 gallons. The petroleum industry has developed 42 gallons as the unit of measure for their barrel and other commodities have their own fixed measures of the barrel.

We have ships today which carry wine just as takers carry oil. A hundred thousand barrels of wine means 3,100,000 gallons while a hundred thousand barrels of oil means 4,200,000 gallons. What then is the cargo capacity in barrels of a bulk liquid product carrying ship? We have to know the product because various products have various meanings of the word barrel.

The 55 gallon oil drum is a common container for many liquids but it is not a standard barrel measure. It serves as a standard for creating calypso musical instruments for steel bands in the Caribbean.

Each business community and profession has developed its own ton and barrel, and each of these groups is comfortable with the use of the terms. Trucking, railroading, shipping, petroleum, wine and many others use ton and barrel daily with little confusion. When an outsider steps in or when one profession moves into the interests of another, confusion can easily develop.

Navy people might want to compare the sizes of ships. It is easy to understand the relationship in size between a 4000 ton frigate, a 7000 ton destroyer and a 95,000 ton aircraft carrier. For each of these three ships we are talking about displacement and we know that displacement is a unit of weight using long tons, 2240 pounds to the ton.

Let's compare the size of a merchant ship and a warship. The re-flagged tanker SURF CITY is a merchant ship of 55,454 gross register tons. USS MIDWAY is an aircraft carrier of 51,000 tons standard displacement and 64,000 tons full load displacement. MIDWAY is 274 meters long, SURF CITY 237 meters. The tonnages of the two ships shows MIDWAY as somewhat numerically larger and MIDWAY is 37 meters longer. Does this mean MIDWAY is larger? Well, you can't directly compare displacement tonnage of one with gross register tonnage of the other. Displacement tonnage is a measure of weight while register tonnage is a measure of volume.

As a long ton of sea water occupies 35 cubic feet, we can make an approximate conversion of displacement to volume. We said earlier that register tonnage is derived by ship designers from a complex process but with this approximation we can come close for comparison purposes.

In this case MIDWAY's 64,000 tons of full load displacement multiplied by 35 cubic feet of sea water for each long ton gives 2,290,000 cubic feet below the waterline. As about half of the aircraft carrier's hull volume is below the waterline, we can estimate the MIDWAY hull volume at about 4,580,000 cubic feet. SURF CITY's 55,454 gross tonnage means 5,545,400 cubic feet. So, although MIDWAY is longer than SURF CITY and MIDWAY's full load displacement is a higher number than is SURF CITY's gross tonnage, we see that SURF CITY's hull is about a million cubic feet larger than is MIDWAY's.

Ships often pay fees for canals, piers, tugs, pilots, etc. These charges are often based on register tonnage. Officers in Navy combatant ships either don't have or don't know the register tonnage of their ships. In a typical situation the officer who fills out and signs the charge form for a harbor pilot writes his destroyer's displacement in the place for gross or net register tonnage on the form. After all they're just tons, aren't they and we all learned as kids that a ton is 2000 pounds? No wonder that Navy ships are treated so well by civilian harbor pilots who are receiving about twice the fee to which they are entitled!

Toward the end of the U.S. involvement in the Vietnam War a merchant ship from the Peoples Republic of China (PRC) was offloading rice at a small anchorage off North Vietnam. The U.S. wanted to close the anchorage with mines but for political purposes didn't want to antagonize the PRC by mining in their ship. This meant that the mining had to take place after the PRC ship left the anchorage. The rice came in 100 pound bags. The PRC ship was listed in a shipping register as 4,000 tons. Surveillance indicated that 6,000 bags of rice were being offloaded each day. As the 4,000 tons represented the cargo carrying ability of the ship to a young intelligence officer, he did some simple arithmetic and determined the number of days it would take to offload the PRC ship.

Four thousand tons meant to the intelligence officer that the PRC ship could carry eight million pounds or 80,000 bags of rice. Off loading at the rate of 6,000 bags per day, the PRC ship would be empty in about 13 days.

As the thirteenth day approached the U.S. forces got into position to mine the anchorage. The thirteenth day came and went and the PRC ship continued to unload rice bags at the same rate. This continued through the fourteenth, fifteenth, sixteenth day and beyond. On about the twentieth day the U.S. forces had to stand down in their readiness and still the PRC ship continued to offload. After 53 days of unloading rice the PRC ship departed, having been replaced by another PRC ship and the anchorage was still not mined. What went wrong?

The 4,000 ton measurement was net register tons, meaning the PRC ship had a volume of 400,000 cubic feet of cargo space. A short ton of rice occupies about 25 cubic feet, so the PRC ship could carry 16,000 tons of rice or 320,000 bags. With 320,000 instead of 80,000 bags of rice on board the ship took 53 days to offload.

Whether it be for comparison, payment or tactical advantage, a simple unit of weight and measure can cause a lot of confusion.

CHAPTER FIFTY EIGHT

SULFUR, SERPENTS AND SARIN

2003

This chapter is an essay that I wrote originally in 1998. I rewrote it a number of times and this is the 2003 version. The original was too long for the Naval Institute Proceedings so I reduced it and that short version was published in the August 1998 issue. I was very disappointed with the short version because I felt it had lost most of the valuable information and messages. This is the long version that I ended up with in 2003.

Just the thought of chemical and biological weapons in the hands of rouge national or terrorist leaders present situations of horror to the civilized world. Finding a means to deal with this threat is extremely difficult, as any remedies must be within the decent world's dimensions, rules and limitations. Chemical and biological agents and weapons are not new, nor are attempts to deal with these threats. What is new is a combination of terrorism with chemical and biological agents in a global high-technology arena. Studying the past may not provide solutions to this problem but past employments of chemical and biological agents do show patterns that might be of use today in dealing with this threat.

History reveals five consistent principles regarding the use of chemical and biological agents and weapons:

- *Biochemicals have been used when there is no fear of retaliation.* Historically, chemical and biological agents have been used when there is reasonable confidence that an enemy cannot retaliate. When environmental conditions have precluded response or a similar agent or delivery system was not available, rogues have used these forbidden weapons with impunity. Saddam Hussein used chemicals knowing the Kurds and Iran did not have the means to retaliate.

- *Deterrence has been the most effective means of stopping the use of biochemicals.* Saddam Hussein didn't use chemicals against coalition forces during the Gulf War of 1990-1991, even when faced with a humiliating defeat. The most likely reason is that he was sure his use of biochemicals would give the coalition justification to respond with similar weapons or, more likely, justification to pursue the war into Iraq. Deterrence can be effective even when the deterrent is a different weapon.

- *Biochemicals are not always used for maximum effectiveness.* Most of the users of chemical and biological agents and weapons have not gone through the development process nor had the training to obtain maximum effectiveness. Iraq has used these weapons with limited results, and if used against U.S. and allied forces, no more effective results can be expected. Terrorists do not spring from an experience base of effective employment of chemical and biological weapons.

- *Laws have not been effective in stopping use of biochemicals.* Users have either disregarded laws, treaties, conventions and agreements (and to this we now can add U.N. resolutions) or have found legal loopholes in interpretation. The 1993 Chemical Warfare Convention, ratified by the United States in 1998, eliminates both response and retaliation. Law-abiding states cannot and will not have or use chemical and biological agents or weapons under any circumstances, but a rogue can break the law and use these weapons, confident that a conforming opponent would not retaliate in kind.

- *Exaggeration is common in reporting results of biochemical use.* The threat of chemical and biological agents and weapons has been so exaggerated that mere suspicion of employment produces near panic. If fear is the objective of Saddam Hussein or any terrorist, rumor of use can produce desired results.

CHEMICALS

World War I stands as the first large-scale use of chemical warfare and most modern references to chemical agents and weapons are based on the employment of poison gas in that Great War, 1914-1918. By one estimate, 125,000 tons of poison gases were used, resulting in 1,300,000 casualties, of which 100,000 died. Although the Germans had used tear gas on the Russian front in January 1915, it is their use of chlorine gas on 22 April 1915 at Langemarck near Ypres in Flanders that is the turning point in chemical warfare.

Modern chemical and biological warfare began in the 19th-century German chemical industry. What started as innocent, peaceful and even humanitarian products has led to the horrors of chemical, nerve and germ warfare. Competition in the world's dye and fertilizer trade called for indigo from China and nitrates from Chile. German chemical companies formed a cartel in an attempt to monopolize the procurement of these materials and to develop synthetic substitutes. The cartel was called an *interessen gemeinshaft,* or community of interests, and became known as the color producers' cartel, or I. G. Farben. From their laboratories came aspirin, sulfa drugs, Atabrine for malaria, heroin, methadone, a cure for syphilis, photo-chemicals and a process for obtaining nitrogen from air. Even today we recognize some of the names of these I. G. Farben companies, such as Bayer and BASF. The nitrates were for fertilizer, but also were necessary for gunpowder, and a substitute indigo was developed through a process that generated chlorine as a by-product.

Fritz Haber, the scientist who developed the nitrogen process, was the director of the Kaiser Wilhelm Institute and a senior chemist of BASF in the I. G. Farben. He was in charge of shifting from fertilizer to gunpowder production, which gave him access to the German General Staff, a relationship he used to convince the German leaders of the value of chemical weapons. Haber developed chlorine gas as a weapon then improved upon it with phosgene, and finally mustard gas. Mustard was the most effective chemical agent used in World War I. It produced eight times the casualties of all other German chemicals and no effective defense was developed against it.

In early April 1915 the French XX Corps had been withdrawn from the line near Ypres and replaced by 17 companies of African colonials and two battalions of the 45th Algerian Zouave Division. Belgium and Canadian units flanked them. Across the mud of no man's land were German troops that had waited, in classic trench warfare routine, through weeks of inactivity.

A little civilian in a dark double-breasted suit, tie, high stiff collar and homburg had been busy supervising the positioning of 6,000 cylinders of pressurized liquid chlorine in the German trenches across a 4-mile front. One hundred sixty tons of the chemical were in position. Haber personally supervised the preparations for what would be the largest employment of chemical warfare in history. After a two-week wait the wind was just right and on 22 April 1915, Haber signaled the release of his gas. A sickly green cloud 5 feet high hugged the ground and moved toward the French line. The African and Zouave troops broke and ran, but not fast enough. Blindness and burning eyes, asphyxiation and choking, throats stripped raw of mucous membrane, lungs with blood, death, screams of pain and panic seized the French colonials. Early estimates reported 5,000 dead and 15,000 wounded; later estimates were perhaps 350 dead of 7,000 total casualties. The *Encyclopedia Britannica* says of this battle; "the casualties were generally not severe, with relatively few fatalities."

With a 4-mile wide hole in the Allied line, the way was clear to the channel ports for the Germans. In fact, the reason Haber had insisted on such a grand-scale first use of his poison gas was to cause a surprising large opening and a quick victory for Germany before the Allies could recover from the gas attack or retaliate. Haber's idea may have been sound, but the German generals had been skeptical. Although German troops moved forward through the Allied lines following the gas attack, there were no reserves in position to exploit the breakthrough. The German troops stopped at dusk and were driven back the following morning by an Allied counterattack.

Once Germany had used poison gas, the British and French felt that all previous prohibitions were voided, and on 25 September 1915, five months after the first German use, the British used 5,500 cylinders with more than 150 tons of chlorine. Three months later, on 19 December, phosgene gas was used by the Germans at Ypres, and in June 1916 the Allies responded with phosgene at the Somme. Both sides used chlorine and phosgene during the remainder of 1916 and into 1917.

On 12 July 1917, the Germans used dichlorethyl sulfide, called mustard because of its garlic like smell. In military terms, mustard gas is an ideal chemical agent. Not only can it kill, but in most cases it only removes the individual from active service and causes that victim to occupy the logistics services of others in the form of transport, medical facilities and personnel in both the front and rear areas. The presence of large numbers of victims and chemical attack casualties can have a profound effect on morale and public opinion. It took the French almost a year, until June 1918, to use mustard and that September the British used it. The armistice followed two months later. By the end of the war the United States had completed development of lewisite, which was faster acting than mustard, and 150 tons were at sea en route to Europe at the armistice. By the end of the war the British had developed an arsenic smoke.

The U.S. expeditionary force suffered 272,000 casualties in World War I, of which 27% were from gas and the remainder from other causes, primarily explosives. Of the gas casualties; 2% were fatal, compared to 26% of the explosives casualties. Of the gas casualty victims; 4% were discharged from the Army as disabled, while 25% of explosives casualties were discharged as disabled. These figures seem to indicate a more humane consideration of chemical warfare. Jacquard Hirshorn Rothschild, in *Tomorrow's Weapons: Chemical and Biological* (New York: McGraw Hill, 1964), writes of gas; "It would appear that they cause less suffering at the time of the attack, and less permanent after-effects, than other methods of causing casualties in war." Major General Harry Gilchrist, the U.S. Army's leading expert on the medical aspects of chemical warfare in World War I said that gas, "—is the most humane method ever applied on the battlefield."

A few days before Christmas of 1936, a chemist at one of the German laboratories, Dr. Gerhard Schrader, prepared an insecticide compound and sprayed it on some leaf lice. All of the insects were killed. During further trials after the holidays Schrader and his assistant spilled some of the substance and experienced distortion of vision and difficulty breathing, taking three weeks to recover. They had developed and were the first victims of the original nerve gas dimethylamineothoxy cyanophosphine acid, named Tabun by Schrader. Tabun represented a considerable advance in toxicity. Where mustard killed in hours, Tabun killed in minutes with paralysis, spasms and asphyxiation. Two years later, Schrader and a team of chemists developed methylisoproproxy fluorophoshine oxide, a nerve gas ten times as powerful as Tabun. They named the new agent Sarin, taking portions of their names: Schrader, Ambos, Rudriger, and von der Linde. Toward the end of the war in 1944, Schrader developed his third nerve gas, Soman. The formula and plans for the process of manufacturing Soman were taken by the

Soviets, who also moved a Tabun plant and a Sarin plant to the Soviet Union. The United States was rumored to have moved thousands of tons of German nerve agents to storage facilities in Denver, Colorado, and in 1969 an accident led the United States to confirm that 1,000 tons of nerve gas was stockpiled in West Germany. Britain and France were estimated to have a considerable supply, and Belgium, Norway, Denmark, Iceland, Luxemburg, Greece and Turkey small amounts.

Chemicals have been used in warfare since ancient and even prehistoric times, some are in common acceptable use today, and some will be in the future. Popular parlance and international agreements have segregated chemicals so that "gas" means weapons not acceptable in modern warfare. A dilemma has developed as some chemicals branded as evil are closely related to agents used by peacekeepers. Tear gas differs from chlorine gas primarily in degree of effectiveness. There is no legal limit to the caliber, shrapnel, type, or quantity of explosive used as propellant or in projectiles, but chemicals that attack a man's internals cannot be used. The ancients used burning pitch and sulfur, then came gunpowder, fuel for machines, chlorine and mustard gas, rocket propellants—all chemicals, but with differences. The differences present dilemmas to military, diplomats and jurists, for why is it acceptable in warfare to use one chemical that throws a jagged piece of steel into a man's throat while it is a violation to use another chemical that constricts breathing? Is it more humane to slash a throat than to close it?

BIOLOGICALS

Each biological agent is a disease existing as a toxin, virus, bacteria, fungus, or parasite. There are more than 350 diseases other than anthrax and smallpox that have historic connections as weapons, including cholera, plague, brucellosis (undulant fever), tularemia (rabbit fever), influenza, Ebola, encephalitis, botulism, and cancer. Most of these diseases have a number of strains, which further complicates protection, as an inoculation against one strain may not protect against another. Like chemicals, biological weapons have been used since ancient times. Examples include shooting poisoned arrows, spreading disease and contaminating drinking water.

During World War II and through the Cold War, the Soviets experimented with a number of diseases before concentrating on plague, anthrax and cholera. The British focused development on botulism and anthrax, while the Americans dealt with anthrax, brucellosis, tularemia, psittacosis (parrot fever) and psycho-chemicals similar to LSD. Separate U.S. research dealt with anticrop agents with varieties specifically directed against rice, beans, beets, potatoes and cotton. British experiments with anthrax led to the contamination of a small island off Scotland that remains quarantined.

Recently developed techniques in genetic engineering permit the manipulation of key biological processes and the transfer of toxic features from one biologic agent to another, allowing the synthesis of biological agents to military specifications. As an example of these modern developments Russia was reported to have used a biochemical against the Mujahidin rebels of Afghanistan that incapacitated people so quickly they were frozen in place, unaware until regaining consciousness many hours later that they had been attacked and immobilized.

AGENTS AND WEAPONS

When U.S. Secretary of State Colin Powell spoke to the U.N. Security Council in February 2003 on national television, he held in his right hand a small, clear vial with a plastic cap containing about a teaspoon of white powder-enough to kill more than a hundred thousand innocent people, he suggested. True. Properly distributed a few ounces of deadly agent could destroy many lives but the key is distribution. Powell was holding a representation of a chemical or biological agent but only when the agent is joined with a delivery system does it become a weapon. Many rogues have deadly agents; fewer have chemical and biological weapons.

To realize maximum effectiveness a chemical/biological weapon must be planned, developed, built and tested. There are no perfect distribution systems and any attempt to deliver the agent results in a compromise where theoretical effectiveness is reduced by practical weaponry. In fact, development of a weapon to deliver a chemical/biological agent often restricts the usage and considerably reduces the effects. Testing and analysis is a lengthy and costly process requiring specially educated and trained personnel, appropriately positioned test and laboratory facilities and an operational training program. Of course all this can be shortcut and a terrorist or rogue leader can obtain chemical/biological weapons from the world arms market. Such minimal process usually produces minimal results as untrained users employ unfamiliar weapons yielding less than maximum effective results.

As World War II commenced, all the major powers had chemical weapons but only Germany had nerve weapons. Tabun was in full production but sarin was not produced in operational quantities during the war. Throughout the war German intelligence and Hitler himself assumed that the United States and Great Britain had nerve and biological weapons. This was not the case, although Britain, the U.S.S.R. and the United States all started programs to develop these capabilities.

During the past 25 years, lack of training resulted in a number of chemical and biological weapons of less than maximum effectiveness. Without adequate training, both sides used chemicals during the Iran-Iraq War, 1980-1988, and even though there were significant casualties the losses were not what they could have been with properly trained and experienced users.

A chemical weapon generally is fast acting where a biological weapon is slow. Chemical weapons tend to be tactical, biological weapons strategic. If a defensive army unit wants to stop an attack, chemical weapons can immobilize the attacking enemy in an hour or in minutes. Use of a biological weapon in this tactical situation would take too long; hours, days or weeks. But use of a biological weapon can spread terror in a city or cripple a large troop encampment over a period of time.

An effective chemical attack takes consideration of toxicity, wind, terrain, humidity and delivery system. Artillery projectiles carry small quantities, bombs a little more. For some time Iraq has had Soviet Scud missiles that can carry a ton of payload, and years ago they developed Al-Hussein and Al-Abbas missiles capable of longer ranges with reduced payloads. In February 2003 U.N. inspectors confirmed that Iraq had the 150-km Al-Samoud missile. By any of these delivery means massive numbers of weapons would have to be placed in an exact pattern and depend on consistent weather and a predictable enemy. Saddam Hussein is reported to have used projectiles and bombs for chemical delivery but there is little evidence of large-scale effectiveness.

What of Saddam Hussein now? Intelligence reports give him chemical and biological weapons, the demonstrated will to use them, and a disregard for public reaction regarding their use. Will Saddam use these weapons against the United States or a multinational force arrayed against him? Not likely, if the pattern of history holds true regarding the employment of chemical weapons. Why? Because the United States and its allies have weapons with which to retaliate, including stronger deterrents such as massive conventional bomb and missile strikes, and even the ability to escalate to tactical nuclear weapons. To a man with complete disregard of adverse international opinion, such extremes are not beyond his perception of others' reason.

For a biochemical attack to be successful a particular concentration or dose of the agent must be given to the target personnel. Dosage must be determined by research. As the agent would spread immediately upon release in the atmosphere the concentration near the middle of the cloud would be stronger, while at the outer volume of the cloud the concentration could be less than desired by the user.

Wind is the greatest diffuser of the chemical cloud. The longer the distance to the target and the stronger the wind, the more diffusion and the less concentration. The agent is absorbed into the atmosphere upon release and the rate of absorption depends on temperature and humidity. High temperature and low humidity mean a higher rate of absorption, and vice versa. The biochemical vapor must be almost the same density or weight as the air in which it will be used. Too heavy a gas will hug the surface and some of it eventually will be absorbed by ground or water. If the gas is lighter than air it will rise and soon be ineffective. The distance the cloud has to travel and the time it takes to intercept the target both influence the effectiveness of the agent.

In addition to missiles, bombs and gun projectiles that can be used as delivery vehicles, chemical and biological agents can be sprayed from canisters carried in aircraft, including helicopters. The delivery system must be capable of reaching the target, which brings into consideration the basic weapon factors of range and accuracy as well as any defensive capability around the target. For example, it may be desirable to apply a chemical agent by spray from a helicopter, like crop dusting, but an army tank or Navy warship might shoot down the helicopter. An aircraft might try to drop a chemical/biological bomb but the aircraft would have to get close enough for accurate placement. A missile from an aircraft would carry a relatively small amount of agent and a long-range missile carrying a chemical/ biological agent would have problems of range, payload and accurate placement in consideration of wind-more so against a moving target.

An artillery projectile might carry 50 pounds of chemical agent. It would take hundreds or even thousands of such rounds to form a significant cloud of mustard gas, the most common chemical warfare agent. It would take hundreds of 500-pound bombs to form an effective mustard gas cloud and the attacking aircraft would have to place the bombs in a tight pattern near the target to ensure sufficient concentration.

During the 1980-1988 war with Iran, the Iraqis used the vesicant (blister) agent known to some as distilled mustard gas. This was delivered in a locally built Iraqi variant of the FROG-7 or, as it was known to the Soviets, LUNA-M. The missile is called by the Iraqis Laith 90 and has a 90-km range. The vesicant agent used by the Iraqis, while not as lethal as the VX nerve agent the Soviets intended for use in their FROG-7, is much easier to produce. This distilled mustard gas can penetrate normal clothing and rubber and potentially is very long lived in a number of environmental conditions. Although it has had marked success against undefended civilian populations, it has had little real effect against military objectives due to poor Iraqi targeting.

Weather combined with a target's defensive systems, resistance and mobility add up to a considerable protection against chemical weapons. Nerve agents such as Tabun, Sarin, and VX are much more toxic than mustard gas. It would take much less nerve agent to immobilize or kill, much less concentration. They also are much more dangerous to handle than mustard, so the user may lose some of his own people in the process. Another problem in developing a biological weapon is that the germs have to survive weapon delivery; the heat and shock of an explosive detonation intended to disperse the germs could destroy them. With all of the natural factors working against the user, higher toxicity means that less of the agent would have to be delivered to targeted personnel.

Saddam Hussein may have chemical and biological agents and delivery systems but whether these can be brought together in practical employment is doubtful.

LAWS, TREATIES, CONVENTIONS, AND AGREEMENTS

Throughout history, chemical and biological warfare has been practiced despite laws, treaties, conventions and agreements attempting to ban their use. Always the user has found justification or legal loophole for the employment of these weapons. Such was the case in the Great War. Germany's use of poison gas in 1915 was intended as a means of ending a costly stalemate and saving lives by quickly ending the war. To the Germans, no treaty or convention of international law had been broken. While the world screamed foul and accused Germany of violating laws, treaties and civilized conventions, each of the allied powers set in motion crash programs to respond in kind-to develop a poison gas capability of their own.

International law dealing with chemical warfare existing in 1915 was based on a series of declarations and conventions starting with the 1874 Brussels Declaration banning the use of poison bullets. The 1891 Hague Gas Convention prohibited, "the use of projectiles for the sole object of diffusion of asphyxiating or deleterious gases," and the Hague Conventions of 1899 and 1907 also dealt with the use of projectiles for spreading poisonous gases. German spokesmen were quick to point out that the release of gas from cylinders fixed in the ground did not violate the rules against the use of projectiles. World War II was not followed by the intense antichemical warfare efforts of international law that followed the World War I, most likely because of the focus on the new weapon, the atomic bomb, and the lack of use of chemical and biological weapons.

The Biological Weapons Convention of 1972 stated that there could be no production or use of biological weapons. As a result of this convention the United States admitted to stockpiling and in 1975 the weapons were publicly destroyed. President Nixon not only renounced biological weapons but also toxin weapons, which occupy a gray area somewhere between biological and chemical weapons. On the battlefield toxins act like chemicals, the difference being that a toxin is synthesized by nature and a chemical is concocted by man. Both are inert and act in minutes or hours. Biological weapons use germs that are living creatures that grow and multiply in days. In this regard, chemicals and toxins might be considered tactical weapons whereas biological agents would be strategic weapons. Time and technology cloud these differences and there now can be tactical biological weapons just as there are tactical nuclear weapons.

Prior to 1993 international law did not prohibit the use of chemical weapons and possession of these weapons by a military force was legal. What international law did prohibit was "first use" of chemical weapons. Once used against him an enemy was authorized to retaliate with chemical weapons, which meant that such weapons legally could be available to all nations. The 1993 Chemical Warfare

Convention declared that even responsive use was prohibited so fear of retaliation no longer would deter a rogue user.

It long has been illegal under international law to have biological weapons. They cannot be produced or used. However, there is always a legal loophole and research in biological weapons is allowed.

International law has not kept up with the increase in sophistication of biochemicals and the need for their controls. It was difficult enough to define the agents in the 1925 Geneva Protocol on Gas Warfare, which dealt with prohibitions on the use of asphyxiating, poisonous or other gases and of biological methods of warfare. The United States did not ratify the Protocol until 1975, 50 years and a number of wars later. A more recent attempt, the 1972 Biological Weapons Convention, which the United States has ratified, allows research but no production of biological weapons. The definition of biochemical agents that would apply today was not foreseen in 1972 and so the Convention does not cover modern or future agents. The most recent agreement, the 1993 Chemical Warfare Convention, ratified by the U.S. in 1998, prohibits existence of any biological and chemical weapons.

If reports are true regarding the toxin used by Russia in Afghanistan against the Mujahidin, it may come close to being the perfect weapon. A weapon that can immobilize an enemy, allow the user to achieve the objective and bring the victims back to health later without knowledge of what has transpired would be nearly ideal. Used tactically in a local situation, the classic hill could be taken without casualties to either side. In a strategic context, a similar biochemical agent tailored to a specific military specification could incapacitate an army or populace long enough for an invader to take a larger objective without losses. With the legal restrictions placed on biochemical weapons by international convention and national legislation, development of such a weapon could take a very long time.

The president of Iraq is still one of the most dangerous leaders in the world, an unpredictable dictator who repeatedly has demonstrated disregard for world opinion, international convention and human decency. For years he has been trying to obtain a nuclear weapon. In

June 1981, Israeli aircraft destroyed a nuclear reactor that had been producing enriched uranium in Osirak, Iraq. On 19 March 1990, British customs agents seized capacitors destined for use as nuclear weapon detonators en route to Iraq. In 2003, U.N. inspectors found aluminum tubes suitable for use in nuclear weapon preparation.

Muammar Qadhafi's German-built chemical plant at Rabat, Libya, that burned in March 1990 was estimated to have the capability of producing up to 40 tons of mustard gas per day, a situation that alarmed most of the West. At the same time, press reports said that Iraq had the capability of making 700 tons of mustard gas and 80 tons of nerve agents each day. More likely those figures should have been per week rather than per day, but even so it gave Saddam Hussein a frightening capability in chemical and nerve weapons. In April 1990 he threatened to destroy half of Israel and the news media acknowledged that he had the weapons, delivery systems and audacity to use them.

Intelligence reports continue to give Iraq a biological weapon capability in addition to its chemical weapons. Very likely Baghdad has disease-related agents such as anthrax, botulism, cholera or perhaps West Nile Fever, the virus sold to Iraq by the Atlanta-based Center for Disease Control in 1985. Whether these have been weaponized is questionable. He likely has chemicals such as the nerve agent sarin and mustard gas, both available as weapons.

Regarding biological weapons, the United States considers any use of these agents contrary to international law and binding on all nations whether or not they signed the 1925 Gas Protocol or the 1972 Biological Weapons Convention. The United States formally has renounced the use of these weapons, has destroyed all of its biological and toxin weapons and restricts research to vaccines for defense.

Since 1975, the United States has been reducing its half-century-old stockpile of chemical weapons due to age, obsolescence, uncertain toxicity and design unsuitability. The reduction program involves rockets, bombs, mines and projectiles variously containing four mustard agents (including lewisite), two nerve agents (Tabun and

Sarin), and a hallucinogenic. Congress had mandated a 1997 deadline on this disposal but the process is continuing.

HISTORIC EXAMPLES

A pattern can be seen after looking at a few historic examples of chemical and biological agent and weapon use. Chemical and biological agents and weapons have been employed when the user is convinced that his enemy cannot retaliate with a similar weapon or escalate to something worse. Deterrence has influenced potential users. Often the agent/weapon is not used for full effectiveness and initial reports can be exaggerated. International agreements and laws have not stopped users.

EXHIBIT A

Chemicals were used in early times as fuel for protective fires, such as coals and oils. Sulfur was used for fire and fumes and various poisons were used on arrows and darts. There are indications that incendiary chemicals were used in Greece as early as 1200 BC. Pitch, sulfur, resins, petroleum, and quicklime were various forms of "Greek fire" used at sea.

In 600 BC at Cirrha in Delphi the Athenians brought in Solon as an advisor. He diverted the river that provided drinking water to the city, contaminated it with hellebore roots, and diverted the river back into town. Cirrhaean soldiers deserted their posts due to obstinate diarrhea and the Athenians took the city. During the Peloponnesian Wars the Spartans used clouds of poisonous sulfur dioxide in the siege of cities.

In 200 BC, the Carthaginians retreated from a city leaving large quantities of wine drugged with mandragora (a narcotic). Roman soldiers took the city, drank the wine, fell asleep, and were killed by returning Carthaginians.

The ancients' use of incendiary chemicals was based on the wind direction. Downwind the enemy could not retaliate even if he had appropriate chemicals. Poisoning drinking water and wine would be based on opportunity not available to the enemy and would be followed by protection of one's own supply. In 600 BC, for example, the Athenians outside the city had access to, and could poison the river supplying water to Cirrha, whereas the Cirrhaeans could not retaliate in kind.

EXHIBIT B

Better known for having earlier taken elephants across the mountains into Rome, the Carthaginian Hannibal in the second century BC won a victory at sea over a larger Roman fleet by having his sailors hurl earthen potfuls of poisonous snakes into the enemy galleys. When the crews saw the wriggling reptiles in their ships, the Roman ships fled the scene. This was more than 2000 years ago and it may be the last time that biological warfare was employed at sea.

Hannibal joined the sea battle equipped with earthen jars filled with snakes to throw into Roman ships, assuming correctly that the Romans had no such weapon with which to retaliate.

EXHIBIT C

An early account of biological warfare took place in 1346. The Mongols had laid siege to the walled city of Kafka on the Crimean coast. After three years the Mongols, dying of plague outside the city, hurled infected corpses over the walls. Plague spread rapidly inside and forced the surrender of the city, with survivors fleeing and further spreading the disease. A few years later the Black Death had killed a quarter of the population of Europe.

In North America in 1736, during the French and Indian Wars, the British commander of colonial forces, Lord Jeffery Amherst, gave infected blankets to a tribe of troublesome Ohio Indians. A few months later the tribe was almost wiped out by smallpox.

The Mongols at Kafka in 1346 were suffering from the Black Death outside the city, so hurling infected corpses over the walls left no retaliation from the besieged city. Similarly, Lord Amherst knew the Ohio Indians had no means of retaliation to his smallpox infected blankets.

EXHIBIT D

During the Crimean campaign of 1854 the British used noxious sulfur fumes at the siege of Sevastopol and at the turn of the century they used artillery projectiles with picric acid against the Boers, contrary to international law. In both situations the British had marginal effectiveness and knew that their enemies could not retaliate in kind. There was no deterrence.

EXHIBIT E

Fritz Haber's massive chlorine use in 1915 is the largest chemical attack in history, and more chemicals were used in World War I than in all the wars of history combined. German use of chemicals in the Great War started with a well-studied understanding of what had to be done and how to use the weapon, resulting in maximum effectiveness. There was no deterrent and existing international law was not violated. Initial casualty reports at Ypres April 22, 1915 were exaggerated; 5000 dead and 15,000 wounded. Later investigation showed 7,000 total casualties including 350 dead.

Fritz Haber was correct. His large-scale use of chlorine in 1915 took the Allies by surprise, opened up the line, and the Germans could have driven through to the channel, perhaps ending the war. Had the termination come in 1915, three years of the highest casualty rates could have been avoided; many thousands of lives saved. Haber was also correct in his assessment that the Allies' chemical industry could not produce the chemical weapons that he could at I. G. Farben, and the Allies could not retaliate in kind. Only the delays of the German generals gave the Allies time to produce a response in poison gas.

EXHIBIT F

The use of chemical weapons did not cease between the world wars. Italy used mustard gas against Abyssinian troops in 1936, and Japan did the same against the Chinese the following year.

In spite of the public outcry and attempts at prohibition following the Great War, why would Italy use mustard in Ethiopia but not against the Allies in North Africa, and why would Japan use chemicals against the Chinese but not against the U. S. a few years later? The answer is that chemical weapons are employed when the user knows his enemy cannot retaliate, but chemicals are not used if the enemy might respond with a similar weapon. It was safe to use mustard against the Abyssinians and the Chinese, but the U. S. and her allies still had chemicals from World War I. Public opinion and international law had little to no effect on the decisions to use chemicals. Deterrence has been active, practiced, and effective long before the age of nuclear weapons.

EXHIBIT G

Generally it is believed that chemical and biological weapons were not used in the Second World War, but this is not so. There was some involvement, small certainly by comparison with the First World War, and accidental, too. The British provided Czech partisans with special anti-tank grenades for use in the assassination of Nazi Reinhardt Heydrich. On May 27, 1942 the ambush took place including grenades containing "agent X," the biological warfare term for botulism. Heydrich and a few other Germans were killed in the attack and some of the survivors later died of botulism. German leaders were unsure of the biological involvement and did not retaliate in kind. Retaliation was by killing civilian non-combatants.

EXHIBIT H

Perhaps the largest use of chemical weapons in World War II came about by accident. The port of Bari, near the heel of Italy on the Adriatic Sea, was heavily congested on December 2, 1943 with merchant ships offloading war supplies needed for the winter drive on Rome by the U.S. army. SS *John Harvey*'s cargo included 100 tons of mustard gas bombs. German JU-88 bombers attacked the harbor, sinking 16 ships and damaging 8 others. *John Harvey* was one of the first hit, blew up, and spread a mixture of oil and mustard across the harbor. Hospitals were unaware of the contamination and not prepared to treat patients. There were at least 600 mustard casualties of which 83 died. The initial exaggerated report was 1000 dead. The Allies were in no position to retaliate, as the chemical weapon had been their own.

Hitler, who had experienced mustard gas as a young soldier, and his top advisors knew that the Allies had chemical weapons and would use them if the Germans did. The Bari accident of 1943 was evidence that chemical weapons accompanied the allied army, and that retaliation was close by. Hitler also was convinced that the Allies had biological weapons and, even though this assumption was incorrect, it could have been the reason that he did not authorize their use.

EXHIBIT I

Egypt used mustard and phosgene in Yemen during the 1960s and Libya used mustard against Chad in 1987, both with very little outcry or objection from the rest of the world and both with marginal effectiveness. Egypt and Libya disregarded international law and knew that neither Yemen nor Chad had the means to retaliate in kind. There was no deterrence.

EXHIBIT J

In what may be the only deliberate biological attack in the United States during the 20th Century, in 1984 at The Dalles, Oregon, Rajneeshees spread Salmonella via restaurant salad bars in an effort to control local county voting. More than 750 citizens were hospitalized and couldn't vote, but the cult failed to elect their candidate and the perpetrators were caught and prosecuted. A trained terrorist would know more effective distribution systems than salad bars. The perpetrators knew that local voters and restaurant customers had no reason or means to retaliate, there was no deterrence other than national and international law that was completely disregarded.

EXHIBIT K

In 1988 Saddam Hussein's military conducted a massive mustard gas attack delivered by aircraft against Halabja, an unprotected city of 45,000 Iraqi Kurds. Saddam Hussein used mustard against the Kurds in his own country knowing that the Kurds could not retaliate. Initial exaggerated reports were 5,000 dead and 20,000 injured. Later investigation showed 5000 total casualties including 200 fatalities. The 200 Kurds killed were fewer than would have been killed by a massive air attack using conventional explosive bombs, showing less than full effectiveness of the chemical attack. His use of chemical weapons in Iran 1980-1988 probably was accomplished with the same reasoning, no possibility of retaliation, although Iran had access to similar weapons in the world market.

Saddam Hussein had no Fritz Haber or Gerhard Schrader, but his cousin and son-in-law General Hussein Kamil al-Majid was responsible for the Iraqi chemical and nerve weapon development and another cousin, Ali Hassan al-Majid, supervised the chemical attack on the Kurds. At Halabja and against Iran there were no considerations of international law by Saddam Hussein, and there was no deterrence.

EXHIBIT L

In 1995 the world was shocked in learning that the deadly chemical nerve agent sarin had been used in a Tokyo subway. Aum Shinrikyo was a cult of wealthy well-educated extremists with worldwide connections intent on destruction of non-believers by causing a major war between East and West, NATO versus Warsaw Pact. Their study, development, manufacture and use of small amounts of sarin was intended to cause one global power to blame the other, with no regard for international law. Aum's elite did not include personnel with training or experience in the use of nerve agents and their attempts, Tokyo subway and others, were less than fully effective, less than successful. They were able to produce the agents but didn't understand delivery or weaponry. There was no deterrence and Aum Shinriko had no fear of retaliation. Initial exaggerated reports of the Tokyo subway attack were 5500 casualties including 300 dead. Later investigation showed 12 fatalities of 300 total casualties.

EXHIBIT M

In 2001, after the 9/11 attacks on the World Trade Center and Pentagon, the nation experienced months of terror caused by Anthrax in the postal system. Millions of Americans were frightened as three died and about ten survived the illness. Inhaled anthrax had killed about 18 Americans during the first ¾ of the 20th century and there had been more than 200 cases of skin anthrax in the early 1900s, rarely fatal. Now the threat of anthrax had returned, by mail, but the postal process is not an effective weapon for distribution of anthrax. A trained terrorist would have used more effective means. There are better diseases for a terrorist to use, better distribution systems and better targets than little old ladies in Connecticut. Still, the word anthrax brings fear, fear means terror, and the perpetrator need not fear retaliation. Initial reports and estimates of the threat were exaggerated, considering that the news media hardly mentioned that the annual flu epidemic killed more than 100 times the number of Americans taken by anthrax. There was no deterrence for the perpetrator nor was he/she concerned with national or international law.

SUMMARY

Biochemicals have been used when there is no fear of retaliation and deterrence has been the most effective means in stopping use of biochemicals. Historically, chemical and biological agents have been used when there is reasonable confidence that an enemy cannot retaliate. When environmental conditions have precluded response or a similar agent or delivery system was not available to their enemy, rogues have used these forbidden weapons with impunity. Now, with the 1993 Convention, any evil-doer can be confident that the law-abiding do not have chemical and biological weapons. In Desert Storm and in Iraqi Freedom Saddam Hussein, who had used chemicals against Iran and the Kurds, didn't use them against coalition forces, even when faced with humiliating defeat. The most likely reason for this non-use is that he was sure his use of biochemicals would give the coalition justification to respond with similar weapons or, more likely, justification to pursue the war into Iraq. Also, in 2003 Saddam Hussein did not use chemical or biological weapons because it would prove his possession or he had either disposed of them or hidden them beyond his control. In either case deterrence, the fear of retaliation, would have driven his inaction.

Biochemicals are often not used for maximum effectiveness and exaggerations are common in reporting results of biochemical use. The threat of chemical and biological agents and weapons has been so exaggerated that mere suspicion of employment produces near panic. If fear is the objective, rumor of intended or potential use can produce desired results. Threats are already exaggerated and, if used, initial reports of casualties are often exaggerated. Most of the users of chemical and biological agents and weapons have not gone through the development process nor had the training to obtain maximum effectiveness. Terrorists do not spring from an experience base of effective employment of chemical and biological weapons.

Users have either disregarded laws, treaties, conventions and agreements, and now to this we can add UN resolutions, or have found legal loopholes in interpretation as justification. The 1993 Chemical Warfare Convention, ratified by the United States in 1998, eliminates response or retaliation. Now, law-abiding states cannot and will not have or use chemical and biological agents or weapons under any circumstances, but a rogue can break the law and use these weapons confident that a conforming opponent will not retaliate in kind.

The original version of this essay included 33 footnotes and a bibliography of 17 items. I have deleted those from this chapter.

CHAPTER FIFTY NINE

TAPS

2017

Betty Schulman and I were at dinner at the Yacht Club and I told her that I was stuck in the last chapter of my book. She's a very bright woman and never hesitates with ideas, good ideas. "Call it 'Taps,' you know, you're military, 'Day is done, gone the sun.'" Another great idea from Betty.

Imagine, if you will, as you read this final chapter that a lonely bugle far away is playing those notes of Taps.

Remember back in this read when I arrived in Mitchell, South Dakota? A cute little nursing student wouldn't let me join her party unless I recited a poem so I rattled off "Gunga Din." Some lines from that poem seem appropriate as we reach the end of this book and I reach the advanced age of 87.

> An' just before 'e died,
> "I 'ope you liked your drink", sez Gunga Din.

I'm sure that Kipling wouldn't mind me borrowing and slightly distorting those words of Gunga Din.

I hope you liked this read.
Taps.